Principles of Marketing

The European Edition

Instructor's Resource Manual

Principles of Marketing

The European Edition

Instructor's Resource Manual

PHILIP KOTLER GARY ARMSTRONG
JOHN SAUNDERS VERONICA WONG

Prepared by

T. C. MELEWAR

PRENTICE HALL

London New York Toronto Sydney Tokyo Singapore
Madrid Mexico City Munich

First published 1996 by
Prentice Hall Europe
Campus 400, Maylands Avenue
Hemel Hempstead
Hertfordshire, HP2 7EZ
A division of
Simon & Schuster International Group

Printed and bound in Great Britain by
Redwood Books, Trowbridge, Wiltshire

ISBN: 0-13-239328-X

1 2 3 4 5 00 99 98 97 96

Dedicated to my beloved wife Hazel
and my darling daughter Amy

Table of Contents

Preface xiii
How to Study xvii

Part I Marketing and the Marketing Process 1
Chapter 1 Marketing in a Changing World: Satisfying Human Needs 3
Chapter Objectives 3
Chapter Overview 3
Teaching Notes 3
Discussing the Issues 10
Applying the Concepts 13
Case 1: Amphitrion: Your Ultimate Host in Greece 14
Jokes and Quotes 18
Chapter 2 Marketing and Society: Social Marketing and Marketing Ethics 21
Chapter Objectives 21
Chapter Overview 21
Teaching Notes 21
Discussing the Issues 27
Applying the Concepts 29
Case 2: Nestlé: Under Fire Again and Again 30
Jokes and Quotes 37
Chapter 3 Strategic Planning and the Planning Process 41
Chapter Objectives 41
Chapter Overview 41
Teaching Notes 41
Discussing the Issues 58
Applying the Concepts 61
Case 3: Trap-Ease: The Big Cheese and Mousetraps 62
Overview Case 1: Kit Kat: Have a Break . . . 67
Jokes and Quotes 72

Part II Marketing Setting 75
Chapter 4 The Marketing Environment 77
Chapter Objectives 77
Chapter Overview 77
Teaching Notes 77
Discussing the Issues 83
Applying the Concepts 86
Case 3: Trap-Ease: The Big Cheese and Mousetraps 88
Jokes and Quotes 93
Chapter 5 The Global Marketplace 95
Chapter Objectives 95
Chapter Overview 95
Teaching Notes 95
Discussing the Issues 100
Applying the Concepts 102
Case 5: Procter & Gamble: Going Global in Cosmetics 104
Jokes and Quotes 109

Chapter 6 Marketing Information and Marketing Research 112
Chapter Objectives 112
Chapter Overview 112
Teaching Notes 113
Discussing the Issues 122
Applying the Concepts 125
Case 6: Ballygowan Springs into New Age Kisqua 126
Overview Case 2: Mitsui & Company 131
Jokes and Quotes 136

Part III Buyer Behaviour 139
Chapter 7 Consumer Markets 141
Chapter Objectives 141
Chapter Overview 141
Teaching Notes 141
Discussing the Issues 154
Applying the Concepts 156
Case 7: Bic versus Gillette: The Disposable Wars 157
Jokes and Quotes 162
Chapter 8 Business Markets and Business Buyer Behaviour 165
Chapter Objectives 165
Chapter Overview 165
Teaching Notes 165
Discussing the Issues 173
Applying the Concepts 175
Case 8: Troll–AEG 176
Overview Case 3: Jacobs Kaffee Wien: Spreading a Golden Light 181
Jokes and Quotes 186

Part IV Core Strategy 189
Chapter 9 Market Segmentation and Targeting 191
Chapter Objectives 191
Chapter Overview 191
Teaching Notes 191
Discussing the Issues 199
Applying the Concepts 203
Case 9: Coffee Mate 204
Jokes and Quotes 211
Chapter 10 Position 213
Chapter Objectives 213
Chapter Overview 213
Teaching Notes 213
Discussing the Issues 220
Applying the Concepts 223
Case 10: Cadbury's TimeOut: Choc Around the Clock 224
Jokes and Quotes 228
Chapter 11 Building Customer Satisfaction Through Quality, Value and Service 230
Chapter Objectives 230
Chapter Overview 230

Teaching Notes 230
Discussing the Issues 237
Applying the Concepts 239
Case 11: Feinschmecker Sauce: Pricey n' Spicey 240
Jokes and Quotes 245

Chapter 12 Creating Competitive Advantage: Competitor Analysis and Competitive Marketing Strategies 248
Chapter Objectives 248
Chapter Overview 248
Teaching Notes 249
Discussing the Issues 256
Applying the Concepts 258
Case 12: BMW: Putting the Brrrrum Back in Brum 260
Overview Case 4: A Cola Challenge: Cola with Breakfast 266
Jokes and Quotes 271

Part V Product 275

Chapter 13 New-Product Development and Product Life Cycle Strategies 277
Chapter Objectives 277
Chapter Overview 277
Teaching Notes 277
Discussing the Issues 282
Applying the Concepts 285
Case 13: The Swatchmobile: Any Colour Combination, Including Black 286
Jokes and Quotes 292

Chapter 14 Products, Brands, Packaging and Services 296
Chapter Objectives 296
Chapter Overview 296
Teaching Notes 296
Discussing the Issues 304
Applying the Concepts 306
Case 14: Colgate: One Squeeze Too Many? 307
Jokes and Quotes 310

Chapter 15 Marketing Services 312
Chapter Objectives 312
Chapter Overview 312
Teaching Notes 312
Discussing the Issues 315
Applying the Concepts 317
Case 15: Tribigarden: Is There Life After Euro Disney? 318
Overview Case 5: Mapanza Breweries 322
Jokes and Quotes 327

Part VI Price 329

Chapter 16 Pricing Considerations and Approaches 331
Chapter Objectives 331
Chapter Overview 331
Teaching Notes 331
Discussing the Issues 335

Applying the Concepts 337
Case 16: Proton Mpi: Malaysian Styling; Japanese Engineering; European Pricing 339
Jokes and Quotes 344
Chapter 17 Pricing Strategies 346
Chapter Objectives 346
Chapter Overview 346
Teaching Notes 346
Discussing the Issues 352
Applying the Concepts 354
Case 17: Stena Sealink versus Le Shuttle, Eurostar and the Rest 355
Overview Case 6: Amaizer: It Tastes Awful but We're Working On It 359
Jokes and Quotes 366

Part VII Promotions 369
Chapter 18 Communication and Promotion Strategy 371
Chapter Objectives 371
Chapter Overview 371
Teaching Notes 371
Discussing the Issues 379
Applying the Concepts 381
Case 18: Absolut Vodka: Absolutely Successful 382
Jokes and Quotes 387
Chapter 19 Advertising, Sales Promotion and Public Relations 390
Chapter Objectives 390
Chapter Overview 390
Teaching Notes 390
Discussing the Issues 395
Applying the Concepts 397
Case 19: Diesel Jeans & Workwear: "We're All Different; But Aren't We All Different in the Same Way" 398
Jokes and Quotes 402
Chapter 20 Personal Selling and Sales Management 405
Chapter Objectives 405
Chapter Overview 405
Teaching Notes 405
Discussing the Issues 412
Applying the Concepts 415
Case 20: Britcraft Propjet: Whose Sale Is It Anyhow? 416
Overview Case 7: Bang & Olufsen: Different by Design 421
Jokes and Quotes 427

Part VIII Place 431
Chapter 21 Distribution Channels and Logistics Management 433
Chapter Objectives 433
Chapter Overview 433
Teaching Notes 433
Discussing the Issues 440
Applying the Concepts 442

Case 21: Freixenet Cava: Bubbles Down a New Way 443
Jokes and Quotes 447
Chapter 22 Retailing and Wholesaling 448
Chapter Objectives 448
Chapter Overview 448
Teaching Notes 448
Discussing the Issues 456
Applying the Concepts 458
Case 22: Pieta Luxury Chocolates 459
Overview Case 8: GTE: Competition Comes Calling 471
Jokes and Quotes 476

Preface

The Instructor's Resource Manual (IRM) for Kotler, Armstrong, Saunders and Wong's edition of Principles of Marketing, The European Edition provides you with a comprehensive package of high-quality, easy-to-use supplementary materials for teaching the basic marketing course. Those of you familiar with the textbook already will find in the IRM an enhanced set of materials that comprise a complete teaching system for helping you in lecture and helping your students get the most possible out of the textbook. For those of you adopting the textbook for the first time, you will find complete resources for any approach you use in teaching marketing principles. Each supplement has been carefully prepared to function either as an independent module for teaching the course or as part of an integrated design of materials chosen by you to enhance your teaching style. For your convenience, each section of this manual is referenced by page number in the Table of Contents. A highlight of the teaching system package is provided below:

- **Colour Transparencies and Lecture Notes.** An integrated set of 100 colour transparencies and lecture notes for the entire book is a key feature of the IRM. More than a lecture outline, each colour transparency is coded by chapter and paired with a full-page of lecture notes in the IRM covering all the key terms in the chapter, discussion points, and extra-textual information to provide you with a complete lecture series for the entire course. For each colour transparency, graphics and text have been redrawn for maximum visibility in even the largest classrooms. No other textbook offers this level of lecture support. The transparencies were created by and the lecture notes prepared by Lewis Hershey of Hershey Consulting Services and John Saunders of Loughborough University Business School. The lecture notes were redesigned and adapted to make them more suitable for usage within the European context.

- **Discussing the Issues.** This feature of the IRM helps students understand the issues that give marketing ideas greater meaning in the larger business world. This section contains suggested responses to the discussion questions at the end of each chapter in the textbook. Historical development, major economic trends, social and cultural forces, and the increase in global marketing are tied to the chapter with real-world examples. Partly prepared by Rick Starr of the University of North Carolina at Chapel Hill, this feature of the supplement also includes examples from the business and popular press relevant to the issues in each chapter as well as references to recent scholarly publications.

- **Applying the Concepts.** This section of the IRM provides answers to hands-on exercises from the textbook that give students experiential knowledge of how the course concepts help marketers make better business decisions. In the IRM these notes are cross-referenced in the chapter outline and index of chapter resources for easy integration into your course plan. These practical applications of course concepts were partly prepared by Rick Starr of the University of North Carolina at Chapel Hill.

- **Answers to Case Discussion Questions.** For each chapter the IRM features a detailed set of responses to the accompanying company case study. Each case provides an opportunity for students to synthesise and apply chapter material in an analytical framework. Answers to three of the case studies were prepared by Lew Brown of the University of North Carolina at Greensboro,

- **Answers to Overview Case Discussion Questions.** Each of the eight sections of the textbook are followed by a comprehensive case study that integrates concepts from the entire section. These exhaustive case studies provide instructors with detailed information for integrating course concepts across each section. Answers to two of the overview case studies were prepared by Lew Brown of the University of North Carolina at Greensboro.

- **Teaching Notes.** The teaching notes provided in the IRM support the transparencies, showing how they relate with the text and giving key definitions and description of the transparencies. You may lecture from the notes although it is recommended that you use both the teaching notes outline and the marketing jokes and quotes provided to prepare for lecture. The lecture notes that accompany the transparencies are designed for easy use in lecture.

- **Jokes and Quotes.** The jokes and quotes found at the end of each chapter of the IRM are means to enhance and add creativity to lectures and tutorials. It is hoped that this section will make teaching and learning of marketing more enjoyable and interesting. The jokes and quotes were prepared by John Saunders of Loughborough University Business School.

- **European Casebook on Principles of Marketing.** Written by Jim Saker and Gareth Smith of Loughborough University Business School, this book contains fifteen previously unpublished comprehensive cases by leading academics covering the scope of Principles of Marketing: The European Edition. The cases are mainly European in origin and are backed by an instructor manual.

- **Interactive Marketing Software.** Written by Fatimah Moran and Mark Smalley, developed by Stephen Cleary and Alan Hawley and led by Ken Randall, all of Staffordshire University, it provides 10 modules of interactive problem solving activities and practical exercises, enabling students to work at their own pace in a supportive and structured environment. It gives instruction and questions students using animated computer graphics and pictorial presentations. It is suitable for student individual use or in a computer lab based seminar.

- **Full-Featured Testbank.** An entirely new testbank has been prepared with over 660 questions in multiple choice format. Each term and concept is tied to multiple questions in the testbank to allow you repeated use of the testbank without duplicating questions. The test bank was developed by Lewis Hershey of Hershey Consulting Services and Andy Hirst of Loughborough University Business School.

As with any text, many individuals contributed to the development of this manual. I extend my sincere appreciation to Professor John Saunders and Dr Veronica Wong in giving me the opportunity to write this manual, to Professor Peter Baron of Leicester Business School in encouraging me to publish the manual and to all of my students and colleagues who assisted me with their comments and insights. Thanks are also due to Julia Helmsley and Ann Greenwood for their understanding and patience in the development of the manual. Since I know that there is always room for improvement, I would appreciate hearing from you any comments and suggestions you might have regarding this manual. I do hope you find this manual helpful in teaching and exciting your students in the marketing arena.

T C Melewar
Department of Marketing
Leicester Business School
Leicester
LE1 9BH
England
Tel: 01162506136
Fax: 01162517548

How to Study

Why

Textbooks are great for storing information and explaining relationships and ideas. But they are not designed to provide you with usable information. You have to *translate* the technology of the written word into a more usable technology - for tests, and for your career. The key to doing this successfully is organising the information into a more efficient (for studying, not storing) form of communication and then maximising your ability to use the new form.

How

Suppose this class meets MWF. You should allocate a couple of hours on S, T, TH to read the chapters before lecture. Below, is a **7 step procedure** you will find works for any class, if you follow it faithfully. It may or may not make you an "A" student. But it will definitely make you a better student. For sure.

Before lecture you should complete steps 1-3.

1. **Read**. First, just read the chapter, starting with the end of the chapter summary. Do not take any notes yet, nor highlight key points. That comes later. Right now it slows you down and breaks your concentration. Even doing steps 1-3 will still take you less time than a stop and go approach to reading.
2. **Highlight**. After you read, go back and highlight the key points of the chapter. This should include all the defined terms and any concepts, procedures, or processes and theories. Do this quickly, do not study them yet - just identify them. Then compare your highlights to the chapter summary, defined terms, and/or chapter objectives. If you left any out then you have just diagnosed an area you need to work on. Try and figure out how the chapter organises information it considers important.
3. **Notecard**. Once you have highlighted, put all the defined terms and any concepts, procedures, or processes and theories onto separate note cards. One definition per card, all on the same side. If you have a concept such as the 5 marketing philosophies, put it on a single card and then follow it with five more cards, each with a definition and example of each philosophy. Try to keep the information on each card to a single idea or definition. Make them easy to read. Your stack of cards forms the basis of information you can now use to study for a test instead of trying to read the textbook.
4. **When & How to Prepare for a test.** A key part to this translation process is understanding the *time* it takes to translate written information into usable information. Do not wait until the night before the test to study. Finish all your study cards a minimum of five days before the test. Now you need to expose yourself to the information in a 100% usable and efficient context. This means reading the cards aloud. Silent reading lets you daydream, hear outside noise, and become bored. Every time you read aloud you have a 100% accurate "practice" of the material. And it does not take long. You can read a stack of 150 definitions and 25 concepts in a few minutes. DON'T TRY TO MEMORISE THE CARDS! JUST READ THEM. Set up a study schedule. 5 days before the test, read the cards all the way through 5 to 7 times. The next day, another 5 to 7 times. By now you can see which chapter you are getting to know and which you need to study more. The last three days, you can adjust as needed. For example, suppose you know you are getting the hang of chapters 1-3. But 4 is a real pain. You still need another full day of reading chapters 1-3 a total of 5 to 7 times, but on day 4 and 5 you can drop to 3 times through chapters 1-3 to remind you of them

and spend extra runs on just chapter 4, maybe 10 times through. Now you are getting ready for the exam.

5. **Be honest**. Only you can say whether you are *really* studying enough. Err on the side of caution. Better to know more than you need than less. If you need more practice, increase the number of times you read the whole stack out loud. If you know the definition of a term but do not understand how to distinguish it from another similar term, go to step 6.

6. **Re-read selected contexts.** Two days before the exam, look up the explanations of terms you have selected as needing more information. Sure you know how to define them but you do not know what is unique about them yet. Now when you read the textbook, you will find the discussion material much more valuable. You are better prepared now to get the most out of the discussion of these ideas your authors have provided. You also have time to get your questions answered, especially when you have a specific idea about what you need to know. USE OFFICE HOURS BEFORE THE TEST!

7. **Relax and rest.** NEVER PULL AN ALL NIGHTER. This is a stupid if fashionable idea. If you divide the same number of hours you spend staying up over the five days before the exam you will find that this 7-step approach actually takes *less* time than studying all night. But you will have the advantage of 25 to 35 repeated, 100% efficient repetitions of the *correct* definitions and terms - you have never practiced a wrong answer! THINK ABOUT THAT FOR A MINUTE. EVERY TIME YOU GO THROUGH THE CARDS, YOU ARE SAYING THE RIGHT ANSWER! Plus, you have enough sleep so you have more energy when you take the test -- which means you will not make as many careless mistakes that happen too often when you are tired. It is even possible that you will find the test easy -- though in fact, it is you that are qualitatively better prepared. When you *know* the material, there is no such thing as a hard test. So prepare early, get some rest, and have confidence in your preparation.

Part I

Marketing and the Marketing Process

Chapter 1
Marketing in a Changing World:
Satisfying Human Needs

Chapter Objectives

After reading this chapter, you should be able to:

1. Define marketing and discuss its role in the economy.
2. Compare the five marketing management philosophies.
3. Identify the goals of the marketing system.
4. Explain the major forces that are now changing the world marketing landscape and challenging marketing strategy.

Chapter Overview

Marketing is part of all of our lives and touches us in some way every day. The marketing system has made all this possible and has given us a standard of living that our ancestors could not have imagined. Many large and small companies make up this marketing system. A recent study of senior managers of major global companies identified their foremost problem as "developing, improving, and implementing competitive marketing strategies." Marketing is a key factor in business success. Marketing and its core concepts, the major philosophies of marketing thinking and practice, goals of the marketing system, and how marketing is used by different kinds of organisations are the topics presented in this chapter.

Teaching Notes

Refer to the following pages for teaching notes.

Core Concepts

Transparency PM 1-1 relates to Figure 1-1 in the text.

Needs

Needs emerge from a state of felt deprivation. Ask students to distinguish among physical, social, and individual needs. Depending upon student level, you may wish to link the discussion to Maslow's Hierarchy of Needs.

Wants

The form taken by human needs as they are shaped by culture and individual experience. Have students provide examples for different wants based upon geographical differences, gender, age, wealth. Link culture to socio-economic-standing, education.

Demands

Demands are wants backed by buying power. Discuss such popular items as dream vacations or favourite cars to illustrate the difference between wants and demands. You may want a Lexus but drive a Nissan Micra. Introduce the idea that demands are often for a bundle or group of benefits and may address a number of related needs and wants.

Products

Products are anything offered for sale to satisfy a need or want. Have students discuss an extended view of products to include services and ideas. Discuss the role of value in distinguishing products. Ask students to identify their product choice set for cars, vacations, dating partners, and, if you are daring, university professors.

Exchanges

Exchanges are the act of obtaining desired objects by offering something in return. Link to barter economies and promises to pay (i.e., credit, cheques).

Transactions

Transactions are an actual trade of value between at least two parties. Transaction marketing is part of the larger concept of relationship marketing in which parties build long-term, economic ties to enhance quality and customer-delivered value.

Markets

Markets are the set of actual and potential buyers of a product. Markets may be decentralised or centralised. Markets exist wherever something of value is desired, such as in the labour market, the money market, even the donor market - for "human" products such as blood or organs.

Notes for PM 1-1

Five Marketing Philosophies

Transparency PM 1-2 relates to the material on pp 14-20.

The Production Concept

One of the oldest concepts, it holds that consumers favour products that are available and affordable. Management emphasises production and distribution efficiency. Examples from the text include Ford's Model T and Texas Instruments.

The Product Concept

This concept focuses on the actual product in an effort to continuously improve quality, performance, and features. May lead to marketing myopia or the tendency to narrowly define the scope of one's business. Consumers buy products for their benefits, not their features.

The Selling Concept

This concept views consumers as unwillingly customers whose inherent opposition must be overcome to make a sale. It is most often used today for unsought goods. The selling concept tends to encourage sellers to misrepresent the true nature of their products or services and can lead to problems in maintaining high customer satisfaction.

The Marketing Concept

This concept links the company's success with the consumer's continuing satisfaction. Its "outside-in" approach starts with a well-defined target market, an analysis of their needs and wants, and then builds the company's offering around meeting those needs better than the competition (Note: the selling and marketing concepts are contrasted in transparency PM 1-3).

The Societal Marketing Concept

This concept adds to the marketing concept the idea that the company should contribute to the betterment of society as a whole (Note: The societal marketing concept is developed in more detail transparency PM 1-4 and the accompanying notes).

> **Tip**
>
> You may find it useful to ask students to give their definitions of philosophy. How do they use philosophies for studying? dating? planning their time? Work from their examples to the idea that businesses too have philosophies about how to get things done.

Notes for PM 1-2

Marketing and Sales Concept Contrasted

Transparency PM 1-3 corresponds to Figure 1-3 and relates to the material on pp.15-18.

Comparisons and Contrasts

The Selling Concept

Takes an inside-out perspective - looking at the company's needs and wants in terms of existing products and ways to find customers for them.

The Marketing Concept

Takes an outside-in perspective - identifying the needs and wants of a clearly defined market and adjusting company efforts to make products that meet the needs.

Tip

Promotional tone may help indicate whether a company practises the selling or the marketing concept. Selling involves persuasion - convincing the customer of their need to buy existing products. Marketing, at its best, involves information - bringing the developed product to the awareness of a target market that recognises need satisfying products.

As the text notes, companies can let their own success lock them into a rigid selling structure. As times change, and they always do, those companies fail to see the need for meeting new and emerging consumer needs. The marketing concept helps companies focus on customer need satisfaction, leading to long-term success by customer retention.

Notes for PM 1-3

The Societal Marketing Concept

Transparency PM 1-4 corresponds to Figure 1-4 in the text and relates to the material on pp.18- 20.

Holds that the organisation should determine the needs, wants, and interests of target markets. In delivering the desired satisfactions more effectively and efficiently than the competition, the company should also maintain or improve both the consumer's and society's well being. Leaving the determination of the "public good" to private business executives can create problems for both society and the company.

Tip

You may wish to consider extra-textual class discussion identifying the pros and cons of the societal marketing concept.

Reasons for adopting the societal marketing concept include:

1. Public expectations. Social expectations of business have increased. 2. Long-run profits. Socially responsible marketing may lead to more secure long-run profits. 3. Ethical obligation. Business should recognise that responsible actions are right for their own sake. 4. Public image. A good public image helps firms gain more customers, better employees, access to money markets, and other benefits. 5. Better environment. Involvement by business can help solve difficult social problems, creating a better quality of life and a more desirable community in which to attract and hold skilled employees. 7. Balance of responsibility and power. Marketers have a large amount of power in society that requires an equally large amount of responsibility. 8. Stockholder interests. Socially responsible companies are considered less risky and safer investments 9. Possession of resources. Business has the financial resources, technical experts, and managerial talent to support public causes.

Reasons for not adopting the societal marketing concept include:

1. Violation of profit maximisation. 2. Dilution of purpose. The pursuit of social goals dilutes business's primary purpose. 3. Costs. Many socially responsible activities do not pay their way. 4. Too much power. Business is already one of the most powerful institutions in society. 5. Lack of skills. Marketers may be poorly qualified to deal with social issues. 6. Lack of accountability. There are no direct lines of social accountability from the business sector to the public. 7. Lack of broad public support. Even favourable attitudes are general and lack consensus on specific actions marketers should take on social issues.

Notes for PM 1-4

Goals of the Marketing System

These notes relate to the material on pp.20-22.

Marketing System Goals

1. Maximise Consumption

This goal uses promotions and advertising to stimulate demand and consumption. The idea is that the greater the level of consumption, the better things are for both the consumer and the seller.

2. Maximise Consumer Satisfaction

This goal stresses the quality of the consumers consumptive experience over its sheer volume. The idea is that marketing ultimately succeeds only if consumers are satisfied with products they consume. Difficulties with this position lie in determining what constitutes satisfaction, compromises between some benefits to the individual consumer versus harm to society, and measuring satisfaction on status items.

3. Maximise Choice

This goal strives to increase the selection and availability of products to expand the consumer's choice among alternatives. Ideally, this goal of the marketing system would generate product forms to suit every imaginable manifestation of consumer wants and needs. Problems arise in implementing this goal in that greater diversity reduces economies of scale, raises inventory and distribution cost, and ultimately raises consumer costs thus reducing consumer choice.

4. Maximise Life Quality

This goal corresponds to the societal marketing concept's view that the marketing system must address the needs of the many as well as the needs of the few. Again, problems arise in defining life quality and balancing individual quality with societal and environmental qualities.

Tip

Under a systems perspective, marketing activities are viewed as an interacting and dynamic whole where change in part of the system affects all the other parts. Use this approach to initiate discussion about the four alternative goals outlined on the slide. Are they compatible? How does each goal affect how marketing is conducted?

New Marketing Challenges

These notes relate to the material on pp.22-27.

Globalisation

Technological and economic developments continue to shrink the distances between countries. Computer and communications technology make possible truly global businesses that buy, sell, manufacturer, market, and service customers easily across international borders. Rising affluence creates new markets. Similarly, more European and Asian companies now compete successfully in the U.S. market.

Changing World Economy

Even as new markets open to rising affluence in such countries as the "newly industrialised" Pacific Rim, poverty in many areas and slowed economies in previously industrial nations has already changed the world economy. Western countries increasingly maintain living standards only by having two incomes per household. Value is hunted for by penny-wise consumers.

Ethics and Responsibility

The greed of the 1980s and the problems caused by pollution in Eastern Europe and elsewhere has spurred a new interest in ethical conduct in business. Many consumers feel business in general has more of an obligation to those who generate profits by buying products.

New Landscape

The new marketing landscape is a dynamic, fast-paced, and evolving function of all these changes and opportunities. More than ever, there is no static formula for success. Only strategies that incorporate and implement constant improvement in product quality and higher delivered customer value stand any chance of long-term success. These needs are featured throughout the text and are covered in detail in Chapter 11.

Tip

As the text notes, rapid changes make yesterday's winning strategies out of date. Challenge students to see marketing as an exciting and creative field needing new ideas and new solutions to emerging business opportunities.

Comments on Discussing the Issues

1. There are many reasons to study marketing:

   • "Everyone lives by selling something." No matter what a person does in life, understanding marketing may help him or her does it better. People who want pay increases must market themselves to their supervisors; people who want donations must market their cause to contributors; people in non-profit organisations must deal with outside suppliers, even if the organisation does not actively market itself; and so on.

   • As shown in the chapter opening, marketing touches every part of our daily lives. People will be smarter consumers if they understand how marketers attempt to turn them into customers.

   • Marketing costs 50 pence or more of the consumers' money. Studying marketing helps show what people are getting for their money.

   • There are many career opportunities in marketing, and marketing is a major route to success in a business career.

   • Marketing is fun. This, obviously, is a matter of opinion, but you, the text, and the supplements package will help students see that marketing is challenging, demanding, interesting, and exciting.

2. Galbraith and many other critics of marketing apparently fail to distinguish between *needs* and *wants*. People realise they need shelter without any help from marketers, but they may need realtors, magazine articles, advertisements, and other sources of information to decide whether to buy or rent, to choose a condo or a house, to learn what part of town has the best schools, and so on.

   The quoted sentence in the question comes from Galbraith's *The Affluent Society*. Have students imagine Dr. Galbraith in a restaurant, ordering the most mouth-watering dish on the menu, only to be brought a cold baked potato. Would he accept it as satisfying his need for food, or would he decide that desires stimulated by marketing are in fact genuine, and insist on the meal he had ordered!

3. When faced with negative demand for a product, marketers can practise the marketing concept by finding why the market rejects the product, then either modifying the product or attempting to change attitudes and behaviours. An interesting example of this approach is given by Jean Boddewyn in the October 1961 *Journal of Marketing*. Most people in North America and Western Europe rejected a nutritious and easily cultivated vegetable—the potato—for over 200 years, despite efforts by many authorities to convince the public of the potato's virtues. Potatoes were not accepted in France until supported by the King and Queen. They did not offer rational arguments in favour of the potato, but instead Louis XVI wore a potato flower as a boutonniere, and Marie Antoinette wore one in her hair—an early but effective form of image advertising.

   The negative demand for mammograms has tragic health consequences. One American woman in ten will get breast cancer in her lifetime, and breast cancer is the second leading cause of cancer death among women. Yet, despite the fact that 30% of all breast cancer deaths could be avoided by regular mammograms, only 10 to 15% of American women who should have had mammograms have ever had them. Price-oriented promotions tend not to be very successful in getting women to have mammograms.

Frightening women with the consequences of breast cancer has even less impact. At the Food and Drug Administration's 1992 hearings on the safety of silicone breast implants, the FDA publicly stated concerns that this issue might hamper breast cancer detection efforts. The logic is complex, but reasonable. Banning silicone implants would make reconstructive surgery seem unavailable after mastectomies, even though non-silicone alternatives are available. If women believed that no reconstruction was possible, they would fear the expected cure, a mastectomy, even more than the disease. More fear would lead not to more *detection*, but to more *avoidance* of mammograms.

The key factor in getting women to have a mammogram is a doctor's recommendation; thus, a health-care service's marketing efforts should target doctors as well as the public in order to overcome the negative demand for mammograms. (These percentages are from the American Cancer Society and the National Cancer Institute.)

4. Military equipment is a unique market. The customer and the seller work together to design the product. This process has been criticised for producing goods that are excessively complex, often unreliable, and very expensive. Military contractors will need to adopt the marketing concept to survive. Because of reductions in world tension, the military has smaller and different needs, and suppliers will need to adapt to them.

There are three major sets of publics the military manufacturers must satisfy: the military, congress, and non-military customers. The military's needs must be well served, for budget cuts mean that not all military suppliers will be kept fully employed as they have been in the past. Government is a public, and also a customer, for it appropriates the monies for all major defence systems. Congress must agree that all major weapons and projects make sense. Finally, cutbacks mean that manufacturers must seek non-military customers to avoid shrinking. For example, Oshkosh Truck in the US depends on the military for 84 per cent of its volume. Any cutbacks in the military business will be difficult to replace with civilian contracts in the short term. Contractors who do not adopt a marketing orientation may not survive.

5. The purpose of this question is to get students to understand the marketing concept better, and to see how it is different from other philosophies. The key difference between the marketing concept and the production, product, and selling concepts is their basic focus. The marketing concept begins with the needs and wants of the *consumer*. A true marketing company achieves its success by fulfilling its customers' desires.

The production, product, and selling concepts all focus on the needs of the seller. The production and product concepts begin with the product, and assume it will generate demand because of price, availability, or quality. The selling concept begins with the product to be sold, and tries to generate demand for it.

The production, product, and seller-based concepts are the easiest to apply in the short run. The company does not need to redefine its business, it just works *harder*: more efficiency, a better product, harder selling. But these measures are only successful if consumer needs are met.

The marketing concept is more difficult to apply. It requires careful study and flexibility to meet the needs of sometimes fickle consumers. This may require a business to rethink its entire mission. But if consumer needs and wants are not met, the business will eventually fail.

6. The quotation is from Dr. Friedman's *Capitalism and Freedom* (The University of Chicago Press, 1962). Friedman supports his argument with several questions (also see John F. Gaski, "Dangerous Territory: The Societal Marketing Concept Revisited," *Business Horizons*, July-August 1985, pp. 42-47): If businesses do have a social responsibility other than maximising profits, how are they to know what that responsibility is? Should unelected private individuals decide what the social interest is? How great a burden are they justified in placing on their stockholders (in lost profits) in serving that social interest?

Dr. Friedman is referring to profit maximisation "within the rules of the game"—that is, open competition without deception or fraud. This qualification eliminates many of the abuses resulting from attempts to maximise profits. It does not address the concerns discussed under "The Societal Marketing Concept," though—environmental pollution, world hunger, and so on. Should packaged-goods manufacturers, for example, act to reduce pollution by spending millions of dollars to develop a biodegradable alternative to plastic containers if they cannot get their investment back through lower costs or higher prices? Who should pay for the costs of this research, the companies' stockholders or customers?

A good way of discussing this question is to take both sides of the issue to extremes. Total social responsibility might prevent people from being able to buy the products they want—bicycles, pre-sweetened breakfast cereals, fatty luncheon meats, and so on. Total profit maximisation might increase prices or pollution, cause safety risks, and reduce the services offered to disadvantaged and less profitable market segments. Either extreme would be unacceptable to most consumers.

Comments on Applying the Concepts

1. The point of this question is to get students to think about effectively serving customer needs. The exact procedure for handling fast-food orders varies from year to year and store to store, but some general trends have been consistent for many years.

   McDonald's is a superb marketing company that uses a carefully tuned production system. To fit this production system, McDonald's has made the strategic decision to offer a standardised product - "one size fits all." Each Big Mac comes with the same mix of toppings unless the customer specifically requests a different mix. If a customer makes a special request, it is treated as a "grill" order: sent back to the kitchen for special preparation. The customer waits, often shunted aside while other customers are served, until the burger is cooked.

   The college's restaurant has more customer-oriented systems: non-standard meals are treated in stride, and prepared to order much faster than McDonald's can handle an exception. This is much closer to the marketing concept: the exact customer need is satisfied.

   The McDonald's system offers the pluses of speed, efficiency, and consistency. If a customer's desires match the average profile that McDonald's targets, this system can provide high satisfaction. The individual-oriented system used by the college's restaurant offers better service for people with specific preferences, but is less efficient overall. McDonald's can offer several short waiting lines with its system, but the restaurant offers only one long queue.

   Overall, all of these restaurants follow the marketing concept, but they execute it differently. Students should be able to spot the differences and to make value judgements about them.

2. All shopping centres are different, but most have several competing stores selling the same categories of goods. It is typical to have many competing clothing and shoe stores, and often at least two bookstores, record stores, or department stores.

   Do shopping centres serve the goals of maximising consumption, consumer satisfaction, consumer choice, or quality of life? To some extent, all of these goals are promoted by shopping centres. The convenient availability of many goods from many outlets promotes consumer satisfaction, consumer choice, and quality of life. However, the overall "shopping centre experience" arguably promotes consumption as an end in itself, making purchasing in itself a primary goal.

   In general, directly competing stores in a centre are usually quite similar in terms of the merchandise they offer, pricing and return policies, and marketing techniques. This type of saturation marketing implies that maximising consumer choice is not the goal of these stores, but that maximising consumption probably is.

   Shoppers clearly have different attitudes about shopping. Some shoppers are very goal-oriented, and want to do an efficient job of buying a pint of milk at Tesco in the shopping centre, or children's shoes for back-to-school. Other shoppers are using the centre as a place for entertainment: shopping itself is a pleasurable activity. The need being served is a desire for activity and diversion, not necessarily the need for a product *per se*.

Case 1
Amphitrion:
Your Ultimate Host in Greece

Synopsis

Mr Constantinos Mitsiou, the owner and manager of the Greek Amphitrion Group of Companies, was thinking of launching a tour in Greece for teenagers. He wanted to show them the historical, archaeological and natural sites of Greece. Mr Mitsiou was not certain about the success of launching this type of tour. Opinions from his friends and other sources are somewhat mixed. Furthermore, he is inexperienced in dealing with people in this age group since the largest part of his touring business comprise mainly of executives and employees of businesses. He was also concerned about the daily programme of this planned tour, the responses of the potential participants and their parents, and the profitability of this tour.

Teaching Objectives

1. Introduce the marketing concept.

2. Acquaint students with the basic elements of a marketing strategy - market targeting and the marketing mix.

3. Introduce students to marketing cases and begin to build skills in case analysis.

Study Questions

1. Has Mr Mitsiou taken a marketing approach to developing his teenage tour idea? What elements of marketing orientation, if any, are missing?

To know whether Mr Mitsiou had taken a marketing-oriented approach, it is best for students to define the marketing approach. Students should then distinguish between the product, production, selling and marketing concept. Mr Mitsiou first developed his product, which is the teenager tour, after a meeting with other agents at an international convention. This is a clear example of a product orientation activity. Hence, we could say that Mr Mitsiou did not follow the marketing orientation approach, i.e. beginning with identifying customers needs and from there developing a successful product, in developing his teenage tour idea.

Students could mention the following elements of marketing orientation that are missing; (1) There has been very limited marketing research. People in the tourism industry and teaching profession, and a lawyer friend who was also a parent have been consulted to a degree. However, there has been no significant research of the consumers i.e. the teenagers who would potentially be going on tour and their parents who will be paying the tour. This suggest that the Mr Mitsiou does not know his customers. We can quote from the text that all he knew about his potential customers' needs came from his knowledge and therefore related to his prejudices. Expressions confirming this point are such as; “He had in mind”, “To Mr Mitsiou, it was obvious”, or even “Mr Mitsiou knew very well”; (2) Identification of the customer. No account has been taken of the wide difference in maturity of teenagers between the age of 13 to 19 nor the variance in the differing ethnic or cultural backgrounds from where the customers may come; (3) No link to corporate goals. The Amphitrion Group specialises in travel and tours for middle and senior executives. It also has a shipping business and a small amount of casual business from "drop-ins" to its agency offices. There is no evidence that the proposed teenage tours are linked to the core business of the Group. This opinion is reinforced by the failure of Mr Mitsiou to consult with his current staff about his idea; (3) Distinctive competency. The Amphitrion Group competency lies in the corporate and family travel market not in the teenager tour market; (4) No formal advertising strategy. Mr Mitsiou has not thought through an advertising strategy. He has a vague notion that a similar operation is successful in Europe and is putting his faith in word of mouth recommendations. There has been no consideration of the variety of potential tourists who would vary in age from 13 to 19 years; (5) Potential competitors have not been identified and researched in depth.

2. Is the teenage tour idea financially attractive? Does it fit the strengths of the Amphitrion Group? Is it a market that the company naturally understands?

Some students will give a financial breakdown such as:

	Dr.	Dr per person
Cost	2,260,000	56,500
7% mark-up	2,418,200	60,455
Profit	158,200	3,955

Assumptions:

1. 40 people go on tour.
2. All costs are accurate as quoted (no other expense will arise)

Provided the assumptions are met, the tour is financially attractive. Any drop outs will put the tour into a loss.

Students should highlight that the Amphitrion Group's business is in the area of travelling and shipping. They cater for various travel tours mainly revolved around executives and employees of businesses. They have little or no practical experience with teenage tours, thus the figures estimated may contain some element of error. Therefore, the company is not ideally suited to the task although they do have some relevant experience in the field of tourism.

The core competence of the company lies in arranging tours for executives. Dealing with teenagers and their parents will prove to be very different. It is highly likely that the executives are on a company expense account while parents will think about the expenses involved. Therefore the market is different and the company does not naturally understand it, yet again by the same token they do have relevant experience in tourism.

This discussion can help lay the groundwork for a discussion of market segmentation and target marketing. Students should begin to develop confidence that they can think about a segmentation problem and identify potential bases for segmentation. They should also begin to see that the other marketing decisions Mr Mitsiou faces will depend on whom he chooses to target.

3. Would the tour have been attractive to you as a teenager? Would it be attractive to teenagers in your country following the Greek tour? Would you

have found a similar tour of your country attractive? Would your parents find it attractive? Who is the customer in this case and what do they want?

With regard to the attractiveness of the tour , some students will say "yes" while some will say "no". Some possible reasons for saying "yes" are; an opportunity to enrich knowledge of Greece and its history, a chance to enjoy by going to discos and visiting the beaches. Possible reasons for saying "no" are; Greek teenagers are familiar with the archaeological and historical sights, too much to do (schedule is too hectic), need more free time, more attractive to travel abroad, do not want teachers to be the guides.

In relation to the attractiveness of the tour for teenagers of your own country, some possible answers; "yes", reasons; exciting to visit foreign country (different culture, language and tradition), Greece is famous for history, beaches and sunny weather; "no", reasons; because the tour would only appeal to those who are interested in art and culture.

The attractiveness of the tour in your own country, some possible answers and reasons; "yes", reasons; exploring different parts of the country that have not been explored before, meeting new people, exchange ideas and having fun; "no", reasons; would prefer to travel abroad, have seen most parts of the country, not as exciting as travelling overseas, do not need an organised tour to visit our own country, we can do it on our own.

Whether parents found the tour attractive, again some possible answers; "yes", reasons; price of tour reasonable, schedule - well planned, parents could spend their holidays independently, educational, safe, ample supervision.

Some students will suggest that the teenagers may be regarded as the consumers as they are the ones who will be utilising the product i.e. going on the holiday. The parents on the other hand, may be appropriately seen as the customers as they are the ones who make the final purchase decision i.e. actually pay for the tour. Therefore Amphitrion must be very tactful in developing their promotional strategy in relation to the teenage tour. This is a good issue to incite class discussion.

4. Is running a tour the only way to see if it would be successful or not? How else do you think its appeal could be tested? How could the tour be changed to be more appealing and less risky?

Running a tour is not the only way to see if it would be successful or otherwise. Students should highlight that in order to assess whether the tour will be a success or not, Amphitrion Group should firstly appraise whether the tour would fit the strengths of the organisation and if the investment in such a project is a viable business venture. Secondly, they could engage in a market research to assess the demand of the product and possible competitors. Ideally, they should engage in an appropriate market research programme using representative sample from schools, students and parents. Such a research would highlight the following points: attractive of the package, time of the year of the tour, duration of the tour, itinerary of the tour, target age ranges, costs, revenues and profits' projections (short and long-term). Subsequently, develop a product based on the findings of the market research exercise.

Students should come up with some possible suggestions as to how the tour could be more appealing and less risky. Some examples are; less activities, giving more time to relax, allowing people to do what they want; less travelling; by reducing the amount of travel and activities, we can assume that cost will be reduced, thus less price means more sales and hence less risk.

Teaching Suggestions

This case was selected to accompany the first chapter because students should easily identify with the product. The case should impress them with the many aspects of marketing. It also introduces them to case analysis. The instructor can use the case to suggest topics that students will cover during the course and to show that these topics have real world applications.

The instructor can ask how many of the students feel there is a need for the kind of product Mr Mitsiou has designed. How many of them would invest in Mr Mitsiou's business? This discussion should lay the foundation for an interesting case discussion.

If the instructor uses the case later in the marketing course, he/she may wish to add a 5th question by asking students to develop a full marketing strategy and plan for the teenage tour.

Instructors can use this case with the pricing chapter or with the product and new product chapters. If used with the new product chapter, students may also be asked to evaluate Mr Mitsiou's actions in terms of the new-product development process outlined in the chapter.

Jokes and Quotes

Marketing is to selling
What seduction is to abduction.

The graveyard of business is littered with companies that failed to recognise inevitable changes.
ANON

A salesman is one who sells goods that won't come back to customers who will.
ANON

We follow the law of demand and supply.
ANON

We're a non-profit-making organisation. We don't mean to be, but we are.
ANON

Almost everything comes from almost nothing.
FREDERICK AMIEL

We don't want to push our ideas on to the customer, we simply want to make what they want.
LAURA ASHLEY

Business is a profession often more requiring for its practice as much knowledge, and quite as much skill, as law and medicine, and requiring also the possession of money.
WALTER BAGEHOT

The only real gauge of success we have is profit - honest profit.
REX BEACH

Civilisation and profits go hand in hand.
CALVIN COOLIDGE

Business has only two basic functions - marketing and innovation.
PETER DRUCKER

In nature nothing can be given, all things are sold
RALPH WALDO EMERSON

Marketing is simply sales with a college education.
JOHN FREUND

Few people at the beginning of the nineteenth century needed an adman to tell them what they wanted.
JOHN KENNETH GALBRAITH

It is not necessary to advertise food to hungry people, fuel to cold people, or houses to the homeless.
JOHN KENNETH GALBRAITH

It is an ill bargain, when no one wins.
SCOTTISH PROVERB

The consumer, so it is said, is the king . . . each is a voter who uses his money as votes to get things done that he wants done.
PAUL A. SAMUELSON

Pan Am takes good care of you. Marks and Spencer loves you. Securicor cares . . . At Amstrad: "We want your money".
ALAN SUGAR

The first rule of business: Find out what the man you are dealing with wants, and give it to him.
WARREN TATE

Advertising can't sell any product; it can only help to sell a product the people want to buy.
JEREMY TUNSTALL

A businessman is a hybrid of a dancer and a calculator.
PAUL VALERY

It is rare enterprise that can assume it will be serving exactly the same market with the same products in ten years time.
JESSE WERNER

Profits are part of the mechanism by which society decides what it wants to see produced.
HENRY WALLICH

Man might be defined as "An animal that makes exchanges".
RICHARD WHATELY

Chapter 2

Marketing and Society:

Social Responsibility and Marketing Ethics

Chapter Objectives

After reading this chapter, you should be able to:

1. List and respond to the social criticisms of marketing.
2. Define consumerism and environmentalism and explain how they affect marketing strategies.
3. Describe the principles of socially responsible marketing.
4. Explain the role of ethics in marketing.

Chapter Overview

A marketing system should sense, serve, and satisfy consumer needs and improve the quality of consumers' lives. In working to meet consumer needs, marketers may take some actions that are not to everyone's liking or benefit. Marketing managers should be aware of the main criticisms of marketing. Marketing's impact on individual consumer welfare has been criticised for its high prices, deceptive practices, high-pressure selling, shoddy or unsafe products, planned obsolescence, and poor service to disadvantaged consumers. Marketing's impact on society has been criticised for creating false wants and too much materialism, too few social goods, cultural pollution, and too much political power. Critics have also levelled criticisms against marketing's impact on other businesses for harming competitors and reducing competition through acquisitions, practices that create barriers to entry, and unfair competitive marketing practices. Concerns about the marketing system have led to citizen-action movements such as consumerism and environmentalism. Many companies originally opposed these social movements and laws, but most of them now recognise a need for positive consumer information, education, and protection. Some companies have followed a policy of enlightened marketing based on the principles of consumer orientation, innovation, value creation, social mission, and social orientation.

Teaching Notes

Refer to the following pages for teaching notes.

Social Criticisms of Marketing

Transparency PM 2-1 relates to the material on pp.36-49.

Marketing's Impact on the Consumer

High Prices

Marketing is blamed for high prices due to distribution, advertising and promotion costs, and heavy mark-ups. Distribution and promotion costs are largely competitively regulated and a close analysis of most businesses will show very close self-regulation in these areas to keep costs to the minimum necessary to deliver them to the consumer. Excessive mark-ups are also often taken out of context, although marketers would do well to admit that some - not all or most - businesses do have excessive margins. However, you may point out that most of these examples come from uncompetitive industries that do not much use the marketing concept, such as the medical and legal professions. Deceptive practices, promotions, unsafe products, planned obsolescence, and high pressure selling do sometimes occur. But the bottom line is that in addition to being illegal in many cases, these practices tend to drive customers to seek other suppliers and eventually self-terminate.

Marketing's Impact on Society as a Whole

Marketing is seen by some as a too powerful influence on the rest of society. While evidence certainly exists that support these criticisms in some cases, you may wish to discuss core values at this point. It may be true that some marketing efforts result in undesirable effects but that it is also true that in most cases people choose to behave undesirably. An advertisement for example may make owning a pair of £100 trainers more desirable but it does not make people want to kill and rob for them. Values are a two way street and marketers are often blamed for individual failures beyond their control.

Marketing's Impact on Other Businesses

Again, much of this criticism attacks straw man positions. Poor business decisions in mergers, acquisitions, and entering new markets are not due to marketing efforts. Moreover, most blatantly exploitative ventures require better laws.

Notes for PM 2-1

Actions To Regulate Marketing

Transparency PM 2-2 relates to the material on pp.49-51.

Consumerism

Many students will be surprised to learn that the beginning of consumerism as a movement can be traced to President Kennedy's Consumer's "Bill of Rights".

Right to Be Safe - Right to be safe refers to consumer's expectation that the product and its proper use should not endanger the user.

Be informed - Be informed means that the consumer should have access to relevant and reasonable product information. Companies should not hide information about products but nor should consumers assume that they have no responsibilities for their own behaviour.

Be Heard - Be heard means that consumers should have the means to tell companies of their satisfaction or complaints and reasonably expect that producer will respond to their wants.

To Choose - To choose means both that consumers should not be coerced into buying and that a competitive marketplace will provide them with some selection among products.

Quality of Life Issues - Quality of life issues arise as consumer groups argue with producers about what a product should do and how marketing can improve life quality through product education and information.

Environmentalism

Ecosystems - Ecosystems refer to how production affects the chain-of-life in the natural environment in which consumers and employees live.

Pollution - Pollution issues centre on harmful by-products of production and packaging. Long-term- issues affect planning of new products.

Growth Issues - Growth issues affect a company's ability to respond to new needs with new plants, suppliers, channels of distribution, and new products themselves.

Tip

The key is to suggest to students that consumerism (and environmentalism) need not be antagonistic towards marketing. In most cases, marketing should view these movements as sources of information about how to meet consumer needs better.

Notes for PM 2-2

Enlightened Marketing

Transparency PM 2-3 relates to the material on pp.53- 56.

The enlightened marketing concept hold that a company's marketing should support the best long-run performance of the marketing system. Enlightened marketing and marketing ethics work together to create socially responsible marketing practices. Enlightened marketing consists of five key principles:

1. Consumer-Oriented Marketing

Means the company should view and organise its marketing activities from the consumer's point of view.

2. Innovative Marketing

Requires that a company seek real product and marketing improvements. Overlooking improvements or settling on "bells and whistles" eventually leads to a loss of competitive advantage.

3. Value Marketing

Holds that a company should put most of its resources into value-building marketing investments. This principle would reprioritise marketing decisions from using incentives to affect reapportionment of demand to long-term incentives to create brand loyalty by constant improvement in the value consumers receive from the firm's offer.

4. Sense-of-Mission Marketing

Means that a company defines its mission in broad social terms rather than narrow product terms. Product use by the target consumer should help advance those social goals to the benefit and profit of consumer, company, and society alike.

5. Societal Marketing

Holds that a company should make marketing decisions by considering consumer's wants, the company's requirements, and society's long-run interests. Desirable products give both immediate satisfaction and long term benefits. Pleasing products satisfy in the short term but may harm consumers. Salutary products are good for consumers but have low present appeal. Deficient products provide neither short term satisfaction nor long term benefits.

Notes for PM 2-3

Marketing Ethics

These notes supplement the material on pp.56-60 and provides additional information on Marketing Ethics for in-class discussion

Distributor Relations

A comprehensive implementation of marketing ethics should include policies and guidelines for defining the company's relationship with distributors. Ethical standards help build trust and confidence in the channel and can be an asset in tough economic times.

Advertising Standards

When considered in light of increasing activism among consumer groups to regulate advertising, marketers have a unique opportunity to proactively address the needs for strong advertising ethical standards. While protecting free speech, marketers could adopt a statement on ethics in advertising that promotes accurate information exchange, encourages creative and innovative message generation. Advertising ethics could go further by denouncing exploitation of women as objects in ads, minorities as stereotypically inferior to whites, and violence as problem-solving or socially acceptable. Without legal regulation, marketers could publicly promise to cease using advertisers who fall to meet the standards.

Customer Service

How to respond to customers and how to treat them while responding says a lot about a company. Customer ethics might be posted or mailed to customers to encourage all employees to live up to a standard known to the customer before the sale.

General Code of Ethics

Corporate marketing policies can provide broad guidelines that everyone in the organisation must follow.

Pricing

Ethics can influence strategic decisions on such pricing decisions as market penetration versus market skimming.

Product Development

May be influenced by ethical codes seeking more desirable products or changes in salutary product concepts to make them more desirable.

Tip

Ask students examples of voluntary bodies that influence activities of companies. Some examples, ASA, ITC, Consumer Association and Trading Standards.

Principles for Public Policy Toward Marketing

These notes relate to the material on pp.60-62.

Toward a Public Policy for Marketing

The Principle of Consumer and Producer Freedom

When consumer and producer freedom drive the marketplace, needs are met more efficiently and profitably than under any other system. Consumer and producer freedom have lead to the highest standard of living in history.

The Principle of Curbing Potential Harm

Political intervention is warranted if and when a transaction or potential transaction creates harm to either party or any third party.

The Principle of Meeting Basic Needs

The marketing system should serve disadvantaged consumers as well as affluent ones. The marketing system should work to solve problems created when large groups lack purchasing power.

The Principle of Economic Efficiency

This principle is essentially "enlightened self-interest." Producers are motivated to cut costs and raise quality to meet the needs of value-seeking consumers.

The Principle of Innovation

Authentic innovation is the most reliable source of long-term profits and business success. The marketing system encourages innovation by constantly monitoring consumer expectations and needs.

Comments on Discussing the Issues.

1. Some students may feel that the manufacturer should have recalled its products until it had proved that the threat of glass fragments was eliminated. These students should be asked to consider the fact that many malicious and nonsensical rumours have been spread about different companies - in the US, Procter & Gamble and satanism, McDonald's and "wormburgers," and others - showing that consumer complaints may be groundless. Where do these students think that the manufacturer should have drawn the line— at 200 consumer complaints? 50? 1? Would an examination by the responsible authority of 80,000 fragment-free jar have satisfied them? 150,000 jars? A million? They will probably be annoyed by these questions, and feel that it is improper to try to quantify this "life or death" decision, but they should come to see that companies *must* weigh the evidence and potential consequences of their decisions— they cannot act to avoid any possible harm, however slight or unlikely.

   These questions can be turned around for students who feel that the manufacturer made the right decision. How does a company make the trade-off between a few million dollars lost in a product recall versus the potential losses in lawsuits if people had died as a result of glass fragments? What about the injuries to babies, the suffering of parents, the emotional burden on the decision makers of the company, and the harm to company morale, if the complaints about glass fragments were valid?

   There is no way to wrap up this discussion to leave everyone feeling good, but it will help students recognise the complexity of questions of social responsibility in marketing.

2. If advertising created barriers to entry, there would be little brand switching from established brands to new ones, new brands would have difficulty challenging the leading brands, and advertising intensity would be higher in industries with few competitors than with many competitors. "Yet, one does not find any of these things.... In summary, the weight of systematic research indicates that advertising is not a barrier to entry into new markets. On the contrary, advertising makes entry possible" (Kenneth E. Runyon, *Advertising*, 2d ed., Columbus, Ohio: Charles E. Merrill Publishing Company, 1984, pp. 240-41).

   The evidence against marketing as a barrier to entry does not say that companies can compete with me-too products and little advertising against established, heavily-advertised brands. To break into the wine cooler business, for example, Miller Brewing Co. set an advertising budget of $40 million to launch Matilda Bay. If a product has something to really set it apart, though, advertising helps get the word out economically and allows products like Cajun Cola and Vernor's Ginger Ale to carve out profitable market niches. Thus, an unknown manufacturer of household cleaning products who developed a cleanser superior to the market leader products could use limited advertising in magazines, direct-response advertising, and publicity to stimulate sales in the face of the market leader's multi-million dollar marketing efforts.

3. Industries often fight against increased government regulations, but for ethical companies, legal constraints may be preferable to voluntary restraints. If the government sets the limits on air and water pollution levels, for example, all companies must comply. If maximum pollution levels are set by an industry code, companies that

choose not to comply gain a competitive advantage by not paying for smokestack scrubbers, low-sulphur coal, or other pollution- control devices that their more principled competitors use. Thus, the chemical company might want to influence the government's determination of what levels are acceptable, but it would probably prefer government regulations to a stringent industry code that some competitors might violate.

4. Procter & Gamble is a good example. It is clearly an "enlightened marketer," practising consumer-oriented marketing. It is also one of the best examples of an innovative marketer. P&G has long emphasised advertising over sales promotion as a way of building customer loyalty. Its official Statement of Purpose describes the company's mission: "We'll provide products of superior quality and value that best fill the needs of the world's consumers." And it follows the principle of societal marketing. P&G's withdrew its highly successful Rely tampons after evidence linked the product to the sometimes-fatal toxic shock syndrome, a strong demonstration of corporate social responsibility.

In considering whether your university or college is an enlightened marketer, look for examples of consumer-oriented marketing, innovative marketing, value marketing, a university-wide sense of mission, and an orientation to serving society's long-run interests.

5. The marketing concept can be expressed as "find a need and fill it, at a profit." The societal marketing concept is more elaborate: "find a need and fill it, at a profit, taking into account the consumer's and society's long-run interests." On the surface, the societal marketing concept appears so reasonable that every company should immediately adopt it. Yet, there are both philosophical and pragmatic objections to this concept. The philosophical objection is that this practice has businesspeople substituting their perceptions of what is in the social good, for consumers' perceptions or the views of elected policymaking officials. The pragmatic objection is that marketing managers have no special expertise in defining and acting in the public interest. Marketers may not foresee the unintended consequences of their "socially responsible" actions. For example, when a cereal manufacturer reduces a product's sugar content to save children's teeth, the result may be a substitution of even sweeter and less nutritious breakfast products rather than a reduction in cavities.

Unfortunately, like most matters of social responsibility in marketing, this question is not as clear-cut as these arguments suggest. Are marketers supposed to *ignore* consumers' and society's long-run interests? Even if consumers are willing to ignore product hazards, is it moral to sell the products to them? As in Q1 and many other questions of social responsibility, the fundamental issue seems to be, where does the marketer draw the line?

6. A major theme in this textbook and this instructor's manual is that marketing is a part of students' lives, now and in the future. The views presented have generally been positive, because there is much that is admirable in our marketing system. It is not perfect, though, and students should recognise that *they can help make it better*. They can improve our marketing system as practitioners by offering value and integrity to consumers, and they can improve it as consumers by demanding the same from the companies with which they interact.

Comments on Applying the Concepts

1. **(a)** Societal marketing is on the increase, but it requires great efforts on the part of the company that undertakes it. Polaroid, for example, has made great strides in reducing environmental impacts. Polaroid has redesigned its manufacturing processes to reduce the amount of toxic waste produced, and to improve the disposal of what is unavoidably produced. The company has made strong efforts to reduce packaging and packing materials, and to use recycled and recyclable materials to the greatest extent possible. These efforts earned Polaroid a place on the "Most Improved" list in *Fortune* magazine's survey of corporate environmental impacts.

   Newer companies are often very conscious of societal marketing. The Body Shop, for example, carefully assesses every corporate action for its social and environmental impact. It has built factories in areas of high unemployment, supported grassroots economic development in the third world, and supported environmental causes.

   (b) What distinguishes true societal marketing from imitation societal marketing is the beneficiary. In true societal marketing, all of society benefits. In imitation societal marketing, the marketer is the primary beneficiary. This type of marketing is very common for alcohol and tobacco products. Beer manufacturers often run ads sponsoring moderation, and asking teens not to drink and drive. These efforts are probably at least partially sincere, but they are also designed to prevent restrictive legislation. Furthermore, the credibility of the campaigns is undercut by other efforts of the beer manufacturers to increase consumption per capita. The hottest trend in beer in late 1993 is larger bottles: 20 to 22 ounce tankers that people can order instead of the usual 12 ounce size. This is hardly the type of marketing that will increase moderation!

2. This question is designed to reiterate one of the key ideas of this course: the purpose of marketing is to find and fulfil consumer needs. Asking students what needs to be done and show them many ways that marketing can aid society.

   Students should be able to list many things that need to be done. Common examples will include such topics as:

improve the environment	provide for the homeless
create more jobs	increase recycling
reduce urban violence	develop a pollution-free car
improve education	reduce tobacco and alcohol use
make health care	more available and affordable
cut the spread of AIDS	

   Listing ways that marketing can help with one of these problems can be eye-opening for your students. They may discover a new way to look at things: that what they had considered as a social problem or a political problem can be recast as a marketing problem. Looked at in this way, some often these problems may appear more tractable, because marketing offers tangible tools that can help in accomplishing objectives.

Case 2
Nestle:
Singled Out Again and Again

Synopsis

Nestle SA is the world's largest food company with annual world-wide turnover of Sfr 57.5 billion. The company employs 200,000 people and produces its products in 494 factories in 69 countries. Many Nestle products and brands are quite familiar such as; Nescafe, Perrier, Libby and many others. In July 1994, Nestle was yet again to face one of many protests the company had faced over the past twenty years. The General Synod of the Church of England was about to call for the ban of Nescafe and for the disinvestment of £1.1 million in Nestle. In the late 1970s and early 1980s, Nestle was under fire from health professionals who charged the company with encouraging Third World mothers to give up breast feeding and use company-prepared formula to feed their babies. Critics have accused Nestle in their use of sophisticated promotional techniques to persuade hundreds of thousands of poverty-stricken, poor educated mothers that formula feeding was better for their children. Formula feeding is not usually a wise practice in such countries. Because of poor living conditions and habits, people cannot or do not clean bottles properly and often mix formula with impure water. Furthermore, due to poverty families cannot purchase sufficient quantities of formula. In 1974, Nestle was heavily criticised by certain parties who produced pamphlets accusing Nestle for behaving in an immoral and unethical manner. These actions won public attention. Nestle sued them for defaming and damaging its reputation and at the end of a two-year trial the company won the case. Due to the significant public attention the company believed its public relations were damaged.

Teaching Objectives

1. Consider the range of marketing activities that raise social criticisms of a company.

2. Evaluate the marketing activities of a particular company in terms of their impact on the company, consumers, and society.

3. Have students explore their own thinking and opinions on several questionable marketing practices.

Study Questions

1. Was and is Nestle's and the other IMF members' marketing of infant formula "unethical and immoral"? Is it the case that ethical standards should be the responsibility organisations, such as WHO and UNESCO, and that the sole responsibility of firms is to work within the bounds set?

In order to determine whether Nestle and the other IMF members marketing of infant formula "unethical and immoral" or otherwise, the following key considerations must be taken into account; (1) Products which are appropriate and acceptable in one social environment may be inappropriate in the social environment of another nation. Infant formula products are demanding products. There must be pure water to prepare them, refrigeration to safely store unused formula and customers must be able to read instructions and have the income to purchase adequate quantities of the products. The greater the existence of these risk factors, the less appropriate the product becomes for marketing. Knowingly marketing the infant formula to countries that has many of the risk factors is considered as unethical and immoral; (2) Good products made without defects may still be inappropriate because of the inherent riskiness of the environment in which those products are to be sold. Nestle and other manufacturers of infant formula often stated that the market they sought to reach consisted only those who could safely use the product and who had adequate income. However, many developing nations continuously showed that vast number of the population did not meet the necessary requirements for safe use of infant formula. By selling these products to such people, the organisation knows with virtual certainty that there would be overdilution, improper mixing or contamination with impure water; (3) Companies may not close their eyes once a product is sold. There is continuing responsibility to monitor product use, resale and consumption to determine who is actually using the product and how. Post marketing review is a necessary step in the process. Naturally, critics attacked the companies for such a careless attitude toward learning the true facts surrounding the products; (4) Products which have been sold to consumers who cannot safely use them must be demarketed. Organisations performed demarketing involve withdrawal or recall of products, limiting the selling of the product or even a halting if future sales of products that has been proven unsafe in the market place; (5) Marketing strategies must be appropriate to the circumstances of the consumers, the social and economic environment in which they live and to the political realities. Consumer advertising to people for whom product use is highly risky is unacceptable and unethical marketing behaviour; (6) Marketing techniques are inappropriate when they exploit consumer's vulnerability. During the 1960s and 1970s, firms in the infant formula industry used "milk nurse" sales personnel who dressed in nurse's uniforms and visited new mothers in hospitals in countries such as Kenya, parts of South America and other developing countries. They would try to encourage the mother to allow their babies to be fed by the formula, rather than breast feeding, to encourage adoption. Mothers who have given birth are vulnerable and the use of milk nurses to take advantage of that vulnerability is seen as unethical and unfair. Considering the above factors, some students will say that the infant formula industry has been pinpointed for its unethical behaviour and immorality for breaching one or more of the above. Uneducated women are particularly susceptible to the promotional materials and marketing tactics used by Nestle and similar companies. The use of promotional leaflets coupled with advice from nurses who had been influenced by Nestle to favour bottle feeding persuaded new mother to abandon breast feeding. By giving samples and discounted formula to nursing mothers, Nestle effectively removed the final barrier restraining mothers from switching to bottle feeding - cost. Once a nursing mother switched to bottle feeding it is not possible for her to return to breast feeding. Nestle has a moral obligation to educate the mothers in Third World countries regarding the need for adequate, continuous supply of formula and the hygiene conditions for its use. Other students will say that Nestle did not foresee the ethical dilemmas in the first instance but have acted to reduce the problems once they were highlighted. Had they gathered better information prior to entering the market they could have predicted the problems. If they had predicted the problems but went ahead anyway then they would have been acting immorally. Nestle believe they are acting ethically and morally as they focus on the beneficial aspects of the market, which are in line with the founders' desire to "save a child's life". It is not a market they need to be in but believe they should, morally, be there.

Some students will highlight that with the rise of multinational corporations operating in many countries of the world, there is an obvious need for the policing of ethical standards. In an ideal world, this would be done by the companies themselves, but as experience has shown us that this rarely, if ever, happen. Therefore, some other form of "police force" is required. While the world's marketplace is becoming smaller, the political stage is becoming more fragmented, so the task cannot be left to individual governments. In any case, public opinion on ethics tends to change in the light of scientific or other revelations via the media and usually far more rapidly than ever the most enlightened governments can change or implement new legislation. Also, in many of the developing countries, governments may be too unstable, too poor, or both to afford what they might well regard as the luxury of such standards. For example in the case of the chemical leak at the Union Carbide plant in Bhopal, India, which resulted in several hundred deaths. The Indian government had an agency which was supposed to enforce safety, but it was seriously understaffed. For all its faults, the United Nations Organisation is the nearest thing in the world that has a cohesive political force and so global policing must be carried out under its authority. WHO and UNICEF have generally over the years earned respect for their humanitarian efforts and therefore are the logical bodies to work alongside governments to set and monitor ethical standards and to encourage compliance throughout the world. Other students should highlight that ethical standards are not merely the responsibility of organisations such as WHO. Social responsibility should be placed in the hands of individual company's part of their wider role in society. Companies should have social conscience and develop corporate marketing ethics policies that serve as guidelines for everyone in the organisation to follow. Large firms such as Nestle should aim to be an economic, intellectual and social asset to the world. They need to look beyond legal requirements and conducts their affairs with honesty and integrity.

2. The WHO code is a recommendation to government. Is it Nestle's responsibility to operate according to the national legislation of any given country, or to follow WHO's recommendations to that country? Who is sovereign? Do international bodies setting international standards, such as WHO and UNICEF, have a moral responsibility to make those standards clearly understood by all parties and to demand action by national governments to enact them?

"... governments have been slow and reluctant to prohibit infant formula promotion. For example, in Taiwan 10% of babies are breast fed, but the government did not restrict promotion until 1993 and then only on TV advertisements".

The above statement proves that the delay in enacting recommendations may result in situation where consumers are relatively unprotected. In light of this, some students will suggest that Nestle should follow WHO's recommendations to that particular country instead of the national legislation. This does not mean that Nestle will not adhere to the national legislation. The national legislation may represent the minimum requirement to be fulfilled but there is no reason why Nestle should not "give more" i.e. by fulfilling recommendations when adhering to legislation. Other students will state that WHO's recommendations are not legally binding therefore Nestle should conform primarily to the national legislation of the countries they have operations. Furthermore some students will be the opinion of that Nestle has a moral obligation, as a wealthy European company, to work within the WHO code. This is a very good question to incite class discussion.

Some students will highlight that with the former approach Nestle would be able to operate within the boundary of legislation as well as the WHO code. Nestle must show their stance is a solid one instead of "exploiting" the respective national legislation. Technically the national legislation is superior but taking into consideration ethical conduct and moral issues WHO's recommendations should be sovereign. Other students will emphasise that guidelines and recommendations by WHO and UNESCO are not legally binding and therefore national legislation is sovereign. Nevertheless, from the moral point of view Nestle should follow the guidelines set out by WHO for the promotion of their infant formula regardless of whether or not these guidelines have been adopted by the government.

Some students will mention that international bodies setting up international standards such as WHO and UNICEF are only responsible to assist the companies in understanding these standards (this is their secondary objective - they have many other primary goals and objectives to fulfil). Ideally it is the responsibility of the firms to make sure that they understand these standards. Nevertheless due to the current situation, it is best for WHO to accept this secondary objective as a primary one at least until they are satisfied that the firms can and will (regardless via enforcement or willingness and ability) take over these responsibility themselves. Other students will suggest that WHO does have a moral responsibility to explain and ensure that standards are understood. It is however not their responsibility to enforce the standards. They serve as recommending bodies but cannot impose mandatory requirements. Students should emphasise that demanding action by national governments to enact the international standards may put constraint in the respective international bodies in carrying out their mission as such it could possibly strain the relationship between the two i.e. when the government "MUST" follow what is being set up. It is up to the respective countries to evaluate and decide as to whether to enact these standards or otherwise. The responsibility of organisations such as WHO and UNESCO are to set standards and make the respective countries aware and understand the benefits of conforming to the standards. Perhaps demanding action is inevitable but it is preferable that these countries enact the international standards at their own free will. Demand should only come after much effort of diplomatic tactics.

3. Are Nestle just unlucky or did their actions precipitated their being singled out by activists? Is the activist's focus on Nestle unjust and itself dangerous? What accounts for Nestle's continuing in the infant formula market despite the protests?

At first, it should be pointed out that Nestle is not just unlucky to be singled out by the activists. As we know, for the activists, the purpose of their actions is aimed at "the entire infant formula industry" (see case, line 33, p65). On the other hand, under fire of their actions, some companies which produced infant formula have been "using furtive branding to hide ownership" (see case, line 14, pp 66). The following are a number of reasons why the activists focus on Nestle; (1) Nestle is the world's largest food company with annual world-wide sales of Sfr 57.5 billion. Large size means greater visibility, making it vulnerable to activists; (2) Nestle has produced infant formula for a long time. Over 100 years ago Henri Nestle invented manufactured baby food and the company have been suppliers ever since; (3) In the 1970's-1980's, although activists called for a boycott on Nestle's infant formula, "Nestle have not shrunk from the controversy, they continue to sell infant formula and display the Nestle name on almost all their brands" (see case, line 12, p.66); (4) In the 1970's, Nestle adopted their defensive strategy to sue the activists for defamation; (5) In 1991, Nestle claimed their sales increased when activists continue to call for ban on Nescafe. The above attitudes and actions lead to the arousal of the activists' indignation. The above gives the impression of Nestle as not being sensitive to the subtle "side-effects" of their "good intention". Students need to emphasise Nestle as a caring organisation must be aware of the local environmental factors of the respective countries. The business world as a global village means that any "hiccups" in one country cannot be concealed from the knowledge of the "village" as this will affect the reputation and goodwill of the company thus their existence as a going concern.

The activists brought the issue to the forefront by targeting a well-known brand name thus creating more impact with the public. The continued controversy keeps the issue in the media but is very damaging to Nestle's public relations, the signalling out of only one of the major companies involved in the marketing of formula to the Third World countries seem to be unfair. If the activists continue to attack Nestle, the company's image may be damaged irreparably. Nestle is aware of the potential damage which the activists may be able to inflict and have chosen to confront them Should the activists continue to attack Nestle, the strength and commitment of the company may result in the activists downfall as Nestle can financially afford any legal action necessary to defeat them.

It is important for students to present that Nestle should continue in the infant formula market but must address the issues raised by the protesters as well as making very clear their intentions of staying in the market. Withdrawal from the market may be interpreted as being in the wrong. This will transform the public's and consumers' perception negatively towards Nestle and all its products. Giving in to the pressure groups means signally to them that their intervention is acceptable. With this, there is a possibility of constant intervention in the future which may interrupt the organisation's operation. Nestle's intention "save a child's life" may also be part of its moral obligation in "giving back" to the world society but it must be carried out in the context of the respective country's environmental factors i.e. political, economic, social and the degree of development etc.

4. Did Nestle benefit from confronting the activists directly in court and winning? Should firms ever confront activists directly? What other forms of actions are available to the company? Should firms withdraw from legitimate markets because of the justified or unjustified actions of pressure groups?

As this particular case has dragged on now for twenty years, clearly Nestle has not gained from its court win. Anyway, as was pointed out in question one, there is often a lag between legislation and public opinion and in the case of large, easily identifiable, multinational corporations companies like Nestle, it is public opinion that matters. "Customers and investors are increasingly demanding higher standards from the companies they deal with. And those that do not match up are penalised". This does not mean that companies should not confront activists groups but they do need to realise that such confrontations carry many risks. For example, Shell taking on Greenpeace over Brent Spar could perhaps be said to have broken even in the publicity stakes after Greenpeace admitted that some of its original facts were wrong, but admission came too late to prevent a boycott of Shell in Germany. Shell is once again in the activists firing line over its current activities in Nigeria, "environmental campaigners and politicians maintain that Shell is responsible for the damage inflicted on the Niger Delta over the past forty years and that it should pull out of Nigeria". In its defence Shell has launched a press campaign with full page advertisement emphasising the potential benefits to the Nigerian people, if they continue with the project. Some students will suggest that for a company that falls into the snare of public image problems regarding its social role, it is best to approach the situation with spirit of co-operation and constructive participation with opposing groups. Other students will suggest that an organisatic should strive to resolve as many of the objections.

There are four basic strategies for systematically dealing with social responsibility issues; defence, reaction, accommodation and proactive. (1) Defence; a business using a defence strategy tries to minimise or avoid additional obligations linked to a problem or problems. Commonly used defence tactics include legal manoeuvring and seeking the support of trade unions that embrace the company's way of doing business and support the industry.

Business often lobby to avoid government actions or regulation; (2) Reaction; a business adopting a reaction strategy allows a condition or potential problem to go unresolved until the public learns about it. The situation may be known to management or it may be unknown. In either case, the business denies responsibility but tries to resolve the problem, deal with its consequences and continue doing business as usual to minimise the negative impact; (3) Accommodation strategy; a business using an accommodation strategy assumes responsibility for its actions. A business might adopt this strategy when special interest groups are encouraging a particular action or when the business perceives that if it fails to react the government will pass a law to ensure compliance; (4) Proactive; a business that uses a proactive strategy assumes responsibility and responds to accusations made against it without outside pressure or the threat of government intervention. A proactive strategy requires management its own free will to support an action or cause.

As mentioned earlier there are dangers involved when a firm tries to counteract adverse publicity generated by pressure groups. Even if a company is innocent of the accusations or not as guilty as originally portrayed, in the public mind, the company's name will have been linked with the controversy and this often lingers long after the details of the original issues have been forgotten as in the case of Nestle. So companies need to carefully weigh the pros and cons of such actions. Earlier this year many of the ferry companies decided against live animal exports as they decided that the benefits of such trade did not outweigh public opinions.

5. How should Nestle respond the threats from the General Synod in 1994? Since Nestle claimed sales increased after the Nescafe Boycott in 1991, should they just ignore the problem?

Students will come up with several ways in responding to the General Synod's threats. Some of them are; (1) Adjusting Nestle's strategy and attitude to make it suitable for new environments. It effectively means that Nestle will chose not to have a "head-on" confrontation with the activists which is subjective in terms of benefits but certain in terms of damages. For example, this can be achieved by as strictly adhering to the standards set by WHO and UNESCO where such conformance will clearly and publicly communicated to the world at large. This proposal is based on the following facts; (i) Nestle is getting into a difficult situation. There is a problem in its relationship with the public; (ii) This difficult situation will worsen if Nestle cannot manage to change its strategy and attitude; (iii) It is felt that Nestle will eventually pay for their indifference should the current situation continues. Perhaps the sales growth will continue in the near future but the rate of growth might be affected. Taking it to extreme the infant formula issues will inflict irreparable damage to the brand Nestle thus affecting the whole range of products under the Nestle umbrella. The advantage of the proposal is that it will improve Nestle macroenvironment i.e. develop and maintain successful relationship with the public (including the pressure group) thus getting out of the long overdue messy situation. On the other hand there is a possibility that an internal rift may also occur as to the decision to give in to the demands of the pressure groups which may give rise to adverse behaviours within the organisation; (2) Nestle may choose to maintain its current approach to the situation. The organisation can confront the pressure groups via legal actions or ignore the activists altogether. This may save Nestle from humiliation of changing their stance but this may also have the effect of deteriorating Nestle's image as well as taking a toll on its market share. Nestle's response must take into consideration the macroenvironment in its totality as well as its recent development. There are a number of new changes in the global business environment; (i) Since the 1970's the number and power of the public interest groups have increased with the like of Greenpeace and WHO. They pressure business executives to pay more attention to consumers rights, environmental issues, infant and minority rights etc.; (ii) People vary in their attitude towards the natural world e.g. food producers have found growing markets for natural products such as health foods, healthy breast feeding methods etc.; (iii) The public pays more attention to their society. They require businesses to undertake more societal responsibility. The above issues must be taken into account by Nestle because its success depends on its responses to changes in terms of the above as well as the global market as a whole.

Teaching Suggestions

A few good infant formula stories will quickly warm up the discussion of this case. Students are likely to have had experiences with siblings, nieces and nephews, or other children to relate to the class. For example, someone may tell about an aunt or a sister who had to change baby formulas several times before a satisfactory one was found. For mothers of allergic babies, it can be a harrowing experience.

Although the issues of the case are closely tied to the chapter on marketing and society, the instructor can also use the case to focus on other marketing topics. The question of mothers' (and physicians') decisions about which formula to use for a particular baby provides an interesting context for examining the buyer decision process presented in Chapter 7, Consumer Markets: Influences on Consumer Behaviour. The infant formula decision can be contrasted with other baby-related buying decisions, such as diapers.

The Nestlé case also provides a fascinating situation for discussing certain concepts in Chapter 18, Promoting Products: Communications and Promotion Strategy.

References

Baby Formula TV Ads in Taiwan, Wall Street Journal, 24th February 1993, p A8.

Hamilton Kirstie (1995), Underfire, Sunday Times, 19 November , pp Business Focus 3.

W. Michael Hoffman & Robert E. Frederick, "The Ethics of Marketing Nestle Infant Formula" in Business Ethics, pp 416-421, Mc Graw Hill, 3rd Edition 1995.

Jokes and Quotes

Marketing: Doing what you can for the customer; not doing the customer for what you can.

The businessman was giving his son a lecture: "In business, ethics are important. For instance, a customer comes in and pays a $20 account in cash. As he leaves, you notice that he's given you two $20 notes stuck together. Immediately you are faced with an ethical question: Should I tell my partner?"
ANON

Business: the art of extracting money from another man's pocket without resorting to violence.
MAX AMSTERDAM

From any cross-section of ads, the general advertiser's attitude would seem to be: If you are lousy, smelly, idle, status-seeking neurotic moron, give me your money.
KENNETH BROMFIELD

Business should be like religion and science; it should know neither love nor hate.
SAMUEL BUTLER

The search for the best possible product at the most possible mark-up with the shortest possible duration for the earliest possible replacement.
JOHN CIARDI

The fact that a business is large, efficient and profitable does not mean that it takes advantage of the public.
CHARLES CLORE?

I always make a point of business ethics, never to tell a lie unless I think I can get away with it
KENNETH & KERRY COOK

I persuade, you educate, they manipulate.
DR ALLEN CRAWFORD

"Do other men, for they would do you! That is the true business concept".
CHARLES DICKENS

It was naive of the 19th century optimists to expect paradise from technology - and it is equally naive of the 20th century pessimists to make technology the scapegoat for such old shortcomings as man's blindness, cruelty, immaturity, greed and sinful pride.
PETER F. DRUCKER

Business that makes nothing but money is a poor kind of business.
HENRY FORD

Every human being has a vote every time he makes a purchase. No one is disenfranchised on account of age, sex, religion, education, length of residence, or failure to register. Every day is election day . . . Moreover minorities count.
W.T.FOSTER and W.CACTHINGS

The customer is an object to be manipulated, not a concrete person whose aims the businessmen is interested to satisfy.
ERICH FROMM

Idealism increases in direct proportion to one's distance from the problem.
JOHN GALSWORTHY

The worst crime against the working people is a company which fails to make a profit.
SAMUEL GOMPERS

I shot an arrow in the air - and it stuck.
GRAFFITI 1980

Business is so much lower a thing than learning that a man used to the last cannot easily bring his stomach down to the first.
LORD HALIFAX

Profit and morality are a hard combination to beat.
HUBERT H. HUMPHREY

The quality of moral behaviour varies in inverse ratio to the number of human beings involved.
ALDOUS LEONARD HUXLEY

When you are skimmimg your customers, you should leave some skin on to grow so that you can skin them again.
NIKITA KHRUSHCHEV

You can fool all the people all of the time if the advertising is right and the budget is big enough.
JOSEPH E. LEVINE

Know your neighbour is not only sound Christianity, it is good business.
DAVID LLOYD-GEORGE

In the jungle of the marketplace, the intelligent buyer must be alert to every commercial sound, to every snapping of a selling twig, to every rustle that may signal the uprising arm holding the knife pointed toward the jugular vein.
DEXTER MASTERS

The consumer today is the victim of the manufacturer who launches on him a regiment of products for which he must make room in his soul.
MARY McCARTHY

Advertising is the place where the selfish interests of the manufacturer coincide with the interests of society.
DAVID OGILVY

The era of low cost energy is almost dead. Popeye has run out of cheap spinach.
PETER PATERSON

There are three classes of men - lovers of wisdom, lovers of honour, lovers of gain.
PLATO

A man of business may talk of philosophy; a man who has none may practise it.
ALEXANDER POPE

If you believe everything you read, better not read.
JAPANESE PROVERB

It is our job to make women unhappy with what they have.
B. EARL PUCKETT

"Faith, hope and charity - but greater than all of these is banking".
SANTANGEL

The truth is, hardly any of us have ethical energy enough for more than one really inflexible point of honour.
GEORGE BERNARD SHAW

Good resolutions are simply checks that men draw on a bank where they have no account.
OSCAR WILDE

Nothing is illegal if 100 businessmen decide to do it.
ANDREW YOUNG

Chapter 3
Strategic Marketing Planning

Chapter Objectives

After reading this chapter, you should be able to:

1. Explain companywide strategic planning and its major steps.
2. Describe how companies develop mission statements and objectives.
3. Explain how companies evaluate and develop their "business portfolios."
4. Explain marketing's role in strategic planning.
5. Describe the marketing management process and the brand plan.
6. Show how marketing organisations are changing.

Chapter Overview

To meet changing conditions in their industries, companies need to look ahead and develop long-term strategies. Marketing plays an important role in strategic planning since it provides information and other inputs to help prepare the strategic plan. Also, strategic planning defines marketing's role in the organisation. An organisation's overall strategic planning and marketing's role in the organisations are discussed in this chapter.

Teaching Notes

Refer to the following pages for teaching notes.

Planning Functional Strategies

Transparency PM 3-1 relates to the material on pp.72-73.

Marketing Role in Strategic Planning

Marketing plays a key role in strategic planning in three ways:

(1) marketing provides a guiding philosophy centred on serving the needs of important consumer groups.

(2) marketing provides inputs to strategic planners by identifying attractive market opportunities and assessing their potential.

(3) marketing designs strategies for reaching objectives within individual business units.

Marketing and the Other Business Functions

Ideally, marketing helps integrate specialised business functions toward meeting consumer needs. This approach places the customer at the centre of the company. All functions must look toward delivering actual customer satisfaction.

Conflict Between Departments

Departments within the firm often compete for scare resources. Further, sometimes the efforts of marketing to improve customer satisfaction lead to increased costs or lost efficiencies in other functional specialities, from their point of view. Marketing must work to help other departments recognise the advantages to the company of achieving customer satisfaction over separate functional efficiencies.

Tip

Ask students why deliver customer satisfactions. The answer is: because it works. Satisfied customers come back and talk to other potential customers - become advocates. Dissatisfied customers talk even more!

This topic is covered extensively in Chapter 11. You may wish to have students preview the discussion on Value Chains, Value Delivery Systems and Total Quality Marketing (Management).

Notes for PM 3-1

Strategic Planning

Transparency PM 3-2 relates to the material on pp.73-91. The following transparencies and notes discuss the portfolio approaches in more detail.

1. Defining the Mission

Mission statements describe what the company wants to accomplish in the larger environment. The text notes the role of mission statements as "invisible hands" that guide operations. You may discuss guidance as an agenda setting function. Mission statements focus organisational attention on some areas and not on others. The dangers of marketing myopia can be addressed here. But the benefits of a focused company in directing energy most productively should also be discussed.

2. SWOT Analysis

It is a summary of the major forces shaping strategy. Strengths and weaknesses relative to the competition and opportunities and threats in the environment. Corporate strategy depends on balancing these.

3. Setting Objectives and Goals

Here strategy begins to be operationally defined. What must each manager do to fulfil the mission? Discuss the need for objective, measurable goals within a specified timetable.

4. Designing the Portfolio

Here you should try and stress the importance of constant evaluation of current businesses in relation to the existing competitive position and the future goals of the company.

5. Planning Marketing and Other Functional Strategies

Discuss with students the concept of marketing as a philosophical orientation for other functional areas. For example, production engineers may design products better if they imagine lay consumers trying to identify usage benefits from the look of a product. Accountants may improve performance and generate business by adapting technical expertise to client's needs and for better understanding and greater information about accounting functions. Point of view differences need not be covered in lecture but you might challenge students to provide specific examples of functional emphasis versus marketing emphasis. Also ethical issues may provide greater competitiveness. For example, marketing may influence company policies on credit. But high interest rates on consumer credit done by an outside bank with the company's name on the card may hurt customer relations.

Tip

Ask students to explain IKEA's dictum: The plan is nothing, planning is everything.

Notes for PM 3-2

Mission Statements

Transparency PM 3-3 relates to the material on pp.73-78 and discusses the importance of Defining the Company Mission from PM 3-2.

A mission statement is a statement of the organisation's purpose - what it wants to accomplish in the larger environment. Good mission statements have the following characteristics:

1. Market oriented

Market definitions of a business are better than product or technical definitions. Mission statements should tell clearly what needs the company meets.

2. Realistic

Mission statements should reflect a careful matching of organisational resources with competitive opportunities.

3. Specific

Concrete, finite and measurable goals and objectives help keep the company focused.

4. Distinctive Competencies

The organisation should focus on what it does best, ideally what it does better than anyone else.

5. Motivating

The company mission should inspire and motivate employees at all levels.

6. Vision

While the statement should be clear and concise, the mission should be guided by an almost "impossible dream" that helps decision-makers guide the company for the next ten to twenty years.

Tip

Give and ask for leaders who effectively communicate their vision. How do they do it? In politics, they could be JFK, Maggie Thatcher or Lee Kuan Yew, in business Richard Branson (Virgin), Lee Iaccoca (Chrysler) or Hayek (Swatch).

Notes for PM 3-3

The Business Portfolio

Transparency PM 3-4 corresponds to Figure 3-2 on p.84 and relates to the discussion on pp.83-88.

Designing the Business Portfolio

The business portfolio is the collection of businesses and products that make up the company. In portfolio analysis, management evaluates the businesses for their strategic fit in meeting company objectives. Strategic Business Units (SBUs) consist of separate units of the company that can be planned independently from other company businesses.

The BCG Matrix

Stars

High growth, high share businesses. Stars often require heavy investment to build/maintain share in rapidly expanding markets. You may wish to discuss the importance of market share to product profitability at this point.

Cash Cow

Low growth, high share businesses. Cows generate profits for investment in other businesses.

Question Marks

High growth, low share businesses. Strategy must decide between further investment to move question marks to star status or phasing the product out.

Dogs

Low growth, low share. Dogs are often targets for divestment but may still be profitable and/or contribute to other organisational goals.

The GE Business-Planning Grid

This matrix (see Figure 3-3 on p.85) uses two dimensions of three zones each. Industry attractiveness is an index made up of market size, market growth, industry profit margin, amount of competition, seasonality & cyclicality of demand and industry cost structure. Business strength is an index of relative market share, price, competitiveness, product quality, customer & market knowledge, sales effectiveness and geographic advantages.

Tip

Draw up some simple portfolios and ask students to comment on them.

Notes for PM 3-4

Growth Strategy: Strategic Focus

Transparency PM 3-5 relates to the material on pp.88-91 and corresponds to Figure 3-4 on p.88.

There are two routes to increasing profitability: increased productivity and increased volume.

Productivity

This means making more profit on each unit sold. Many businesses have reduced cost in recent years. Capital cost can be reduced by lean manufacturing, or buying in rather than making. Delaying reduces fixed costs by reducing managerial overheads. Flexible working also does this. Technological process or value engineering can reduce variable cost as can increased labour productivity. Increased margins can come from changing the product mix so firms sell more of what makes the most money, by justifying a high price or adding value by doing more for the customer.

Volume

Winning competitors' customers is the most direct and often the hardest way of increasing volume. Large firms often buy competition to gain instant volume. Often firms try to gain volume by increasing usage rate, such as suggesting alternative uses for breakfast cereal. Creating customer involves innovation. New segment of the market can be uncovered, such as the provision of mobile phone by car breakdown services. New markets in South East Asia and Eastern Europe are where many firms seek growth. Innovation, like Internet or multi-media PC can create rapidly growing new demand.

Tip

Ask students to say how each of the branches could be used to increase profitability of a company making a consumer item like toothpaste. Help them recognise how the action at each branch change - you capture competition and customer differently in entering new markets.

Notes for PM 3-5

Product Expansion Grid

Transparency PM 3-6 relates to the material on pp.90-91 and corresponds to Figure 3-5 on p.90. It further develops the growth strategies in PM 3-5.

Developing Growth Strategies

Market Penetration

A penetration strategy involves increasing sales to present target customers. The product itself remains unchanged although there may be a substantial change in how the product is promoted. You may wish to link market penetration with other company-wide strategies such as market leader if appropriate to course progress at this time.

Market Development

A market development strategy involves identifying new segments for the current products offered by the company. Market development can be successful for old products like baking soda (used as a refrigerator deodorant). You may wish to link market development to emerging technologies such as geodemographics for identifying new market segments.

Product Development

A product development seeks growth by modifying existing products or introducing new products to serve an existing market. Line extensions in snack foods are often useful for illustrating this strategy to students. You may ask your class how many flavours of Doritos they can name as an example.

Diversification

This strategy involves taking profits from existing products or businesses to acquire or enter new markets, usually in different industries from previous company efforts. RJR buying Nabisco is an example.

Tip

Ask which are the most difficult quadrants and why? The answer is diversification. Explain how they often fail because firms have few strengths in the diversified areas.

Notes for PM 3-6

The Marketing Process

Transparency PM 3-7 corresponds to Figure 3-6 on p.91. This material previews the focus on later chapters. You may wish to show this transparency as an introduction to the following discussion on target consumers. The lecture information below is provided if you wish to cover the strategic background information prior to coverage of details.

This begins as an extended discussion of planning, organisation and specific-actions that includes slide transparencies on the 4Ps, factors affecting marketing strategy decisions and a general outline of the contents of a marketing plan. These topics are covered in more detail on subsequent transparencies.

Market Analysis (and Planning)

Marketing must conduct a complete analysis of its situation and all relevant environmental influences. Further, marketing must provide each functional area of the company with the information from this analysis that affects their area-specific tasks.

Selecting Target Markets

In evaluating analysis, it should become clear that the company cannot service each market opportunity equally well. Target market selection occurs by matching strengths and weaknesses identified in analysis to particular target markets.

Marketing Implementation

Plans must be co-ordinated and launched with realistic logistical support if they are to succeed. Marketers must be able to translate plans into concrete action.

Marketing Control

The need to measure, assess and evaluate performance all relate to control issues. These are discussed in more detail later.

> **Tip**
> Ask what is the alternative to targeting? If a firm does not target, who chooses their customers for them? The competitor does.

Notes for PM 3-7

Managing the Marketing Effort

Transparency PM 3-8 corresponds to Figure 3-7 on p.92 and the discussion overview on p.92. You may find that marketing planning and strategy are an on-going process. Each area of the Marketing Effort is broken out into separate transparencies.

Analysis

Tools of analysis include marketing research, marketing information systems, demand forecasts models and systematic if more subjective sources of information such as sales force composites and expert judgements. Even while taking advantage of constantly improving technologies, marketers must know when their own judgement must be relied on as well. If there is much science to marketing, there remains a great deal of art to it as well.

Planning

The marketing plan is discussed in PM 3-12.

Implementation

Through implementation, the company turns the strategic and marketing plans into actions that will achieve the company's strategic objectives. You may wish to remind students that planning can become self-absorbing activity that needs constant re-connection to real world marketing constraints.

Control

Control consists of measuring and evaluating the results of marketing plans and activities and taking corrective actions to make sure objectives are being reached.

Tip

Ask students to discuss how these steps in managing the marketing effort are interdependent and mutually influencing. For example, how does the experience a manager gains from taking corrective actions influence the planning process? Does it in turn affect how analysis is conducted? Resources used for analysis?

Notes for PM 3-8

Target Consumers

Transparency PM 3-9 relates to the material on p.93. For marketers, the consumer is the centre or focal point of the marketing management process. Target consumers and meeting their needs underscore the entire decision making process.

Four Steps

1. Demand Measurement and Forecasting

The company must make careful estimates of both the current and future size of the market and any market segments within it. Estimates of current market size require looking at competing products and estimating their current level of sales. Also, the company will want to know the rate of growth and overall growth potential to determine if entering the market offers an opportunity for profitable return on the initial investment.

2. Market Segmentation

A market segment consists of a group of consumers who respond in a similar way to a given set of marketing stimuli. Market segmentation is the process of dividing the total market into these distinct groups of potential buyers. Each segment will have differing needs, characteristics and behaviours that will require different products and marketing mix variations.

3. Market Targeting

This involves evaluating each market segment in terms of its attractiveness to the company and selecting which segments to enter. Sustaining customer value relative to the competition is a key factor in market targeting. Very few companies have the resources to enter all market segments successfully. In the global marketplace, this trend towards greater selectivity is likely to continue.

4. Market Positioning

Positioning is the process of differentiating the company's products offer from the competition. The company seeks to have the product occupy a clear, distinctive and desirable place relative to the competition the consumer's mind. Value creation is again a key success factor. The company must both communicate and deliver greater value than the competition to position its product successfully.

> **Tip**
>
> Ask students to identify strongly positioned products. Comment on the positioning of Club Med, Bali as a holiday destination (it sounds nicer than Indonesia) or Hard Rock Cafe.

Notes for PM 3-9

Competitive Marketing Strategies
Transparency PM 3-10 relates to the material on pp.95-96 and introduces the competitive marketing strategies concept covered in detail in Chapter 12.

Industry Position
Marketing strategies are often influenced by the position the company holds in the industry. Additionally, strategies can be identified by how the competitor behaves in a given position. For example, market leaders like Coca Cola, IBM and Boeing have made poor strategic choices that jeopardise their positions and even their survival.

Market Leader
Market leaders must decide between attack and defence strategies. Leaders have more resources than most competitors and may choose to dominate the market. Many competitive moves by the leader set the tone for competition in the industry.

Market Challenger
Challengers are runner-up companies that aggressively attack competitors to gain market share. Challengers may attack market leaders, firms its own size, or smaller firms.

Market Follower
Followers are also runner-up firms but choose not to attack competitors. Followers seek stable market shares and profits by matching competitive offers.

Market Nicher
Nichers specialise in serving smaller segments of the market overlooked by competitors. Market niches often have specialised needs that serve as the basis for how the nichers design their business.

Tip
Pick a market, say cars, and ask students to identify from: Market Leader - GM, Market Challenger - Toyota, Market Follower - Nissan, Market Nicher - Land Rover.

Notes for PM 3-10

The Four Ps of Marketing

Transparency PM 3-11 corresponds to Figure 3-8 on p.97 and the material on pp.96-97. Mix decisions are covered extensively in Chapters 13-22.

The Marketing Mix

Product

In the contemporary mix, product is the term for the "goods and service" offering sold by the company. As technology makes everything from stereos to computers more accessible to the average buyer, service increasingly makes the competitive difference, especially in creating brand loyalty and generating repeat customers.

Place

Place refers as much to how the product arrives to the final outlet as where the customer actually buys it. Later in the course, when students distinguish between convenience, shopping and speciality goods the logistics of getting the product to the "place" of purchase can be emphasised again. It may also be appropriate to discuss the role of infrastructure on placing decisions - highway, rail and waterway conditions and/or airfreight costs.

Price

Price too is an excellent source of discussion content. Students will undoubtedly know about list and discount prices as many will have had shopping experiences in discount shops. The manipulation of price in the channel of distribution through allowances, credit and payment arrangements may be new to them.

Promotion

Promotion covers most of what students will stereotypically identify as "real marketing". While the role of promotion is important you may remind them the dangers of too much emphasis on a single component of the mix.

Tip

Ask how the marketing mix changes for segment of the same market such as air travel: compare business class and discount fares.

Notes for PM 3-11

Brand Planning

Transparency PM 3-12 relates to the material on pp.97-102, continues the discussion on managing the marketing effort and summarises the information in Table 3-1 on p.98.

Marketing Plan Components

1. Executive Summary

This opening section provides a short summary of the main goals and recommendations for action. It should prepare the reader in anticipation of full explanations later. Hint for students: write this section after completing the plan.

2. Current Marketing Situation

This section describes the market and the company's position in it. A product review should compare all market entries. A distribution section reports sales trends and channel developments.

3. SWOT Analysis

This section distils environmental scanning efforts into an appraisal of how those forces and trends affect the company and compares the company's strengths and weaknesses with those of the competitors.

4. Objectives and Issues

This section begins the process whereby the manager translates analysis into terms for action. Based upon the preceding two steps the manager can set goals that will successfully implement company strategy.

5. Marketing Strategies

Just as the company has strategies for growth, the manager must define the marketing logic or "game plan" to be used in running the specific product or business. The marketing plan here must provide specific strategies for target markets, the marketing mix expenditures and how strategies complement and support overall marketing goals.

6. Action Programmes

This section will tell the who, what, when and how much of the plan.

7. Budgets

This section is essentially a projected profit-and-loss statement.

8. Controls

All marketing plans must specify the means for evaluating their effectiveness. Financial goals by market by quarter are common.

Tip

Discuss how marketing planning ensures continuity of focus. Most good brands hold steady to their position. Examples are BMW, AMEX, Chanel and Coke.

Notes for PM 3-12

Marketing Audits

These notes relate to the material on pp.98-99 and summarise the information in Table 3-2 on pp.100-101.

Topical Areas for Marketing Audits

Marketing Environment

This includes the macroenvironment and the task environment. Macroenvironment questions address demographic, economic, natural, technological, political and cultural questions that affect the companies marketing efforts. Task environment questions address markets, customers, competitors, channels, suppliers and publics in relation to how the company interacts and responds to them.

Marketing Strategy

This audit questions the business mission, marketing objectives, marketing strategy and budgetary issues. Audits here seek to ensure a clear sense of mission and strategic fit for the company.

Marketing Organisation

This audit examines the formal structure, functional efficiency and interface efficiency of the company.

Marketing Systems

This audit deals with the adequacy of the marketing information system, marketing planning system, marketing control system and new-product development. In particular, audits in this area seek to identify whether or not each of these functions work well and meshes synergistically with the others.

Marketing Function

This audit evaluates the products, price, distribution, advertising, sales promotion, publicity and salesforce efforts of the company. Efforts here correspond to a strategic review of the elements of the marketing mix with traditional promotional elements broken down into two related categories.

Tip

Compare the marketing audit using the military analogy: know your enemy, know yourself, the battlefield (the customer) and the climate (the economic and political climate).

Marketing Department Organisation

These notes relate to the material on pp.102-104.

Functional Organisation

In functional organisation marketing specialists are in charge of different marketing activities such as advertising, research, sales management, promotions and the like. The main advantage is that functional organisation is simple to administer. The main disadvantage is that company growth complicates how a given function is defined.

Geographic Organisation

In geographic organisation marketing activities are arranged by regional proximity. For the sales force and distribution channels, geographic organisation offers advantages on time and travel considerations.

Product Management Organisation

In product management organisation activities are grouped by individual products, product lines or groups of similar product offerings. In a large company a product manager may have group managers who in turn have individual brand managers reporting to him or her. Product management organisation provides advantages for co-ordinating the marketing mix and speeding reaction time in responding to product or line specific problems. Product management also helps train well-rounded managers, since product decisions involve all areas of company operations management. Disadvantages include conflict among products, limits on product manager authority, escalating cost structures for personnel and greater demand for decentralised, local responsibility to meet market and competitive demands.

Market Management Organisation

This method is often used when a company sells one product in several different markets. Computer companies often sell their basic computer to government, educational, military and business markets, each requiring marketing mix variations.

Tip

Discuss how marketing structures are now being questioned by leading firms: category management, etc.

Marketing Control

These notes correspond to Figure 3-9 on p.104 and the material on pp.104-105.

Marketing control is the process of measuring and evaluating the results of marketing strategies and plans and taking corrective action to ensure that marketing objectives are attained. Four steps of control include:

1. Set Goals

It is important that students understand that the control process is proactive in nature. Management starts by deciding which goals it wants to reach. Goals are integrated into all marketing plans and should be reasonable and specific.

2. Measure Performance

In determining the success of the marketing efforts, performance in the marketplace and the company must be objectively measured. The measurements then become the basis for considering how things are working out for the company.

3. Evaluate Performance

Many students will bring with them a negative connotation of the evaluation process. You may want to encourage them to think that the evaluation step is a diagnostic one. Few companies use this step or the following one for strictly punishing marketing personnel. Evaluation may identify a need for improvement for the marketers, but it may also indicate changed environmental conditions, new competitive threats, unrealistic goals or faulty strategic assumptions.

4. Take Corrective Action

Again, many students will see "corrective" as a necessary evil. Invite them to consider that all organisations seek feedback on performance in order to make changes in their competitive behaviour. Coaches use half-time and time-outs to take corrective action. Marketing managers use the control process to "tinker" with the plans in order to help all members of the marketing team perform well.

> **Tip**
>
> Discuss positive aspects of control (positive feedback). A pat on the back is only a foot above a kick in the backside but it makes a world of difference.

Marketing Implementation

These notes relate to the material on pp.105-107. Students may have initial difficulty in developing a solid approach to implementing marketing plans. After working through the planning process itself is often hard for students to focus again on the more concrete activities required to implement their ideas.

Marketing implementation is the process that turns marketing strategies and plans into actions in order to accomplish strategic marketing objectives.

Action Programme

This element of the implementation process co-ordinates the activities - what people do - of the plan. Decisions and deadlines for actions are specified. Lines of authority and reporting are specified. Procedures for resolving conflicts should also be provided.

Organisation Structure

It should be emphasised to students that there is no one "right" organisation structure. Structure is appropriate to the kind of market and competitive conditions that exist. Fast changing markets in high technology are best served by decentralised structures. Management styles from formal to informal serve company interests better if they linked to the kind of decisions that need to be made rather than personal preferences of management. While decentralised, informal approaches are popular in fast changing markets, formal and centralised structures are often more competitive for organisations in stable markets.

Decision and Reward Systems

These must include issues of compensation but management will also benefit from attention to information networking opportunities and the role of praise and honour as effective additional roles that build a sense of company identity.

Human Resources

Recruitment and training of motivated people with the necessary skills and abilities to perform specific tasks are crucial to successful implementation of marketing plans. Combined with reward systems, you may wish to introduce extra-textual discussion of theories of management such as Herzberg's motivators and hygiene factors here.

Climate and Culture

Company culture is a system of values and beliefs shared by people in the organisation that provide collective meaning and identity. This system serves as the context for determining meaning and identity. This system serves as the context for determining meaning and guides decision making.

Tip

Ask which is the most important: obtaining and retaining the customer or obtaining and retaining the best staff.

Comments on Discussing the Issues

1. Businesses are frequently criticised for focusing too much on short-term results. Long-range plans help firms prepare for the future by anticipating changes in customer needs, resource supplies, competitive strategies, and so on. A long-range plan is updated each year to reflect the company's progress toward its goals and to respond to changes in the marketing environment. While the annual marketing plan offers short-term responses to changes in the environment, the long-range strategic plan forces a longer-term outlook. Managers must look at the long-term implications of changes in the marketing environment. Better planning should result.

2. A marketing audit should be carried out in the context of the overall strategic analysis. It must be carried out to determine weaknesses and strengths of the company relative to competitors and identify threats and opportunities to improve the marketing performance within the macroenvironment. It requires a comprehensive, systematic, independent and periodic examination of a company's marketing environment, objectives, strategies and activities. The importance of the marketing audit being a relative assessment lies in the continuous environmental, technological, industrial (external) and organisational (internal) changes that occur. Since all these factors are not static, the effectiveness and efficiency of business activities will change, thus requiring periodic auditing. Changes in consumer needs and technological advances may change the position and strength of the company. A leading company may tomorrow find itself in the awkward position of needing to follow competitors' actions. Moreover, the degree to which a company can exploit its strengths depends on the competition's ability to match theirs. Relative strengths provide the distinct competencies of the company, and must be identified. Therefore relative analysis is crucial in gaining and keeping competitive advantage over rivals which subsequently ensures survival and provide opportunities for success.

3. The first part of this question involves classifying the SBU into one of the four cells of the Boston Consulting Group matrix. As described in the question, the SBU is smaller than competing firms, so it is classed as either a Dog or a Question Mark. Semiconductors are a high-growth industry, so the SBU is a Question Mark.

The second part of the question is designed to get students thinking about limitations of the matrix approaches to portfolio analysis. This SBU sounds like a good prospect for divestment or phasing out, though the company could consider investing enough in it to build it into a Star. But as a *guaranteed source of supply* for a critical element of other products of the firm, the SBU may be an important resource of the company. As noted by George S. Day ("Diagnosing the Product Portfolio," *Journal of Marketing*, April 1977, pp. 29-38), $20,000 worth of a particular raw material can affect the production of $10,000,000 worth of finished parts. Therefore, a company might be willing to lose money on a subsidiary to avoid price gouging by suppliers or possible production delays in its major line of business.

4. In order to assess the possible growth opportunities and strategies, it is essential for students to determine the position of the company. The sales of the company's main product line of video cassette recorders (VCR) are stabilising in a mature market with low growth potential. Let us assume that the company has a high market share. At the maturity stage only the main competitors survive while the weaker ones either withdraw or are gradually squeezed out. Along with maintaining its position in this market, the company should look for growth opportunities. If the ultimate objective of the company is growth in sales and share, then using profits generated from the VCRs, the company has the following opportunities; (1) Market development - the company may wish to capitalise on it existing strengths to develop and expand into new market segments using the same product line. This will save the cost to develop new product. Market development can be directed towards new markets (abroad), nonusers and new segments; (2) New product development - where the company already operate globally, it may pursue developing a new product focusing both the current users and nonusers. The company may develop a product related to the VCR thus saving costs of developing completely new technology. If it is a well known brand it may use brand extension, thus reducing costs of introducing new brands; (3) Cash generated from the VCRs can be used to invest in product lines with low market share in high growth markets, in order to increase their market share; (4) Diversification - develop new products for new markets. This is the riskiest strategy where the company enters a market based not on it core competencies. Sony is an example of a company that used existing VCR technology and its core competence of miniaturisation to develop the mini-camcorders which were a growing market. VCRs were not Sony main product line and by 1988 were in a mature market. Sony saw the growing camcorder market and developed in 1989 the mini-camcorders (8mm) to satisfy consumer's need for easy to carry camcorders. The mini-camcorders enhanced Sony's VCRs line. Philips on the other hand saw the opening of Eastern Europe as an opportunity for product extension into a growing market.

5. Students should understand that the GE approach, like the BCG approach, is a useful means of analysis, but it is only a *guide* to decision making. The GE grid is helpful as a way to analyse and summarise many factors about a company's business portfolio, but it is not a substitute for careful consideration of the issues. The company must decide exactly what constitutes "attractiveness" for industries, and then consider how its businesses rank within those industries. This highlights the strengths and weaknesses within the portfolio.

The grid is useful for resource allocation decisions. Companies always have a limited amount of resources, and it is important to use them in the most advantageous way. The grid highlights which businesses are likely to have good returns, and which are not. It can help in setting business objectives for specific units. The grid is also helpful in guiding decisions on whether to acquire in a given industry or divest a specific business.

The GE grid is not, however, a way to set mission or strategy. Management must set a clear vision of the company's mission to guide all portfolio and resource allocation issues. McDonald's, for example, would not invest in pharmaceutical or computer companies. These industries are highly attractive, but they do not fit McDonald's mission of seeking sales, growth, and profits in fast food.

6. This question is designed to help students understand the differences in competitive marketing strategies. It can also demonstrate the linkages between strategy (what to do) and execution (how to do it). Related issues will be explored in depth in Chapter 9 and 10, Market Segmentation and Targeting, and Positioning respectively.

A market challenger would attempt to take customers directly from Sony. It would probably offer most of Sony's benefits plus an additional advantage or difference such as a lower price or broader selection. A market follower would closely imitate Sony in most respects. It would probably enter locations where there was not a conveniently located Sony store. A market-nicher would compete by offering more specialised service to a different clientele. A market-nicher could differentiate itself in many different ways. Ask students to come up with some examples.

Comments on Applying the Concepts

1. This question asks students to consider the issue of starting a business (a restaurant, clothing store, or music store) in the shopping area near where they live. This requires creative thought, and may be difficult for some classes. If the discussion gets stuck, ask the class to list the drawbacks of the existing restaurants in the area. This may point out some opportunities that were not immediately apparent.

   Try to discipline the class to consider their target audience: who it is, and how it might be different from current businesses. Remind them that marketing consists of filling consumer needs, which implies that you must know the consumer in order to know her needs.

   Finally, the marketing mix should be a straightforward issue for students to grasp. Students may consider this issue to be *so* obvious that they assume that there is only one marketing mix possible. If they cannot expand their thoughts, first ask them to name some marketing mix elements that are *inappropriate*. Have the class explain why these mix elements are unsuitable for this business. Then challenge them to name some businesses for which these marketing mix elements would fit. This will illustrate that there must be a fit between the target audience, business positioning, and the marketing mix.

2. Basically students should conduct a SWOT analysis of the company they have chosen. The next step is to discuss what specifically the firms should do in responding to the external forces such as technology, politics and legal developments, economic upheavals, social and cultural trends. The last section asks for a strategy to be developed taking into account both the internal and external factors. This is a good question in that it allows the students to look at a real organisation and analyse its operation comprehensively. In addition, students are asked to come up with a marketing strategy which will encourage them to apply the marketing plan that they have studied earlier. This will enable the students to appreciate the relationship between what is happening in the real world and the academic side of marketing.

Case 3
Trap-Ease:
The Big Cheese of Mousetraps

Synopsis

A group of investors has purchased from an inventor the US rights to sell a patented, innovative mousetrap. The group has hired Martha House to manage the company including assuming responsibility for sales and marketing. Trap-Ease America has targeted the trap to housewives whom it believes will be attracted to the safety and cleanliness that its trap offers. The trap lures the mouse into a square tube in which it finds itself trapped alive. Thus, there is no danger in baiting and setting the trap, and there is no "mess" resulting from the trap's operation. Martha is marketing the trap directly to large retail store chains such as Safeway and K mart. The traps are sold in packages of two and are priced at $2.49 -- about five to ten times the price of the traditional, spring-loaded trap. Martha has been promoting the mousetrap basically through trade shows and personal selling. As the case opens, she has just returned from a trade show at which the mousetrap received the award as Best New Product of the Year. However, despite the innovativeness of the mousetrap and its success at gaining public attention, sales are disappointingly slow. Martha finds herself wondering why the world is not beating a path to her door, as Ralph Waldo Emerson would have predicted.

Teaching Objectives

This case was selected to accompany Chapter 3 since it does an excellent job of introducing the student to the concepts of the mission of the firm and the elements of a marketing strategy in a simple but rich case.

The teaching objectives of the case are:

1. Introduce the idea of a firm's "mission".

2. Introduce the basic elements of a marketing strategy.

3. Drive home the point that customers seldom beat a path to a firm's door.

Study Questions

1. Martha and the Trap-Ease investors feel they face a "once-in-a-life" opportunity. What information do they need to evaluate this opportunity? How do you think the group would write its mission statement? How would you write it?

The case paints a very typical picture of a group of business people who believe they have an outstanding product that will be readily accepted by the market. There is little evidence in the case that the investors have done any real thinking about customer needs or have followed the marketing concept as it is introduced in the chapter. The investors believe they have a mousetrap which will satisfy customer needs and, therefore, customers will buy it. Students needs to realise that even though a firm may have an excellent product, it needs to understand customers' needs and how they respond to those needs. There is no indication in the case that the investor group has any marketing information about its potential customers or has done any real marketing research. The investors would need to know the size of the mousetrap market in the United States. Who buys mousetraps? What kinds do they buy? What prices are charged for the various kinds of mousetraps? How are these mousetraps sold to consumers? What customer needs do existing mousetraps solve, and which needs do they fail to solve adequately? How do consumers deal with their mice and rat problems? Answers to these and other "marketing research" types of questions would give the investors a better feel for the challenges facing them in marketing the mousetrap.

Probably, however, like many new, small businesses, the investors would write a mission statement which focused on making money for themselves. Their statement might be, "Make a lot of money by selling a patented mousetrap." Discussing this with the class will allow the instructor to raise the oft-repeated slogan, "maximise shareholder wealth." Proponents of the marketing concept might well argue that making money is not the goal of the firm. Rather, if one follows the marketing concept, the goal of the firm must be first to satisfy the firm's customers and to do that better than the competition. Only then does a firm have the opportunity to "make money."

2. Has Martha identified the best target market for Trap-Ease? What other market segments might the firm target?

The case indicates that Trap-Ease is targeting housewives, and implies that housewives are reluctant to set and bait traditional spring-loaded mousetraps. They also are concerned about the safety of children and pets who may be around the home. Further, once the spring-loaded trap has worked, one often has a mess resulting from its action. Besides being unpleasant, the mess presents health concerns due to the diseases which may be carried by mice.

There are a number of other market segments which the firm could target. The issue of disease control suggests several other potential targets. First, the instructor might ask students where disease control concerns would be important. Any business which handles or stores food and, therefore, is attractive to rats and mice, would be a potential target. Restaurants should come to mind here both because of the presence of food and food products and also due to the fact that these establishments cannot use chemicals near food. This also should suggest food wholesalers or warehouses where large quantities of food may be stored in the channel of distribution. Food manufacturers also need rodent protection.

Another potential market is research laboratories. Here, researchers often have large numbers of mice involved in research projects. It is not unreasonable to think that some of these mice occasionally get loose. A researcher would be interested in the ability to recapture a mouse without harming it - something that the researcher would be able to do with the Trap-Ease.

Another potential target market is exterminating companies themselves. Because they must work in areas where chemicals would not be allowed and traditional traps would have the same messiness problem about which housewives are concerned, these companies might be a target market. These companies might also sell the traps directly to consumers with whom they deal. This possibility will allow the instructor to talk about channels of distribution and the impact of Trap-Ease's decision to go directly to the end customer.

3. How has the company positioned the Trap-Ease in its chosen target market? Could it position the product in other ways?

As suggested in the answer to question 2, Trap-Ease has been positioned from the point of view of the customer as meeting safety and cleanliness needs. Because of its pricing and distribution, Trap-Ease is positioned for use by the individual homeowner who has these concerns.

The major alternative positioning for the product focuses on its ability to control disease. Because the mouse would be trapped in a fully enclosed device and would be captured live, there is little opportunity for disease to spread as a result of its capture. It should be noted, however, that positioning the product this way would make substantial differences in the entire marketing strategy. This allows the instructor to make the point that will be reinforced throughout the semester that the full marketing mix must be co-ordinated to position the product properly in the customer's mind.

4. Describe the current marketing mix for Trap-ease? Do you see any problems with this mix?

In summary, Trap-Ease marketing mix is as follows:

Product: As noted above, Trap-Ease's product is the patented mousetrap which is designed to allow consumers to avoid the safety and cleanliness problems associated with traditional mousetraps.

Perhaps by this point in the discussion someone will have already suggested one of the obvious problems with this product. That is, what does one do with a live mouse caught inside the trap! The inventor had designed the product to capture the mouse alive and to suffocate it over a period of several hours. However, this presents a problem for the user. If the consumer discovers the trap has worked while the mouse is still alive, he/she must pick up a trap containing a live mouse which may be squirming and squealing. Then, what does the consumer do with the mouse? It might be flushed down the toilet or let out in the woods, if one lives near woods. However, we might wonder if the target market, housewives, will be comfortable carrying the trap containing the live mouse and then opening the door to let it out. Later market research revealed that few people felt comfortable in this situation.

On the other hand, if the consumer allows the mouse to simply suffocate in the trap, he/she will find that mice, like most animals, do not die quietly. You can imagine the trap bouncing around under a sink like a large Mexican jumping bean as the mouse tries to free itself. Experience indicated that the mouse also made a lot of noise prior to suffocating. The targeted housewife may find herself presented with the dilemma of how to handle a live mouse or how to put up with the noise and unpleasantness of its suffocating. Thus, while the trap works well to catch a mouse, it fails to deal with the problem of what does one do with the mouse.

Price: The price of approximately $1.25 per trap, when sold in packages of two, also creates a problem in that it is five to ten times more expensive than traditional traps. This problem is complicated by the fact that if consumers have significant mouse problems, they would need a number of traps to address the problem. Or, if they decide to simply throw away traps which contain mice to solve the disposal problem, the cost could again become prohibitive.

Place: Martha House has made the decision to distribute the products directly to national chains. Although on one hand this decision makes sense given the company's desire to achieve rapid sales growth, it creates problems for the company due to its small size. As noted in the example which concludes the case, the company does not have its own truck and distribution facilities. It must depend on outside firms to deliver its product. Because national chains have very strict time schedules, this makes it difficult for Trap-Ease to control its distribution.

Promotion: Trap-Ease is relying basically on appearances at trade shows and some limited advertising. In fact, it is relying on word-of-mouth advertising. Primarily, the firm depends on point-of-purchase displays to sell its product. One might wonder, however, how quickly consumers passing point-of-purchase displays for the product will understand it. Further, the firm is dependent on whatever advertising the chains may do to generate end-customer awareness. Even early in the semester, students should understand that generating such awareness is extremely expensive and difficult. It is not clear that Trap-Ease has adequate resources to do significant advertising aimed at end customers, and it is not clear that the chains will devote sufficient resources to advertising the product.

All of these marketing mix problems should suggest that Trap-Ease has a number of significant hurdles to address if it is going to improve its performance.

5. Who is Trap-Ease's competition?

Even though Trap-Ease has a patent on its mousetrap, it does have competition. Students may tend to think that with a patent a firm is protected from competition. Obviously, the traditional, spring-loaded trap is competition. Although the Trap-Ease trap has significant advantages, its price means that for many low-income consumers who probably have more mice problems, Trap-Ease is too expensive. Consumers who have better incomes and who may not be excited about dealing with dead or live mice will probably simply turn to exterminators to take care of their problems. While exterminators are more expensive, the benefits of having someone else take care of this unpleasant problem for you will be attractive to many consumers. Thus Trap-Ease finds itself with competition both above and below it relative to price. This competition significantly reduces the size of the target market.

6. How would you change Trap-Ease marketing strategy? What kinds of control procedures would you establish with this strategy?

There are, of course, numerous possibilities which students might suggest. Many students will focus on trying to make specific changes to elements of the established market mix. For example, some students may suggest that simply by lowering price the Trap-Ease trap will become more competitive with traditional traps and be more attractive to consumers. However, any attempt to manipulate the existing marketing mix allows the instructor to make the point that the marketing mix should flow from the target market. At this point, having discussed previous questions, it should be clear to students that there is some question about the size and viability of the selected target market. In fact, there may not be a real market given the product's positioning -- at least not a market which is big enough to support the firm and reach the investor's goals.

To revise the firm's marketing strategy, the firm needs to begin by thinking about its target market selection. First the student could suggest that the product has been positioned improperly. While health and cleanliness concerns are of interest to consumers, the other aspects of the marketing mix make the product unattractive. However, the disease control aspects of the product are important. It would be possible to reposition the product for disease control purposes and to select the industrial/ institutional target market. Thus, the target market would become food manufacturers, wholesalers, and others who store quantities of food which are subject to rat infestation and also restaurants and other institutions where food may be handled and where poisons and other rat control measures may be inappropriate.

With respect to the marketing mix for this new target market, the firm needs to develop larger sizes of the trap. Some of the potential customers will have larger rats with which to deal. These firms will also often have maintenance employees who will not be squeamish about dealing with and disposing of rats which are caught in such traps.

With respect to price for this new strategy, there is really no information in the case to allow the instructor to figure what the price might be. We can imagine that, in connection with the place decision, the firm might decide to deal directly with larger exterminating companies or food wholesaling chains. The company will probably find itself in a negotiation situation as it has with the large retail chains. This will make it important that the firm understand its costs and be able to figure what prices it can agree to which will allow it to make an adequate profit.

With respect to place, the firm will be required to continue to sell to a limited number of customers due to the lack of any real sales force. This would imply that it will have to sell to food wholesalers or exterminating companies themselves unless it can find a distributor who caters to these kinds of operations. Looking for distributors who could handle some or all of the sales effort would be appropriate given the firm's limited resources. This may put additional pressures on margins, but the firm will have to evaluate accepting smaller margins versus absorbing the cost of improving its own distribution system.

The new strategy would continue to imply a trade promotion strategy. Appearing at trade shows for food wholesalers or exterminators would be a first step, and one with which the firm is familiar. This strategy avoids the necessity for having to pursue expensive media options for developing end-customer retail demand. Advertising in trade magazines should help bring the product to the attention of targeted customers. Further, if the firm is successful in selling to exterminators, they will become its sales force.

As to control procedures, the process of revising the marketing strategy allows one to ask the students how they will monitor their progress. In the case, Martha has no connection with the end customer. She is dealing with buyers for the large retail chains. She is not sure who is buying the mousetrap or why or how they are using it. A first control procedure for any strategy then is to identify the target market and establish mechanisms to monitor the target's use of and satisfaction with the product. Chapter 6, Marketing Research and Information Systems, will introduce students to techniques which might be used by Trap-Ease to evaluate the success of the strategy.

Teaching Suggestions

This case is an excellent early case because it deals with a product and a need with which students are familiar. Further, as the discussion unfolds, students will have little trouble spotting some of the marketing problems and marketing concerns that the firm faces. While cases can sometimes intimidate students early in the semester, this case should begin to give them some confidence that they can deal successfully with a marketing situation even though they do not have a lot of experience.

If the instructor is interested in any field research, you might ask a group of students to check local retail and hardware stores to see what devices and methods are available for helping people deal with their mice and rat problems.

If the instructor does not use this case at this point in the text, it may be used in connection with the Marketing Research and Information Chapter (Chapter 6) or in connection with the Consumer Behaviour Chapter (Chapter 7).

Overview Case 1
Kit Kat: Have a Break . . .

Synopsis

The chocolate confectionery market is a concentrated, stable and highly competitive market. The UK market is dominated by Cadburys, Nestle Rowntree and Mars who together share 68% of the market. Nestle Rowntree has grown to become the largest confectionery company since the acquisition of Rowntree by Nestle SA for $3.8 billion in 1988. Selling to over 120 countries, Nestle UK Ltd is UK's largest exporter of chocolate and sugar confectionery. The main markets of operation are Europe and the Middle East. Nestle Rowntree divides the market into three categories; (1) Chocolate box assortment market - a gift market segment (e.g. Quality Street); (2) Countline market - a "self-eat" consumer product segment (eg. Kit Kat four-finger); (3) Chocolate biscuit countline (CBCL) market - a segment created by Nestle, nonpersonal, "family consumption" sector (e.g. Kit Kat two-finger).

Kit Kat was originally launched in 1935 by Rowntree as Chocolate Crisp. It was renamed twice; in 1937 as Kit Kat Chocolate Crisp and then in 1949 as Kit Kat. By 1950 it was Rowntree's biggest brand. At first Kit Kat was positioned as both confectionery and a snack. Now it is positioned half way between a snack and an indulgence. The widely known slogan "Have a break, have a Kit Kat" was launched in 1957. Kit Kat is being sold in two formats in the UK; (1) The two-finger format that belongs to the CBCL sector. It is purchased in multipacks at superstores and large grocers and its usage is non-personal, "family" consumption as well as snack and lunch boxes for children's consumption; (2) The four-finger format belongs to the chocolate countline sector. This format is purchased at confectioners, tobacconists and newsagents (CTNs). It is purchased for personal consumption, broad usage and for the "adult" and "self" eats categories. It belongs to the consumer-product category. The four-finger format had the higher sales volume in the UK until it was overtaken by the two-finger format in 1989, in the light of the rise of the grocery sector and superstores sector at the expense of the CTNs. Eighty per cent of the four finger format goes to CTNs compared with only about 18% of the two-finger. Outside the UK the four-finger Kit Kat is sold more than the two-finger Kit Kat. In addition, the European retailers emphasise the demand of Kit Kat minis. This portrays the diverse markets in which the company operates and the complexity of arriving at a comprehensive marketing plan.

Teaching Objectives

1. Acquaint students with the SWOT analysis.

2. Expose students the effect of Europoean Union to marketing of products in this region.

3. Encourage students to start designing the marketing plan.

Study Questions

1. **What is the situation facing Kit Kat; the strengths and weaknesses of the brand and the opportunities and threats it faces?**

The situation that Kit Kat is facing can be analysed in the form of a SWOT analysis that explores the current strengths and weaknesses as well as future opportunities and threats. Students should highlight the following SWOT. Strengths; (1) Number one confectionery brand in the UK; (2) Marketing orientated; (3) Strong brand image; (4) High investment; (5) Low inventory cost; (6) Pioneer in exploiting new market (CBCL); (7) Number one seller in CBCL sector; (8) Price dictator in CBCL sector; (9) Customer brand loyalty. Weaknesses; (1) Limited investment of capital to supply the European markets; (2) Low sales margin in European markets; (3) Low ROCE; (4) Low productivity (below target); (5) Low customer service level due to capacity limitations; (6) Adverse total sales of confectionery sector; (7) Operating profits going down; (8) Consumption of four-finger format is biased towards female buyers; (9) Four-finger format remained a weak number two position after Mars bar; (10) No effective differentiation between the two product category (two-finger and four-finger) in the customer's eyes. Opportunities; (1) Rising customer spending on confectionery; (2) Overseas sales increase; (3) Growing power of multiple grocers for CBCL; (4) Growth of confectionery market; (5) High level of penetration to young customers for the two-finger format; (6) Increase demand for minis by large grocery stores; (7) High demand for four-finger format abroad. Threats; (1) Economic forces e.g. recession; (2) Diminishing power of CTNs poses threat to four-finger format; (3) Decline in 15-24 years old population; (3) Intensive competition; (4) Inability to meet increased demand for two-finger format; (5) Competitive price cutting activities; (6) Kit Kat reaching end of life cycle and market saturation; (7) Risk of market not following premium prices of Kit Kat two-finger. The above SWOT is not exhaustive. Students will mention other elements.

2. Why are the two-finger and four-finger Kit Kats marketed differently? How do the customers for the four-finger Kit Kat differ from those for the two-finger Kit Kat? What are the differences in the way the company addresses the two target markets?

The two formats of Kit Kat are marketed differently due to the different segments they are aimed at. The two formats are used by different segments, on different occasions. The four-finger Kit Kat belongs to the chocolate countline group of products competing against other countline brands such as Mars Bar, Twix, Sneakers, etc. It is mainly sold at CTNs and is purchased as a snack on the street by individuals for "self-eating" and by 16-24 year olds. The four-finger is purchased for self consumption where the purchaser is the decision maker and the user of the product. In this format Kit Kat is packed individually and competes against both chocolate snack bars and wafer based snacks. The two-finger on the other hand, belongs to the CBCL group. It is mainly sold in multipacks at superstores and large grocers. This is a different segment where the purchase is made by housewives for "family" and domestic consumption. The two-finger is sold as biscuits rather than just as snack. It is purchased by housewives for their children's lunch boxes as well as for "family" consumption while having a cup of tea for example. The CBCL products are non personal and it may be that the purchaser is not the decision maker nor the only user of the product. Children may ask their parents to buy Kit Kat two-finger when they go to the superstore. Another important element is the size of the product. Parents who purchased Kit Kat for their kids are concerned with their health and would rather they have a small sized snack.

Clearly, these are two distinctive segments requiring different marketing strategies. In order to successfully satisfy the two segments Kit Kat employs different ways of marketing. The two-finger format marketing is aimed the 30-44 year olds through advertising in the morning TV, which is generally watched by housewives bearing in mind that housewives are more likely to do the shopping (this may not be the case in other countries and cultures). The four finger sector of the 16-24 year olds is targeted rather differently using different means of media. In order to enhance Kit Kat's image and appeal to the younger generation, the company advertises in youth press including trendy young people's magazines, on TV and independent radio stations. Promotion strategies are also different. The promotions for the two-finger are value and grocery trade orientated, including "one bar free" and "10p of next purchase". The latter also encourages repeat purchases to take advantage of the discounted price. The four-finger promotions are more consumer orientated and aimed to gain competitive advantage of the "on the spot" decisions by offering for example "1p off", which stands out amongst the competing products and brands. An annual promotion also takes place, regardless of the format, which emphasises brand awareness. There are also different pricing policies. The two-finger format is a market leader and can therefore dictate price. It is priced 2p above its competitor, Penguin. The four-finger format is priced parallel with Twix and 2p below the Mars bar which is more hunger satisfying. Thus pricing policy is vital in order to retain volume. Overall, the competition in the chocolate countline sector is tighter and the four-finger format position is comparatively weaker and more price sensitive, thus requiring more extensive advertising than the two-finger format.

3. What is the effect of European integration on the marketing of Kit Kat? What are the barriers to the brand's standardisation across Europe? Should the company now move towards standardising its brands and packaging across Europe?

In light of the unification of the European market many directives had been written in order to make the necessary changes to intra-EC trade and create the Single European market. These 1993 directives eliminated most trade barriers, including taxes, etc. between the EC countries. The direct benefits include the removal of bureaucratic obstacles to imports, the ability to realise economies of scale and hence achieve lower costs and reduction in packaging and labelling costs. Nevertheless, the removal of limitations has also allowed many imports and has increased in-house competition. These changes to the European market structure meant that companies now need to adapt to the new directives and work within their measures. Nestle in its marketing policy must consider the differences between the various European countries.

The barriers to standardisation across Europe are; (1) Requirements for a different type of chocolate; (2) Varying pricing policies; (3) Different state of product life cycle; (4) Different styles and types of promotions and advertising required; (5) Various types of consumers; (6) Different cultures with different norms; (7) Different languages; (8) Different packaging.

Some students will say that standardisation of brand and packaging is seen as a risky decision while other will say that it is too early to standardise these two aspects of the product. It is seen as risky to standardise the brand due to the significant barriers of standardisation exist in Europe which at this point in time cannot be overcome. There is a wide variety of taste which exist between consumers in different countries e.g. habits and tastes vary between the UK, Germany and France. Despite good intentions of standardisation, there are many national differences in product standards, safety regulations and distribution systems. Linguistic differences will hamper pan-European communication strategies despite advanced satellite technology which serves the single European market e.g. the language used in the UK promotion activities might not be translated the same way in France or Italy. In addition the packaging of Kit Kat is also restricted from being standardised. The flow-wrapped German Kit Kat may not be suitable for the UK since the consumers in the UK are used to the foil and band packaging. These students will suggest that the company should try and standardise as much as possible the production procedure for the brand and packaging. However, where strong national differences in taste persist, the company has to adopt decentralised marketing and promotional strategies to meet the needs of the different consumers across Europe. Some students will suggest that Nestle should conduct extensive market research to determine opportunities for standardisation. The main benefit is cost reduction in production and packaging. In addition, standardisation would also lead to a projection of uniform and consistent image globally.

4. How would you describe the organisational structure of the company and its marketing department? In what alternative ways could the company organise the management of its wide range of confectionery? What structure would you recommend?

The overall organisational structure of Nestle Rowntree is a functional structure. There are several functional managers who report to the managing director. The sales and marketing departments comprise the commercial unit. The commercial unit has a product management structure. The marketing director supervises several product group managers who in turn supervise brand managers who are in charge of specific brands. Hence the structure of the marketing department is decentralised in terms of products and brands having their own managers who have closer relationship with their target market and therefore able to make quick decisions. This product based structure provides special attention to each and every product and brand. The brand managers co-ordinate the business management of their brand which includes dealing with advertising, promotions, market research and product development. This ensures that attention is provided to the development of a co-ordinated marketing mix for each brand. The brand manager is directly responsible for the commercial success of his brand and therefore responds quickly to market changes. This however is a costly structure as brand managers require assistants and when new brands are launched new brand managers and assistants are required. Hence, there are a lot of management levels. Thus, Nestle is basically a functional organisation with a product orientated marketing structure.

There are alternative ways the company could organise the management of its wide range of confectionery. These include; function-oriented structure, regionally orientated structure, customer type orientation and divisionalised marketing structures. (1) Functional-oriented structure; this is a line and staff structure where the different marketing activities are separated into groups each under a functional head who has line authority. The major drawback of this structure is that people may get orders from more than one individual. This may lead to direct lines of communication being ignored and salesmen dealing straight to staff executives. There is always a danger of conflicts between executives in the marketing function which may ultimately result in dysfunctional. (2) Regionally-oriented marketing structure; this structure is utilised by many companies operating over wide geographical areas. The exact allocation of other services in the hierarchy varies with their relative importance and regional variation in the market. In such an organisation some duties may be duplicated at more than one level causing problems of co-ordination. A variation of straight regional organisation is one where products are sold in two or more dissimilar types of market. We may then find either regional marketing managers for each type of market or national managers dealing with the full range of goods in their type of market. This type of division is not often found in consumer goods market although it is fairly common for industrial markets.

This type of organisation is particularly useful for a policy of maximum market penetration. (3) Customer-type orientation; there are potentially as many different customer-orientated marketing structures as there are customers but we shall only consider a few different types. Customer types in large companies often tend to divide by product, providing a convenient division. Marketing managers in charge of each channel or group are purely line executives responsible to the marketing manager and responsible for a single group of salesmen. They have no staff function. Each salesperson would deal with a full line of products. (4) Divisionalised marketing structure; the biggest single problem of a divisionalised organisation is the allocation of functions between corporate headquarters and operating units. There are two principal parts to the problem. First, the responsibility for profit and costs, and direct functional control. The more that can be passed down the structure the better. However, there is a proviso that the division must be large enough to keep such services fully occupied and of sufficient size to employ executives of the required calibre. The second problem that arises concerned with whether management posts should be purely staff post or whether they should have line authority as well. When the organisation becomes sufficiently large it is often found desirable to have some functions carried out at each level. The corporate level has a staff officer and at divisional level the staff are part of line. A structure of this type is advantageous when certain common data may be collected or when specialist advice may only be required occasionally. There is no single best form of structure for any organisation. The organisation might have to change or alter the whole or part of the structure in a particular division or sector according to circumstantial changes. Different students will suggest different structures. Again, ask them to justify their choices and open the discussion to the whole class.

5. Prepare a brand plan for Kit Kat.

Essentially the brand plan should cover the following components; Introduction, Market Situation, Product Situation, Distribution, Target Markets, SWOT Analysis, Issue Analysis, Brand Objectives, Brand Marketing Strategy and Action Programme. Most of the answers to the above have been discussed in the previous questions. As far as brand objectives are concerned they can be divide into financial objectives and marketing objectives. For example financial objectives will be; (1) to increase UK sales; (2) to increase capital employed (ROCE); (3) to increase profitability. While marketing objectives could be; (1) to increase productivity in the confectionery business; (2) to become a clear leader in the UK; (3) to increase the efficiency of the supply chain; (4) to improve customer service. The brand marketing strategy should discuss the 4P's in some detail. The action programmes are tactical in nature. Again the students have to be very specific in discussing the action programmes. Answers will vary between one student and another.

Teaching Suggestions

This case study could also be used to illustrate Chapter 7 (Consumer Behaviour) and Chapter 14 (Designing Products).

References

Hayhourst, R. and Wills, G. (1972), Organisational Design for Marketing Futures, London George Allen and Unwin Ltd.

Jokes and Quotes

The best way to succeed in business is to be a genius. If you're not a genius, hire a genius. If you can't find a genius, plan.

The man who attends strictly to his own business usually has plenty of business to attend to.
ANON

Where there is no vision, the people perish.
THE BIBLE

One must change one's tactics every ten years if one wishes to maintain one's superiority.
NAPOLEON BONAPARTE

In action, be primitive, in foresight, a strategist.
RENE CHAR

An optimist sees an opportunity in every calamity; a pessimist sees a calamity in every opportunity.
SIR WINSTON CHURCHILL

You've removed most of the road-blocks to success when you've learnt the difference between motion and direction.
BILL COPELAND

Make sure you're right, then go ahead.
DAVY CROCKETT

One cannot govern with buts.
CHARLES de GAULE

Annual income one pound,
annual expenditure, nineteen and six (£0.975),
result happiness.
Annual income one pound,
annual expenditure one pound and six (£1.025)
result misery.
CHARLES DICKENS

The secret of success in life, is for a man to be ready for his opportunity when it comes.
BENJAMIN DISRAELI

When you see a successful business, someone once made a courageous decision.
PETER F. DRUCKER

In preparing for battle I have always found that plans are useless, but planning is indispensable.
DWIGHT D. EISENHOWER

People who don't mind their own business either have no mind or no business.
LEOPOLD FECHTNER

Once the toothpaste is out of the tube, it's hard to get it back in!
H.R. HALDEMAN

He who every morning plans the transaction of the day and follows out that plan, carries a thread that will guide him through the maze of the most busy life. But where no plan is laid, where the disposable of time is surrendered merely to the chance of incidence, chaos will soon reign.
VICTOR HUGO

I always wanted to be some kind of writer or newspaper reporter. But after college . . . I did other thing.
JACQUELINE KENNEDY ONASSIS

Don't agonise. Organise.
FLORENCE R. KENNEDY

For the building of a new Japan
Let's put our mind and strength together,
Doing our best to promote production,
Sending our goods to the peoples of the world,
Endlessly and continuously,
Like water gushing from a fountain,
Grow, industry, grow, grow, grow,
Harmony and sincerity.
MATSUSHITA ELECTRICAL

All growth is a leap in the dark, a spontaneous unpremeditated act without benefit of experience.
HENRY MILLER

Act quickly, think slowly.
GREEK PROVERB

What's small, dark and knocking at the door? The future.
ROMANIAN PROVERB

Luigi Cortillo operates a hot dog stand in New York. One day a friend asked, "How's business?" ". . . ", Luigi smiled. "I already save t'ousand dollar in banco". "Ai, ai, ai", said the friend. "So you can lend me ten dollar". Luigi sighed, "I no allow". The friend said, "What you mean you no allow". Luigi said, "I make deal with banco: They no sell hotdogs, and I no lenda money".
ROSTEN

Business is like riding a bicycle. Either you keep moving or you fall down.
JAMES BEASLEY SIMPSON

It is a bad plan that admits of no modification.
PUBLILIUS SYRUS

Before wars erupt, weigh the strengths and weaknesses of both your own and the enemy's forces.
SUN TZU

Know your enemy and know yourself, one can go through hundred battles without danger.
SUN TZU

Though know not the other, yet know yourself, the chance of victory is only half.
SUN TZU

It is better to err on the side of daring than the side of caution
ALVIN TOFFLER

Part II

Marketing Setting

Chapter 4
The Marketing Environment

Chapter Objectives

After reading this chapter, you should be able to:

1. Describe the environmental forces that affect the company's ability to serve its customers.
2. Explain how changes in the demographic and economic environments affect marketing decisions.
3. Identify the major trends in the firm's natural and technological environments.
4. Explain the key changes that occur in the political and cultural environments.

Chapter Overview

A company must start with the marketing environment in searching for opportunities and monitoring threats. The marketing environment consists of all the factors and forces that affect the company's ability to transact effectively with the target market. The company's marketing environment can be divided into the microenvironment and the macroenvironment.

The microenvironment consists of five components: the company's internal environment, marketing channel firms, types of markets, competitors, and publics. The macroenvironment consists of six factors: demographic, economic, natural, technological, political, and cultural. Marketing management cannot always affect environmental forces, but smart marketing managers can take a proactive, rather than a reactive, approach to the marketing environment.

Teaching Notes

Refer to the following pages for teaching notes.

Environmental Forces

Transparency PM 4-1 relates to the material on pp.134-160 and gives an overview of the chapter. Each area of the micro and macroenvironments is covered on the following transparencies.

Microenvironmental Forces

Suppliers - Suppliers are the firms and persons that provide the resources needed by the company and competitors to produce goods and services.

Company - Marketing plans must accommodate the needs of other functional areas of the firm to co-ordinate product/service delivery effectively.

Competitors - Competitors are usually considered those companies also serving a target market with similar products and services, although broader definitions may apply.

Publics - May consist of any group that perceives itself having an interest in the actions of the firm. Publics can have positive as well as negative influences on the company's objectives.

Intermediaries - Intermediaries include various middlemen and distribution firms as well as marketing service agencies and financial institutions.

Customers - Customers usually consist of consumer, industrial, reseller, government, and international markets.

Macroenvironmental Forces

Demographic - Population characteristics on such items as size, density, age, location.

Economic - Economic include income and spending pattern concerns.

Natural - Indexes pollution concerns, energy costs, and raw materials.

Technological - Fast pace of change, unlimited opportunity, high R&D.

Political - Regulation by government, social engineering.

Cultural - Values and subculture memberships that affect purchase decisions.

Tip

Ask students to discuss some current examples and issues relating to the above forces.

Notes for PM 4-1

Company's Microenvironment

Transparency PM 4-2 relates to the material on pp.134-138 and corresponds to Figure 4.2 (p.135), Figure 4.3 (p.136) and Figure 4.4 (p.137).

Internal Environment

The internal environment consists of all those groups marketers must consider when developing marketing plans. Top management sets the company mission, objectives, broad strategies and policies. Finance is concerned with finding and using funds. R&D focuses on designing safe and attractive products. Purchasing worries about getting supplies and materials. Manufacturing produces the desired quality and quantity of products. Accounting measures revenues and tracks costs.

Customers

The company is concerned with five types of customer markets. Consumer markets consist of individuals and households that buy goods and services for personal consumption. Business markets buy goods and services for further processing or for use in their production process. Reseller Markets buy goods and services for repackaging and reselling at a profit. Government markets buy goods and services to produce public services or to transfer them to needy constituents. International markets consist of those various types of buyers located in other countries.

Publics

A public is any group that has an actual or potential interest in or impact on an organisation. Financial publics influence the company's ability to gain funds. Media publics carry news, features, and editorial opinions. Government publics regulate many business activities. Citizen-action publics forward particular social and political agendas. Local publics include communities that house the organisation or are affected by its operations directly. General public consists of the overall population. Internal publics include employees, owners, and other vested stakeholders.

Notes for PM 4-2

Demographic and Economic Environments

Transparency PM 4-3 relates to material on pp.140-145 and is the first slide in the series that breaks down the macroenvironment for lecture discussion. The remaining macroenvironmental forces are discussed on following transparencies. Demographic and economic environments can be discussed as foundations for marketing strategy.

Demographic Environment

Definition

Demography is the study of human populations in terms of size, density, location, age, sex, race, occupation, and other aggregate statistics.

Key Aspects of the demographic environment include:

Age Structures (esp. Baby Boomers)

The post WWII Baby Boom is the most significant demographic feature by its sheer size. This bulge in age distribution leads growth strategies in industries serving age-specific markets. Where boomers go, marketers must follow. More proactively, marketers need to identify emerging boomer. They also need to plan strategically for an ageing population that also lives longer than previous ones.

Family Structure

The typical family rarely exists anymore. Increasing age of those marrying, delayed child-bearing, increased two-income families, and non-family households are key demographic trends.

Increasing Diversity

Moves towards European integration have escalated. In its enlarged form it presents huge challenges for domestic and international marketers. In the US the term "salad bowl" has been coined where various groups have mixed together but maintained their ethnic and cultural identities.

Economic Environment

Marketers must address income and changes in spending patterns. Income is rising slowly for some groups, especially "baby boomers".

> **Tip**
>
> Tax and census data indicate a declining middle class earning power. Spending patterns are consistent with Engel's Laws for income groups. However, upper income households are generally unaffected by changes in the economy.

Notes for PM 4-3

Natural and Technological Environments

Transparency PM 4-4 relates to the material on pp.144-152.

Natural Environment

There are several areas affecting marketing that stem from the natural environment. Raw material shortages both increase demand and sprout counter-movements aimed at conservation. Both sides of the "green" movement utilise sophisticated database marketing and lobbying techniques. Energy costs make long-term growth of high energy industries and goods difficult to predict. Changing philosophies on the role of government in managing natural resources also blends into the legal environment. Marketers must take care in identifying natural environmental trends.

Technological Environment

Most texts emphasise the dramatic nature of technology to shape the future of business and create marketing opportunities. You might point out to students raised on Star Trek and Star Wars how much of yesterday's sci-fi is already coming true. Cellular phones as Star Trek-type communicators might get class discussion going. That technology also affects the rate of change itself is important as marketers seek to plan product introduction strategies. Other areas of concern to marketers in the technological environment include the high cost of R&D for technological innovation. Risk factors associated with high costs of development often lead to minor improvements over substantive product changes. While minor improvements help keep products "fresh" to the market, marketers must anticipate that changing consumer needs will limit the competitiveness of too little innovation. Regulation of technology is also a key influence marketers need to consider and leads well into discussion on political and cultural macroenvironmental forces.

> **Tip**
>
> Natural forces can serve as exciting discussion topics for some students. Many universities now have active student groups involved in "green" issues and you may be able to use local campus recycling and energy conservation issues in class. Technological issues are also highly relevant to students, especially those already involved in personal computers.

Notes for PM 4-4

Political and Cultural Environments

Transparency PM 3-5 relates to the material on pp.152-158.

Political Environment

The political macroenvironmental forces consist of laws, government agencies, and interest groups that seek regulation of business activities to forward their own interests. Business in general, more than other groups, uses lobbying efforts to try and obtain legislation favourable to their competitive interests.

Legislation

Laws generally attempt to protect companies from each other to create more competition that in turn creates more value for the consumer. Laws also aim at protecting consumers from unfair and sometimes dangerous business practices. Laws sometimes seek to protect society as a whole from practices that endanger whole communities or other publicly owned resources such as rivers, forests, and parks.

Enforcement

The effect of laws depends upon the emphasis given to enforcing them within the regulatory agency responsible for administering the law. Regulation varies in intensity with political agendas of public officials and budget allocations. Public interest groups too affect the degree of legislative activity and administrative enforcement.

Cultural Environment

The key elements of understanding the cultural macroenvironment lie in values, subcultural influences, and shifts in secondary cultural values. Core values are relatively enduring and must be considered by marketers positioning products. For example, product innovations that conflict with core values are unlikely to be adopted. Secondary values change over time and change more often than core values and may provide positioning opportunities. Subcultures consist of homogeneous ethnic or lifestyle groups within the larger culture.

Tip

The Government's role in business activities as we enter an increasingly global marketplace is being re-examined and re-defined in light of world standards. As students learn about cultural influences in their home markets, they may be motivated by opportunities to apply knowledge of cultural influences abroad later in their careers.

Notes for PM 4-5

Comments on Discussing the Issues

1. This question is designed to give students a way to gauge how the cultural environment has changed by looking at one particular issue. A president or prime minister would not be seen smoking today because it would reflect badly on his image. In the 1950s and 1960s most politicians, celebrities, and public figures smoked, and it was regarded as a popular and sophisticated habit. Cigarettes were everywhere, and they became part of a person's image. Humphrey Bogart, for example, is still remembered for the way he gripped his cigarettes.

   The cultural environment has changed dramatically. Smoking is now seen as a dirty and unhealthy habit which is unpleasant to be near. Many county councils have passed anti-smoking ordinances which restrict where a person may smoke. Cigarette ads are banned from television, and many advocate a total ban on tobacco advertising in all media. Interestingly, these cultural trends are occurring throughout the Western world. Canada is reducing smoking through taxes that raise cigarettes to $5.80 per pack, and France has banned all advertising and sponsorship of sporting events by tobacco companies.

   There are many ethical issues concerning marketing tobacco products. For this question, it is best to keep the class focused on how a cigarette maker might respond to these trends most effectively. Students may see the ethical issues even more clearly when the discussion focuses on effective marketing. A cigarette marketer might work to *adapt* to the new environment. This could include new product development. RJR tried innovation with Premier, a smokeless cigarette. Unfortunately, smokers said it tasted like "burning insulation." Other products could include a conventional cigarette with less sidestream smoke, or cigarette substitutes such as snuff. The company could *combat* the cultural environment with advertising and public relations that stresses the pleasures or benefits of smoking, such as increased mental alertness and muscle relaxation. The company could *circumvent* the cultural issues by working to grow its business abroad, in cultures which are not opposed to smoking.

2. Let us look at the Disney adventure parks. The Walt Disney Company must consider many trends in its planning for the 1990s. The declining birthrate means that Disney should continue its expansion into non-child oriented areas (such as movies for older audiences developed by Disney's Touchstone Films). Technological improvements in home entertainment may make programmable or interactive cartoons possible. A downturn in the economic environment or gasoline shortages might limit attendance at Disney's theme parks (though park attendance seems to have been relatively unaffected by the economy in the past), but could boost sales of Disney videos. Cultural trends in foreign countries (for example, increasing openness in the Soviet Union) may expand markets in new areas for Disney. Tokyo Disneyland has been around for a number of years and is doing very well but EuroDisney is not doing as well since its inception. The Disney Company needs to assess why EuroDisney has been unsuccessful. Many factors attributed to the failure of EuroDisney so far. Refer to Case 15 for a full account of the situation.

3. There are many pressure groups, lobbyist and public interest groups that are currently in the limelight. Let us take Greenpeace International for example. It has been in existence for 25 years and has been one of the most established and aggressive "direct-action" pressure groups. Operating in at least 30 nations, it has an estimated budget of

100 million pounds which are largely donations from millions of its members and supporters world-wide. The organisation's causes have been the concern for the deteriorating natural environment and to a lesser extent the human environment (Peattie, K. (1992), Green Marketing, M& E Handbooks, Pitman Publishing). In 1995, Shell has been embroiled in the tussle over the dumping of the Brent Spar. The tremendous pressure and lobbying by Greenpeace has tarnished the image of Shell and has cost them million of pounds of lost sales. The final outcome however, was that Shell was right in planning to dump the Spar into the sea but the loss revenue can never be recovered. The lesson from this episode was that, had there been a proper forum where Shell and pressure groups like Greenpeace could discuss the most appropriate way of solving the problem, the former could have earned such revenues while the latter could have save enormous cost of the operation. It is important for Shell to maintain a forum to discuss any environmentally sensitive matter concerning its operation on an on-going basis. This will help Shell in projecting a better image to the market world-wide.

4. Many marketers are facing situations in which their products do not fit well with growing environmental concerns. In some cases, the solutions are straightforward. A manufacturer of aerosol cleaner can reformulate and convert to a trigger-spray non-aerosol bottle. Car manufacturers, bowing to regulation, reworked their engines to run on unleaded gasoline, and refineries retooled to make it.

   A plastic sandwich bag manufacturer faces a more difficult task: the product has some inherent environmental problems. They can be minimised, but not eliminated. There are several ways to manage this situation. The manufacturer could, for example:

   - make bags thinner, so there's less waste
   - print a "Recyclable" logo on each bag
   - fund plastic recycling efforts for good public relations exposure
   - develop and use a biodegradable plastic
   - diversify and develop biodegradable bags of treated paper

   None of these solutions is perfect, but each helps to reposition the company for the future.

5. This question is based on an American company, Anheuser-Busch's introduction in the late 1970s of "Chelsea," an "adult soft drink" intended to be a socially acceptable substitute for alcohol. Like many other soft drinks, Chelsea contained a small amount of alcohol; by reporting on the label that the amount was less than 0.5 percent, Anheuser-Busch aroused intense opposition to the product. Religious and other groups, and even the Secretary of Health, Education, and Welfare, objected so strongly to a product that they perceived as being designed to introduce children to alcoholic beverages that Anheuser-Busch withdrew the product from the market for modifications. (See "Felled By a Head of Foam," *Fortune*, January 15, 1979, p. 96).

   Several environmental factors might contribute to the success of a similar product today. The cultural environment is less receptive to heavy drinking in social situations, the political environment supports stiffer penalties on drinking and driving, and a healthy economy supports the sale of more expensive luxury items. However, the enthusiastic response to several brewers' of adult soft drinks such as Hooch and Two Dogs suggests that the time may now be right for an adult soft drink in the UK and Europe.

6. The purpose of this question is to get students to think of marketing in broader terms: marketing need not always consist of an exchange of dollars for a tangible product. Marketing to an internal audience uses a similar approach to any other marketing task: look at the audience's wants and needs, and structure a way to satisfy them that also meets the company's objectives.

Employers must first attack any issues of credibility or mistrust. The best way to do this is through displaying trust to the employees themselves: giving them information about company objectives and empowering them as real partners working towards fulfilling the company mission. Workers sometimes think that goals are arbitrary or unimportant. Explaining why better quality products or more courteous service is important will increase workers' willingness. Communication in many forms is needed: meetings with management, newsletters, posters, performance measures that support the new goals. Asking for and accepting employee input is critically important.

The employer meets an number of needs for the employee by providing money, meaningful work, group affiliation. A company can internally market by tying its goals to satisfying these employee needs better. It might offer a bonus for improved quality, increase the meaningfulness of the work by adding an element of mission ("Quality is Job 1"), and foster affiliation needs by building a more cohesive, goal-oriented team.

Comments on Applying the Concepts

1. There seems to a growing trend to use adjectives in brand names to help position products. Students should be able to come up with many examples. In cigarettes, many brands have a regular and a light version, such as Camel and Camel Light. Beers use the same terminology, so we see Coors and Coors Light. Variations occur as well, with some brands changing their brand names to a greater degree, such as Budweiser and Bud Light and Miller and Lite. Some brands have chosen not to modify the base brand: Heineken offers its light version under the name of Amstel Light.

   Foods have offered a wide range of "light" versions, which generally means lower fat or calorie content. This marketplace is rapidly changing, however, with the adoption of new standards by the EEC regulations. In the future, all food claims of this sort will need to meet very specific requirements. Similar claims in non-regulated products, such as light air fresheners, or "unscented" products (which are sometimes fragranced with a "masking" perfume) will continue to be made.

   The use of an adjective generally means that the product is being positioned against another product that already exists. In the computer field, we can find facsimile transmission software under the names of Winfax Pro and Winfax Lite. Winfax Pro was the original product, and Winfax Lite was introduced as a cheaper, less featured version designed to be bundled at a package price along with a modem. In general, brands with adjectives tend to be newer versions. This can often be an effective strategy to adapt to changing market conditions.

2. Many industries will potentially feel the effects of a changing political environment. In some cases, governmental action will potentially have a direct effect on the industry. Different countries face different political environments for example in the US continuing cuts in the defence budget, including military base closings and fewer and smaller weapons systems contracts, will directly impact military suppliers. Similarly, proposals to change the American health care system can have dramatic effects on the insurance industry. The Clinton administration's original health care proposal, made in late 1993, advocated the creation of giant pools of people to be insured, with insurers bidding for this business. This proposal appears to be very favourable for large insurers, but could potentially put medium and small insurers out of business. Other effects will be felt by doctors, hospitals, drug companies, and health maintenance organisations (HMOs). Students may list many more types of industries that could be affected.

   There are no clear right and wrong answers when students suggest strategies to cope with change. The instructor should judge the answers by two criteria. First, is the student's assessment of the likely changes reasonable and plausible? If so, is the strategy suggested likely to improve the industry's performance in the face of this change?

   Environments change, and these changes are rarely "set in stone." Furthermore, a company's reaction to an environmental change often creates even more changes in the environment as consumers and competitors respond. Companies can easily do some planning for change: demographic trends develop slowly and predictably, and smart companies are not caught unaware. A nappy (diaper) maker can easily and accurately predict the likely number of babies for several years in advance. Other changes, such as the state of the economy or of consumer confidence are not easily predicted. In these cases, companies should have a most likely scenario to guide their planning, with contingency plans in the event that the environment changes in an unanticipated way.

Case 4
Angelou's Restaurant (and Snack Bar?)

Synopsis

This case depicts the growing competition in the restaurant market, focusing specially on fast food restaurants and traditional restaurants. The case opens with Mr John Angelou who has owned and run a traditional Greek restaurant in an Athens suburb for nearly twenty years. It then recounts that business is not too good at the moment, with his family having to work long hours to keep the restaurant going. Although the restaurant has seating for up to 80 guests, it rarely has more than 40-50 guests at a time, usually only on Friday or Saturday evenings. Trade has mainly been affected by the growth of fast food restaurants and changing in customers' tastes. He has had an offer from a friend for business, plus there is a vacant restaurant unit in a new shopping centre in a rapidly developing suburb. Mr Angelou has to decide whether to sell his business and move to the shopping centre or continue with his existing restaurant. The case concludes that he has to make his decision within one week.

Teaching Objectives

1. Allow students to examine the impact of macroenvironmental changes on companies' marketing strategies.

2. Show students how those macroenvironmental changes produce microenvironmental changes.

3. Familiarise students with a very competitive consumer market and allow them to make recommendations for marketing action.

Study Questions

1. What are the major influences on Mr Angelou's decision to set up a new restaurant? Will moving to a new location change the balance of favourable and unfavourable influences?

Students should suggest that the strongest influence is that; lifestyle and behaviour are changing, which in turn leading to changing eating habits. This has led to a proliferation of a large number of fast food outlets being established in Greece such as McDonalds, KFC, Pizza Hut and Greek franchises. This development has resulted in increased competition faced by Mr Angelou. His restaurant is seen as not being competitive in its present form and location. This lack of competitiveness is highlighted by the fact that he is unable to use the full capacity of his restaurant and losing money through wasted resources. Students should mention that at most the restaurant has about 40-50 guests at any one time, working approximately half its capacity and Mr Angelou is fully aware of this. On the personal side, students should cite that one of the major factors contributing towards Angelou's zest to move is his concern about the working hours that both he and his family have to endure in order to keep the restaurant going. Evidently, John Angelou is unhappy about working very hard yet achieving mediocre results. Students can also mention that Mr Angelou is concerned about the long run viability of his present restaurant, the future seems quite bleak. He recognises the business opportunity in moving to the new shopping complex. He seems fully aware of the various benefits that a move to the new premises would bring.

Students should highlight briefly the current unfavourable circumstances such as lack of custom, long hours, being in a declining market and lack of job satisfaction. Students then could explain several favourable factors in moving to a new location. The new shopping centre, in a relatively wealthy population area of Athens, presents a great business opportunity for Mr Angelou. Potentially he has 200,000 relatively wealthy customers to tap for custom, In addition, there are also the office workers and the shopping centre employees who will possibly eat at the restaurant. He could also attract the school children and construction workers during their lunch break. If Mr Angelou decides to move to the new location it will give him the option of changing the style of the restaurant from the present style. This may seem attractive because the number of traditional restaurants are declining in Greece. He could move to a more popular format of restaurant e.g. becoming a franchise. Furthermore, he already has someone interested in his present restaurant even though he is not receiving a fair price. It will save him the trouble of finding a buyer. Another favourable point is that Mr Angelou's restaurant will be the only restaurant apart from the snack bar in the supermarket, he will not have direct major competition. The regular booking of the restaurant by the shop owners' association is a favourable point that should not be overlooked. Students should highlight some unfavourable points such as; the price offered by a friend was less than fair price. If Mr Angelou chooses to obtain a franchise, he would need extra money to cover the franchise charge; it would take Mr Angelou two years (operating at 80% capacity) to recover the value of his investment and the franchise fee; the threat of the snack bar in the supermarket; the popularity of the fast food restaurants is becoming widespread in Greece, thus this sector will be the strongest force of competition for his new restaurant. This can be overcome by Mr Angelou opening his own fast food restaurant through taking out a franchise.

2. What markets can Mr Angelou serve with his new restaurant? Does he need to choose between them or can he serve them all? Is it the right time to open another traditional Greek restaurant?

There are several markets Mr Angelou can target; (1) The suburb is a rapidly growing one with most its 200,000 inhabitants with high incomes. This mean that many of the people would have greater disposable income and more likely to eat out. Of the 200,000 inhabitants many are likely to be young people. They will be shopping at the centre for clothing and etc. and may like to eat a light snack while shopping. They will be inclined to purchase a takeaway; (2) The employees in the shopping centre would be on short lunch breaks which could mean they would want a reasonable sized snack for lunch. There is also a possibility that they want a nice hot meal, thus use the restaurant; (3) The professional people working next door i.e. the dentist, doctors, architects and civil engineers are more likely to have sit down meals at lunch time, if they are not too busy. However, if they are too busy somebody may be sent to purchase a large order of sandwiches and other snacks. Some may even bring prospective clients to the restaurants for business lunches; (4) The construction workers are unlikely to dine in the restaurant but will require a filling meal and may purchase large amounts of sandwiches and drinks that could be financially beneficial; (5) With a school of 1500 students 2 blocks away, it seems the students are possibly another market Mr Angelou can target. The students are likely to hang out in the centre during lunch time which could mean that they would require snacks during the lunch hour. At the end of each school day the children are again likely to want more snacks; (6) The restaurant would be used for the twice monthly meetings of the association. This means that Mr Angelou has the chance of impressing colleagues, who then may recommend his restaurant to others.

By segmenting the target market Mr Angelou can meet the desired needs of all the different customers. Professional (e.g. business executives) and some shoppers will prefer a sit-down restaurant, especially in the evenings. This would be aiming at the higher end of the market, potentially more profitable, but he may have problems keeping the restaurant busy during the day. However, many shoppers and students will prefer a snack bar. This has the advantage of high turnover but would be difficult to attract custom when the centre closes at night. He can therefore serve all his potential markets if his restaurant caters for snacks and sit-down meals. Some students may have different view points. Ask them to justify their opinions.

The figures show that in the last 10 years the number of traditional Greek restaurants has fallen which could be attributed to the change in social eating habits and a change in lifestyle. The figures also show that the number of fast food outlets has increased (be it Greek or international like McDonalds). This could mean that there is a very large demand for fast food due to an increased pace of life. Thus, it would not be a viable proposition to continue in the traditional Greek food market. On the other hand, considering the shopping centre is situated in a developing suburb, it can be assumed that this neighbourhood is not saturated with Greek restaurants. There will be a proliferation of fast food outlets in due course but Mr Angelou is not competing in this market. He will be able to build a good reputation within the suburb as long as the customers are satisfied with his food and services.

3. Mr Angelou computed the cost of a franchise but what are the benefits? Why pay for a franchise from one of the national or international chains when a restaurateur, like Mr Angelou, already knows about food and how to serve it? What do large chains gain from having franchisees rather than running outlets themselves? If you were a franchiser, what would you control most carefully?

The benefits of a franchise are; a tried and tested product is used. An established trade name which is easily recognised by the customer is adopted by the franchisee e.g. many people will eat in McDonalds not because they know that an individual outlet is particularly good but they know what they will receive, as McDonalds' products are internationally recognised. There is a restriction of competition in the local area, as a franchiser is unlikely to franchise more than one outlet in the immediate vicinity. Training is given by the franchiser in standardised business management and administration. The franchiser assists the franchisee with many aspects of the business such as finance, marketing , quality control systems, accounting and management control systems, and distribution. The franchisee is provided with a set format with which to run the business and receives the benefits of national and international promotion. A franchiser will also often have carried out its own market research to identify whether or not an outlet is likely to succeed. A franchiser will some times supply part of the set up capital, for example some fast food companies supply the furniture and cookers in a new franchise. A local restaurateur may know about food and how to serve it but franchiser is likely to have superior all round knowledge of the industry. With a minor loss of control Mr Angelou is still in effect his own boss.

At present the restaurant run by Mr Angelou is not proving to be feasible. Mr Angelou would benefit from purchasing a franchise due to the change in social habits where there is an increasing demand for fast food. Franchising has been the fastest growing development in recent years; national and international chains have proven successful. Their trading name is established and they have known products. With an established name and known products behind you, it is obviously less risky to open a franchise than to go on your own. If the marketing of the product are already in place, the franchisee can concentrate on other matters such as quality of food served. The new competition in retailing is no longer between independent business units but between whole systems of centrally programmed networks.

Students should mention some of these gains; (1) The royalties obtained by the franchiser provide a positive cash flow; (2) Increase in the number of markets and outlets with minimal capital investments; (3) Franchisee is the owner and therefore highly motivated in contrast with a manager of a "normal" retail outlet; (4) It is an easy entry in the local community. Local knowledge that the franchisees possess is an advantage; (5) Often it is a contractual requirement for the franchisee to purchase certain inputs from the parent company; (6) The majority of the risk is borne by the franchisees.

There are many aspects of a firm that need to be considered and controlled. Quality must be observed at all times so as to present a uniform image. This also ensures continuity of the product and service throughout the chain. Financial matters must be controlled and analysed to forecast demand for a particular product or to detect an upturn or downturn in demand. Some marketing activities should be controlled while others should be regularly monitored and inspected by the parent company.

4. Should Mr Angelou go ahead and open the new restaurant? What will be the influence of the supermarket's snack bar and the other business and people in the area? Which floor plan should he adopt?

Some students will suggest that John Angelou should go ahead and open the new restaurant. Others will add that he should not go for the franchise deal because they feel that after 20 years in the restaurant trade, Mr Angelou has sufficient experience in running a restaurant. In the long term the rewards will surpass the capital outlay he has to put into the new business. By not being part of a franchise Mr Angelou will have complete control over the restaurant, be more in tune with the needs of the customers and also understand fully what services the restaurant should provide for the customers. He has been offered a shade less than the fair price for the old restaurant which means that he does not have to delay starting up the new restaurant. The projected figures mentioned in the case study shows that the new restaurant will break-even within six months. If these forecast are accurate than the new restaurant seemed attractive. In addition, Mr Angelou will recover his investment cost within the first two years of trading. With the above forecast the new restaurant seemed to be financially rewarding which his old restaurant was not. The location of the new restaurant is very appealing, with attributes such as being in a developing suburb of Athens where there are 200,000 residents in the upper end of the social class. There is a small office block nearby with about 40 to 50 potential customers. Two new offices moving to the centre with a further 15 employees. Also, a new secondary school being built in the vicinity. The last reason John Angelou should open the new restaurant is because the restaurant has already been booked twice-monthly by the shop owner's association.

Some students will suggest that if Mr Angelou had more time he should carry some market research such as; what the customers want from the restaurant and if they need another snack bar. In addition, he could also find out more about the supermarket's snack bar. As stated in the case study this snack bar is a loss leader thus making it very hard for Mr Angelou to compete on the basis of price. Mr Angelou may do better in terms of offering a better service. The influence of other businesses and people in the area will have a positive effect because basically they are the market Mr Angelou will want to capture. It is vital for Mr Angelou to plan ahead in order to counter competition. In particular, he should be very aware of a McDonald's, KFC or Pizza Hut arriving in the future in one of the un-let units in the shopping centre. His main forte will be the production of high quality Greek food.

Some students will favour one layout over the others. The majority will be partial to the second floor plan that has the following characteristics; kitchen in the middle creating two areas with separate entrances. He can use part of the restaurant as a snack bar which will trade steadily whilst the shopping centre is open. The remaining area would be the traditional Greek restaurant for those who want a sit-down meal. This would trade well in the evenings, with his customers coming from the affluent local area. He could use different names for the two areas if he was worried about his restaurant's name being cheapened by the snack bar. The main issue here is to ask students to justify why they prefer one layout over another.

Teaching Suggestions

This should be an interesting case because students will be familiar with some of the facts discussed and can find additional information easily.

The instructor may wish to ask students to survey local fast food and ethnic restaurants in preparing the case. How many fast food outlets are there in the area? How many ethnic restaurants are there in the vicinity? What prices are charged for the various foods? Is there any evidence of decline or upsurge in each category of the restaurant business? Have the macro and micro environments affect this type of business endeavours? Are their specialised offerings targeting to certain groups? The students may want to talk to restaurants' managers about how their businesses are doing and determine their views on the individual restaurant's strategies.

Students may also wish to talk to representative members of different target markets to determine if they use certain types of restaurants and why or why not.

This is an excellent case for use with the Market Segmentation Chapter (Chapter 9) and with the Consumer Behaviour Chapter (Chapter 7). It can also be used with the Retailing and Wholesaling Chapter (Chapters 22).

Jokes and Quotes

Environmentalist: Concern about the things that other people do that you do not like.

Education is an ornament in prosperity and a refuge in adversity.
ARISTOTLE

Boundary: In political geography, an imaginary line between two nations, separating the imaginary rights of one from the imaginary rights of the other.
AMBROSE BIERCE

Learning without thought is labour lost; thought without learning is perilous.
CONFUCIUS

Since a politician never believes what he says, he is always astonished when others do.
CHARLES DE GAULLE

We are locked into a system of "fouling our own nest," so long as we behave only as independent, rational, free-enterprises.
GARRETT HARDIN

The command *Be fruitful and multiply* (was) promulgated, according to our authorities, when the population of the world consisted of two persons.
DEAN WILLIAM R. INGE

Economics is a subject that does not greatly respect one's wishes.
NIKITA KHRUSHCHEV

The importance of geology to geography is that, without geology, geography would have no place to put itself.
ART LINKLETTER

Planned Economy: Where everything is included in the plans except economy.
CAREY MCWILLIAMS

First you forget names, then you forget faces, then you forget to pull your zipper up, then you forget to pull your zipper down.
LEO ROSENBERG

Greater love hath no man than this, that he lay down his friends for his political life.
JEREMY THORPE

We have been God-like in our planned breeding of our domesticated plants and animals, but we have been rabbit-like in our unplanned breeding of ourselves.
ARNOLD TOYNBEE

Young men want to be faithful and are not; old men want to be faithless and cannot.
OSCAR WILDE

Chapter 5

The Global Marketplace

Chapter Objectives

After reading this chapter, you should be able to:

1. Discuss how foreign trade, economic, political-legal and cultural environments affect a company's international marketing decisions.
2. Describe three key approaches to entering international markets.
3. Explain how companies might adapt their marketing mixes for international markets.
4. Identify the three major forms of international marketing organisation.

Chapter Overview

Companies today can no longer afford to pay attention only to their domestic market, no matter how large it is. Many industries are global industries, and those firms that operate globally achieve lower costs and higher brand awareness. At the same time, global marketing is risky because of variable exchange rates, unstable governments, protectionist tariffs and trade barriers, and several other factors. Given the potential gains and risks of international marketing, companies need a systematic way to make their international marketing decisions. The company must understand the international marketing environment. Next, the company must decide whether it wants to go abroad and consider the potential risks and benefits. Third, the company must decide the volume of foreign sales it wants, how many countries it wants to market in, and which specific markets it wants to enter. Next, the company must decide how to enter each chosen market. Then it must decide how much products, promotion, price, and channels should be adapted for each foreign market. Finally, the company must develop an organisation for international marketing.

Teaching Notes

Refer to the following pages for teaching notes.

Major Decisions in International Marketing

Transparency PM 5-1 corresponds to Figure 5.1 on p.173 and relates to the material on pp.173-185

Understanding - comes from looking at the international marketing environment. Multinational companies operating in many countries have proliferated and in a global economy more companies must consider international markets if they are to grow.

Deciding - whether to go abroad may be the best growth opportunity, even for relatively small companies. More foreign markets can increase volume.

Which Markets - to enter is also based upon environmental conditions.

How to Enter - involves choices about how to compete.

The Marketing Programme - the marketing programme appropriate to international markets includes variations on the product and promotion.

The Marketing Organisation - choices available in international marketing include export department, international division, and global organisation.

Looking at the International Environment

Trade System - concerns identify opportunities and obstacles for firms abroad. Companies should investigate tariffs (taxes on imported goods), quotas (which restrict import amounts), and other obstacles such as nontariff barriers that may affect ability to compete.

Economic Environment - concerns relate to the industrial structure of the host country. Subsistence and raw-material exporting countries may be limited markets for some kinds of consumer goods, for example.

Political/Legal Environments - vary from country to country and in each country in their attitude toward foreign firms. Scrutiny of legal regulation is a must.

Cultural Differences - are very important in international marketing. Most advertising and even product images are culturally-based and may be inappropriate, ineffective, and even offensive in another culture. Care is required.

Tip

Ask students to discuss the impact of European Union, ASEAN, etc. in the context of international marketing.

Notes for PM 5-1

Market Entry Strategies

Transparency PM 5-2 corresponds to Figure 5.2 on p.188 and relates to the material on pp.188-190.

Market Entry Strategies

Exporting

Exporting may be of two kinds. Indirect exporting works through independent international intermediaries and involves less investment by the exporter. Risk is also smaller. Direct exporting involves more risk and investment as the firm sets up its own presence in the host country but the potential return is also greater.

Joint Venturing

Firms have four types of joint venture available to them. Licensing occurs when a company enters into an agreement with a licensee in the foreign market. Licensing means little risk but also little control. Contract Manufacturing arranges for a foreign producer to make products in the host country for that market. Management Contracting has the exporting firm provide the management team with the host country supplying the capital. Joint Ownership consists of one company joining with another in the host country to create a local business in which they share owner ship and control. While this option commits both companies to the enterprise, it demands close agreement on both the goals and the methods for doing business.

Direct Investment

This option occurs when the exporting firm enters a foreign market by developing foreign-based assembly or manufacturing facilities. Direct investment can be especially attractive when the firm needs firm local control and when there are substantial cost savings. Risks also rise due to unfamiliar environmental conditions, changes in government in some areas, and generally uncertainty of the firm's position in the country.

Notes for PM 5-2

The Global Marketing Programme

Transparency PM 5-3 corresponds to Figure 5.3 on p.195 and relates to the material on pp.195-197.

Product Strategies

Straight Product Extension

Involves marketing a product in the foreign market without making any changes. Some products may have very strong brand awareness and already be desired as is in the new market.

Product Adaptation

Involves changing the product to meet local conditions or wants. Often product forms need to be altered. Size and tastes, for example, are usually at least partially preferred on some culturally related dimensions.

Product Invention

Consists of creating something entirely new for the foreign market.

Promotion

Communication Adaptation

Adaptation is often required. Although some companies can use a single theme and meaning internationally, it is often the case that the local variation on even a universal theme may require some modification. Language, both literal and figurative, must be very carefully considered in international promotion. Also, media vary in the reach and effectiveness, even their availability.

Dual Adaptation

Involves a combination of promotion and product alternations for the foreign market.

> **Tip**
>
> Some examples of language blunders are; Coke's Chinese "bite the wax tadpole" and General Motors' "No Go" (Nova) in Spain are legend.

Notes for PM 5-3

Global Marketing Organisation

These notes relate to the material on pp.199-200.

Three Organisational Structures

Export Department

During early international marketing efforts, companies typically just create a new department to co-ordinate international operations. The sales manager may take on larger staff if and as the international business grows in importance and more marketing services are needed to support it.

International Division

As the level of involvement in and complexity of international operations increases, companies commonly organise an international division. In addition to running international operations, the division oversees strategic growth and investigates different types of foreign entry opportunities in new countries. Operating units in foreign markets under division control may be organised by geographical organisation, world product groups, or international subsidiaries.

Global Organisation

For many large companies, the scope of operations grows to the point where they are no longer a firm involved in many foreign markets, they are a truly a multinational company. Recruitment, management, suppliers, manufacturing, and financing are no longer linked to a single-country mentality. The entire world becomes a single market whose segmentation is base upon strategic and tactical competitive advantage, not national affiliation.

Comments on Discussing the Issues

1. An article by Douglass G. Norvell and Sion Raveed (*Marketing News*, October 17, 1980, pp. 1-2) gives "Eleven Reasons for Firms to 'Go International'":

1. To escape from recessions in the domestic market.
2. To counter adverse demographic changes (such as declining birth rates).
3. To keep up with or to escape competition.
4. To enjoy economies of scale in production.
5. To dispose of inventories.
6. To export technology to less developed nations.
7. To increase political influence.
8. To extend a product's life cycle.
9. To enjoy tax advantages.
10. To create research opportunities (by testing products in foreign markets).
11. To establish a progressive image.

2. Marketers have various responses to consider in the face of different trade restrictions. Tariffs have the effect of raising prices, so marketers may increase advertising to stimulate demand and overcome the price disadvantage. Alternatively, the company could be willing to accept a lower profit margin on the product because of other benefits of competing in the country. The company could also try to influence the political environment and have the tariff reduced or eliminated.

Quotas may allow an exporting company to follow a price- skimming strategy. Because the quota limits the amount of the product that can be sold, the company is able to target the consumers who are willing to pay the most for the product. (This may sound like a profiteering strategy, but if the price is set at a low level where demand exceeds supply, there will be consumer frustration due to product shortages and ways of rationing the product that benefit other channel members rather than the manufacturer, such as bribes to middlemen.)

With an embargo, the company does not have a marketing mix—the product cannot be exported to the country. Instead, the company may consider other forms of international operations in the country, such as joint ventures with local investors, or direct investments in the country.

3. International marketing can be exceptionally difficult. A company must cope with all the market threats it faces at home, and learn to operate in a very different business and consumer environment as well. The Japanese have been successful in international trade because of their willingness to keep learning until they succeed. This long-term outlook is a hallmark of Japanese business: Mitsubishi has a 500 year business plan, for example! The Japanese would stay and learn to work in difficult conditions. European firms may need to show similar patience in international efforts.

4. As described in the text, prices are often higher in foreign markets because of the extra costs of transportation, tariffs, and extra layers of middleman mark-ups. Also, the possibility of exchange rate fluctuations leads the exporter to want a higher rate of return in foreign markets to compensate for the extra risks.

There are several factors that may lead prices to be *lower* in foreign markets than in domestic ones. Incomes may be low, and higher prices might severely limit the market. If the product is made in the foreign country, production costs may be lower and there may be cost-saving product modifications (for example, putting fewer safety or pollution control devices on cars, or sweetening diet drinks with saccharin rather than the more expensive aspartame (NutraSweet)). The lower costs allow an adequate profit margin with lower prices. Government policies in the foreign market may limit the price that may be charged, and domestic government practices may subsidise lower prices to boost exports. The company may also set a low price to penetrate the market in hopes of raising prices later. Thus, higher prices in foreign markets may be the norm, but perhaps the only universal rule is that pricing decisions are complicated in international marketing.

5. The test of injury resulting from dumping is whether the effect of the dumping is to "cause or threaten material injury to *an established domestic industry*, or is such as to retard materially the establishment of a domestic industry" (General Agreement on Tariffs and Trade, Article VI, italics added). Dumping is prohibited not because of its effects on the consumer, but because of its effects on an industry, or more broadly, on competition.

The disadvantages to the consumer of dumping are indirect and long-term. Dumping has some impact on the country's economy, its balance of trade, and the health of its industries. If a company is unable to compete with dumpers, it may leave an industry, reducing the choice available to consumers and possibly giving dumpers the power to raise prices or reduce service at some future time.

6. The situations presented in the question illustrate the different stages of marketing organisation described in the text. Raleigh, selling only three bicycle models in the Far East, would probably use an export department organisation. A US toy manufacturer might use an export department, or if exports made up a substantial part of its sales, it might set up an international division. Rover and other car manufacturers often sell in many countries, so a large international division or a true global organisation would be most appropriate for its international marketing activities.

Comments on Applying the Concepts

1. **(a)** This part of the question asks simply for a list, and a first impression of whether this brand is local or foreign. Relate this question to products that originate from your students' country and those that are foreign.

   (b) Determining country of origin is not always easy. This question compares different ways of classifying the origin of goods: by the sound of the brand name, by the home country of the parent company, and by the country in which the goods were manufactured. There are some surprises here: Some Sony and Philips televisions are manufactured in the United States, National (Japanese) air conditioners are manufactured in Malaysia. Many Honda cars sold in the UK are made in Derby and Nissan cars are made in Swindon (UK), and some of these cars are now being shipped back to Japan for domestic consumption. Mercedes Benz plans to begin manufacturing in the United States. And "domestic content" legislation makes the picture even more confusing. Ford has managed to get its full-size Crown Victoria model (in the US) classified as an import by using many imported components. This allows Ford to average the Crown Victoria's abysmal fuel economy with much smaller imported cars, thereby meeting CAFE fuel economy standards and avoiding a "gas guzzler" tax. -

   Brand names often change hands, and this can affect country of origin. Garrard was a venerable British manufacturer of turntables in the 1960s, but the brand name now graces a line of cheap portable radios manufactured in the Far East. Fisher, a highly regarded American manufacturer of high fidelity equipment, has met a similar fate.

2. **(a)** Entertainment is the second biggest export of America and the American influence on world culture is even large than this number implies. American entertainers are popular abroad, and students will find many American stars in foreign equivalents of *Us* or *People* magazines. Scandal is just as popular around the world as it is here, so racy gossip about American entertainers gets great attention. Occasionally, there are some surprises. David Hasselhoff, the former star of the little-missed *Knight Rider* television series which featured a talking car and the current star of Baywatch, is little known in America. He is, however, a major pop singer in Germany, and gave an outdoor concert on top of the Berlin Wall as it was being torn down.

   (b) Indian movies are not popular in Europe primarily because they do translate well into the European culture. Although Sanjit Ray has received many acclaims for his films, they are really known in then West only by the serious student of film. The Indian culture is rich, complex and ancient. Many traditions, both strong and subtle, have developed in this subcontinent. The cinema of India includes its country's cultural richness in plots and subplots. Some elements of a movie, such as the barriers of the caste system, may be blatantly obvious to an Indian native, but completely escape the grasp of a Westerner.

   There are other differences in acting style, plot structure, and production quality that are very different between European and Indian films. At the present time, it is likely that this gulf is too large to be overcome for the mass market. If Indian movie companies do wish to tap the European market, they could consider making special efforts to distribute films through the smaller theatres that specialise in art films.

Indian film companies could also study European films and European audiences, and consider making films directed to meet the needs of this target audience.

Case 5
Procter & Gamble:
Going Global in Cosmetics

Synopsis

This case recounts the moves Procter & Gamble has made to enter the cosmetics industry. In doing so, the case provides students with a good look at an international business and the competitors' strategies. First, P&G purchased Noxell Corporation with its Noxzema, Cover Girl, and Clarion brand names. P&G focused on strengthening Cover Girl and realised success. Then, P&G's chairman, Edwin L. Artzt, went shopping again. This time he landed Revlon's Max Factor and Betrix lines because 80 per cent of their sales were outside the United States. Artzt also saw that he could use the new products' distribution channels to help make Cover Girl an international brand. P&G put its resources to work to revitalise Max Factor's US franchise. Like Revlon, it had to find ways to attract younger women. But every other company was trying to do the same thing, and P&G had other problems as it learned the cosmetics business.

P&G overhauled the Max Factor line and undertook its first world-wide product introduction during the Spring of 1993. It will pursue a global strategy, using the same products in each market. No other company has tried to develop a world-wide, mass-market cosmetics brand. As P&G tries to go global, it also continues to face aggressive competition in the US market. To succeed both domestically and globally, it must develop new marketing strategies.

Teaching Objectives

1. Allow students to apply the ideas presented in the chapter.

2. Give students insight into a well-known industry and help them understand the trends shaping competitive strategies.

3. Provide students an opportunity to use competitive and marketing strategy concepts to develop a strategy for Procter and Gamble and to consider potential competitive reactions.

Study Questions

1. Who are Procter & Gamble's competitors, from an industry point of view and from a market point of view? Are there strategic groups in the industry? Why are these questions important for P&G?

From an <u>industry</u> point of view, all of the firms mentioned in the case are competitors. The products are close substitutes . As the text suggests, if the price of one product rises, the demand for other products will rise. This is especially true if one takes a global perspective on the industry.

However, from a <u>market</u> point of view all of the firms do not compete with each other. The text suggests that direct competitors are firms that are trying to satisfy the same customer need or serve the same customer group. Students can identify different <u>strategic groups</u>. One group is based on <u>distribution strategy</u>. Some competitors, like P&G and Revlon, compete only in the mass-market outlets. Others, like Estee Lauder or Chanel, compete primarily in department or speciality stores. Although P&G must watch competitors in the department store arena, it does not compete directly with them day-to-day. The difference in distribution strategy also matches a difference in product quality. The higher-priced, higher quality cosmetics and perfumes use the department store channel where their higher margins can support personal selling efforts. The firms using the mass market use lower prices to build volume, but that volume is only available in mass-market outlets. Some firms, like Betrix, had product lines at different price points. Betrix had the mid-priced Ellen Betrix women's products and the upscale Laura Giagiotti line

Other strategic groups are based on geography. P&G and Revlon are attempting to be global competitors. Betrix competes primarily in Germany and western Europe. L'Oreal, while it has a more global presence, is a primary competitor with Betrix because of its dominance in its home market, France.

Determining your firm's competitors is obviously important. P&G does not worry about Estee Lauder, but it does watch Revlon closely. Revlon may not have seen P&G as a global competitor until it purchased the Max Factor line and decided to relaunch the brand globally.

Students may want to develop a 2-by-2 matrix using price (low and high) and market presence (regional to global) to place each company. This will help them "see" strategic groups.

2. What trends are shaping competitors' objectives in the cosmetics industry?

First, there is the ageing of the US population. As the case notes, ageing baby boomers had decided to focus on skin-care products rather than cosmetics. As a result, firms were having to attract younger women who use more cosmetics. But the youth market was limited. This meant that to grow, US companies had to examine the international markets. This is the source of the pressure to establish a global presence. Finally, in the US market in particular, women were deserting department stores' cosmetics counters. They did not like being assaulted. Further, because more women were working and had less time to shop, they wanted to be able to buy their cosmetics in places where they normally had to shop. This produced the boom in mass-market outlets. However, this trend was making it harder to get shelf space in mass-market outlets. This means that smaller firms will have a more difficult time competing. Firms must get bigger to have the resources to fight the marketing wars. Going global also helps control costs if the company can use standard products and marketing approaches.

Students should see how these various forces work together to shape strategic changes in the industry.

3. Based on information in the case, which of Michael Porter's competitive positions have the various cosmetics competitors pursued to gain competitive advantage?

Students will have some trouble clearly distinguishing among the companies in terms of cost leadership, differentiation, and focus strategies. Some students will argue that P&G and Revlon are pursuing cost-leadership strategies. They focus on mass distribution where cost and value pricing are important. By going global, increasing volume, and using standard products and marketing, P&G and Revlon can develop a cost leadership strategy.

Other students will argue that the cosmetics business is not one where you want to be low cost and therefore low price. They will suggest that P&G and Revlon are pursuing differentiation. Each cosmetic line wants consumers to see it as different and better. Does one want to wear the low-priced perfume or cosmetics? The firms may want to charge prices that are low enough to appeal to the mass market, but having the lowest-priced products is not necessarily the best goal.

Students will also say that Estee Lauder, Chanel, and other upscale marketers are pursuing a focus strategy. They serve upscale customers primarily through the department/speciality store outlets.

In terms of the leader, challenger, follower, and nicher strategies, students will identify P&G and Revlon as pursuing leader strategies. Revlon has been a leader and is attempting to maintain its position. P&G has not been a leader, but its acquisitions and resources have put it in a leadership position. In some markets, it may continue to challenge established competitors, but its overall strategy is to be "number one." Revlon and P&G are trying to expand the market while protecting and expanding their market shares.

Maybelline pursues a challenger strategy. It has lost share to Cover Girl in the mass market. However, at the end of the case, Maybelline has decided to target women over 35, in contrast to the other firms who are targeting younger women. This is a flanking attack strategy. Unilever, with its Elizabeth Arden and Faberge brands, is also pursuing a challenger strategy. With its size, it may launch a frontal attack on Estee Lauder and L'Oreal. Betrix is a challenger at the regional level.

Students will suggest that L'Oreal, although relatively large, pursues a nicher strategy by serving women who are willing to pay more for their perfumes and cosmetics. Estee Lauder and Chanel also pursue niches, but they are aggressive in their efforts. Kao Corporation and Shiseido Company are nichers who compete only in Japan

It is difficult to identify any true followers. Perhaps the industry is in a situation where it is hard just to follow. Unless a firm has an aggressive strategy, it may not survive.

4. What actions should P&G take in order to expand the total cosmetics market and to protect and expand its market share?

The text suggests that market leaders can expand the total market by finding new users or new uses or by increasing usage. P&G has focused on the women's market. Students may suggest it should target men also. It could acquire a men's fragrance line and develop it as it has Max Factor. P&G could also work to expand the entire market by promoting perfumes and cosmetics in general. This could tie in with the effort to target men. It could encourage men to wear cologne. It could also promote skin-care products for men and develop a line of men's products for that purpose. Especially in the area of skin-care products, P&G can promote more usage. As the baby-boom population ages, the case indicates that its members become more concerned about their skin. P&G could promote good skin care. It could include sunscreen in more products and encourage consumers to use them more. Finally, P&G could examine the market potential in the republics of the former Soviet Union or China. These emerging markets could be very lucrative.

To protect its market share, P&G will have to continuously introduce new products. This will help keep competitors off balance. The case also mentions that P&G has had distribution and delivery problems. Solving these problems will be important to protecting its share. Students may recommend closer co-ordination between marketing and manufacturing to help avoid these problems. P&G should also listen to retailers' reactions to its consolidation of the salesforce. It should monitor salesforce performance and retailer/distributor satisfaction with the salesforce. If the retailers and distributors continue to be dissatisfied, P&G should make changes. This situation offers a good opportunity to point out that the retailers and distributors are just as much customers as are the end customers. P&G will also want to watch its flanks. Competitors who have been focusing on the department store channel may decide to pursue customers who are moving to the mass-market outlets. If so, P&G must be prepared to meet them. This may mean having a line of upscale, mass-market cosmetics and perfumes ready for introduction.

To expand market share, P&G should deliver more value to customers than the competition. Students should suggest that P&G should monitor customer satisfaction closely and invest in market research to keep track of consumer trends. It will then have to be ready to respond to what it learns. P&G will also want to keep its promotion efforts at a high level. This will force smaller competitors to respond. Such a strategy keeps the competitors from spending money where they want to spend it, such as on R&D, and keeps the price of competing in the industry high.

5. What competitive strategies would you recommend for P&G's competitors?

Revlon should see P&G's efforts to become global as a direct attack on its position. As the case suggests, it should consider taking some of its regional brands global. It is important that it remain on the aggressive and not just react to P&G's moves. Revlon should also consider stepping up its efforts in the US market where it has had some success against P&G. This might divert some of P&G's resources from its international efforts.

Estee Lauder, L'Oreal, and Unilever hold the top spots in department stores. Yet, at least in the US, women are shopping for cosmetics and fragrances in other outlets. These firms want to protect their positions, but they must also consider the mass-market outlets. They should evaluate the potential of upscale products at the higher end of mass-market pricing. Perhaps they could introduce products that took advantage of their upscale heritage without hurting the firms' department store sales.

For niche players, the key will be to get bigger. Smaller firms will want to pursue acquisitions or position themselves to be purchased. P&G and Revlon are raising the stakes in the cosmetics business. These smaller firms must have the resources if they are going to play in the international market.

Teaching Suggestions

Women students will enjoy this case because they will be familiar with the products. Males may feel as though they are lost. The instructor can ask males to investigate the male cosmetics and toiletries markets to find out what the trends are. They may find that Japanese men use many more cosmetics than American men. Some analysts predict that US men will begin to use more cosmetics over time.

Students may want to survey local discount stores and drug stores to find out which companies are represented. They can talk to sales representatives at the stores to find out what products are selling and why. They can also talk to department store personnel to find out if women are still deserting those stores and what marketing steps the stores are taking to counter the trend.

This case can be used with the Competitive Advantage Chapter (Chapter 12), the Place Chapter (Chapter 21), the Retailing Chapter (Chapter 22), and the Marketing Environment Chapter (Chapter 4).

Additional Information

In late 1991, P&G began to investigate the cosmetics market in the former Russian republics. It has invested millions to study Russian consumers, develop products for the Russian market, advertise those products. It offers Oil of Ulay (instead of Olay), Head and Shoulders, Camay soap, and Pert Plus (marketed as Vidal Sassoon) products.

The products are very expensive compared to the average Russian's income, but the products sell well. Oil of Ulay night cream costs $2.40, almost one-tenth of the average Russian's monthly salary. A bar of Camay soap is $.37--enough to buy eight bars of normal Russian soap.

Chairman Artzt predicts that the Eastern European market will be between $8 billion and $10 billion by 2000. P&G wants to capture one-third of the market. Unilever and L'Oreal have also set up shop in Russia.

For more information see, Valerie Reitman, "P&G Uses Skills It Has Honed at Home to Introduce Its Brands to the Russians," The Wall Street Journal, April 14, 1993, p. B1.

Jokes and Quotes

If all the world's a stage, why are all the players singing different songs?

Young and Rubicam had problems launching "Big John's" canned pork and beans in the French Canadian market. The direct translation to "Grand Jean" was weak so they went for "Gros Jos". Then, just prior to launch they noticed that "Gros Jos" meant "Big Breasts" to French Canadians.
ANON

A hot air balloon was sinking fast so the captain appealed to the character of his passenger to lighten the load. He told the English it would be unsporting not to jump; the French that it would be smart to jump; he ordered the Germans to jump; he told the Italians that jumping was prohibited.
ANON

Heaven is where the police are British,
the chefs French, the mechanics German,
the lovers Italian
and it is all organised by the Swiss

Hell is where the police are German,
the chefs British, the mechanics French,
the lovers Swiss
and it all organised by the Italians.
ANON

Not only is England an island but every Englishman as well.
ANON

The Englishman is very fond of animals - especially roasted with two veg.
ANON

Everything in France is a pretext for a good dinner.
JEAN ANOUILH

Whatever else may divide us, Europe is our common home; a common fate has linked us through the centuries, and it continues to link us today.
LEONID BREZHNEV

And yet there are some things that most countries do without difficulty that others cannot get a grasp of at all. The French, for instance, cannot get the hang of queuing. They try and try, but it is beyond them. The British, on the other hand, do not understand certain of the fundamentals of eating, as evidenced by their instinct to consume hamburgers with a knife and fork. Germans are flummoxed by humour, the Swiss have no concept of fun, the Spanish think there is nothing at all ridiculous about eating dinner at midnight, and the Italians should never, ever have been let in on the invention of the motor car.
BILL BRYSON

We are asking the nations of Europe between whom rivers of blood have flowed to forget the feuds of a thousand years.
WINSTON CHURCHILL

How can you be expected to govern a country that has two hundred and forty-six kinds of cheese?
CHARLES DE GAULLE

I've come to think of Europe as a hardcover book, America as the paperback version.
DON DELILLO

The Spaniard . . . shuns abstractions as much as any Englishman and is as free from inhibitions as any Frenchman can be.
SALVADOR DE MADARIAGA

The French want no-one to be their superior. The English want inferiors. . ."
ALEXIS DE TOCQUEVILLE

The problem of economics in Britain is very much like that of sex in the United States. Both countries have enormous difficulties in keeping it in perspective.
J.K. GALBRAITH

In Europe life is histrionic and dramatised and . . . in America, except when it is trying to be European, it is direct and sincere.
WILLIAM DEAN HOWELLS

The merchant has no country.
THOMAS JEFFERSON

The Irish are a fair people; they never speak well of one another.
SAMUEL JOHNSON

That grand drama in a hundred acts, which is reserved for the next two centuries of Europe - the most terrible, most questionable and perhaps also the most hopeful of all dramas . . .
FRIEDRICH NIETZSCHE

In Western Europe there are now only small countries - those that know it and those that don't know it yet.
OBSERVER

It may be the way the cookie crumbles on Madison Avenue, but in Hong Kong it's the way the egg rolls!
ROBERT ORBEN

The situation in Germany is serious but not hopeless: the situation in Austria is hopeless but not serious.
AUSTRIAN PROVERB

To trust is good, not to trust is better.
ITALIAN PROVERB

The nail that sticks up will be hammered down.
JAPANESE PROVERB

I have come to the conclusion that Americans treat "neurotic" as a synonym for "nuts"; that Englishmen think neurotic as adjective applicable to foreigners; and that Jews consider "neurotic" a synonym for "human".
ROSENBERG?

Whatever it is, I fear the Greeks even when they bring gifts.
VIRGIL

When a Swiss banker jumps out of the window, jump after him, there must be money to be made.
VOLTAIRE

The world is a stage, but the play is badly cast.
OSCAR WILDE

Chapter 6
Market Information and Marketing Research

Chapter Objectives

After reading this chapter, you should be able to:

1. Explain the importance of information to the company.
2. Define the marketing information system and discuss its parts.
3. Describe the four steps in the marketing research process.
4. Compare the advantages and disadvantages of various methods of collecting information.
5. Discuss the major methods for estimating current market demand.

Chapter Overview

In carrying out their marketing responsibilities, marketing managers need a great deal of information. Despite the growing supply of information, managers often lack enough information of the right kind or have too much of the wrong kind. To overcome these problems, many companies are taking steps to improve their marketing information systems. A well-designed marketing information system first assesses information needs. The MIS next develops information and helps managers to use it more effectively. Marketing research involves collecting information relevant to a specific marketing problem facing the company. Finally, the marketing information system distributes information gathered from internal sources, marketing intelligence, and marketing research to the right managers at the right times.

Marketers need accurate measures of current and future market size. A market is the set of actual and potential buyers of a market offer. Consumers have interest, income, and access the market offer. The marketer must distinguish among the various levels of the market including the potential market, available market, qualified available market, served market and the penetrated market. Marketers estimate total market demand by the chain ratio method which multiplies a base number by successive percentages. Area market demand can be estimated by the market-build-up method or the market-factor index method. Estimating actual industry sales requires identifying competitors and using some method of estimating the sales of each. For estimating future demand the company can use one or a combination of seven forecasting methods based on what consumer say (buyers' intentions surveys, composite of sales force opinions, expert opinion); what consumers do (market tests); or what consumer have done (time series analysis, leading indicators, and statistical demand analysis).

Teaching Notes

Refer to the following pages for teaching notes.

The Importance of Information

Transparency PM 6-1 relates to the material on pp.210-211 and provides a context for discussing marketing research and marketing information systems. It synthesises much of the introductory material about the research function and may help students link research to the marketing planning process more clearly.

The Marketing Environment

Companies compete in an environment of social, legal, cultural, technological, natural and competitive dimensions. Information on each aspect of the environment is crucial to effective marketing planning. You may wish to discuss the role of environmental monitoring or scanning in class. Information gathering can be serendipitous or it can be planned. While not all environmental information needs can be identified in advance, it is possible to approach research and information systems planning with an eye to setting up ways of collecting information in an on-going fashion.

Customer Needs and Wants

If environmental forces cause the company to seek information in a larger context, customer needs and wants focuses the attention to the target market. Even meeting customer needs with products affects how the consumer expects to be serviced the next time. Constant timely information of needs and wants and how they change must be part of any marketing effort.

Competitors

The actions of competitors cannot go unnoticed by the company. Innovative companies not only identify competitive actions and offerings, they also consume competitors' products - in small quantities of course! For example, to understand the value of a competitor's automobile it makes sense to drive it for a while as a customer would and evaluate it in that fashion.

Strategic Decision Making

Strategy formulation depends upon accurate and timely information most of all.

> **Tip**
>
> Ask students what critical information would be necessary when setting up a new undergraduate degree course.

Notes for PM 6-1

The Marketing Information System

Transparency PM 6-2 corresponds to Figure 6-1 on p.212.

Definition

The MIS consists of people, equipment and procedures to gather, sort, evaluate and distribute needed, timely and accurate information to marketing decision makers.

Components of the Marketing Information System

1. Assessing Information Needs

- Knowing what is needed or likely to be needed is a key feature of the MIS that underscores the importance of information. Quantity alone in not the answer; too much information can obscure important details.

2. Distributing Information

- Requires organising the MIS in a flexible and responsive manner that allows each use access to the combinations of information they need to make better decisions.

3. Internal Records

- Provide a wealth of information which is essentially raw data for decision making. An effective MIS organises and summarises balance sheets, orders, schedules, shipments and inventories into trends that can be linked to management decisions on marketing mix changes.

4. Information Analysis

- Requires that the MIS director anticipate how the information is to be used. But if users from all business functions use the MIS on-line for short deadline decisions, then the analytical tools each area needs must be available on demand.

5. Marketing Intelligence

- Provides the everyday information about environmental variables that managers need as they implement and adjust marketing plans. Sources for intelligence may vary according to needs but may include both internal and external sources.

6. Marketing Research

- Links the consumer, customer and public to the marketer through an exchange of information. Research is often project oriented and discussed in more detail on the following transparency.

Tip
Describe how these components could help make the decision about starting a new degree course.

Notes for PM 6-2

The Marketing Research Process

Transparency PM 6-3 corresponds to Figure 6-2 on p.215 and relates to the material on pp.215-231. Many students see marketing research as a dull, if necessary side, of marketing. Share your excitement about how stimulating and creative the research process can be. Cite for example, Unilever's uncovering of the need for a strong detergent that became Radion.

1. Defining the Problem and Research Objectives

Before researcher can provide managers with information, they must know what kind of problem the manager wishes to resolve. Specifying a behaviourally-based information problem clearly is often hard to do. One key is to remind students that people report problem symptoms more often than they identify problems. Objectives for research can only be linked to clear problem definitions. Objectives for research may be exploratory, descriptive or causal.

2. Developing the Research Plan and Collecting Information

Developing the plan includes the following steps: (1) Determining specific information needs; (2) Surveying secondary information sources; (3) Planning the primary data collection if necessary; (4) Choosing the contact method and sampling procedure appropriately; (5) Presenting the plan to the client for approval.

3. Implementing the Plan - Collecting and Analysing the Data

In implementing the plan care must be taken that all personnel involved in collecting and analysing data understand clearly the purpose of the research and are adequately trained and experienced to complete it professionally.

4. Interpreting and Reporting the Findings

Interpreting research findings may involve statistical analyses or not, but these tools of analysis should not be confused with the action-oriented information needed by the marketing managers. Research is valuable only in its use to make better marketing decisions. Reports of findings should always be in the style and language of how the information will be used by the manager.

Tip

Ask why new products fail even after spending so much money on marketing research. Possible answers; research asked the wrong questions, reject by management, too late to change plans, etc.

Notes for PM 6-3

Kinds of Information

Transparency PM 6-4 relates to the material on pp.219-230. You may have students that do not realise research seeks both primary and secondary information for marketing decision making. The need for careful and complete research information requires attention to both kinds of information.

Secondary Data

Some of these sources are given in Table 6-1. Data collected from other sources for other reasons serves as a secondary data. To be useful to the researcher, secondary data must be in a form usable to solve the problem being researched. Data from incomes from a census, for example, must be in intervals meaningful to the current project. Secondary information must also meet project requirements that the information is impartial, current, accurate and relevant.

Primary Data

Decisions on primary information needs include:

1. Research Approaches

There are three common approaches for gathering primary data. Observations are linked to actual behaviours but may not help in understanding why people act as they do. Surveys can help describe reasons for people's behaviour and provide the research with flexibility. But surveys can be plagued by problems in completion and demand characteristics from several factors. Experimental methods help identify cause and effect relationships but controlling for extraneous variables is usually difficult in real world situations.

2. Contact Methods

Include mail, telephone, personal and group interviewing. These are covered in more detail on the following transparency.

3. Sampling Plans

Address the who (sampling unit), how many (sample size) and how to choose decisions of drawing a sample (probability or nonprobability). These are given in Table 6-5.

4. Research Instruments

May include mechanical or electronic devices although the survey questionnaire is the most common instrument.

Tip

Question when to use direct or indirect questions. Indirect questions are often used in exploratory research or investigating sensitive issues.

Notes for PM 6-4

Collecting Information

Transparency PM 6-5 corresponds to the material in Tables 6-2 and 6-3 on pp.221 & 223 respectively and relates to the material on pp.221-226. Table 6-4 shows how the use of these information collection method varies from country to country.

Data Collection Methods

Mail Questionnaires

This method provides excellent control over the effects of having an interviewer influencing the respondents' answers. Since no interviewer is present, no interpersonal influences are possible. Mail questionnaires may elicit more honest and in-depth information. Discuss with your class the kind of problems that may require this kind of information, such as social marketing issues on health care concerns. Still, lack of ability to distinguish respondents from nonrespondents makes inference to the general population difficult.

Telephone Interviewing

Being able to control the sample and complete the data collection quickly are assets of telephone interviewing. Many marketing contexts, such as person marketing in political campaigns, need almost overnight information on the effectiveness of the latest promotions. Telephone technology can reach diverse geographic markets of interest and can be linked to computers for easy data analysis. Problems with respondent co-operation may becoming increasingly important over time.

Personal Interviewing

Personal interviewing is very flexible and can provide a rich and deep volume of data for the researcher. Also, personal interviewers can follow-up unexpected or unusual responses that other collection methods are not prepared to handle. Using groups in personal interviews can also reveal social influences that may be important in consumer decision making.

Tip

Ask which method is best for finding out who watches a particular TV programme, find the range of products consumed over a week or explore the market for new fashion products.

Notes for PM 6-5

Defining the Market

Transparency PM 6-6 corresponds to Figure 6-4 on p.233 and relates to the material on pp.231-233. You may wish to emphasise the critical importance of market definition to all subsequent forecasting and measurement activity.

Market

A market is the set of all actual and potential buyers of a product or service.

Industry

An industry is the set of all sellers for a market

Potential Market

The potential market is the set of consumers who profess some level of interest in a particular product or service.

Available Market

The available market is the set of consumers who have interest, income and access to a particular product or service.

Qualified Available Market

The qualified available market is the set of consumers who have interest, income, access and specific qualifications for the product or service. Qualifications may stem from legal restrictions (such as those for alcohol consumption) or prerequisite skills or knowledge levels (such as home computers).

Served Market

The served market is the part of the qualified available market the company decides to pursue. Here segmentation decisions and company resources must be considered.

Penetrated Market

The penetrated market is the set of consumers who have already purchased the product. This may include consumer who own either the company's product or the product of its competitors.

Planning

Marketers should use market definitions to focus their planning efforts. Strategic goals can be addressed at different levels of market definition. Planners need to assess which level of the market they can work with to meet company expectations and objectives.

Tip

Ask what is the most critical measure in developing a marketing plan.

Notes for PM 6-6

Measuring Current Demand

These notes correspond to Figure 6-5 on p.234 and relate to the material on pp.233-237. Note that the graphs illustrate general factors regarding the relationship between demand, forecasts and the economic environment (total market demand). Students are often confused that they do not illustrate the methods for estimating area market demand.

Total Market Demand

Total market demand for a product or service is the total volume that would be bought by a defined consumer group, in a defined geographic area, in a defined time period, in a defined marketing environment under a defined level and mix of industry market effort. Total market demand is a function of stated conditions. It is not a fixed number. A change in any of the defined conditions leads to a change in total market demand.

Market Minimum

The market minimum refers to the levels of sales that would take place without any marketing expenditures.

Market Potential

The market potential is the level of sales at which no further increase in marketing expenditures will lead to an increase in sales.

Primary Demand

Primary demand is the total demand for all brands of a given product or service.

Selective Demand

Selective demand is the demand for the company's own product or service.

Estimating Area Market Demand

Market-Build-up Method

This method identifies all the potential buyers in each market and estimates their potential purchases. It is especially applicable to business markets. It is very important that students understand that the bases for determining potential purchases varies in method and accuracy across different industries.

Market-Factor Index Method

This method identifies the market factors that correlate with market potential and combines them. The method can help the company determine its current market share.

Tip

Ask student to explain the S-curve in the top table: Why does it saturate? Why is their threshold level sales start rising quickly?

Forecasting Future Demand

These notes correspond to Table 6-8 on p.238 and relate to the material on pp.237-243.

Forecasting is the art of estimating future demand by anticipating what buyers are likely to do under a given set of conditions.

Sales Forecasts

Companies typically use a three-stage procedure for estimating sales. First, an environmental forecast is made to determine likely operating conditions. Environmental forecasts project likely inflation rates, unemployment, interest rates, consumer spending and savings, business investment and other factors. Then and industry forecast estimates likely competitive conditions within that environment. Finally, a company sales forecast is made using one or more of the following methods **(Common Sales Forecasting Techniques):**

1. What People Say

A survey of buyers' intentions asks buyers directly their plans for future purchases. Surveys are especially valuable when the buyer has clearly formed intentions, will carry them out and can describe them to interviewers. A composite of salesforce opinions is based upon what the salesforce thinks it can sell in a coming period. Salesforce composites may be biased when compensation is linked to performance but they are also informed by those who do the selling. Expert opinion is obtained from specialised vendors or can be obtained from progressive surveys of top executives (Delphi method).

2. What People Do

The test market method is used to measure how the product performs on a smaller scale. Test markets are especially useful for new products. A key consideration is matching the environmental, competitive and product conditions in the test with those in future periods.

3. What People Have Done

Time-series analysis consists of breaking down the original sales into four components: trend, cycle, season and erratic. Use of leading indicators relies on other time series that change in the same direction but in advance of the company sales. Statistical demand analysis is a set of statistical procedures used to discover the most important real factors affecting sales.

> **Tip**
> Ask how forecasting is carried out for a new product when there is no sales history?

Comments on Discussing the Issues

1. An article by Alan Andreasen ("'Backward' Marketing Research," *Harvard Business Review*, May/June 1985, pp. 176-82) shows the importance of close collaboration between the researcher and the client in determining the success of a research project. Andreasen suggests starting the research project by *determining how the results will be implemented* (which helps to define the problem). If this step is skipped, the client may not be able to act on the findings.

   The second step in this "backward" research process is determining what the final report should contain and how it should look. The client may be asked, "What would you do if we got this result?" The answer may suggest better ways of wording a question, or other questions that need to be asked to give management more guidance. The answer may even show that the question is irrelevant because the client's actions will not be affected no matter what the results.

   The remaining steps in the process implement the standard "forward" approach to research planning, as described in the chapter. Putting the last steps first ensures that clients will get their money's worth from a research project, because the research will be usable rather than just "interesting."

   Students may suggest many different answers to this question—use large sample sizes, word questions carefully, validate interviews to reduce interviewer error, and so on. These steps may improve research quality, but if the research is addressing the wrong problem, it is a waste of the client's money no matter how carefully it is conducted.

2. This question builds on the material in Chapter 4, the Marketing Environment. The purpose of the question is to get students to recognise that the marketing environment is always changing, and research information must be kept up to date.

   Market research can go stale. Research information is always collected at some point in time, and it may or may not represent the trends into the future. It is like driving forward by watching in the rear view mirror: you can see only where you have been. What lies ahead must be predicted from what has been passed.

   Research tends to be a good predictor of the future trends if no significant elements of the situation change. If there are few changes in consumer preferences and habits, competitive brands and their marketing plans, and the macroenvironment, current trends will probably continue. In these cases older market research will probably remain useful for some time.

   However, either a single event or gradual changes over time can make information obsolete. The launch of a new brand can greatly change consumer preferences.

   Managers must always look at the context in which research is collected, and make a careful judgement about the ways in which the future is going to be like the past. If the research is older, the manager must decide if it is applicable, or if the environment has changed enough so that it is outdated. Market research provides guidance and perspective, but not clear-cut answers. Managers, not researchers, must make key decisions.

3. **(a)** In investigating the effect that young children have on parents' purchasing decisions, Nestle might use focus groups, surveys, observation, and experiments.

Experiments and observation would give the clearest results, because parents may not realise (or not want to admit) how much their purchases are influenced by their children. Questioning parents and children could be quicker and cheaper, reveal children's influence in a wider range of purchase situations, and explain *why* parents respond as they do.

(b) Focus groups are a good source of insights about marketing situations. A college bookstore could use focus groups to get ideas about how students perceive its merchandise, prices, and service. Before implementing changes suggested by the focus group findings, the store could do a survey to find out how the student body in general feels about the focus group suggestions.

(c) Gillette could estimate the demand for a line of children's deodorants with focus groups and surveys, but experimental research would be more conclusive. A simulated test market would suggest initial purchase levels, but only a full-scale test market allowing actual product use would give the information Gillette needs before introducing the product line.

(d) In selecting a site for a new outlet, Virgin needs information on population density in different areas, incomes, ages, ethnic characteristics, family sizes, locations of competing music stores, and traffic patterns at different times of day. In a fast-growing suburb, census data might be too outdated to be useful, but most of the information Virgin needs could still be obtained from secondary sources, such as the local chamber of commerce or utility companies. Virgin might need to commission traffic studies in different parts of the suburb to help locate a specific worthwhile site.

4. Overestimating demand can lead to huge losses. The most extreme cases occur when overestimating the volume of an unproven new product. In this instance, a marketing company that overestimates volume must absorb not only the losses on unwanted products, but also the cost of capital that was spent for unneeded new plant and equipment.

   Underestimating demand usually leads to opportunity costs—profits that cannot be made because there is not enough product to sell. These sorts of lost opportunities are much less visible to stockholders than the real losses caused by overestimating demand. For this reason, managers have an incentive to underestimate demand: they look like heroes if their forecasts are exceeded, and do not have to incur tangible dollar losses because of the mistake. If this is carried to extremes, however, a company can miss opportunities from excessive conservatism.

   The best course is to develop realistic and reliable estimates of demand whenever possible. Astute companies put many resources into developing good forecasts for their businesses.

5. The first step in forecasting Pedigree Chum's cat food sales for the coming year is to find out *why* sales jumped so much during the past year. If sales increased because 50% more stores took on distribution of the product, the current sales level might well be sustainable. Likewise, if sales were up because of a favourable review in *Consumer Reports,* sales might also stay up. If, however, sales went up because temporary production problems made a competing brand unavailable, the sales level will probably

decline from this one-time peak. Once the reason for the past year's increase is known, it can be considered, along with the forecasting methods described in the chapter, in predicting sales for the coming year.

6. The *Survey of Current Business* reports monthly levels of many leading indicators, including average workweek hours, manufacturers' orders for consumer and durable goods, stock prices, and many more. For any given manufacturer certain indicators will be more relevant than others. A baby foods manufacturer will be most interested in the number of births annually. A car and mobile phones' manufacturer will be more interested in economic conditions, consumer sentiment, and interest rates. In searching for useful leading indicators, the first step is to identify variables that precede other variables, such as first-time house buyers used as a precursor to appliance and furniture sales. This relationship can be checked with historical data to confirm that first-time house buyers are, in fact, a good predictor of appliance sales. If so, this leading indicator is likely to be helpful in predicting future appliance sales.

Comments on Applying the Concepts

1. Students will know of dozens or even hundreds of new product ideas. On average, most of these ideas will have been unsuccessful, so coming up with negative examples is likely to be much easier than positive ones.

   Students will have many personal impressions of what caught their interest about these new products. Most comments are likely to centre around either real fulfilment of a consumer need, or novelty value. Try to steer the discussion towards abstracting the marketing principles that students can apply in evaluating future new products they encounter.

2. A live example of research can help students become far more aware of the potential for bias in market research There are some precautions to take in this exercise. First, it is helpful to have a confident and outgoing student as a moderator. The moderator should have some brief training, and preferably a list of four or five prearranged questions to ask the group. At least one of these should be a very biased approach to the issue.

   In discussing the focus group, try to encourage a constructive tone to the discussions of the moderator's performance. Criticisms can easily grow harsh, especially from those who have never moderated. If the moderator is being heavily criticised on one point, the instructor can always say, "I told the moderator to ask that question."

   In general, classes find this exercise interesting. Seeing research in process illustrates its strengths and weaknesses in a very immediate way.

Case 6
Ballygowan Springs Into New Age Kisqua

Synopsis

Ballygowan Spring Water Company was established in 1981. By 1991 it exported to 15 countries and held 77% of the 12.5 million litres of the Irish water market. The bottled water market in both Ireland and the UK was then one of the fastest growing markets in light of the deterioration in tap water quality and the demand for natural, low calorie, healthy foods and drinks as part of a trend towards healthier lifestyle. The company's success came from still and sparkling water. In 1988 Ballygowan extended its product range to include flavoured spring water. By 1990 their turnover was £10 million. Ballygowan hoped to double this figure within two years by launching soft drinks, where the company saw an opportunity for growth. The products were to be consistent with consumer trends towards healthier lifestyles. The company identified three stages in the product development process; (1) product development; (2) brand development; (3) business plan. To commence the process Ballygowan recruited a marketing consultancy firm. The first stage was product sourcing, using certain criteria for selecting a suitable manufacturer of fruit juice. The next stage was product formulation. Six products were produced. Ballygowan used results from a quantitative market research conducted by a market research agency to establish the tastes that should be focused on. Further research was required to isolate performance from packaging and advertising. Six prototype brand names were selected out of hundreds of names. To explore the attitudes of consumers, five positioning strategies were considered. The same market research agency conducted four focus group interviews representing market segments with different attitudes to soft drinks. To assess the impact of the brand name, label design, price, positioning and advertising options a further research was undertaken. Based on the results the target market was defined, an advertising concept was adopted and bottle and pack design was selected. The business plan proposed the product to be made available in three sizes. Distribution was to take place through existing Ballygowan's network of distributors. After some deliberation a pricing strategy was adopted. A test market revealed discouraging results and Ballygowan needed to decide on a new strategy.

Teaching Objectives

1. Expose students to the problems of market research in a fast moving consumer product such as Kisqua.

2. Involve students in thinking the relationship between marketing research process and new product development.

3. Enlighten students in the importance of designing appropriate marketing research activity that commence with a clear definition of the objectives of the research exercise.

Study Questions

1. **Examine the types of market research used by Ballygowan in the development of Kisqua. What sort of information were they hoping to get from the different**

methods they used? Is quantitative marketing research intrinsically more reliable than qualitative research?

The market research undertaken by Ballygowan can first be identified to be an external ad-hoc research in which the company conducted a research into usage, attitudes, advertising, promotions, positioning, branding, etc. With regard to a specific purpose of launching a new product. In order to conduct the research Ballygowan recruited the services of both a marketing consultancy and a marketing research agency. The research was custom designed for Ballygowan in light of their briefing and requirements and included the following; (1) Manufacturer selection and taste test (product sourcing) - involved a few stages of quantitative research to provide descriptive data. The first stage began with the assessment of the technological and production capabilities of three companies and then involved the assessment of the performance of laboratory-scale products produced in terms of aroma, appearance, taste and overall opinion. This was a structured research in which the proposed products were compared with successful brands. A further stage included revision of the product in view of the results of the previous stage. This process was repeated six times until a German company was finally selected; (2) Product formulations - a quantitative market research survey was undertaken using questionnaire developed from the earlier survey to gather information regarding flavour, aroma and appearance. The results indicated the preferences for orange combination drinks. Ballygowan saw this as unsatisfactory and decided to undertake a second quantitative market research that would isolate the various variables (performance, packaging and advertising); (3) Product concept and brand name development - focus group interviews were conducted in order to decide on positioning, pack design, brand name and bottling formats. This was research in the form of group interviews in which respondents were first free to discuss their own use and purchase of soft drinks. Thereafter, the discussions were more focused towards the need of the research; (3) Marketing mix - a quantitative research was conducted which revealed the preference of Kisqua in relation to another brand. This nevertheless was a very restrictive research as it could only differentiate between preference on the grounds of taste and preference to the whole product. The research did not explore the reasons for the differences. Ballygowan concluded that it was the colour and sweetness that needed some improvement. The research did not provide the reasons for not liking a certain attribute nor did it provide provide information about people's preferences regarding colour, taste, etc. It can be seen that Ballygowan used different techniques of market research at different stages of the product development process. Each research was aiming to reveal certain information.

Qualitative research provides insights and understanding of the problem setting, while quantitative research seeks to quantify the data and typically applies some form of statistical analysis. Whenever a new marketing research problem is being addressed quantitative research must be preceded by appropriate qualitative research. Sometimes qualitative research is undertaken to explain the findings obtained from quantitative research. However, the findings of qualitative research are misused when they are regarded as conclusive and are used to make generalisations to the population of interest. It is a sound principle of marketing research to view qualitative and quantitative research as complementary rather than in competition with each other.

2. Relate the market research to the stages in the product development process and explain their use? Were the methods appropriately used? What alternatives would you suggest? How did they contribute to Ballygowan's understanding of the strategy for launching Kisqua?

To some extent this question has been answered in question 1. To recapitulate, quantitative research was used at the first stage of the product development process. The process began with product sourcing which consisted of a research survey using structured questionnaire. The research was designed to identify possible supplier. The second stage consisted of product formulation. Once again structured questionnaires were used to choose which flavours were the most suitable for the market. At the third stage product name and brand development were examined. The research consisted of focus groups' interviews investigating prototype names, pack design, bottle formats and direction for brand positioning. The focus groups were able to probe deeper into people's opinions. The marketing mix was then developed using more surveys which were used to back the results of the focus groups. At the business plan stage experiments were used to determine what pricing strategies were the most appropriate. Experiments were also used at the final stage to examine the popularity of the products. This would help determine whether any changes were needed for the marketing mix strategy.

Some students will say that although some of the marketing research conducted by Ballygowan was appropriate, this was not always the case. The qualitative research using focus groups would have been far more useful at the beginning of the process because it explores how consumers feel about broad concepts. By identifying and selecting a strong concept at this early stage Ballygowan could then research the market to establish whether the product concept has sufficient potential to make further development worthwhile. If so, the company could then have invested in selecting a manufacturer and developing a product to fit with the concept. Some students will suggest that Ballygowan's final research into reasons people preferred either Kisqua or Club would have been much more useful at an earlier stage whilst there was still scope to make changes to the product. There are other suggestions such as; (1) Qualitative information regarding the segments could be useful at the product formulation stage; (2) Group interviews could inhibit honest answers - therefore in-depth interviews could be useful to reduce errors due to pressure; (3) Several label suggestions could be shown as part of many others; (4) Advertising effects could be measured in a similar manner; (5) Bottle design was decided upon arbitrarily - the effect of the bottle formats could be measured using the same taste, name , label, etc. on different bottle formats and observe the one which is more appealing i.e. leave them all as refreshments and see those which were mostly used.

Ballygowan used various methods to establish a launching strategy for Kisqua. Quantitative data was used to establish the most preferred tastes, labels and brand name. Qualitative information was used in understanding people's attitudes towards soft drinks and their preferences for design and brand name. Ballygowan used the information to develop the product and the launching strategy as well as confirm the target market and adjust the advertising concept. On the other hand, it seems that Ballygowan failed to account all of the variables that impinge the launching of Kisqua. This may have been the result of misinterpretation of information or even errors in research design. For example, the reactions to the design could be interpreted differently and a different design might have been more appropriate. It also seems that decisions regarding the bottle design have been made based on Ballygowan's assumptions rather than on concrete research.

3. Why could in-depth marketing research lead to wrong strategic choices? Do marketing research errors explain Kisqua's poor test market showing? What does explain the poor showing? Was too much or too little, market research done by Ballygowan?

In-depth marketing research could lead to wrong strategic choices because it is virtually impossible to remove all sources of error in a behaviourally based field such as marketing. The type of error include; (1) Sampling errors - these are errors in the specification of the target population and errors caused by the selection of a non-representative sample; (2) Data collection errors - these include occasions where respondents provide answers to please, impress or irritate the interviewer. In responding to a question, the respondent may be unable to articulate a response accurately. Data collection errors may also be caused by leading questions and the way interviewer read out the question to respondents, with a positive or negative bias in the tone of the voice; (3) Analytical and reporting errors; (4) experimental errors - may arise if uncontrollable events occur during the experiment for example if a competitor launches a new product during a test period.

Students need to emphasise that there were several pitfalls in the marketing research conducted on behalf of Ballygowan. Having selected Dohler as their manufacturer, Ballygowan's first test for its new product was for taste, aroma, appearance and likelihood of purchase. Ballygowan used only Club as a control and seemed unconcerned by the fact that Dohler was rated lower than Club on almost every occasion. The company did, however, pick up on the particularly poor results for the orange drink but instead of trying to further improve the product they did a second round of tests with "performance isolated from packaging and advertising effect", suggesting that this had not been the case in the first round of tests. The qualitative research using focus groups gives even more cause for concern. Ballygowan's product had been developed with a "sophisticated, self-righteous and reasonably health conscious adult" (aged 18-30) in mind, who was likely to "prefer 7-up or Club Orange to Coke or Pepsi". The consultancy brief stated that "a superior but competitively priced product" with a "premium but accessible imagery" was required. The four focus groups selected for the research seem inconsistent with this concept and contains some startling gaps; (1) Young teenage girls, middle class - why only young teenagers when the product is aimed at adults? What exactly is middle class?; (2) Young men, 18-24, C1 C2 - why research C's and not B's? What about more sophisticated men aged 25 and over?; (3) Women, 22-32, C2 with children - why C2 and the children? This group seems totally incompatible with the product concept!; (4) Women, 22-32, B1 B" with children - where are the single/ married with no children women? Where are the women under 22? And the C1 women? Finally the results of the quota sample taken during the final stages of the process are clearly inaccurate. A sample quota of 200 respondents was taken with 100 being asked to taste Kisqua and Club Orange blind, and the remaining 100 being asked to do the same test with both products branded. The results, however, equate 106 respondents on the blind test and only 67 on the branded test. Based on these figures, the number of respondents preferring Club outweighs the respondents preferring Kisqua by 3:1 on the blind test and almost 10:1 on the branded test. If these were the figures presented to Ballygowan, it is extremely difficult to understand why they believed that they could develop much higher ratings by "fine tuning Kisqua's advertising strategy". The poor results at this late stage may therefore have been attributable to marketing research errors. On the other hand, the entire product development process seems to have been managed in a haphazard way, with inconsistencies in the product concept and target market at almost every stage. The consultancy's brief contained a fairly specific outline of the product that Ballygowan wished to develop before they had even established whether there was a market for the product, and if so, who that market was. The product concept itself then becoming increasingly vague and inconsistent. For example the expected positioning of the product was changed several times in an apparently haphazard way - the initial concept was "consumers who would prefer to drink 7-up or Club Orange to Coke or Pepsi", whilst the consultant's brief was for a product that would target the soft drink sector, including "Coke, 7-up, Club, Lilt and so on". The consultancy then proceeded the whole process and the new product was finally positioned to compete "directly with Club Orange" without ever properly identifying the target market. Moreover, Ballygowan appeared to disregard the fact that its new product never, at any stage performed particularly well against Club. The company seemed determined to carry on regardless, convinced that they could overcome any shortfalls by fine tuning the product, the marketing mix or the advertising. In conclusion, the problem was not so much that Ballygowan did either too much or too little market research, but that the quality of market research was poor and that the results did not appear to be taken seriously (with no apparent link between the two!).

4. Where should Ballygowan go from here? What extra research should they do, if any? Should they go ahead with the existing marketing strategy, reposition the product, start again or give in?

Students will come up with all kinds of answers to this question. Some will say that Ballygowan have invested heavily in the development and launch of Kisqua and will have to write off the costs of product development, market research and capital investment if they decide to abandon the product completely. On the other hand, we have seen that the product has never performed particularly well at any stage, particularly when compared with Club Orange against which it has been positioned. The best option for Ballygowan may be to research the market further in order to determine whether or not there is a place for a product such as Kisqua. If so, the company needs to establish who is the target market in terms of its profile so that the marketing mix and advertising strategy can be tailored accordingly. And if not, it's "back to the drawing board", or more specifically, to a marketing audit and SWOT analysis!

Other possible suggestions; (1) Get consumers involved in idea generation; (2) Drink should not be targeted to a specific group; (3) Further exploitation of the flavoured spring water should be considered; (4) Need to understand what factors lead to test market failure; (5) Test market the product in another geographical area; (6) Need to look at current positioning and pricing strategy; (7) Focus on the healthy product image; (8) Questionnaires directed to retailers; (9) Pack was identified as unpopular - further research and development of the pack.

Teaching Suggestions

This case could be used with the Strategic Planning Chapter (Chapter 3), Product Chapters (Chapter 13 and 14), and Market Segmentation and Targeting, and Positioning Chapter (Chapters 9 and 10)

Overview Case II
Mitsui & Company

Synopsis

Mitsui & Co. is one of Japan's largest trading corporations which comprises of 70 large Japanese firms with 219 overseas subsidiaries and 165 overseas offices. In 1974 it established a regional headquarters (RHQ) in London to manage operations in Western and Eastern Europe. By 1989 Mitsui had 26 offices and 32 affiliated companies in 19 European countries. It was very important that Mitsui responded very positively to the unification of the European market.

Teaching Objectives

1. Enlighten students the importance of marketing research and information system as competitive tools.

2. Expose to students the realities of the pan-European marketing.

3. Assess the activities of a foreign owned company operating in a foreign market.

Study Questions

1. Describe each of the steps taken by Mitsui in reaction to the Single Market. Explain the reason for each step. Why is it necessary for Mitsui to react in the way it did?

Students should highlight that the first step taken to fortify its already strong position in Europe was to establish an EC92 task force to monitor the progress of the Single Market. The task force was set up simultaneously in the Tokyo head office and in the London RHQ. After its establishment the task force focused initially on internal corporate education, collecting information on developments in the EC. It also held educational seminars for company executives and managers to keep them fully briefed on developments. By 1989 this had been largely accomplished and the task force then focused on assisting the various operating groups helping with individual problems and helping them to determine their strategies. The task force acted as an information clearing house and consultant for Mitsui group committee. Assisted by the Information and Research Division, reports on significant events were distributed among Mitsui and other business companies. Mitsui's long term direction towards globalisation combined with the discussions co-ordinated by the EC 92 task force resulted in a strategy for EC92. It emphasised the need to reorganise Mitsui's operations on a pan- European basis and establish Mitsui and its associates as European "insiders" through a massive increase in investment. The number of investments in affiliated companies doubled from 33 to 67 between August 1987 and August 1988. Mitsui entered into joint ventures and also assisted small companies set up in the EC. They believed by using this approach the opportunities for a general trading company in the EC were enormous. Mitsui also made a variety of investments in the retail field to enhance its sales network. In response to the European Company Status (ECS) Mitsui strengthened the RHQ and raised the ceiling for investment without approval from Tokyo thus creating a separate and independent "inside" owner not controlled by Tokyo. Albeit the primary responsibility for strategy would still rest in Tokyo. EC matters were resolved by the RHQ.

Some reasons students should mention why it was necessary for Mitsui to react are; (1) Mitsui had a large interest in Europe built up over many years which it had to protect. Mitsui had to conform to EC 92 requirements particularly the European Company Status otherwise their presence would diminish in Europe; (2) In keeping with their overall strategy of globalisation Europe was seen as one of the major markets which they could not afford to be excluded from. Their belief and goal is "Mitsui is at home everywhere in the world"; (3) Mitsui saw that the unification of the European market would allow them to realise significant economies of scale in administration and trading activity.

2. How does Mitsui handle information about European integration? What sort of information do you think should be in Mitsui's information system for Europe? How much importance do Mitsui attach to information and education? Is their interest in education and training typical of other Japanese or European companies?

Mitsui established an EC 92 task force with the aim of monitoring the progress of the Single Market. Mitsui set up a centralised location in Tokyo to collect all documents, press articles and other materials from banks and private companies in EC. This information was disseminated to the company executives and managers using seminars. They also published an EC newsletter on the progress of EC integration. The IR&D also gathered information on the progress of EC integration. The IR&D sometimes drafted reports on significant events and distributed them around Mitsui and other business people. When EC92 task force had accomplished its internal education programme they concentrated their efforts on solving individual problems and determining strategies for various operating groups. The IR&D eventually found that requests for assistance focused on concrete business questions rather than general information. However, they found that very specialised information strictly connected with business activity, was needed by Mitsui's affiliates and clients.

The information gathered by Mitsui should cover all areas of the business activities these include; import, export, commercial, development, technology transfer, off shore trade, etc. The information covering these activities should be fairly generic. When considering these generic issues the list of required information should include; (1) Removing barriers to trade; (2) Abolition of frontier controls; (3) Standards (EC mark); (4) Public sector procurement; (5) Financial currency; (6) Community patent/trademark; (7) Distribution; (9) Future/current joint ventures; (10) Co-operation agreements; (11) Subsidiaries and branches; (12) Mergers and take-overs; (13) Working conditions and the social dimension; (14) Community law; (15) Consumer protection; (16) Company law; (17) Mobility of labour. The list could become exhaustive . In order to cover these areas in sufficient detail it is essential that the key representatives from the corporate divisions are involved. Mitsui has set out to accomplish this by forming the EC 92 task force comprising individuals from ; finance, accounting, tax, legal, credit, corporate planning and information and research. The list should also include representatives from marketing and a technical function. Although Mitsui currently has a strong presence in Europe, segmentation and differentiation should be reconsidered to enable them to; understand their existing customers, identify new potential customers, adapt their products, innovate new products.

Students need to emphasise that Mitsui appears to attach great importance to information and education, evidence to suggest this; (1) The establishment of the EC 92 task force in 1988 which focused on information and internal education four years before

European integration; (2) The creation of a newsletter to inform personnel of EC92; (3) The holding of seminars to inform managers and executives of the change; (4) The drafting of reports by the IR&D defining the progress of integration. This combination of resource deployment resulted in the formulation of Mitsui's business strategy. This strategy resulted in reorganisation of Mitsui's European operations on a pan-European basis and a campaign to establish Mitsui and its associates as European insiders through a massive increase in investment. Without applying great importance to information and education Mitsui would have been running blind in 1992.

Japanese companies have always believed in a highly trained workforce. Education is taken very seriously by the Japanese. Japanese children currently go to school 257 days a year, for 9.5 hours a day. Japan is next after Korea in terms of having the highest number of PhDs per head. It has numerous universities most of which are owned by private companies. This is believed to be the prime reason for their success. In Britain children do only six hours a day for less than 200 days per year. The number of young people who stay on in some kind of education or training after 16 has of late grown at an unprecedented rate, but overall levels of achievement in Britain still lag behind other more competitive nations. To meet this challenge the government, the CBI and the TUC have introduced a challenging set of national targets for education and training. The targets tell us what the UK need to do to compete effectively as a nation beyond the year 2000.

3. Why do you think American and Japanese companies have been faster in taking a pan-European approach than many European companies? Given the diversity of economies and consumers is Mitsui too early in adopting a Pan European strategy?

Some students will suggest that it is by no means certain that the formation of the single European market will create a united (pan) European marketing approach across the EU. The basic concept of a "free flow of products, services, capital and people" should promote a pan-European approach but the very influential issue of local tastes and preferences will have the effect of reducing the "standardisation of marketing strategies between countries". The success of this standardisation depends greatly on the product types; consumer durables (cameras, watches, radios, etc.) can be easily standardised; FMCG (food and drink) are more dependent to local tastes, preferences and customs i.e. McDonalds in Norway sells salmon sandwiches whilst in Italy the preference is for salad bars. The introduction of trade restrictions as a result of "Fortress Europe" has encouraged foreign companies to increase their direct investment in the EU and exploit the benefits of the Single European Market. This applies especially to Japanese and American companies. Both countries have a tradition of investment in the European market and in the case of Mitsui, have been trading in Europe since 1880, building a presence in at least 14 European countries. The increase in investment by Japanese and American companies have given them a much stronger position in Europe, placing them in an ideal situation where they can control their own destiny. Because of these investments and subsequent control over the European market "Fortress Europe" proved to be not as protective and exclusive as may have been imagined. Many Japanese and American companies are much more experienced in the international business market, providing "a potentially intense competitive environment". In their home market, American companies have gained much more experience in marketing over a large continental area, managing a variety of cultural, economical and political differences. Japanese companies, putting their previous encounters aside, also have the experience of selling in the American market. The limited size of the Japanese market forces them to expand into other industrialised markets such as the USA, Europe. Subsequently, both the USA and Japan have developed a better foresight of the benefits of a united market i.e. economies of scale, fewer technological variants, etc.

Along with many other Japanese and American companies, Mitsui and Co. have a well-established integration into the European market. As such it was relatively simple for them to identify the build of "Fortress Europe". They realised that they must react quickly and positively before the gates to the European markets were eventually closed to foreign investments i.e. 1992. With their strong position in the EU market prior to 1992, Mitsui can easily take the initiative and establish themselves as major contributors in the creation of a united Europe. The strategy of "insiderisation" developed by Mitsui provided the necessary information to determine the correct timing for their adoption of a pan-European strategy. With their past experience in other diverse markets, Mitsui are ideally placed to not only survive but to dominate the market.

4. What does Mitsui gain from having a strengthened RHQ? What advantages are gained from the pan-European and sector responsibilities of the country offices? Why do you think they were only "encouraged" to take on these roles? Do you think the new structure will slow down Mitsui's decision making and make their European operations slower and more difficult to control than it was before?

By strengthening its RHQ, Mitsui will gain the following; (1) Mitsui would be able to maximise the opportunities emerging from the pan-European sector; (2) Mitsui would be able to react to the disadvantages emerging from the pan-European sector and display a greater commitment to its customers. This could facilitate Mitsui in scale building; (3) Mitsui could be perceived as an indigenous supplier hence improving chances of market success; (5) Mitsui would be able to handle its sales distribution and promotion better . Creating both customer satisfaction and greater value than the competitors. Thus enhancing its competitive advantage.

The degree of pan-European marketing is likely to differ between industries and markets. Where large scale economies combined with convergent tastes, Pan European marketing is likely to thrive. However, where strong national differences in taste persist, marketing is likely to remain fragmented. Mitsui will be able to respond very effectively where "commonalities" (pan-European) and "non commonalities" (sector responsibilities) exist among Euro consumers. Examples of "commonalities"; (1) Young Europeans appear to share similar tastes (music, clothing) and general cultural values; (2) Affluence is not determined by national boundaries. For example the "Gold Circle" which extends for 250 mile ring around Cologne contains many Europe's wealthiest consumers and is multinational; (3) The advent of multinational communication systems e.g. satellite television and the growth in multilingual consumers means that the Pan European advertising messages may be possible in the future; (4) The growth of global brands reflected in the merger activity within certain industries will promote the development of a pan-European culture. For example in the West European from 1988 to 1990 in the food and drink industry there were over 400 mergers and acquisitions. Mitsui can also respond to the threats arising from the European Union; (5) Sales distribution network and promotion activities will also benefit from economies of scale. Mitsui can also respond to the threats arising from the non commonalities of the EU as follows; (1) The wide variety of tastes which exists between consumers in different countries and within countries; (2) Despite good intentions, many of the national differences in product standards, safety regulations and distribution systems will remain post 1993; (3) Linguistic differences (unlike the USA) will hamper pan-European communication strategies; (4)

Entrenched national competitors will fight penetration of their markets by pan-European marketers.

Mitsui only "encouraged" to take on these roles for the following reasons; (1) If "forced" then the existing Tokyo office might perceive loss of control and power, resulting in lack of co-operation from it personnel. Also if the European operations failed, Mitsui Tokyo would withdraw and change its strategies without "loss of face"; (2) By "encouraging" only Mitsui provided an opportunity for its managers to realistically investigate the feasibility/viability of adopting a pan-European strategy resulting in "ownership" leading to smoother implementation.

On the contrary this approach would make Mitsui more effective. It will improve the ability of managers in local markets to react and make decisions quickly in the ever changing EU environment. Mitsui needed to give the authority to local managers to make this happen. The strategy for Europe will be directed through the RHQ in London therefore Mitsui's overall strategy will not be compromised. Local offices will be able to react quickly in a consistent manner whilst maintaining the corporate strategies developed in Japan.

References

British Institute of Management, Doing Business in Europe, 1994.

OECD Figures for Education at a Glance, OECD, 1993.

Business and Technology Education Council Report, 1994.

Jokes and Quotes

Marketing Research: What you do to avoid marketing.

Research is cheap if you want to stay in business, expensive if you don't.
ANON

Forecasting is very difficult, especially if it is about the future.
ANON

Two hat manufacturers sent salesmen to Africa. Within a few days one of the salesmen cabled back to his company, "Disaster - no one in Africa wears a hat! Am returning home immediately." At about the same time, the second salesman sent a cable to his company, "Great news - no one in Africa is wearing a hat! Start production immediately."
ANON

A group of numbers looking for an argument.
ANON

Can't act, can't sing, slightly bald. Can dance a little.
ANON

The teenage vogue for beat music and rock 'n' roll is over. Now the demand is for pop music shows with broad family appeal.
ANON

Research is the process of going up alleys to see if they are blind.
MARSTON BATES

A statistician is one who collects data and draws confusions.
HYMAN MAXWELL BERSTON

You can never plan the future by the past.
EDMUND BURKE

A trend is a trend is a trend
But the question is, will it bend?
Will it alter its course
Through some unforeseen force

And come to a premature end?
SIR ALEC CAIRNCROSS

Prolonged statistics are a lethal dose, which if it does not kill will certainly dispel your audience.
ILKA CHASE

Consumer's delusions result in producer's blunders.
JOHN BATES CLARK

The singer will have to go; the BBC won't like him.
ERIC EASTON (COMMENTING ON THE ROLLING STONE)

No amount of experimentation can ever prove me right; a single experiment can prove me wrong.
ALBERT EINSTEIN

Economic forecasting houses like Data Resources and Chase Econometrics have successfully predicted fourteen of the last five recessions.
DAVID FEHR

If you can keep your head when all about you are losing theirs, perhaps you have misunderstood the situation.
GRAFFITI

The way to do research is to attack the facts at the point of greatest astonishment.
CELIA GREEN

If Beethoven's 7th Symphony is not by some means abridged, it will soon fall with disuse.
PHILIP HALE

Forecast: Is the act of knowing what would have happened if what does happen hadn't.
RALPH HARRIS

Statistics are the lowest grade of information known to exist.
O. HENRY

Research men in advertising are really blind men groping in a dark room for a black cat that isn't there.
LUDOVIC KENNEDY

He uses statistics as a drunken man uses a lamppost - for support rather than illumination.
ANDREW LANG

Flight by machines heavier than air is impractical and insignificant, if not utterly impossible.
SIMON NECOMB

The secret of business is to know something that nobody else knows.
ARISTOTLE ONASSIS

If you understand everything, you must be misinformed.
JAPANESE PROVERB

With optimistic expectations
I started my own explorations,
And swore to move without a swerve
Along my sinusoidal curve.
Alas! I knew how it would end;
I've mixed the cycle and the trend
SIR DENNIS H. ROBERTSON

Research is to see what everybody has seen and to think what nobody else has thought.
ALBERT SZENT-GYORGYI

A commander who does not want to buy information about the enemy, thus resulting in his defeat is inconsiderate. Such a commander is not a good military leader. He can never win in battles.
SUU TZU

All the business of war and indeed all the business of life, is to endeavour to find out what you don't know from what you do; that's what I called "guessing what was at the other side of the hill".
DUKE OF WELLINGTON

Fools make researchers and wise men exploit them.
H.G. WELLS

Part III

Buyer Behaviour

Chapter 7
Consumer Markets

Chapter Objectives

After reading this chapter, you should be able to:

1. Define the consumer market and construct a simple model of consumer buying behaviour.
2. Tell how culture, subculture and social class influence consumer buying behaviour.
3. Describe how consumers' personal characteristics and major psychological factors affect their buying decisions.
4. Discuss how consumer decision making varies with the type of buying decision.
5. Explain the stages of the buyer decision and adoption processes.

Chapter Overview

Markets have to be understood before marketing strategies can be developed. The consumer market buys goods and services for personal consumption. Consumer behaviour is influenced by the buyer's characteristics and by the buyer's decision process. Buyer characteristics include four major factors: cultural, social, personal, and psychological. For new products, consumers respond at different rates, depending on consumer and product characteristics. Manufacturers try to bring their new products to the attention of early adopters, especially opinion leaders.

Teaching Notes

Refer to the following pages for teaching notes.

Model of Consumer Behaviour
Transparency PM 7-1 corresponds to Figure 7-1 on p.270 and to the material on pp.269-270.

Consumer Behaviour
Consumer behaviour refers to the buying behaviour of final consumers - individuals and households who buy goods and services for personal consumption.

Model of Consumer Behaviour
The model shown on the transparency corresponds to Figure 7-1 in the text. The following transparencies and accompanying notes discuss the influences on consumer behaviour in greater detail.

Tip
You may wish to discuss the "buyer's black box" at this stage. Students sometimes become involved in the controversy regarding the presence or absence of consciousness in consumers. Experimental psychologists argue that what we call consciousness is merely a set of complex learned responses - an ordinary physiological function. Sociologists and social psychologists argue that consciousness is greater than the sum of its physiological parts. For marketers, the issue is sometimes linked to free will: Do marketers create needs by conditioning consumers? Do marketers offer need-fulfillers to needs consumer's create in their "black box"?

Notes for PM 7-1

Influences on Consumers

Transparency PM 7-2 relates to Figure 7-2 on p.271 and previews the material on pp.270-288. The factors influencing consumers stem from a combination of forces over a consumptive lifetime. Marketers cannot control these factors but in understanding them can better predict how the factors shape consumer preferences. Consumer needs are shaped and often given importance from the influences discussed here.

Cultural

Culture is the most basic influence on a person's values, priorities and beliefs. Cultural shifts make marketing opportunities although most such changes are in secondary rather than core cultural values. Subcultures are important markets as these groups are often significantly different in their needs to warrant different marketing approaches. Social class is determined by a combination of income, occupation, education, wealth and other variables.

Social

Social factors within one's class that affect consumer behaviour include reference groups and aspirational groups. Families also exert strong social influences. Finally, each relationship a person has with his or her group carries with it certain roles and status that may carry consumptive responsibilities.

Personal

Major personal factors are age and life cycle stage, occupation, economic situation, life style and personality/self-concept. Texts vary in their treatment of the life cycle stages but it is clear that singles buy different products than do young marrieds with small children. Occupations differ in time constraints and social pressures to conform that affect consumption decisions. Lifestyle typologies can reveal different consumption patterns across otherwise dissimilar groups. The unique characteristics of each person that make up their personality also affect behaviour.

Psychological

Maslow's hierarchy reminds marketers that need states vary in their intensity or motivations. Perception is the process of organising stimuli and is influenced by selective exposure, distortion and retention. Learning occurs in response to the presentation of information linked to relevant drives, cues, responses and reinforcement only some of which is under the control of the marketer. Beliefs and attitudes, though shaped by cultural and social forces, may vary considerably on the individual level.

Tip

Ask students what factor(s) influences their choice of clothes? Note how many wear jeans. Why?

Notes for PM 7-2

Group Influence on Brand Choice

Transparency PM 7-3 corresponds to Figure 7-3 on p.275 and relates to the material on pp.273-274. Groups vary in their influence on product and brand purchases as illustrated on the transparency.

Consumers belong to several different membership groups:

1. Primary Groups

Primary groups are those with which we have regular but informal interaction. These include family, friends, neighbours and co-workers.

2. Secondary Groups

Secondary groups are those with which we have more formal and less regular interaction such as religious groups, professional associations and trade unions.

3. Reference Groups

These groups serve as direct (face-to-face) or indirect points of comparison and evaluation in a person's formation of attitudes or behaviour.

4. Aspirational Groups

This type of group is one to which the individual wishes to belong and emulates in adopting behaviours appropriate to that group.

5. Opinion Leaders

These are people within a reference group who exert influence over others due to special knowledge, skill, personality or other characteristics.

Tip

Ask how students would classify premium priced beers. How do the products reflect their position as a public luxury good? What groups influence the purchase?

Notes for PM 7-3

Consumer Buying Roles

Transparency PM 7-4 relates to the material on p.275-276. Involving students in a discussion of different consumer buying roles can be challenging. You might wish to link a discussion to social influences or family roles and have students describe purchasing responsibility each role has. Expanding from this kind of imaginative role playing to a model of small group decision making for a product like a personal computer might help students see how each role contributes to consumption decisions.

Initiator

The person who first suggests or thinks of the idea of buying a particular product or service. For example, Bill may suggest a Euro Disney trip for a family vacation.

Influencer

The person whose views or advice carries some weight in the final decision. This person may influence the decision criteria used as well. For example, Dad's feelings about France may influence the Euro Disney trip.

Decider

The person who authorises the purchase. For example, Mum's vacation time may be limited by her schedule as a lawyer, so she decides when and where the family goes.

Buyer

The person who actually makes the purchase. For example, Jane may telephone the reservation at Euro Disney once given the authorisation.

User

The person who consumes the product. For example, the whole family would use the Disney product. For equipment purchases like computers at universities, it might be students enrolled in courses coming to the computer lab.

> **Tip**
>
> Ask students about the role played by a new father sent out to buy baby products for his new born child. Also, consider the purchase of children's sweets.

Notes for PM 7-4

Family and Lifestyle

Transparency PM 7-5 corresponds to Table 7-2 on p.277 and Table 7-3 on p.278 and the material on pp.276-282.

Personal Factors

1. Age and Life-Cycle Stage

Buyers' choices are affected by changes in their age and family structure over time. Young singles have different tastes in clothes, furniture, food and recreation than do middle aged persons with their own children. Older consumers continue to change in their preferences and additionally acquire new buyer needs such as increased health care needs.

2. Occupation

A person's occupation carries with it distinct consumptive needs. White collar workers need different clothes than blue collar workers. Also, occupations usually carry their own subcultural norms and values that influence buyer behaviour.

3. Economic Situation

Will constrain buyer behaviour for almost everyone except for the most wealthy (see Table 7-1 on p.272 on social class).

4. Lifestyle

Lifestyle is a person's pattern of living as expressed in his or her activities, interests and opinions. Psychographics - lifestyle measures combined with demographic information can identify distinct market segments for consumer products and services. The best known of these methods, VALS 2, is addressed on the following transparency. If you do not wish to cover the material in-class, you can refer students to Table 7-4 on p.279.

5. Personality and Self-Concept

Personality refers to the unique psychological characteristics that lead to relatively consistent and lasting response to one's own environment. Self-concept is the basic perception that people have about who they are.

> **Tip**
>
> How does a person's need change through the family life cycle for (1) cars (2) holidays (3) savings products.

Notes for PM 7-5

SRI VALS 2 Segments

Transparency PM 7-6 corresponds to Table 7-4 on p.279 and lists the VALS 2 typologies. It divides people according to self-orientation (principle-oriented, status-oriented or action-oriented) and resources.

Self-Orientation

1. Principle-Oriented

Fulfilleds - are mature, responsible, well-educated professionals. Leisure centres around the home but they are also well informed about the world. High income but practical, value-oriented consumers.
Believers - have more modest incomes, are conservative and predictable consumers who favour local products.

2. Status-Oriented

Achievers - are successful work-oriented who get satisfaction from jobs and families. Conservatives who respect authority. Products show off success.
Strivers - seek to emulate achievers but have fewer resources.

3. Action-Oriented

Experiencers - are young people who like to affect the environment in tangible ways. This group is active and outgoing and likes new things.
Makers - also like to affect their environment but in more practical ways. They value self-sufficiency, family and have little interest in the larger world.

4. Resources

Actualisers - are people with the highest incomes and so many resources that they can indulge any or all self-orientations. Image is an expression of taste, independence and character. They can buy anything; need nothing.
Strugglers - have the lowest income and tend to be brand loyal.

Tip

Ask the students to imagine they are selling homes to each of these groups. How would the homes differ? How would the selling of them differ?

Notes for PM 7-6

Maslow's Hierarchy

Transparency PM 7-7 corresponds to Figure 7-4 on p.286 and the material on pp.283-284. Maslow's Hierarchy of Needs provides a theoretical framework for understanding how humans seek need-filling products. After discussing each level in the hierarchy you may wish to ask students to explain situations in which higher level needs are met before lower needs are addressed.

Need Levels (Lowest to Highest):

Physiological

Physical needs such as hunger, thirst and bodily functions are the lowest level need and require satisfaction before other needs become important to the individual. Sometimes this helps students understand the difference between needs and wants. A thirsty person may still want an expensive car but if thirsty enough will take a drink of water.

Safety

Safety needs for security and protection are the next level needs in the hierarchy. So long as physiological needs are met, safety needs will take precedence over other needs. Fear appeals for consumer products are often linked to safety needs.

Social

Human beings are social, gregarious animals. We group together in part to fulfil physiological and safety needs but also because we enjoy and need the company of others. Going to shopping centres to "hang out" fulfils social needs.

Esteem

To be recognised as an individual fulfils esteem needs. self-esteem is the value a person places on himself or herself. As lower needs become more stable, esteem needs become more important to the individual.

Self-actualisation

Beyond esteem needs very successful people may still be driven to improve themselves and "accomplish something". These people are driven to self-actualise their potential.

Tip

Ask if the hierarchy is universal. If so, what makes rich people take up dangerous sports and the military risk their lives? If it is internationally true, why do the Japanese put social needs on top?

Notes for PM 7-7

Types of Buying Decisions

Transparency PM 7-8 corresponds to Figure 7-5 on p.289 and relates to the material on pp.289-291.

Types of Buying Decision Behaviour

1. Complex Buying Behaviour

Consumers undertake this type of behaviour when they are highly involved in a purchase and perceive differences among brands. Involvement increases when the product is expensive, infrequently purchased, risky and highly self-expressive.

2. Dissonance-Reducing Buying Behaviour

Consumers engage in this behaviour when they are highly involved with an expensive, infrequent or risky purchase, but see little difference among the brands. Without objective differentiation to confirm the purchase, buyers often seek support to reduce postpurchase dissonance - the feeling they may have made the wrong decision.

3. Habitual Buying Behaviour

This behaviour occurs under conditions of low consumer involvement and little significant brand differences. Consumers do not search extensively for information about brands. Brand familiarity aids in promoting products under essentially passive learning conditions.

4. Variety-Seeking Buying Behaviour

Consumers may seek variety when involvement is low and there are significant perceived differences among brands. Differences may be product features - new taste, improvements, extra ingredients - or promotional benefits such as coupons, rebates and price reductions.

Tip

Ask student to comment on buying decision they have made; (1) choosing a college; (2) choosing a mate; (3) choosing a soft drink.

Notes for PM 7-8

The Buyer Decision Process

Transparency PM 7-9 corresponds to Figure 7-6 on p.291 and relates to the material on pp.291-297.

Stages in the Buyer Decision Process

1. Need Recognition

Problems are recognised when people sense a difference between an actual state and some desired state. Problem recognition can be triggered by either internal or external stimuli.

2. Information Search

Consumers vary in the amount of information search conduct. Information search may be a survey of information stored in or may be based upon information available externally. Search effort varies from heightened awareness corresponding to increased receptivity for relevant information to active information search modes where the person spends some energy to obtain information that is desired. External information vary in their informational and legitimising characteristics. Riskier decisions usually elicit more search behaviour than non-risky decisions.

3. Evaluation of Alternatives

Following information search, the person compares decisional alternatives available. Criterion for evaluation compares product attributes of the alternatives against degrees of importance each attribute has in meeting needs, beliefs about the product or brand's ability and utility, and an evaluation procedure that ranks the alternatives by preference that forms an intention to buy.

4. Purchase Decision

The individual buys a product. Purchasing other than the intended product may be due to attitudes of others exerted after the evaluation of alternatives is completed or unexpected situational factors such as point of purchase promotions that affect the alternatives' ranking.

5. Post-purchase Behaviour

Involves comparing the expected performance of the perceived performance received. Cognitive dissonance describes the tendency to accentuate benefits and downplay shortcomings.

Tip

Consider asking students to describe some of their purchases decisions made at the beginning of the term and link them to steps in the process. Or you may provide them with a brief description of a purchase and ask them to identify passages linked to each stage.

Notes for PM 7-9

New Product Adoption Process

These notes relate to the material on pp.297-298.

Stages in the Adoption Process

The new product adoption process parallels the buyer decision process but focuses more on the interaction of consumer needs with product adoption. The new product adoption process may work best to explain how regularly used products requiring re-purchase are considered for inclusion in the consumer's consumptive behaviour patterns but may also apply to some durables as well.

Awareness

In this stage the consumer is aware of the new product but lacks further information about it.

Interest

The consumer is motivated to seek information about the new product.

Evaluation

The consumer determines whether or not to try the new product.

Trial

The consumer tries the new product on a small scale to test its efficacy in meeting his or her needs. Trial can be imagined use of the product in some cases.

Adoption

The consumer decides to make use of the product on a regular basis.

Tip

Ask how media may help in each of the stages. Ad for awareness, PR for interest, store for evaluation, sales promotion for trial, product for adoption.

Buyer Adopter Categories

These notes correspond to Figure 7-8 on p.298 and relate to the material on pp.298-299.

Individual Differences in Innovativeness

Innovators

Innovators include the first 2.5% of buyers who adopt a new product idea. Innovators help get the product exposure but are not often perceived by the majority of potential buyers as typical consumers. Innovators like risk taking and enjoy buying new products. Innovators may purchase at skimming prices.

Early Adopters

Early Adopters comprise about 13.5% of the buyers who adopt new products. This group serves as opinion leaders to the rest of the market and their product usage outcomes serve as motivation to later buyers to get the product.

Early Majority

Early Majority are some 34% of buyers adopting the product. They are deliberate consumers who adopt new ideas before the average person but seldom lead the market.

Late Majority

Late Majority comprise another 34% of buyers adopting the product. This group is sceptical of new products and only buys after the majority of the market has tried it.

Laggards

Laggards are the final 16% of adopters and are tradition-bound. They are suspicious of change and only adopt innovation that have already become something of a tradition.

> **Tip**
>
> Ask for suggestion of product in the various stages and their uses: innovators (digital audio tape), early adopters (mobile phones), early majority (CD players), late majority (foreign holidays), laggards (VCRS).

Rate of Adoption

These notes relate to the material on pp.299-300. The adoption of innovations may be initially confusing to students but they will usually become involved in discussion when new products of importance to them are used as examples.

Product Characteristics Influences

1. Relative Advantage

This refers to the degree to which the innovation appears superior to existing products. The greater the perceived relative advantage, the sooner the innovation will be adopted.

2. Compatibility

This refers to the degree to which the innovation fits the values and experiences of the potential consumers. Increased compatibility will accelerate adoption of the innovation.

3. Complexity

This refers to the degree to which the innovation is difficult to understand or use. Greater complexity will slow the rate of adoption of the innovation.

4. Divisibility

This refers to the degree to which the innovation can be tried on a limited basis. Greater divisibility will help increase the rate of adoption of the innovation.

5. Communicability

This refers to the degree to which the results of using the innovation can be observed or described to others. Greater communicability will increase the rate of adoption of innovation.

Tip

Ask about a clear success/failure: How about the Channel Tunnel? Euro Disney? DAT (Digital Audio Tape - a failure)?

Comments on Discussing the Issues

1. Many factors affect the decision to buy a hi-fi system.. The buyer has a number of brand choices to make, for example Bang & Olufsen, Sony, Hitachi, Technics, Aiwa, Panasonic and so on. He or she has to decide on the price, design, features, functions, size and quality of the system. When purchasing a hi-fi, cultural and subcultural elements play fundamental roles. The buyer may belong to a group which values music and technology highly. The buyer will identify with a brand which he thinks is acceptable to his social class. Buyers from the upper classes will probably want a brand which is exclusive and expensive, whereas a buyer from the lower classes will probably be looking for a hi-fi which gives the basic features at a reasonable price. Membership and primary groups will have an effect on the decision of the buyer. For instance the buyer may wish to impress his family and friends. The family members of the buyer will affect the buyer's decision depending on how dominant the members are and how much their opinion is valued. If the hi-fi is for personal use other family members may not have a major influence. If the hi-fi is to be used by the family then their needs will have to be taken into consideration. Age and life cycle stage will affect the buyer's evaluation of the hi-fi system. For example, a teenager would want a trendy, good-looking system whereas a middle-aged person may want a system with excellent sound quality. Income plays a very important role. Hi-fi's are priced according to perceived quality. A hi-fi is a luxury item and the amount of disposable income a person has would directly affect the brand and price chosen. As far as lifestyle is concerned, brands are marketed so that they identify with a particular type of person. A Bang & Olufsen hi-fi would be suitable to affluent, status seeking buyers and perhaps not to lower income groups. The purchase of a hi-fi is a psychogenic need. This recognises the need for self-esteem, recognition and status. Certain features may motivate the buyer to make a particular decision, e.g. a CD player and a certain brand name may be the deciding factor.

2. The buying behaviour of consumers is quite different in the purchase of a new album, a laptop, jogging shoes and cereal. Some students will say that the purchase of Bruce Springsteen's new album can be an impulsive purchase. There is no real problem of evaluation of alternatives. The buyer probably has been told that there is a new album of his or her favourite singer. He just wants to buy it. Relatively the price is inexpensive and pretty much the same in every shop, so there is no room for information search. The purchase will be influenced by personal and social factors. The purchase of a note book computer is an extended problem solving behaviour. More time will be spent on "information search" because of for example it is quite expensive. Some criteria that will be used are; performance, convenience, durability, reliability, memory capacity, expansion possibility, software compatibility and so on. This purchase is a long term investment thus has the highest level of involvement in comparison to the other products. Jogging shoes could be categorised as limited problem solving product. Some need jogging shoes because they are busy executives living in New York and it is "in" to wear such shoes - recognition, status. Some need them for sports. Some consider them as comfortable shoes. Information search is slightly complex but still simple. Buyers can visit specialised retailers or read sports magazines. Then they need to try the product. Influencers will play a role in the buying process. The purchase of breakfast cereal is generally a habitual problem

solving where involvement is low. The information search is also low and the evaluation of alternatives is as quick as the purchase. Taste plays an important role. Buyers buy the product on a weekly or monthly basis or when they run out of it.

3. A detailed understanding of the buyer decision process will enable marketers develop a more effective marketing strategy. First and foremost the marketers will know who their market is as well as the buyers characteristics. Marketers will be able to understand what the customers are thinking at each stage of the buying process and will design appropriate strategies in each of the stages. From the model marketers will be able to identify problems relating to the product and appropriate improvement and modification could be implemented. Ask students how universal is the model. Could it be used for impulse purchase products or in instances where there is strong brand loyalty.

4. In developing advertising strategies and messages, lifestyle information works best in conjunction with demographic information. Demographics help show who is in the market and suggest when and where to run advertising to reach the target audience without paying for wasted coverage of probable nonbuyers. Lifestyle information gives extra psychological insights for fine-tuning a message or media schedule. For example, one study revealed "Family Oriented" and "Rigid and Resistant" lifestyle groups, who had similar demographics but preferred different kinds of television programs. An advertising media plan based on demographics alone would have ignored important information about the audience.

5. Some factors that should be taken into account : (1) In some sector of the society this is a sensitive issue where it go against religious beliefs; (2) Which gender buys male contraceptives most often; (3) Age group; (5) Lifestyle; (6) Life cycle stage; (7) Possible outlets; (8) Price; (9) How receptive are the male consumers with regard to this new albeit innovative form of contraception. There will be other factors mentioned by students. Try to generate as many factors as possible.

6. According to Tony Wainwright, President of the Bloom Companies, "Perception is reality." People act on the basis of their perceptions, whether or not their perceptions match the facts of the situation, so as far as an individual's attitudes, beliefs, and behaviour are concerned, there is no difference between perceptions and reality.

Selective exposure, distortion, and retention all operate to turn perception into reality. Customers who have had a bad experience with a company's products may pay more attention to information about the company's shortcomings than about its strong points; they may interpret advertisements in a way that makes the company look inferior; and they may remember unfavourable information and forget positive information about the company. The obvious marketing implication is that companies must pay attention to their images as well as to their actions.

Comments on Applying the Concepts

1. Students may have oversimplified ideas about the types of needs that different products fulfil. This exercise is designed to clarify this issue by making them articulate exactly what sorts of needs are fulfilled by different products.

   The first part of the question asks students to list products based on their personal level of interest. Usually making these distinctions is quite easy. The second part of the question requires more thought: students are to list adjectives describing how they *feel* about the products. The question is not to describe the products themselves, but rather the feelings that they elicit. This is likely to be easy for the high-interest products, but it may prove difficult for the low interest items. It is entirely possible that some students have no real feelings at all for the lower interest items.

   When the exercise is complete, the contrast between the low and high interest products should be quite apparent. It is useful to remind students of the marketing concept once again: marketers attempt to fulfil consumer needs, and different needs require different types of marketing responses.

2. Many items that students buy are influenced by peers as a reference group. In some cases the influence is rather subtle: two peers may simply share the same taste in music, and may not be aware that the other person owns the same CD. Other cases are quite clear, such as cars or clothing. Consider asking the class if anyone knowingly owns exactly the same piece of clothing as another peer. This is virtually certain to be the case in a college or university community, especially if college logo clothing is considered. Probe the type of influences that affected these purchases.

   Many product purchases are influenced by what our parents used. This influence often has its effect when people enter a new and unfamiliar product category for the first time, and search for a familiar reference point. Thus, young men often follow the shaving product preferences of their fathers. Students of both sexes are often faced with buying laundry detergent for the first, and are more likely to pick the brand of laundry detergent that was used in their home. The idea of using a heuristic ("I'll buy what I know from home") rather than thinking through the entire issue is more common in low interest, habitual purchase categories.

Case 7
Bic versus Gillette:
The Disposable Wars

Synopsis

After their introduction in the United States in 1976, disposable razors grew so rapidly that by early 1989 they accounted for 40 per cent of the dollar sales of shaving products and over 50 per cent of the unit sales. This case focuses on the men's wet-shave market.

Gillette dominates the wet-shave market with a 62 per cent U.S. market share. Gillette has historically pursued a strategy that focuses on blade-and-razor systems as opposed to disposables because it makes about three times as much money per unit on cartridge refills as it does on its disposable shavers. Thus, even though Gillette's disposable entry, the Good News!, had captured 58 per cent of the disposable market, each share-point gain for Good News! reduces the company's profits to the extent that it takes sales away from Gillette's Atra and Trac II systems.

The case also presents information on the Bic Pen Company, whose Bic shaver is challenging Gillette in the disposable shaver market. Bic and the other disposable entries have produced significant price competition, resulting in even lower margins for the players. While Gillette has pursued a strategy emphasising disposable cartridges but permanent handles. Bic has pursued a disposable-only strategy (as it has in the pen and cigarette lighter markets).

The case also outlines the psychology of male shaving, both to prepare the student to deal with the questions at the end of the case and to depict the challenge facing Gillette as it tries to get men to switch from disposable shavers to its blade/razor systems.

Teaching Objectives

1. Introduce students to the psychology of men's shaving and acquaint them with how Gillette and Bic have developed strategies to serve this market.

2. Provide a framework in which students can utilise the major concepts in the chapter: consumer buying roles, types of buying decision behaviour, stages in the buyer decision process, and buyer decision processes toward new products.

3. Allow students to develop recommendations for dealing with the problems facing Gillette.

Study Questions

1. Who is involved in a man's decision to buy a disposable razor and what roles do the various participants play? Do these participants and roles differ for the decision to buy a system razor?

The chapter indicates that the consumer buying roles include initiator, influencer, decider, buyer, and user. With respect to purchasing a *disposable* razor, any number of persons in a household can be the initiator. If a man uses the same kind of razor as his wife or sons or daughters, then any of these family members might initiate a particular buying decision--that is, whoever notices that the supply of blades is getting low will suggest to the person who typically does the shopping that a new purchase is needed. Obviously, in this scenario, any member of the family can also be an influencer. A man might also be affected by the opinions of other men with whom he associates, who may share views on the merits of various types of shaving systems. The decider might not be the man, especially if the same type of shaver is used by other family members. The person who actually does the shopping may make the decision as to what brand will be purchased. Thus, the decider and the buyer may be the same person. So in the decision to buy a disposable razor, a large number of people can be involved in various consumer buying roles.

A *system razor*, however, is a more personal decision. A man might have a Trac II system that he has been using for many years. Thus, he would have to be the initiator for a particular purchase. Again, however, there could be a number of influencers. Other men might influence his decision to switch brands, or his wife or other family members might complain about him not having a good shave, and this could influence his product decision.

These two hypothetical scenarios show that there may be a significant difference between buying a disposable razor and buying a system razor. The system razor would seem to have a higher probability of being a personal decision, or at least a decision influenced by past decisions.

2. What types of buying decision behaviour do men exhibit when purchasing razors?

For a first-purchase decision, a man might pursue limited problem solving or extensive problem solving. A teenager might simply use the same brand as his father, or he might find out from his friends what king of shaving systems they are using. Initially he would have to decide between a wet or dry shave system, but once the initial decision is made, most men move quickly toward a routine response behaviour. As we have seen, for may users of disposables, this means a generic decision to buy disposables rather than a decision to buy a particular brand of disposables.

3. Examine a man's decision process for buying a wet shaver. How have Gillette and Bic pursued different strategies concerning this process?

Problem Recognition: The buyer decision process as outlined in the text runs from problem recognition to postpurchase behaviour. Gillette's strategy is based on the premise that shaving is an important ritual to every man and that men recognise the value of a good shave and the problems associated with obtaining it. Gillette believes that a man will take the necessary steps and spend the extra money to get the best possible shave. Bic, in contrast, believes that a shave is a shave is a shave. It operates on the premise that men have adopted a routine, price-driven decision-making process and really do not think too much about what particular razor they use. Bic also believes that, for most men, almost any shaver will provide an adequate shave.

Information Search: Although Gillette appears to believe that men will seek information about their shaving problems, Bic believes that men will decide on a shaver on the basis of price and availability. By constantly introducing new and improved products, Gillette has encouraged information search on the part of consumers. Its ads and the information it provides on its products give men lots of knowledge about how razors work and how they can provide a closer shave. Bic, on the other hand, would like men to skip the information search process.

Evaluation of Alternatives: Gillette has invested heavily in trying to understand how razors work and how men use them so that it can present information based on the degrees of importance and salient attributes that come to a consumer's mind. Bic, on the other hand, conducts little research. These different strategies have led to two very different brand images. Gillette has developed a brand image that is associated with high quality and higher price, technological advancement, and innovation. Bic has developed a brand image that, it hopes, is associated with maximum service at minimum price. Where Gillette emphasises functions and features in its promotion, Bic emphasises convenience and price. It is important for the student to see that brand image conveys much information that is involved in the consumer buying decision process.

Purchase Decision: With respect to the purchase decision itself, both Gillette and Bic have pursued strategies to make their products widely available so that the consumer can easily buy them once the decision has been made. Although this purchase decision may be affected by the attitudes of others, unexpected situational factors, or perceived risk, most consumers probably follow through on their decision to purchase a particular kind or brand of shaving system.

Postpurchase Behaviour: Shavers provide the consumer with immediate feedback. Most people probably cannot tell whether they are being shaved with a single blade (the Bic shaver) or a dual-blade system (Gillette Good News!). But a blade that is not sharp or that cuts may cause the consumer to stop using the product immediately.

It would be interesting to discuss with students what they do when they encounter an unsatisfactory shaving system. Those who use disposables might be tempted to simply throw the shaver and any unused shavers or blades away because the investment is not too significant. However, those who use a razor/blade system have made a greater outlay, so they might stick with the system for a while to see if their attitude toward it changes.

4. **What marketing strategy should Gillette adopt to encourage men to switch from disposables to system razors? How would buyer decision processes toward new products affect your recommendations?**

By this point in the discussion, students should realise that Gillette has a big problem to solve. With disposables growing rapidly and accounting for over half the market, it is clear that many consumers feel that one blade is as good as another and that price is the driving force. Further, society in general seems to be more and more inclined to use disposable products. Gillette is going to have to swim against the tide of disposables.

The instructor might suggest that Gillette's first task should be to try to make the shaving decision a more personal one. To the extent that family members share razors and that the purchase decision has become routine, it is probable that a man will pursue the low-cost, disposable alternative. Therefore, Gillette would want to emphasise the personal nature of the decision and the right of a man to have a shaving system that suits his own needs. To do this, they have to make men aware of product features and other information related to shaving, which suggests a heavy investment in advertising and promotion. Probably Gillette should switch most of its advertising from disposables to system razors, and remind men of the aura, mystique, and manliness of shaving. Most contemporary men do not remember the "old days" when shaving was a more difficult, and sometimes dangerous, task.

Finally, Gillette needs another new product or technological breakthrough in order to raise the issue of deciding about shaving systems again for most men. Following the new-product adoption process outlined in the text, Gillette would then try to identify innovators who could influence their peers to consider a new system. Given Gillette's long association with sports, it would be natural for the company to use famous athletes in advertising programmes emphasising the manliness of shaving and the value of the close shave provided by the new product.

5. What explains Bic's differing success in competing against Gillette in the disposable pen, lighter and shaver market? Why do you think Bic perfume failed?

Bic's differing success in competing against Gillette in the disposable pen, lighter and shaver market was due firstly to the fact that they both entered the pen and lighter market at the same time. This resulted with Bic being the cheaper of the two and also been marketed better, thus ended up with Bic doing better in these markets. Basically Bic's philosophy stated that it wanted to make status into commodities via mass production and due to this they had great success with the lighters and pens. Secondly, lighters and pens were seen as status products in the past but now are seen as everyday items which everybody will be using without regard to their quality. However, in the shaving market Gillette faired better, possibly due to the fact that Gillette was an established and recognised name. The company had patented their first razor in 1904 and Bic entered this market later in 1975 in Europe. Also, during this time Gillette's name had given confidence to the consumer about offering the ultimate shaving experience; Gillette was associated with quality shave. Lastly, Gillette faired better because unlike pens and lighter which can be very similar from one brand to another, razors can be very different and therefore the consumer will not buy the cheaper product if it means that he would cut himself.

On the question of why Bic perfume failed, this could be due to the fact that perfume is sold through selected outlets but Bic pursued a policy of selling the perfume at any outlet. Therefore, due to this and the fact that the company had an image of selling cheap things this did not fit in with the perfume market. In the perfume market the name of the perfume offers a degree of status i.e. people pay the higher price for Chanel No. 5. If a room full of ladies were discussing the type of perfume they were wearing and one of the ladies said she was wearing Bic perfume she would lose status within that group. Also, the perfume sector is seen as a more luxury market than that of practical items such as pens and perfumes are bought as gifts for loved ones. Finally, the perfume sector is more to do with the idea of spending more will give in return a greater self confidence and therefore it would be better to buy a perfume for twenty pounds than Bic's five pound perfume.

Teaching Suggestions

Because this chapter comes after the Marketing Research and Information Systems Chapter (Chapter 6), the case offers the opportunity for some field research. Student groups could examine the number of shaving systems offered at the typical drug or grocery store and their prices. Or each student in the class could be assigned to interview five men about their shaving habits. Either the instructor or the students themselves could develop a simple set of questions designed to examine what products men use, how long they have used them, if they have switched and why, and if they use disposables, what would make them switch back to a system. (This assignment might be especially helpful for women students since the case focuses on men's shaving.)

Additional Information

Gillette has pursued the strategy of introducing a new shaver, the Gillette Sensor, to catalyse its drive to reduce disposables' share of the market. First, the company adopted a new theme for its promotional program in 1989: "Gillette: The Best a Man Can Get." Rather than focusing on product features and benefits, the campaign features pictures of men in action, often in sports situations, to remind men of the "masculinity" of shaving. Gillette has also altered its advertising emphasis: In 1989, it spent about 70 per cent of its ad budget on system razors and only about 30 per cent on disposables--the reverse of its spending pattern just two years earlier. This decision to put most of the company's advertising dollars into shaving systems was made by John Symons, the new head of the North American Shaving Group, who had used this strategy very successfully when he headed Gillette's European shaving operation.

"The Best a Man Can Get" campaign became Gillette's strategic platform. The theme carried two messages: Gillette will give men the best shaving products and, by using Gillette products, men will be at their best in terms of their feelings about their personal appearance.

In January 1990, Gillette introduced the Gillette Sensor in advertisements during the Super Bowl. Sensor represented a true technological breakthrough. The razor featured individually spring-mounted twin blades and pivoting action allowed the blades, the narrowest produced to date, to respond automatically to the nuances of each man's face. In addition, the skin guard, also independently spring mounted, works in concert with the blades to stretch the skin for a more efficient shave. The ergonomically designed handle produced the proper weight and balance to fit a man's hand while shaving. The product incorporated 22 patents and carried a $200 million final development cost.

Gillette launched Sensor in 19 countries simultaneously, probably the largest new consumer product introduction in history and supported the launch with $100 million advertising, promotion, and public relations campaign.

The market's reception for Sensor was so enthusiastic that demand exceeded supply for much of 1990. By the end of 1990, Sensor had captured 9.3% of the market's dollar sales. By the end of August 1991, Sensor held an estimated 13% market share and system razors held a 51% share, up from 49% at the end of 1990 and 46.5% at the end of 1989. Gillette's share of the system's market had risen from 69.7% at the end of 1989 to 73.9% by August 1991, and its share of the disposable razor market had fallen from 54.2% to 52.4% over the same period. Gillette's overall market share was holding steady at 62.2%. Overall, its strategy to slow if not halt the growth of disposable razors seemed to be working.

Jokes and Quotes

Marketing is about making what customer want today; innovation is about making what customer don't know they will want tomorrow.

"I used your soap two years ago and not used another since then".
PEAR SOAP ADVERTISEMENT

There is a sucker born every minute.
P.T. BARNUM

Commerce is the art of exploiting the need or desire someone has for something.
EDMOND and JULES DE GONCOURT

The philosophy behind much advertising is based on the old observation that every man is really two men - the man he is and the man he wants to be.
WILLIAM FEATHER

What do we want? Everything. When do we want it? Now!
GRAFFITI

My next-door neighbour had a great holiday this year. He bought a big new Volvo estate, put all the kids in the back - and then took himself off on a cruise.
JOKE

It is intelligent to ask two questions: (1) Is it possible? (2) Can I do it? But it is unintelligent to ask these questions: (1) Is it real? (2) Has my neighbour done it?
SOREN KIERKEGAARD

Look, it's like a fight. One guy comes into the ring in a gray pin-stripped robe and across the back in small black letters it says REASON. He's wearing glasses and his hair is thinning. Into the opposite corner leaps a guy in a robe of scarlet satin and across the back in orange and purple letters it says THE IRRESTIBLE URGE. He looks like a bull and there's foam at the corners of his mouth. Where you gonna put your money, kid?
ERIC KRAFT

Why, a four-year-old child could understand this report. Run out and find me a four-year-old child. I can't make head or tail out of it.
GROUCHO MARX

Doesn't a fellow feel good after he gets out of a store when he nearly bought something.
FRANK MCKINNEY-HUBBARD

Today the tyrant rules not by club or fist, but, disguised as a market researcher, he shepherds his flocks in the ways of utility and comfort.
MARSHALL MCLUHAN

(Consumption is) a quantity always indefinite, for there is no end to the desire of enjoyment, the grand concern is to increase the supply.
JAMES MILL

When asked why he buried an axe in a bar, Murray Clyde of Aberdeen explained, "I was having difficulty in catching the barmaid's eye".
NEWS

The public is an acute as well as merciless beast neither over-sees a failing, nor forgives it - but stamps judgement and execution immediately, tho' upon a member of itself.
SIR DUDLEY NORTH

The consumer is not a moron. She is your wife. And she is grown up.
DAVID OGILVY

Economists know a lot about what makes producers tick, while they know almost nothing about the motivation of consumers.
TIBOR SCITOVSKY

Can one desire too much of a good thing?
WILLIAM SHAKESPEARE

Daddy, what did YOU do in the Great War.
SLOGAN

You Know What Comes Between Me And My Calvins? Nothing!
SLOGAN

Perhaps We Could, Paul. If . . . You Owned A Chrysler.
SLOGAN

Desperation, Pacification, Expectation, Acclamation, Realisation.
SLOGAN

Conspicuous consumption of valuable goods is a means of reputability to the gentleman of leisure.
THORSTEIN VEBLEN

With the exception of the instinct of self-preservation, the propensity for emulation is probably the strongest and most alert and persistent of the economic motives proper.
THORSTEIN VEBLEN

Chapter 8

Business Markets and Business Buyer Behaviour

Chapter Objectives

After reading this chapter, you should be able to:

1. Explain how business markets differ from consumer markets.
2. Identify the major factors that influence business buyer behaviour.
3. List and define the steps in the business buying decision process.
4. Explain how institutional and government buyers make their buying decisions.

Chapter Overview

Businesses make up a vast market. There are three major types of business markets: the industrial market, the reseller market, and the government market. In many ways, business markets are like consumer markets, but in other ways they are much different. Business markets usually have fewer but larger buyers who are more geographically concentrated. Business demand is derived, largely inelastic, and more fluctuating. More buyers are usually involved in the business buying decision, and business buyers are better trained and more professional than consumer buyers are. Business purchasing decisions are more complex, and the buying process is more formal.

Teaching Notes

Refer to the following pages for teaching notes.

Characteristics of Business Markets

Transparency PM 8-1 relates to the material on pp.310-315. This summarises the areas where business markets differ from consumer markets.

Characteristics of Organisational Markets

1. Market Structure and Demand

Business markets have far fewer buyers than consumer markets. Business markets are much more geographically concentrated. Business demand is derived demand coming from the demand for the consumer goods the organisation produces. Demand is more inelastic and more fluctuating.

2. Nature of the Buying Unit

Business markets have more buyers and more professional purchasing procedures. Purchasing agents may be career professionals highly trained in how to buy better. As purchases become more complex, more people are likely to become involved in the purchase decision.

3. Types of Decisions

Business buying decisions may be more complex due to the large amounts of money involved, technical specification considerations, and the interaction and co-ordination of more people in the buying process.

4. Decision Process

Beyond the complexity of the decision business buying is more formalised, often with written procedures. Also, business buying decisions feature buyer-seller relationships that are more dependent upon each other than consumer buying situations. Both buyer and seller have fewer options to do business elsewhere than do consumer buyer and sellers.

Other Characteristics

5. Direct Purchasing

Business buyers usually buy direct from producers.

6. Reciprocity

Business buyers often practice reciprocity, selecting suppliers who also buy from them.

7. Leasing

Many businesses lease rather than buy equipment. Leasing gains a number of advantages over buying such as having more capital, having newer products, and tax incentives.

Tip

Ask students why the Third World is so dependent upon fluctuating price of raw materials such as cocoa beans (for chocolate) and titanium (for aircraft engineer). Relate to Figure 8-1 in the text on pp.310.

Notes for PM 8-1

Stages in Business Buying Process

These notes correspond to Table 8-1 and relate to the material on pp.325-328.

Stages Include:

1. Problem Recognition

Problem recognition can result from internal or external stimuli. They may emerge from an identified shortage or ideas for improvements recognised by buyers.

2. General Need Description

The buyer describes the overall characteristics and quantities of the needed item. For complex items, this step may require co-ordinating the efforts of many specialists.

3. Product Specification

A developmental team must translate general needs into product specifications. An engineering value analysis team may look at alternative designs to reduce production costs.

4. Supplier Search

The buyer conducts a search for the best vendors for the product specifications.

5. Proposal Solicitation

The buyer invites qualified suppliers to submit proposals covering the terms of supply and support. Selected proposals may be asked to make formal presentations.

6. Supplier Selection

The buyer selects suppliers based upon a combination of technical competence and service record and reputation. Negotiation of specific terms may occur before final selection, especially on price.

7. Order Routine Specification

The buyer specifies the details of the supplier's contract listing technical specifications, delivery terms, policies for return and warranties, and quantities needed. Sellers will seek blanket contracts binding them closer to the buyer.

8. Performance Review

The buyer will review how the supplier contract is working for the company and may continue, amend, or drop the seller.

> **Tip**
>
> How could a copy selling a radically new product (say laser hole punch) influence the early stage in the process. How and when could a non supplier break into for a "straight rebuy"?

A Model of Business Buyer

Transparency PM 8-2 corresponds to Figure 8.2 on p.315 and the material on p.315. Elements of the model are discussed in greater detail on the following transparency.

The Environment

The business buyer operates in a competitive environment consisting of two categories. Marketing stimuli consist of the product, place, price, and promotion. As with consumer markets, other stimuli consist of the forces in the economic, technological, political, cultural, and competitive environments. However, group membership in the business organisation and participation in the business buying process affects how these environmental forces influence decision making.

The Buying Organisation

The buying organisation is influenced by the overall organisation - its corporate culture and values, traditions, and procedures and regulations. The buying centre and the business buying decision process also differs from consumer buying influences and is discussed on a following transparency.

Buyer Responses

Buyer responses in business buying situations often consist of more alternatives than those available to consumers. Supplier choice, order quantities, delivery terms, service options, and payment terms are often more negotiable than they are to the consumer.

> **Tip**
>
> Ask, are business buyers rational and consumers not rational? If so, why do industrial sellers spend so much on entertaining the customers? Why may a business buyer be more scared of taking a risk with a business purchase (say fleet of trucks) than a purchase for themselves (new sports coat). Answer - it could be a "jobs worth" of a decision.

Notes for PM 8-2

Major Types of Business Buying Situations

Transparency PM 8-3 relates to the material on pp.316-317 and Figure 8-3.

Major Types of Buying Situations

1. Straight Rebuy

This is an industrial buying situation in which the buyer routinely reorders something without any modifications in the order. Marketers of industrial supplies seek to establish this type of relationship with the customer. When buyers place straight rebuys, competitors have little or no chance of making a sale.

2. Modified Rebuy

This is an industrial buying situation in which the buyer wants to modify product specifications, prices, terms, or suppliers. This increases the number of participants in the buying decisions thus increasing the combination of influences on the decision. "In" suppliers worry that competitors will gain some business. "Out" suppliers recognise the situation as an opportunity.

3. New Task Buying

This is an industrial buying situation in which the buyer purchases a product or service for the first time. New task buying is the most complex of buying decision processes made by a company. It is also both the greatest opportunity and challenge to the marketer. Marketers must consider that new task buying situations often arise in response to still-emerging problems seeking solutions.

Tip

Ask students how an industrial buyer reduces the risk of a "new task buy"? Could lease, rent, use existing supplier, maintenance contract, etc.

Notes for PM 8-3

Buying Centres

Transparency PM 8-4 relates to the material on pp.317-319.

Participants in Business Buying Centres

Users

These are members of the organisation who will use the product or service. Users often initiate the buying proposal and help define product specifications.

Influencers

These are people who affect the buying decision. They often help define specifications and provide information for evaluating alternatives. Technical personnel are particularly important influencers.

Buyers

These are the people with the formal authority to select the supplier and arrange terms of purchase. Buyers may influence product specifications, but their major role is in selecting vendors and negotiating.

Deciders

These are the people who have the formal or informal power to select or approve the final suppliers.

Gatekeepers

Gatekeepers are those people who control the flow of information to others. Gatekeepers are extremely important to anyone trying to gain the co-operation of buying centre members, especially in widely- dispersed organisations.

Tip

Take an industrial purchase such as a new student accommodation (hostel) and ask about the people (users, influencers, etc.) involved in the process.

Notes for PM 8-4

Major Influences on Business Buying

Transparency PM 8-5 corresponds to Figure 8.4 on p.320 and the material on pp.319-324.

Major Influences Are:

1. Environmental Factors

Industrial buyers are heavily influenced by the economic environment especially the level of primary demand, economic outlook, and the cost of money. Materials shortages are also increasing in importance.

2. Organisational Factors

These factors stem from each organisation's objectives, policies, procedures, and ways of doing business. Marketers must identify how each of these elements are manifest in a particular company.

3. Interpersonal Factors

Interpersonal influences centre on group dynamics and the interplay of personalities and organisational roles. Buyer roles within the buying unit may differ not only from organisational factors but from the interpersonal interaction of the individuals involved as well.

4. Individual Factors

A person's age, status, education, professional speciality, and overall personality and attitudes affect how they participate in organisational buying decisions. It may be difficult for the marketer to identify individual factors directly.

Tip

Use the student accommodation example again. How might the building be influenced by the four major factors? What would increase the chance of it being built and what would reduce it?

Notes for PM 8-5

Institutional and Government Markets

These notes relate to the material on pp.329-332.

Institutional Markets

Characteristics of Institutional Markets

Institutional markets are characterised by low budgets and captive patrons. Those marketing to institutions need to be aware that buyers may not be seeking strict cost minimisation nor addressing profit maximisation.

Government Markets

Characteristics of Government Markets

Governments engage in centralised buying. Governments are also carefully watched by outside publics and subject to public review. Non economic criteria also influence government buying decisions. Governments require suppliers to submit bids. Identifying who participates in government buying decisions is important. Each agency has some say in how it buys and institutions attempt to centralise common purchases.

Major Influences

Major influences on government buying decisions include not only employees charged with buying responsibilities but also lobbying for political favours by professional lobbyists. Government paperwork is also a significant influence on the process. How government makes decision is frustrating to many business people. The red tape, bureaucracy, regulation, cost over value emphasis, delays and personnel changes often discourage small suppliers from attempting to crack government markets.

Comments on Discussing the Issues

1. Students could discuss and distinguish the 4P's of both the fashion clothing and military uniform market. They could also explain the decision processes that transpire from idea generation to post purchase evaluation for both markets. In addition, they need to explain who participates in the buying process in both instances. As far as product is concerned, for the military market, fashion is not perceived as important. Quality (ability to perform functions, durability, reliability) is of primary importance. On the other hand, fashion item is a highly personal product. People want to buy clothes which reflect their self-image..

2. **(a)** BMW's first purchase of a new form of car computers would be a new-task buying situation, with many details to be worked out regarding performance, reliability, and price.

   (b) Volkswagen's purchase of spark plugs from a familiar supplier would be a straight rebuy, unless VW wanted some modifications in product prices or terms, which would make the purchase a modified rebuy.

   (c) Honda's purchase of light bulbs for its Legend model could involve any of the three buying situations. Honda could treat the purchase as a straight rebuy, it could use the leverage of higher production volumes to negotiate better prices or terms, or it could keep Honda and Acura production completely separate and treat the purchase as a new task.

3. Identifying the members of the buying centre may be difficult or even impossible. Some can be identified by asking the original contact person, such as a purchasing agent, who else will be involved in the purchase. However, this person may not know - or may not want to reveal - everyone who is in the buying centre. Therefore, the company may use advertising media to reach a variety of organisation members in order to persuade people it cannot reach in person.

   In selling dictation equipment to a law firm, for example, a company would want to identify users (lawyers and secretaries), influencers (such as an office manager), and buyers and deciders (a purchasing agent, partner, or even the head of the firm). Gatekeepers could be an important factor, too. If a single member of the firm made the purchase decision, his or her secretary could have a large impact on the decision by making it easy or difficult for a salesperson to see the decider.

4. One important environmental factor that would affect the purchase of radar speed detectors is the political climate: Do national and local governments support "get tough" approaches to law enforcement? Is any form of public funding tied to the percentage of people speeding on the motorways? Is it easy or hard to convict speeders on the basis of radar detection?

   Another environmental factor is the economic environment. If the economy is troubled, tax revenues may be down, and national and local governments may not have funds for radar equipment.

   Technological developments are another relevant environmental factor. These developments allow prices to go down, improve quality (for example, laser speed detectors have been developed that speeders cannot tell are in operation, as they can with radar devices), and even reduce manpower requirements. As in many European cities), a Swiss-made robot detects and photographs speeders automatically!

5. The rationale for promoting the industrial product to the general public is explained by the concept of *derived demand*. Industrial demand is affected by consumer demand for the product. Generating consumer demand for industrial product was an effective way of creating industrial demand, despite the high costs of the promotion.

This strategy is known as a "pull" strategy: Consumer demand pulls the product through the channel of distribution, creating industrial demand and stimulating resellers to carry the product. This strategy is not limited to industrial markets, it is frequently used with reseller markets. For more discussion of pull strategies (and the opposite approach, "push" strategies), see "Push versus Pull Strategy" in Chapter 18.

6. The reason why some industrial companies advertise their products to the general public is that they want to stimulate demand in an indirect way. The best way to explain this fact is to look at some examples. Some steel manufacturers tend to use this strategy. By increasing customer awareness about steel cans, these companies could persuade customers to buy drinks in cans made of steel instead of aluminium or glass. They use such arguments as quick chill properties, weight differences or recycling possibilities. This advertising policy increases the use of such cans and thus stimulates the sales of steel. Boeing has used this strategy as well to promote the benefits of air travel. By doing so, the demand in this kind of transportation is increased and in a derivative way, the demand for aircrafts (industrial product) is also increased.

Comments on Applying the Concepts

1. Students are advised to use the business buyer behaviour model in answering this question. He or she needs to; (1) Find out what kinds of books that the college/university needs; (2) Demonstrate a differential advantage e.g. price or quality; (3) Understand the decision making unit of the university/college. This is essential since this will affect the "approach" method; (4) Provide relevant information for the decision making unit members to make rational choices. As buyers increasingly treat suppliers as partners, good buyer-seller relationships should be built which can be achieved by; (1) Helping customers by providing free or low cost services, suppliers can build goodwill and foster close relationship with them ; (2) Giving free sample (books) to the decision making groups and proactive follow-up should be done in order to provide customers with reassurance; (3) Creating systems that link the customer to the supplier e.g. through reorder system or just-in-time delivery. The business buyer behaviour model helps sales representatives to analyse the buying part thoroughly and strategies can be employed effectively. There are various parties involved, for example; (1) Library and bookshops as buying centres; (2) Course team members who agree on the books to recommend for student adoption as deciders; (3) Librarians as deciders; (4) Individual tutors could be initiators and influencers; (6) Students as buyers. The initiators, deciders and influencers can be dealt with through personal contact or interaction approach. Buyers could be dealt with by offering more economical textbooks e.g. soft cover textbooks. Where decision making unit members are inaccessible, advertising or direct mail may be used.

2. Key factors that a local government institution should consider when deciding to purchase new coffee-making machines for users in its offices are: (1) The number of workers in each of the offices; (2) The total number of coffee-making machines needed; (3) The types of coffee that most employees drink; (4) The location to place these machines; (5) The usage level of these machines; (6) The variety of choices and prices of these machines; (7) The services (for maintenance and servicing) of the supplier of these machines. As a potential supplier, students need to emphasise the product's price, quality, different functions, durability, warranty, instalment and maintenance service. Products can be sold at discounted rate depending on the number of machines needed. Examples of companies that are current users of the product could be given to this customer (Government institution) in order to raise credibility.

Case 8
Troll-AEG

Synopsis

In January 22, 1992, two manufacturers of lighting elements (lamps), one Spanish and one German, were schedule to sign two (mirror) reciprocal international distribution agreements. AEG-LT, the German partner, would sell in Germany the indoor accent lighting elements manufactured by JFP-TROLL, the Spanish partner. Vice-versa, JFP-TROLL would undertake to sell, in Spain and France, the lighting elements manufactured by AEG-LT. The case describes the gestation of this multinational marketing alliance from the point of view of JFP-TROLL, up to the evening of January 21, 1992, that is, just the day before the signing of the agreements.

Teaching Objectives

1. Encourage students to become more familiar with the SWOT analysis.
2. Identify the different parties involved in a buying and selling situation.
3. Apply the consumer behaviour model on an international basis.

Study Questions

1. What are the major strengths and weaknesses of the Catalan company? How and why did they change over time? What were the major strategic shifts of JFP and what stimulated them?

Some strengths that students should mention are; (1) JFP has developed a diverse range of products which they manufacture or buy from other companies. Originally the company had a very small product portfolio; (2) The company has created an extra incentive to its sales people by offering higher commissions than other companies; (3) In some ways the company has been innovative, which in their domestic market is seen as having a competitive advantage: (4) JFP is an old, well established company which always had a reputation for reliability and quality; (5) JFP has developed some products that are very distinctive in comparison to the competitors products; (6) The company has in some respects moved towards a more marketing based approach to manufacturing; (7) The leaders of the company are strong and highly-motivated; (8) The alliances which the company has developed with three non-competing companies give strength to its bargaining power; (9) An effectively managed and economically sound company. Some weaknesses students could highlight are; (1) The company in many circumstances has displayed a lack of strategic planning ; (2) In new areas such as those relating to prescribers, the success rate of 1 to 10 is very low and a waste of resources; (3) The company's margins are being reduced; (4) The company is based on the entrepreneurial spirit of its owners. In many ways as the company expands the owners may lose control of the organisation. Red tape may also increase. These are just some examples of strengths and weaknesses. Students are encouraged to add more to this list.

It is best for students to answer this part by looking at the company from 1974 to 1992. In 1974, Miguel and his brother Xavier became owners of the business which is at that time described as small and outmoded with only 15 employees. The change - started selling

Nordart Industria SA's entire output of spot projectors, power tracks and adaptors under the TROLL brand name. In 1978, the managers realised that the future was TROLL. The change - merger between JFP and Nordart Industria SA. This leads to an increase of the workforce, a rise in sales and JFP becomes the market leader in accent lighting elements. The firm wanted to succeed in this market and so decided to create a competitive advantage with a differentiated product. The change - changes in distribution channel and continuous improvements and redesign of its products. Around this time also, their distribution channel moved from a traditional approach (lamp retailers) to a pioneering one i.e. developing the concept of the wholesales-stockists. An alliance was formed between JFP, a wire company, a transformer company and a cable fastener company whose products were sold through the same electrical goods stores. The aim of this alliance was to reinforce JFP's negotiating power with its wholesalers. In addition, JFP reduced the colour range of its lamps from 16 to 4 and a new system of universal connector was implemented. The aim of these changes was to reduce the number of stock-keeping units. The result was a dramatic increase in turnover for the warehouses. In 1985, JFP started to commission original designs of lighting elements from the freelance industrial designers. JFP wanted its lighting elements to be immediately recognisable. In 1988, JFP decided to expand abroad choosing France as a starting point (46 pta million of exports). This was a response to a fiercer competition in Spain (price wars and an increase of lamps' manufacturers). Other activities around this time period are: JFP decided to offer an integral, complete and coherent product range in France. The aim was to achieve a significant level of sales in France. Development of a new generation of lighting elements. This is done to create a competitive advantage by the way of differentiating products within a highly competitive market where all competitors provide similar designs. In 1989, the recruitment of Javier Rocasalbas as general manager because of strong increase in demand and Miguel is becoming more and more overwhelmed with the complexity of the company's business. In 1990. Phillipe Martinez became the new TROLL France general manager. JFP entered into a contract to supply a Dutch outlet. A proposal was made of a contract between AEG and JFP. In 1991, they terminated relationship with Barcelona and Madrid representatives. 21st January 1992 JFP's owner Miguel de la Pena had cold feet.

Basically we have answered part 3 in part 2. To reiterate some of the vital strategic shifts are: (1) Merger with Nordart Industria SA. Stimuli - outdated products and success of the previous agreement; (2) JFP make an alliance with three non-competing companies and change distribution policy. Stimuli - limited negotiating power, new products difficult to promote and limited range of products; (3) Improve quality and increase production capacity. Stimuli - increasing demand, lack of capacity supply, too long lead times, lack of internal organisation in production and good design but poor technical aspects; (4) Decide to influence prescribers. Stimuli - environmental changes, understanding of the buying process and sophistication of the sector; (5) Decide to penetrate the European market (internationalisation). Stimuli - intuition, fiercer competition in Spain and price wars.

2. What are the roles in the buying centre for lamps towards the end of the case? How does the market vary across Europe?

A buying centre is "all those individuals and groups who participate in the decision making process, who share common goals and the risks arising from the decisions". The individuals who take part in the buying process can be grouped under six headings; initiators, users, influencers, buyers, deciders and gatekeepers. As far as the lighting market is concerned, the buying centre could be described as follows; (1) Initiator - this would be the precribers who creates the interest and awareness of a need for a specific lighting type for the business. This is communicated to the owner of the business; (2) Users - the owner of the company who the prescriber is working for and perhaps the people working in the building and offices; (3) Influencers - accountants may point out financial implications while the people who will install the system (electricians) may point out practical implications. Both of these implications could affect the decision; (4) Decider - Possibly the owner of the firm; (5) Buyer - actual purchase could be made by the purchasing manager; (6) Influencer - the prescriber would supply information and advice relating to the possible lighting which could be purchased; (7) Gatekeeper - There is no obvious gatekeepers to be identified in this situation. It should be noted that these roles will differ from organisation to organisation i.e. the buyer may be the production manager or perhaps the contractor.

A number of differences can be observed between the various lighting markets within Europe. This fact has hindered JFP's attempts at internationalisation. The variations are best noted if the countries which JFP tried to enter are looked at individually. Diversity of taste is a main factor for example, the Belgians are bias towards the classic light design whereas in Germany there is a trend towards technical decorative indoor lighting. These differences create a need for product modification. The diversity demanded also differed. JFP observed that the limited product range which was successful in Spain was not sufficient for the French market, who demanded an integral, complete and coherent lighting elements. In addition the products did not meet French standards. Price differentials also exist. Austrians tend to prefer the premium price lighting elements while the Spanish looked for the lower priced products. These differences suggest that just because a product is successful in Spain it does not mean the same product will be successful throughout Europe. It is required for a light manufacturer who wishes to expand on a European scale, that products are differentiated and diversified to suit the target market. This fact was identified by JFP's management. There are many other answers that student could highlight in this question.

3. How does JFP seek to influence people in the buying process? What mistakes were made in Spain and France?

Since 1978 JFP influenced people in the buying process in three different stages and ways. The first stage was characterised by trying to motivate the self-employed representatives with a 10% commission. This proved successful. Other measures that were not part of a wider planned strategy include; trying to influence people in the buying process by cutting prices in the face of competition and creating a second "fighting" brand name; TROLL. This strategy seemed to work reasonably well for JFP's basic products, but for the selling of technical architectural lighting the company changed their tactics. For the technical architectural lighting products JFP recognised that they had to influence three sets of people in the buying process; the prescriber, contractors and owners. JFP concentrated primarily on the prescriber as they recognised that it is this group who carried the most influence in the buying process. Prescribers were made up of architects, interior decorators, shop window designers, engineers and technicians specialising in lighting and so on. JFP decided that is vital to influence the prescriber during the early stages of building. Firstly, this was done through the original reps (who wanted to be fully independent by this time and who were not familiar with the new products) and four new "well-groomed" female employees to help the reps promote to the prescriber. It soon became clear that this arrangement was not working. It was then that the total solution idea took shape i.e. solving the prescriber's problem from design to installation or at least help them solve it by providing them with the necessary technical data, free product samples and so on. The third and final stage was the opening of the sales office and showroom and the ending of the link with the sales reps in Barcelona and Madrid. At the end of 1991, JFP started to target the prescriber market specifically with their new sales force using "maturing process" method of attempting to influence them during the blue-print stage, Salespeople continued also to target wholesalers with the original products.

The major mistake in Spain was the failure to hold onto market share. Two internal problems were partially responsible for this; technical quality was poor and JFP suffered from a mediocre image. For the technical lighting there was the significant distribution problems. The tried and trusted wholesalers-stockholders did not buy and did not distribute the technical products because they were too sophisticated. This leads to the central problem of JFP. JFP can be characterised as having a reactionary management style. They rely more on reacting to situations and problems rather than planning. Moreover, they are not a marketing led company. They remain product centric and evidently do not hold marketing research as important.

". . . if Troll products sold well in Spain, they should also be successful in France". This summarises JFP's entire marketing strategy concerning their movements in France. This lack of planning and research was the sole reason for their lack of immediate success and problems. The quality was not right, the prices were not right and the products were not even certified as conforming to French standards. Furthermore, JFP suffered from an incomplete and non-integrated product range. They did not market fluorescent panels in offices for example. This mess is all as the result of lack of research in their French target market and therefore a total lack of planning.

4. Was JFP internationalisation wise and successful? What are they looking for in their joint ventures? Would you recommend them to sign the deal with AEG-LT?

Students will generally say that JFP's internationalisation was not so much wise but essential. From 1988 onwards the market in Spain became much fiercer with profits being slashed through increased competition and the erosion of the market share. As the case study indicates, prices slashed sales margins from 30 per cent in 1988 to around 15 per cent in 1991. JFP was indeed wise to go international because the Spanish market had reached its short-term potential and competition had become severe. Unfortunately as detailed in the answer to the previous question, JFP's internationalisation to France has not been wildly successful due to lack of careful planning and ignorance of the French market. However, JFP appear to be learning from their mistakes and are making a modest success of their exploits in the French market.

The managers at JFP are certainly not looking to lose control of their company through joint ventures. JFP is primarily concerned with expanding into foreign markets. The problem with this is their lack of knowledge of the countries they would like to expand into. Joint ventures serve to draw on the partnering company's knowledge of the market in that particular country. JFP are specifically looking for knowledge that covers distribution and the demands of the particular foreign market. They are evidently eager to not repeat the learning curve they had in France. A joint venture is a way of short cutting this painful learning curve.

Most students will say to go ahead with the contract after considering all of the above issues. JFP should sign with AEG because they need AEG's knowledge of the German market and the distribution network. However JFP needs to direct attention to its product specifications and product quality in order to protect the company. It needs to tailor its product and promotional strategy towards the German market. Failure to do this, even with the might of the AEG distribution network, may well result in failure.

Teaching Suggestions

This case can also be used in the Global Marketplace Chapter (Chapter 5).

Additional Information

Just a few months after the signing of the contracts, the Spanish peseta was devalued three times in less than one year. The exchange rate which had been around 62-63 pesetas per deutsche mark, went to 76 pesetas per dm in May 1993. In October 1994, the exchange rate was around 83 pesetas/DM. Some general conclusions; (1) Overall the Spain to Germany stream of business was a modest success. The Germany to Spain side was a failure; (2) Alliances should be made between companies of similar sizes and similar corporate cultures; (3) Complementary at first sight - product lines can turn out to be relatively less complementary than expected due to the subsegments of the market, which require different salesforce and different ways of serving the subsegment; (4) Language and cultural barriers should not be underestimated especially regarding the hard, day to day implementation efforts; (5) The implementation of alliances will involve many organisational levels in participating companies, well beyond the general managers who negotiated and signed the agreement; (6) The feared (hidden agenda) did not exist but unexpectedly strong difficulties appeared, due to environmental factors (economic decline and devaluation) and the hardships of the Daimler-Benz Group.

Overview Case III
Jacobs Kaffee Wien:
Spreading a Golden Light

Synopsis

Klaus Jacobs founded Kaffee Wien in 1961 as the first foreign subsidiary of Jacobs Kaffee Bremen. Jacob's business is involved in four areas; (1) Coffees for private households; (2) Coffees for the catering sector; (3) Coffees of the Hag Company (Cafe Hag and Colombian); (4) Food sector - including ready to serve meals, soft cheese, etc. With the household sector, Jacob's has positioned his brands to be identified with different segments; premium or quality segment - Monarch; decaffeinated segment - Night and day; mild segment - Mild and Fine; price segment - Meisterrostung, Edelmocca and Merido. The brand managers of the various countries are responsible to take into account variations in coffee taste of the local inhabitants. In Austria, competition in the coffee industry is fierce. Jacob's Monarch is the market leader with 10.6% market share. There is high penetration in the Austrian market with 96% of Austrian households buying coffee. There is little brand loyalty where only 15% of purchasers are loyal to a single brand. Coffee drinkers switch brands depending on the consumption occasion. The brand used depends on whether it is a weekday or holiday, daytime or night-time or for own consumption or as a gift. Consumers make the choice at the point of sale except when they go to specialised coffee shops where the choice of shop determines choice of brand.

In Austria people develop brand preference when they are young. The love of coffee is part of the traditional coffee-house culture. Coffee is part of social ritual and a natural part of everyday life. The Austrian coffee advertisement show harmony, atmosphere, enjoyment and self-actualisation. German advertisements on the other hand, often show problem situations - where social recognition of the buyer depends on the choice of the correct or wrong coffee. There are two significant trends within the European market; (1) The market is polarising towards premium or price-conscious segments; (2) Lifestyle issues are growing in importance. People care more about their health and prefer "green" products and socially responsible producers. Jacob's plan to launch a new product containing less caffeine and irritants than the regular coffee but still offering complete enjoyment and flavour. Jacob's tested a few names and has found that the name Monarch Golden Light is perceived as a high quality mild coffee. The incorporation of the name Monarch is to counter the association of "light" with no flavour and transfer the image of high quality and full flavour coffee.

Teaching Objectives

1. Provide students with an opportunity to apply some of the ideas presented in Part III of the text.

2. Help students to see how the major factors affecting consumer's behaviour in the purchase fast moving consumer goods such as coffee.

3. Allow students to discuss market and positioning between existing brand/product and new extended product/brand.

4. Allow students to apply concepts from Part III to Jacob's situation.

Study Questions

1. Describe an extensive, a limited and a routine coffee purchase. Which of them occurs most often and why?

Extensive problem solving is usually associated with three conditions; (1) The alternatives are differentiated and numerous; (2) There is an adequate amount of time available for deliberation; (3) The purchase has a high degree of involvement. Extensive coffee purchases are made by those consumers who feel it is important to buy the right kind of coffee. This happens when the coffee buyer wants to buy coffee of the highest in quality or flavour, either for his or her own consumption or for social occasions such as Christmas, as a gift and etc. This type of purchase involves a high degree of information gathering and high level of search and examination of alternative coffee brands, ingredients, packaging and price. Other factors include, type of coffee, e.g. a rich, dark roast or mild decaffeinated, country of origin such as Kenya and Colombia.

Limited problem solving occurs when buyers confront an unfamiliar brand in a familiar product class. He or she is fully aware of the product class but may not be familiar with all the brands and their features. In the case of coffee, one would assume that the customer has already used the product or a small range of the product, but still check a few factors such as price. The final choice may be made based on price and can be influenced by advertising and other promotional activities. This type of consumer is likely to switch brands regularly rather than being loyal to one brand

Routine purchase is generally the simplest type of buying behaviour. It occurs when consumers buy low-cost, frequently purchase items. These buyers have very few decisions to make. They know a lot about the product class and major brands available, and they have fairly clear preferences amongst the brands. Routine coffee buying is made by purchasers who do not evaluate the possible alternatives. This is due to the fact that they have bought the product before and are satisfied with its quality. Repeat buying may be reinforced by advertising which keeps the brand name in the consumers mind.

Some students will say that coffee buying is a limited problem solving purchase while others will say that is a routine response behaviour. Ask students for reasons why they say it is "routine" or "limited". Generally, it is a routine behaviour because; (1) Coffee's price is relatively low compared with major purchases such as cars etc.; (2) Coffee has high penetration (96% of Austrian households buy coffee); (3) There is little brand loyalty (only 15% according to the case study); (4) Buyers usually decide the brand at the point of sale.

2. What are possible stimuli that may start the buyer decision process? How can the process be influenced in Jacobs' favour?

The buying process starts with problem recognition. This stage can be referred to as the perception of difference between the desired state of affairs and the actual situation sufficient to activate the decision making process. To activate the purchase process the need must be of sufficient importance and the consumer must believe that the solution is within his or her means. Students should mention that here are different factors that influence the likelihood of a need to be activated: (1) Time - as time passes the actual state of the consumer may change. For example, a person may gradually run out of coffee and thus his actual state changes. A change can also occur in the desired state as the consumer may change his taste and thus will realise a need for a different type of coffee; (2) Changed circumstances - a person who is promoted to a highly regarded position in his organisation may change his lifestyle and purchase brands that will suit his new status; (3) Product acquisition - the purchase of a certain product may activate the need for other products. For example a person purchasing a new coffee machine may have the desire to buy more types of coffee or a different type of coffee; (4) Product consumption - the actual consumption of a product creates a need. The coffee may be running out creating a need to purchase more. If the coffee that was purchased previously did not live up to expectations, a need may be created to buy a different type or brand of coffee; (5) Marketing influences - marketer can activate the needs of the consumer. A basic objective of many advertising is to stimulate consumers' awareness of their needs. For example, selective need recognition occurs when there is a need for a specific brand within a product category. Jacob's may use this to his advantage by creating advertising that will activate the need for his coffee amongst consumers. As the Austrians buy coffee for self actualisation and enjoyment, Jacob's can produce advertising relating his coffee to self enhancement. By knowing people's attitudes, values, beliefs and trends, Jacob's can produce advertising that associates his coffee with those attributes mentioned earlier. For example, the Monarch Light brand can be associated with the trend towards "health" and premium coffees. Need recognition can also be activated by marketing tools at the point of sale. Consumers may see a display that reminds them of an unrealised need or alternatively the display may directly activate a previously unrecognised need. Product innovation can also creates a need. The new innovative coffee by Jacob's may trigger a need for that coffee as it may solve a recent created need for consumers; (6) Individual differences - at one extreme are the actual state types, for whom need recognition is triggered typically by changes in the actual state, while at the other extreme are the desired state types, for whom the need is recognised from changes in the environment. As an example, for actual state types, the need for a new jar of coffee tends to be recognised only when they have run out of coffee, whereas for desired state types, the need for a new jar of coffee may be the desire for something new due to an advertising influence, etc.

Consumers make decision based on their perceptions rather than objective reality. It is therefore vital for marketers to recognise the efficiency of targeting their products to the perceived needs of consumers in order to maximise the likelihood that their products will be perceived by the potential prospects. Students will provide a variety of answers. Some students will mention that marketing research is important i.e. to determine what consumers consider to be ideal attributes of coffee. The marketer can then segment the market based on these needs. As there is a trend towards healthier coffee drinking Jacob's should try and create the image of the new product as the healthy alternative. In terms of advertisements, many factors need to be considered. Jacob's should take into account the steps in developing effective advertising campaign such as; (1) Determining the target audience; (2) Effect sought; (3) Message; (4) Medium; (5) Source; (6) Feedback. For example, to promote the high quality Monarch brand they could use magazines and quality newspapers for their advertising campaigns. Television advertising would be an appropriate medium to promote their coffee product at the lower end of the market. In addition, with respect to packaging, it is important that every aspect of the package - its name, shape, colour, label, copy - provide sufficient sensory stimulation to be noted and remembered.

3. How does the buyer decision process for Jacob's coffee compare with that for Eduscho coffee? What factors affect the behaviour of coffee consumers? Would you recommend introducing Monarch Golden Light into the German market also?

For the Jacob customers, in their buyer decision process, it may start with the problem recognition that there is a short of coffee or a need for drinking coffee. They may then decide to put it into their shopping list. The information search for the coffee will be derived only from their past experience of Jacob's coffee and the awareness of coffee brands through advertising. At the point of sale, the customer begins to evaluate the alternatives, packaging, special offer or shortage of other brands, all may influence the decision. However, the time spent on this purchase decision is not long. It may just be a glimpse on the shelf and then a decision to buy is made as it is only a low involvement item. After consumption of Jacob's coffee, consumer may form an opinion; whether it satisfies their need and become a habitual drinker/purchaser of Jacob's or otherwise. For the Eduscho customer, the problem recognition may be the same with Jacob. However, it could also be based on their past experience with Eduscho or visiting one of Eduscho coffee shop as there is a high degree of brand loyalty with Eduscho coffee drinkers. They may then remind themselves to stop at Eduscho to buy the coffee. The evaluation of alternatives will be, for Eduscho brands within Eduscho shops, or they have decided already at home. The purchase decision will also be made within a short period of time. The post purchase behaviour will be stronger than Jacobs' users. They may remember their preference of drinking Eduscho as they make a greater effort to go to the Eduscho shop and purchase the item. They perceived it as a better than average coffee. So, if Eduscho can fulfil their needs, they may become loyal customer.

Students should highlight factors such as; (1) Culture - Austrian culture of having coffee to "spoil oneself"; (2) Price; (3) Occasion which coffee will be consumed; (4) Taste - either strong or mild with less irritants to the stomach; (5) Caffeine and irritant content - important to health conscious; (6) Brand name and qualities associated with it; (7) Advertising and promotional activity.

Students will pose two arguments here. Some will say that at this stage they will not recommend the introduction of Monarch Golden Light to the German market. The use of the brand name Monarch Golden Light which is used in the Austrian market may not bring the same effect for the German market. The German premium coffee brand is called Kronung which has a different recipe and taste to suit the German preference for fine sour coffee. As Monarch taste is strong it would not be suitable for the German market. Other students will say that Monarch Golden should be considered for introduction into penetrate the German market. The health and "green" awareness among consumers will make Monarch more appealing. Nevertheless, further details should be analysed before making the final decision.

4. Why should consumers judge a coffee Monarch Light differently from a neutral light coffee? What dangers are inherent within the proposed brand extension?

Monarch is the brand leader in Austria. Its name is synonymous with quality and flavour. By associating the new coffee with Monarch it will persuade current drinkers of Monarch who enjoy the taste but would prefer less caffeine and irritants to try Monarch Light. It will also attract those coffee drinkers already in the coffee-light segment. The current consumers of light-coffee will be influenced by the brand strength of Monarch and may be persuaded to try the new Monarch Light coffee.

There is a danger that the introduction of the new product may cause existing regular buyers of Monarch to switch to Monarch Light thus reducing sales of Monarch. Consumers may try the new Monarch Light product and dislike it, this feeling of dissatisfaction may be extended to the original brand and undermine its strength on the marketplace.

Teaching Suggestions

Instructors may ask students to contact manufacturers of coffee and light coffee and supermarkets that carry the different types of coffee. The students might interview brand managers to discuss the current market situation of the different types of coffees in your area or country.

This case may also be used with the New Products Chapter (Chapter 13) and the Promotion Chapter (Chapter 18).

Jokes and Quotes

Said of one industrial product; It may be fertiliser to you but it's my bread and butter.

A bribe is when the giver says, "Thanks", and the receiver says, "Don't mention it."
ANON

Businessmen get together and complain about bad business over the most expensive dinners.
ANON

A businessman is one who talks golf all morning at the office and business all afternoon on the links.
ANON

The formula for achieving a successful relationship is simple: you should treat all disasters as if they were trivialities but never treat a triviality as if it were a disaster.
QUENTIN CRISP

Remember, the client's indecision is final.
KEN HORNSBY

The role of the receptionist is an important one. She is the first person you see when you visit a company. And, if she's doing her job right, she's the only person you see.
JOKE

The two industrial giants after the Acme Paint's business arranged a meeting with the chairman of Acme to argue the matter out. But the bargaining had no sooner begun than one tycoon shouted, "You're a liar!". The other responded, "You're a cheat!". Now that you two have identified each other, "said the paint company boss, "let's get on with our business."
JOKE

Always go for the top man.
WENDELL PHILLIPS

The best salesman we ever heard of was the one who sold two milking machines to a farmer who had only one cow. Then this salesman helped finance the deal by taking the cow as down payment on the two milking machines.
HERBERT V. PROCHNOW

A dinner lubricates business.
WILLIAM SCOTT

A civil servant is still to me an arrogant fool till he proved otherwise.
NEVIL SHUTE

The one thing that has been proved abundantly in aviation is that government officials are totally ineffective in engineering development.
NEVIL SHUT

A diamond is forever.
SLOGAN (DE BEERS)

Part IV

Core Strategy

Chapter 9
Market Segmentation and Targeting

Chapter Objectives

After reading this chapter, you should be able to:

1. Define market segmentation and market targeting.
2. List and discuss the major bases for segmenting consumer and business markets.
3. Explain how companies identify attractive market segments and choose a market-coverage strategy.

Chapter Overview

Sellers can take three approaches to a market. Mass marketing is the decision to mass-produce and mass-distribute one product and attempt to attract all kinds of buyers. Product-variety marketing is the decision to produce two or more market offers differentiated in style, features, quality, or sizes, designed to offer variety to the market and to set the seller's products apart from competitors' products. Target marketing is the decision to identify the different groups that make up a market and to develop products and marketing mixes for selected target markets. Sellers are moving away from mass marketing and product differentiation toward target marketing. The key steps in target marketing are market segmentation, market targeting, and market positioning.

Teaching Notes

Refer to the following pages for teaching notes.

Markets

Transparency PM 9-1 corresponds to Figure 9-1 on p.354.

Market Segmentation

Market segmentation is the process of dividing a market into distinct groups of buyers who might require separate products or marketing mixes. All buyers have unique needs and wants. Still it is usually possible in consumer markets to identify relatively homogeneous portions or segments of the total market according to shared preferences, attitudes, or behaviours that distinguish them from the rest of the market. These segments may require different products and/or separate mixes.

Market Targeting

Market targeting is the process of evaluating each market segment's attractiveness and selecting one or more segments to enter. Given effective market segmentation, the firm must choose which markets to serve and how to serve them. In targeting markets to serve the firm must consider its resources and objectives in setting strategy.

Market Positioning

Market positioning he process of formulating competitive positioning for a product and a detailed marketing mix. Marketers must plan how to present the product to the consumer. The product's position is defined by how consumers view it on important attributes.

Tip

Ask students to consider the holiday market and ask how firms have segmented it, what targets they have chosen and their positioning; examples are Saga aimed at retired people, Mark Warner aimed at families, Club 18-30 aimed at them.

Notes for PM 9-1

Market Segmentation

Transparency PM 9-2 relates to the material on pp.355-369.

Bases for Segmenting Markets

1. Geographic Segmentation

Geographic segmentation divides the market into different geographic units based upon physical proximity. While location determines how geographic segmentation is done, it is also true that many consumer products have attribute differences associated with regional tastes.

2. Demographic Segmentation

Dividing the market into groups based upon variables such as sex, age, family size, family life cycle, income, education, occupation, religious affiliation, or nationality are all demographic segmentation. Consumer needs often vary with demographic variables. Demographic information is also relatively easy to measure. Age and life-cycle stage, sex, and income are three major demographic bases for segmentation.

3. Psychographic Segmentation

Psychographic segmentation divides the market into groups based on social class, life style, or personality characteristics. Psychographic segmentation cuts across demographic differences. Social class preferences reflect values and preferences that remain constant even as income increases. Life style helps to group markets around ideas such as health, youthful, or environmentally conscious. Personalities may transcend other differences in markets and may be transferred to products themselves.

4. Behaviour Segmentation

Behaviour segmentation divides markets into groups based on their knowledge, attitudes, uses, or responses to a product. Types of behaviour segmentation are based upon occasions, benefits sought, user status, usage rates, loyalty, buyer readiness stage, and attitude.

Tip

Ask how the clothing market could be segmented on each of the above lines. Ask for more than one way in each major base such as wealth and climate in geographic.

Notes for PM 9-2

Geodemographics

Transparency PM 9-3 combines text and extratextual information. It also relates to Table 9-1 and Marketing Highlight 9-1.

Innovative research companies (featured in chapter 6) utilise geodemographic segmentation variables to describe potential markets.

Geodemographics combine demographic, geographic, psychographic, and behaviouristic segmentation variables to identify markets for products much more narrowly than other segmentation strategies. Geodemographics lends itself best to marketing mix strategies utilising technological innovation to reach consumers with product information. The two marketing areas that benefit most from geodemography are direct marketing via mail and telephone and computer-based marketing. These are discussed more in chapters 18, 19, 20, 21, 22 on communication and distribution.

Direct Marketing

Use of telephones and postal mailings without prior qualification of leads are generating grass roots movements for regulation. Geodemography makes it more likely that direct marketers will contact more people who have already expressed an interest in the product or are very likely, statistically speaking, to appreciate information on a relevant product for their geodemographic group. In discussion, you may want to raise questions about the role of marketing ethics in generating and using these increasingly specific databases.

Computer-based Marketing

In the US over 300,000 people now subscribe to computer shopping services such as PRODIGY that provides consumers with on-line information and services via their personal computer and modem. With PC consumers can bank, order from catalogues, receive information, check stock prices and do trades - all right at their desktop. While the user requests information on-line, mainframe computers track their information search patterns and record orders and requests for more detailed information to create more databases segmentation.

Tip

Ask how geodemographic databases influence the amount of junk mail people get. Most people think it creates more but marketers say targeting reduces inappropriate materials being sent.

Notes for PM 9-3

Segmenting Business Markets

Transparency PM 9-4 relates to the material on pp.369-371 and Table 9.4.

Major Segmentation Variables for Business Markets

1. Demographics

Industry segmentation focuses on which industries buy the product. Company size can be used. Geographic location may be used to group businesses by proximity.

2. Operating Variables

Business markets can be segmented by technology (what customer technologies should we focus on?), user/nonuser status (heavy, medium, light), or customer capabilities (those needing many or few services).

3. Purchasing Approaches

Five approaches are possible. Segmentation can be by purchasing function organisation (centralised or decentralised), power structure (selecting companies controlled by a functional speciality), the nature of existing relationships (current desirable customers or new desirable customers), general purchase policies (focus on companies that prefer some arrangements over others such as leasing, related support service contracts, sealed bids), or purchasing criteria (focus on noncompensatory criteria such as price, service, or quality).

4. Situational Factors

Situational segmentation may be based upon urgency (such as quick delivery needs), specific application (specific uses for the product) or size of order (few large or many small accounts).

5. Personal Characteristics

Personal comparisons can lead to segmentation by buyer-seller similarity (companies with similar personnel and values), attitudes toward risk (focus on risk-taking or risk-avoiding companies), or loyalty (focus on companies that show high loyalty to their suppliers.

Tip

Ask how the market for mail is segmented by how secure (Securicor) or how quick (Data Post) a piece of mail needs to be.

Notes for PM 9-4

Developing Market Segments

Transparency PM 9-5 relates to the material on p.375.

Qualitative Research

Exploratory research technique such as focus groups or depth interviews, that give clues about how people think about the market. This stage identifies what to measure quantitatively.

Quantitative Research

Survey based gathering of quantitative information on consumer attitudes, behaviour, etc. using pre-determined measures.

Analysis

Sorting of the quantitative information into segments using one or more statistical techniques (Marketing Highlight 9-2)

Validation

Statistical or experimental test to see if the segments are reliable. Questions could be, are there statistically significant differences between the segments, can they be reproduced using other data, are they managerially useable.

Profiling

Describing the segments using a memorable name, picture and their statistics.

> **Tip**
>
> Get the students to "brainstorm" the sorts of dimensions that could describe the market for writing implements, restaurants or trainers.

Notes for PM 9-5

Effective Segmentation

Transparency PM 9-6 relates to the material on pp.379.

Requirements for Effective Segmentation

1. Measurability

- Refers to the degree to which the size and purchasing power of the segments can be measured. The accuracy and availability of measures of market potential are important.

2. Accessibility

- Refers to the degree to which a market segment can be reached and served. Identifying a segment is useless if the marketer has limited access to the customer.

3. Substantiality

- Refers to the degree to which the segments are large or profitable enough to service.

4. Actionability

- Refers to the degree to which an effective marketing program can be designed for attracting and serving segments. Company resource limitations figure prominently in actionability issues.

Tip

Ask students to think of the airline market and how its discount, tourist, business and first class segments are measurable, accessible, substantial and actionable.

Notes for PM 9-6

Market Targeting

These notes relate to the material on pp.380-387.

Evaluating Market Segments

1. Segment Size and Growth

The company must collect and analyse data on current dollar sales, projected sales-growth, and expected profit margins for each market segment.

2. Segment Structural Attractiveness

Long run attractiveness includes an assessment of current and potential competitors, the threats of substitutes, and the power of buyers and suppliers.

3. Company Objectives and Resources

The company's resources and core business strengths should also fit well with the market segment opportunities.

Market Coverage Strategies

1. Undifferentiated Marketing

This strategy uses the same marketing mix for the entire market. This strategy focuses on the common needs of the market rather than differences in it. Undifferentiated marketing provides economies of scale on product costs but may be limited in application.

2. Differentiated Marketing

This strategy targets several market segments and designs separate marketing mixes for each of them. Product and marketing variation also helps company image and may produce loyalty in consumers as they change segments.

3. Concentrated Marketing

This strategy commits a company to pursue a large share of one or more submarkets. Economies and segment knowledge and service are strengths of this approach but risk due to smaller market size is greater.

Tip

What attracted Toyota and Honda to the luxury car market and how did it fit them? Why did they choose a differentiated marketing strategy for Lexus and Acura?

Comments on Discussing the Issues

1. In the UK, British Telecom employs mass marketing techniques such as advertising in the newspaper, television and magazines in an attempt to reach as many people as possible. Almost everyone has a telephone at work and at home, British Telecom is able to fulfil the needs of every potential customer but must compete with other suppliers such as Mercury Communications on service and price. Many consumer foodstuffs are mass marketed because nearly everyone uses them. Products such as baked beans, toilet rolls and bread are mass marketed as they are bought by the majority of customers in the marketplace. In the US, Ford Motor Company is a good example of a company that has evolved from a mass-marketer to a market-targeted. Ford originally made one car for the entire market—customers did not even have a choice of colours. Over time, Ford added other cars to its line (product-variety marketing), and eventually developed cars for nearly every market segment (target marketing).

   Most companies that have been around for a long time have shown a similar evolution. Procter & Gamble, for example, had been in existence more than 80 years when it introduced Ivory Flakes to supplement Ivory Soap (product variety), and was almost 90 years old when it first developed a product (Camay) to compete with an existing P&G product (Ivory) ("150 Years of P&G," *Advertising Age*, August 20, 1987, p. 10). Now, of course, P&G is one of the pre-eminent market targeting companies in the world.

   Mass marketing can be beneficial as the product has a much larger potential customer base, sales volume should therefore be significantly higher than those products aimed at a specific market segment. Not many products are suited to mass marketing as the majority of products do not meet the needs and wants of all potential consumers at a price which they can afford. Everyone may wish to own a Rolls Royce but the price restricts the number of people who are able to fulfil that wish. In the case of Rolls Royce cars mass marketing would clearly be inappropriate.

   Airlines for example offer two distinct services, one for business travellers at a premium price with a high level of service both in flight and passenger handling, the other for economy travellers such as holidaymakers, these customers receive a more austere service in flight and at the terminal but pay significantly less than the business travellers. Both services meet the needs of the market segments which has been targeted at a price acceptable to each group of travellers. By differentiating their product - the transportation of people - the airlines capture two differing segments of the market.

2. **(a)** The casual clothing market is segmented in many ways; by benefit sought (smart casual clothing to go out or something to lounge around at home), by purchase occasion (for own wear or given as gifts), by lifestyle and personality (target the trend-setters or individuals with dress sense), by gender (for example, Levi's 501 is targeted to both male and female, ask students if they have seen latest Levi's 501 advertisement), by age (younger people tend to dress more casually), by income (designer casual wear cost more than casual clothes form a department store), by geographic location (Londoners are considered trendier people than those in the North).

(b) The beer market is segmented in many ways: by region (through regional brewers and brands), income and social class (premium beers and imports versus budget beers), life style ("The original party animal"), race (especially beer versus malt liquor, which is much more popular with black consumers than white), purchase occasion ("Here's to good friends"), and usage rate ("The one beer to have when you're having more than one"). Benefit segments are also served; Miller Lite is a good example, pursuing both the "Great taste" and the "Less filling" segments.

(c) The holiday market can be segmented in may ways; by type of holiday (foreign holiday, package or camping), by benefits sought and purchase occasion (activity holiday or relax-in-the-sun holiday), by usage (those who travel a lot and those who hardly travel), by lifestyle (young and out-going or conservative and traditional), by income and social class (far-flung holiday destinations probably targeted to the upper end of the income bracket), family life cycle (young parents with children).
These are just some examples. Ask students to provide other examples.

3. The advent of the European Union (EU) has resulted in the removal of barriers to trade between the member states. The newly established trading block means that companies now have the opportunity to sell their goods in a much larger arena. Some students will say that the EU cannot be viewed as a single market segment because within that segment many sub-segments exist. A product which is successfully marketed in one country may not necessarily achieve success in another in its original form. This may be due to differing tastes, demographics, competing products, market maturity and cultures which exist in each country. Changes in packaging, pricing, promotional activity and even taste, for food items, may have to be made for the product to be successful in a different country. These changes which manufacturers have to make within the EU, implies that market segmentation is still very important because of the different market segments that exist within the EU.

Clearly marketers cannot address the EU audience as a homogeneous group. The segments must be examined for their similarities and differences, and a product or service positioned appropriately to meet the individual consumers' wants and needs. Ultimately, a marketer must sell to individuals. Market segmentation is a process of aggregating individuals with some factors in common, so they can be reached in a practical and cost-effective manner.

4. Service, selection, and reliability can all be used in benefit segmentation of industrial markets. Suppliers who want to emphasise these characteristics must identify firms that need these benefits. By better satisfying these firms' needs, the supplier is able to charge higher prices than competitors who offer fewer services or less selection. Of course, other suppliers can find market segments that do *not* need these benefits, and sacrifice service, selection, and reliability to reduce costs and be able to sell at a lower price.

5. The main advantage of the undifferentiated approach is that it requires only one, undifferentiated product, thus development costs and promotional costs will be kept to a minimum. The launch of a single product will also simplify distribution and minimise the training required for the sales force. On the other hand, whilst undifferentiated marketing requires minimal resources, it is extremely unlikely that these resources will be used to maximum effect because, by definition, they will not be focused on those segments of the market that are most likely to buy and gain satisfaction from the product or service. It is very difficult to find examples of products or service providers that have used undifferentiated marketing, probably because developed economies have such highly sophisticated and competitive markets that such organisations will probably fail to survive, if indeed they ever get going! In the Third World or developing countries, where disposable income is much lower and markets are less sophisticated, examples of undifferentiated marketing should be easier to identify.

The merits of the differentiated approach are that resources (for product development, advertising and promotion) are channelled in a way that is likely to maximise customer satisfaction thereby generating and sustaining the highest possible level of sales and profits. The Burton Group for example, identified several different market segments for its clothing, including the style market (Principles), younger women and teenagers (Dorothy Perkins), larger women (Evans) and family (Debenhams). The company set about developing a different marketing mix for each specific market segment, by designing the clothing styles and the shop names, decor and ambience for each segment as appropriate and by carefully selecting the advertising media accordingly. The Burton Group's differentiated marketing strategy has therefore resulted in the duplication of some resources and the loss of some economies of scale.

The main advantage of the concentrated marketing is that resources can be concentrated in meeting the needs of just one, specific market segment. Consequently, niche markets are often suitable for smaller companies with limited resources. Another advantage is that market niches, are by definition usually small which means that competition will often be limited. Some examples of successful niche markets are "Kingshill" (designer clothes by mail order) and "Long Tall Sally" (clothes for women of 5' 10" and over). Both companies place small advertisements in the back of quality women's magazines. Body Shop for example created a niche market for environmentally friendly toiletries and cosmetics aimed at teenage girls and young women. By precisely identifying the needs, wants and values of its target markets and by developing a strong brand image and a marketing mix which reflected these values in every aspect of the company's activities, Body Shop enjoyed phenomenal success which resulted in fierce competition from Boots, M & S, Avon and many others.

6. In the UK the financial services market has been changing considerably in recent years, a trend which is likely to continue as the government increasingly promotes and encourages personal choice and self sufficiency. The resulting growth resulted in increased competition and more discerning consumers. In addition, the industry is faced with considerable scepticism and mistrust as a result of many unscrupulous salespeople knowingly selling pensions and endowment policies that were not in the best interest of their customers. In segmenting the market, firstly, the financial services providers need to find out which categories of consumer are likely to buy which type of service. Pensioners and teenagers for example are unlikely to be interested in buying pension plans. The sellers of pension plans need to know exactly which age group is likely to be interested, together with their gender, demographic profile, income level, lifestyle and so on. Secondly, the company then needs to identify the various wants and needs of the group. For example, what benefits do they want from their pension plan, in terms of when they retire, how they receive the benefit, etc. Having developed the product that meets these requirements as closely as possible, the next stage will be for the company to develop a promotional strategy for the pension. For this to be effective, the financial services provider needs to carefully consider the most effective way of reaching and appealing the target market segment within the necessary budget constraints. For example, the company may decide to increase awareness of their pension plan through press advertising, in which case it will need to identify those newspapers and/or magazines which are more likely to be read by the target consumers and to design advertisements which are carefully tailored to appeal to this group. There is no reason why a similar approach could not be taken for any other aspect of financial services. Life assurance for example is most likely to be bought by people with dependants, so it would seem foolish to use an undifferentiated approach to marketing when valuable resources can be used to target this category specifically. In conclusion, segmentation would enable resources to be focused in a way that is most likely to satisfy the wants and needs of financial services consumers whilst producing the highest levels of return for the providers.

Comments on Applying the Concepts

1. Students will come up with different types of groups and the mnemonic to each group. The groupings will depend on whether the students are in their first or last year of the undergraduate programmes or they are in the full-time, part-time or executive MBA programmes. Students should use their creative ideas in segmenting and marketing specific products and services to these groups. This question allows the students to apply the segmentation theory in a real and applied situation.

2. Again here students will suggest different advertisements. It is important to look at for example the headline, subheadline, copy, illustration, etc. of the advertisements in order to identify the markets. Some advertisements are very clear in projecting their product and image for a particular target market such as, car advertisements, while others are not as clear as to whom the advertisements are directed to, for example beer advertisements. Ask students for more examples.

Case 9
Coffee-Mate

Synopsis

The coffee creamer market has grown consistently since the first creamers were introduced in the early 1970's. However, since then the market place has changed. The increasing numbers of women in the labour market, increased health consciousness, awareness of the benefits of low fat and exercises and the disadvantages of higher sugar intake, have all contributed to a further segmentation of the market. Thus, there is a need to re-examine the market. The undisputed king of the creamer market has to be Coffee Mate. As a result of increased advertising expenditure, a strong brand image has been created and maintained. It acquired 62.9% share of the 26 million market. The introduction of Coffee Mate Lite at the end of 1990, indicated that it has a distinctive character and market of its own. Cannibalisation of volume has been minimal and it has secured 10% growth in sales volume since its introduction.

Creamers compete not only with the real thing, such as milk and cream, but also with dried and powdered milk. Due to its powder base, creamer is often associated with the latter and subsequently thought to be a poor taste substitute, a distress product which is only used in emergencies when the milk bottle is empty. Regular users of Coffee Mate see it as an indulgence, a luxury to be savoured. Research shows that the level of awareness of the product was high but that the taste's perception was low. Non users are negative and suspicious of the product, dislike its sweet taste and do not see it as substitute to full blown calorie rich cream. Lapsed users are becoming health conscious, wary of the cream association and the glucose and vegetable fat content of the product. Consequently, Coffee Mate Lite was introduced, which gives the same results, but less sweet, less fattening and lower in cholesterol. In this case study several areas need to be address such as, Coffee Mate benefits, marketing strategy, segmentation methods, positioning and promotion.

Teaching Objectives

1. Demonstrate the need to segment, identify target markets and to position a product clearly in the minds of consumers.

2. Illustrate a typical market-segmentation problem facing a specific company.

3. Let students practice creating a marketing strategy for a developing target market.

Study Questions

1. What are the main benefits of Coffee-Mate and what is limiting its sales? How would the promotion of Coffee-Mate change with the benefits promoted and the competition targeted?

Students should highlight the following main benefits of Coffee Mate; (1) Cheaper alternative to the real thing; (2) A decent milk substitute if the fridge is empty; (3) Complements rather than destroy the taste of coffee; (4) Has a longer shelf life than milk; (5) Convenient product, easily transported; (6) New packaging considered convenient and environmentally friendly; (7) As a brand it has a high profile, strong brand image and a backing of a large multinational organisation (Nestle, better understanding of the European culture, where coffee is more heavily consumed); (8) It has an indulgent, rich and relaxing image; (9) The introduction of a Lite option has a possibility of being a major player as a health conscious choice for consumers who still wish to experience the "creaminess of a cup of coffee". Other students might add; (10) An increased demand for convenience food with long shelf life; (11) A growing number of working career women looking for a little luxury at work.

Some factors limiting its sales are; (1) A lack of versatility compared to dried milk, you can't put creamer on your cornflakes; (2) It does not mix well with tea; (3) Its perception is clouded by its generic resemblance to dried milk, which tastes awful and tends to congeal and become lumpy in hot drinks; (4) Too close to cream, high in glucose and vegetable fat and out of sync with the current health fad; (5) Launch of cheaper own brands which are suitable for tea and coffee; (6) Launch of instant packet beverages such as instant cappuccino; (7) Launch of Kenco Coffee Top to compete in luxury creamer market; (8) Over dependence on coffee sales; (9) A recent study stated that people are changing to tea due to health scares centred on coffee (cancer, caffeine poisoning and Alzheimer's disease from decaffeinated); (10) Market characterised by low interest level - an occasional purchase; (11) Diverse competition - milk, dried milk and whiteners.

Some students will suggest that Coffee Mate is never going to be better than the real thing and is inherently so close to dried milk that its taste perception is tainted. Consequently, it is necessary to create a perceived image. It should not be sold on its "negative" benefits i.e. if the milk runs out it's a noble substitute. Therefore, the promotion should focus on its convenience. Currently, there is a growing demand for convenience products. Coffee Mate represents the closest thing to real cream (an aspirational goal for the coffee drinkers) with the added benefit that you can take it with you and leave the fridge at home! In addition, the powdered milk connection should be broken. Non users should be informed that Coffee Mate is a complement and not a substitute, a smooth alternative to its lumpy competition, the taste of real cream with fewer calories. Lapsed users with health concerns should be converted to new Coffee Mate Lite, a healthy alternative to the real thing, with no compromise on flavour. An indulgence that does not breed guilt. As said previously, the convenience element is perhaps the key concept. Coffee Mate is consumed in many office type environments where milk storage is a problem. Coffee Mate and Coffee Mate Lite should be personified as a friend, a luxury to be treasured, something which is there to help you unwind and forget the rigours of the day for "one glorious coffee break moment". It is a "go-anywhere" product, drink it at home, at work, abroad, wherever you are take a cup of luxury with you!

2. Should Coffee-Mate be mass marketed, aimed at one segment or multiple segments? How would the different alternatives alter the marketing mix used to market Coffee-Mate? Why launch Coffee-Mate Lite?

Coffee mate needs to identify which market segments(s) to target. There are three main target marketing strategies which can be selected for the Coffee Mate case. These are undifferentiated marketing (mass marketing), differentiated marketing (multiple segments) and focused marketing (one segment). A mass marketing approach is usually adopted when market analysis shows that there are no strong differences in the characteristics of the market. Another reason is that it may not be cost effective to produce several strategies for marketing different consumer segments. Some students will highlight that for Coffee Mate the customer characteristics are different. Therefore to mass market the product with one marketing mix in inappropriate. For example, some people use Coffee Mate because it is convenient while other use because of its good taste. The product has already been segmented into two markets which are Coffee Mate and Coffee Mate Lite users. These are two very different segments which have many different views on what they want from a creamer. The one segment strategy is used when a company identifies several segments and targets the most promising. This could be for a number of reasons including cost and the fact that the company may wish to concentrate its resources on one segment rather than stretch them over several. Thus one marketing mix is developed for one segment. This approach would not be suitable for Coffee Mate because there are two differing products. If the brand is to stay as market leaders in both segments, then Nestle will have to target them both. Students may add that Nestle being a major player in the food industry has the resources to target both segments. Some students may say that it is highly dangerous to concentrate efforts on a single segment because of the large number of competitors which exist. The multiple segments approach is used when market segmentation shows that there is more than one potential market. Thus, different marketing mixes are developed for the different segments. In this strategy the company cannot benefit from cost economies as suggested in a mass marketing strategy. This approach is seemed to be the most suitable for Coffee Mate. The market is already segmented into two groups as mentioned previously. Different marketing mix should be constructed because the two segments use the product for different reasons and benefits. Generally, Coffee Mate users respond to the luxury and taste aspects of the product whereas Coffee Mate Lite users respond to the health and weight issues involved. A third segment might emerge, coffee drinkers who are non-users but are potential users that would be attracted to use Coffee Mate or Coffee Mate Lite.

Health and weight are very much topical and influential factors in today's society. Coffee Mate Lite is a product which has identified a customer need. The product gives Coffee Mate users who want the taste and benefits of the creamer but without the side effects of putting on weight and causing health problems. In addition, consumers are switching from cream and full fat milk to skimmed and semi-skimmed milk. This is in alignment with health issues especially those related to weight. The development of Coffee Mate Lite is in tune with what consumers want. One of the reasons why consumers have stopped using Coffee Mate is because they perceived Coffee Mate as being fattening and unhealthy. Although, Coffee Mate is the leading creamer brand in the UK, the brand was becoming somewhat stagnant. Since its introduction Coffee Mate Lite has grown at a much faster speed in comparison to Coffee Mate. Coffee Mate Lite was launched because it was what many Coffee Mate users wanted.

3. Evaluate the alternate ways of segmenting the Coffee Mate market? Make your choice and defend your choice of segmentation method, segmentation strategy and target segment.

First, students should provide a brief explanation of the various bases of segmentation for Coffee Mate. There are many ways by which markets can be segmented. In segmenting the Coffee Mate market there are three broad segmentation bases that we can follow. Under behavioural segmentation there are four possible alternatives; (1) Benefit sought - with regard to Coffee Mate the type of benefit sought by the consumers will be that they want a creamy tasting coffee without having to use cream, they want the affect of cream without the high fat content and also they may want the status linked to having cream in coffee; (2) Purchase decision - in the Coffee Mate market the consumer may buy the product as an emergency item which is only used occasionally if there is no milk or cream, or it could be purchased as a routine item which is used all the time; (3) Purchase behaviour - Some customers may become completely brand loyal and only purchase Coffee Mate whereas others may show no loyalty whatsoever and move from one brand of coffee creamer to another depending on price or special offers; (4) Usage - This is based on the degree of usage of Coffee Mate, whether the consumers of Coffee Mate are heavy users, light users or non users. With regard to psychographic segmentation the market is divided into groups according to their lifestyle as reflected in their activities, interests and opinions. This can be related to the Coffee mate market as shown by the TGI survey in the case study which highlighted different clusters of lifestyles and their tendency to drink Coffee Mate. Another basis of segmentation which is appropriate to Coffee Mate is Demographic segmentation. Here for example the Coffee Mate market can be divided into age, sex, family size, income, occupation, education and race.

In relation to the Coffee Mate market all of the above segmentation bases could be used. In other words the multiattribute segmentation base could be used. Under the behavioural segmentation base, the market can be segmented using the befits sought and usage variables. With the benefits sought variable the market can be segmented into the following area; people who want creamy coffee, people who want the status linked to drinking coffee with cream and with Coffee Mate Lite, people who want creamy coffee without the fat content in cream. The usage variable can also be used because Coffee Mate market can be split into high users, low users (lapsed users) and non-users. From the psychographic area of segmentation, lifestyle of the consumers can be used. The evidence is already shown by the TGI survey. The survey shows the kinds of people more likely to use Coffee Mate and their respective lifestyle. Finally the socio economic variable can also be used. Certain people from a particular socio-economic background are more likely to drink coffee with cream.

From the above rationale students can suggest that the target segment is derived from a combination of segmentation bases. First and foremost it is essential to target the coffee drinkers for the obvious reason that Coffee Mate's sole purpose is for the use in coffee. Secondly, the target market are people who prefer a creamier taste of coffee thus those people who may use cream in their coffee. They are the target market because the producer want them to consider Coffee Mate as a norm rather than cream. In addition, the target market could consist of low or occasional users of Coffee Mate, in the hope that they will switch to using Coffee mate on a regular basis. Therefore, increasing the size of the Coffee Mate market. The target market will be in the socio-economic classes ABC1, the reason being the TGI survey highlighted that these types of people are more likely to use Coffee Mate and cream in their coffee. By highlighting these people, people in the lower classes will buy Coffee Mate in order to be seen as having the status of the higher classes.

4. Evaluate the segments from TGI's user for target attractiveness and their fit to Coffee-Mate's strengths. Which of the segments would you target and why? Evaluate the proposed ad for target market and benefits promoted. Will the ad help propel Coffee-Mate's further growth? Create an alternate ad for you chosen target market?

The TGI user surveys have come up with five possible consumer groups. However, for Coffee Mate to be marketed effectively it is important to target specific group or groups. Therefore we must consider the five groups individually to assess their attractiveness as potential customers of Coffee Mate. The first group was the "Sharon and Tracy" group who are considered to be "experimentalists". As the name depicts this group is one that does not care about much and shuns responsibilities in favour of enjoying themselves. This group is very materialistic but has no interest in politics and environmental issues. At first sight this group does not seem to be the one we need to consider. However, there is a possibility here because the group is a materialistic one who could mean that they like to be seen to be trendy and more like the rich. The added advantage is that this group is a heavy user of coffee and cream. This tells us that they have not really had the experience of Coffee Mate or have had the experience but did not like it. The household income of the people in this group is fairly reasonable, between £15,000 and £30,000 which is likely to be the incomes of two people. The socio-economic grouping of C2/D in combination with other factors indicate that these people aspire to be yuppies of the middle class. The media plays a large part in the lives of the experimentalists thus making them very accessible to advertising. The lifestyle of this group indicates they socialise very often and like to portray an image of being successful. At present their consumption of Coffee mate is small. The reason for this seems to be that they do not consider Coffee Mate to be a good or trendy enough product to go with their lifestyle or image.

The second group is the "Eileen and Mary" group, who are regarded as cost constrained, older and conservative. This group is always looking for the lowest price when shopping, thus they have no brand loyalty. They are health conscious but do not have the financial resources to do anything about it, as their household income is between £5,000 and £11,000. With a low disposable income it is obvious the lifestyle of this group is very different from those of the on higher incomes, which will dictate the types of products purchased. The social implication for this group is that they are likely never to try new products except on the odd occasion. Also the use of luxury products will be limited to mere indulgences, as in cream. The social lifestyle of this group means that they are open to the influences of the media and other advertising. This group's spending on shopping is relatively low, they decide what to purchase before entering the supermarket and on its cost. This group always enters competitions. This could be a way of introducing Coffee Mate to a new target market and a way of getting them out of their routine existence. It appears this is a group least likely to be targeted as they neither have the financial resources nor the interests to purchase the product.

The third group is "Sarah and Anna" who is young and affluent with a socio economic grouping of A/B/C1 and above average household incomes. This group at present is the second most likely to use Coffee Mate and also tend to use cream often. This tells us that they may not be totally satisfied with Coffee Mate but use it on a daily basis for personal use but use cream on occasions when they are entertaining. An important factor with this group is that they are willing to pay extra as long as the quality is there. The group's affluent lifestyle allows them to spend freely and try new and different things. They also socialise considerably more than other groups which will allow them to experience new things and pass their views to others. This group asks whether the food is healthy, is it environmentally friendly product and whether it has any additives. One reason this group is a good target market is because people aspire to be like them for example wealthy, healthy, socialites and environmentally friendly. Therefore, if this group is seen to be using Coffee Mate then other people will want to use it too.

The fourth group is the "Dawn and Lisa" group who are cost constrained and mainly young families. This group is like the "Eileen and Mary" group - low disposable incomes. The only difference is that this group is young with children. The occupation of these people is mainly part time employees or students and possibly currently unemployed. Also, many are uneducated with little concern for the environment or their health. An explanation for this, being their low disposable incomes. The financial situation of this group can also explain their lifestyles. This group never uses cream but is a heavy user of coffee. In combination with their income, this tells us they do not use cream because they cannot afford to purchase it on a regular basis. This group is very receptive to advertising through the media. However, they still shop at cost saving stores and look out for special offers. This could be used by Coffee Mate to introduce the product to another target market. This group tries to save as much as it can but finds it difficult. They do not socialise very much and do not worry too much about health and environmental issues. It is for these reasons this group would not be selected as a target market and also because the usage rate of Coffee Mate would be very low.

The final group in the TGI survey is the "Dorothy and Amy" group, who are the most affluent of all the groups. This group is prudent with money but it does not worry too much about the price of goods. The socio-economic grouping is A/B/C1. This group as a whole is not does not pay much attention to the media, but they are health and environmentally conscious, yet fairly traditional. This group is the one uses Coffee Mate the most, it also socialises a lot, but it is a group that likes its own company and has a relatively high standard of living. The expenditure on weekly shopping is above average. A reason for it not being the highest is because the group usually consists of just two people. The group is willing to pay extra money as long as the quality is there. Generally, those in this group are retired or have part time jobs (not for the money but for the mere fact of having something to do).

Based on the above evaluation some students will target groups 1, 3 and 5 as they hold potentially more consumers than the other clusters. Cluster 1 are not heavy users of Coffee Mate but due to the above reasons are potential users, thus highlight an opportunity. Clusters 3 and 5 are currently heavy consumers who just need to be reminded to purchase the product. All three segments are in the higher income bracket therefore are not price sensitive. They are eager to invest in branded name products as they show the characteristics of preferring manufacturer's brands to own labels. These groups will not be treated alike for example, clusters 3 and 5 who are both users of cream and health conscious, Coffee Mate has to be promoted as a product that gives the same taste as cream but having less fat than cream.

Some students will suggest some strengths of the ad; aimed at the correct segments, namely affluent people with out-going lifestyle; it creates the "I want to be like that" atmosphere, a lifestyle the lower classes aspire to be; correct settings for affluent people. Students should also highlight some weaknesses of the ad; it makes the product to be the last alternative after cream and milk; it infers Coffee Mate is only used occasionally not purchased on a regular basis. The ad may help Coffee Mate maintain their position in this market, possibly even encroaching on other coffee creamer company's market share. However, it is unlikely to help the expansion into the market share of cream or milk because of the above weaknesses.

Students will give a variety of advertisements. Some aspects that should be highlighted in the advertisement are; product should be pushed as the first choice as opposed to the last resort; the setting could be a social occasion or an individual enjoying a cup of coffee with Coffee Mate; should focus on the convenience aspect of the product.

Teaching Suggestions

Because some students are familiar with the products discussed here, it should generate lots of interest and involvement. The instructor may want to begin discussion by asking students to say in one or two words the first thought they have when they hear the word Coffee Mate. They can then show how many of them use Coffee Mate or another creamer. When do they use Coffee Mate? Why do they use one brand versus another?

Students may want to visit local supermarkets and convenience stores to see what kinds of creamer are available and to note their prices. Ask them where normally creamers are located in the supermarket. Why is this? What impact does it have on complementary products and competitive strategies?

Instructors can use this case with many other chapters. Because the products are so well known, the case can be used with Chapters 1, 3, or 4. It goes well with the Consumer Behaviour Chapters (Chapters 7 and 8), the Promotion Chapters (Chapters 18, 19 and 20), and with the international chapter (Chapter 5). It also fits with both product chapters (Chapters 13 and 14) because of the interest in developing new products to target new markets.

Jokes and Quotes

Segmentation lets the strong thrive and the weak survive.

Used gravestone for sale. Ideal gift for family called Ellsworth.
ADVERTISEMENT

Women come in two types: young and not-so-young.
ANON

Every crowd has a silver lining.
PHINEAS TAYLOR BARNUM

I don't know the key to success but the key to failure is trying to please everybody.
BILL COSBY

If Mr. Vincent Price were to be co-starred with Miss Bette Davies in a story by Mr. Edgar Allan Poe directed by Mr. Roger Corman, it could not fully express the pent-up violence and depravity of a single day in the life of the average family.
QUENTIN CRISP

Keeping up with the Joneses was a full-time job with my mother and father. It was not until many years later when I lived alone that I realise how much cheaper it was to drag the Joneses down to my level.
QUENTIN CRISP

I tried selling doorbells door-to-door. But when I rang, the people who needed the product didn't know I was there.
JOKE

If you just torture the data long enough, they will confess.
T. MAYER

Having money is rather like being a blond. It is more fun but not vital.
MARY QUANT

To sell no matter what, no matter how, to no matter whom; behold in three words the whole diplomacy of the peasant at the fair.
JOSEPH ROUX

Sell when you can; you are not for all markets.
WILLIAM SHAKESPEARE

Planning ahead is a measure of class. The rich and even the middle class plan for future generations, but the poor can plan ahead only a few weeks or days.
GLORIA STEINEM

People in the higher income groups, have greater spending power than those with smaller incomes.
TEACHER UNION CONGRESS STATEMENT OF ECONOMIC

In advertising terms, an intellectual is anybody who reads a morning newspaper.
ARNA-MARIA WINCHESTER

Chapter 10
Positioning

Chapter Objectives

After reading this chapter, you should be able to:

1. Define differentiation and market positioning.
2. Explain why companies seek to differentiate their markets and use positioning strategies.
3. List and discuss the major ways companies can differentiate their products.
4. Explain how companies can position their products for maximum competitive advantage in the marketplace.

Chapter Overview

A firm's functional strengths give its competitive advantage. Market positioning is about managing customers' view of the company and its products. It is about perception. Perceptual maps are a way of revealing how customers see markets. They show which products customers see as alike and those that are not. They can also show segments and the dimensions customers use to split up the market. There are several positioning strategies for shifting and holding customers' perceptions. Positioning works by associating products with product attributes or other stimuli. Successful firms usually maintain a clear differential advantage and do not make violent changes to their market position.

Teaching Notes

Refer to the following pages for teaching notes.

The Other BCG Matrix

Transparency PM 10-1 relates to Figure 10-1 and based on material on pp.401-405. This shows how differentiation is harder in some industries than others.

Volume

Few ways of dominating these markets where size is very important. The oil industry is an example.

Stalemate

Industries making products with few opportunities for advantage and these are small. Agricultural products fall here along with many other commodity industries such as steel and the building industry. Own brands are strong here.

Fragmented

There are many small ways of differentiating but they are small. Alcoholic drinks and confectionery are good examples. Own branding is not strong here.

Specialised

The many and big advantages available leads to a diversity of strong companies. Defence and ethical drugs are specialised industries.

> **Tip**
>
> Explain how it is the role of marketing managers to "differentiate something, anything" for them to break out of stalemate markets. Show how some differentiation can exist in fragments of volume markets.

Notes for PM 10-1

Differentiation Advantage

Transparency PM 10-2 relates to the material on pp.405-409.

Competitive Advantage

Competitive advantage is created by differentiating the product from those of competitors.

Product Differentiation

Product differentiation can be based upon features or performance.

Services Differentiation

Services differentiation may come from delivery, installation, repair or training advantages.

Personnel Differentiation

Personnel differentiation is derived from a superior workforce.

Image Differentiation

Image differentiation can be generated from effective use of symbols in association with product consumption.

> **Tip**
>
> Ask how a car hire company could differentiate by the four ways. Why don't they?

Notes for PM 10-2

Ries and Trout Positioning

Transparency PM 10-3 relates to material on pp.409-412.

Product Position

Product position is the way the customer defines the product. For example, maker of the best burger.

Competitive Advantage

Competitive advantage is a strength of the company that the company has. This could be a cost effective distribution system.

Ries and Trout Suggest Four Positioning Alternatives

1. Number One

The top company or brand; Coca-Cola, McDonald, Chanel, Kodak and Shell all hold these positions.

2. Current Position

Maybe not number one but could be the best in its class or chosen position; BMW, Land Rover, Hard Rock Cafe, U2.

3. Latent Position

Realising a gap in the customer needs and filling it. Club Med did this as did Sony with their Walkman and Unilever with Radion and Wash 'n' Go.

4. Depositioning or Repositioning

Remove the ground from underneath competitors. Porsche was depositioned when Mazda showed some of it saloon cars outperformed cheaper versions of the sports car. Airbus attacks Boeing number one position by showing it also has a full range of product.

> **Tip**
>
> Ask how politicians deposition their opponents. Is deposition someone easier than positioning yourself?

Notes for PM 10-3

Product Positioning

Transparency PM 10-4 relates to the material on pp.414-420.

Positioning for Competitive Advantage

A product's position can be based on a number of variables including:

1. Product Attributes

This positions the product on unique or distinguishing features it possesses such as low price, unique technology, versatility or other features.

2. Benefits Offered

Positioning can be based upon specific value provided.

3. Usage Occasions

The product usage associated with special occasions or values

4. Users

A product can be positioned to its most important users.

5. Activities

Castrol's synthetic oil is for racing while expensive Champagne usually means a celebration.

6. Personalities

Well-known personalities can quickly bestow an authority to new products like Carlsberg ICE beer.

7. Origin

Countries or region have associates that can help positioning. An example is Baccardi from Jamaica or Russian Vodka.

8. Other Brands

Well-known brands such as Rolls-Royce cars and Disney are so powerful that they can influence the perception of a brand appearing next to them.

9. Against a Competitor

This strategy is appropriate for substitutes that cost less.

10. Away from Competitors

Thos positions the product as unique in some respect and/or worth it.

11. Product Class

The company may vary positioning as needed in relation to one or more competitors.

Notes for PM 10-4

Promoting Differences

Transparency PM 10-5 relates to the material on p.425. The key to selecting the right competitive advantage is to develop a unique selling proposition (USP) for the product and stick to it.

Selecting the Right Competitive Advantage

Differences selected to promote competitive advantage should satisfy the following criteria:

1. Important

The difference must deliver a highly valued benefit to target buyers.

2. Distinctive

Competitors do not offer the difference or the company offers the difference in a more distinctive way.

3. Superior

The difference should be superior to other ways that customers might obtain the same benefit.

4. Communicable

The difference is communicable and visible to buyers.

5. Pre-emptive

Competitors cannot easily copy the difference. This may be a result of innovative technology, production economies, distribution economies and/or proprietary rights.

6. Affordable

Buyers in the target market must be able to pay for the difference.

7. Profitable

The difference must be profitable for the company to offer.

Tip

Ask students to consider an appropriate competitive advantage for their college.

Notes for PM 10-5

How Many Differences

Transparency PM 10-6 is based on the material on pp.421-425.

Unique Selling Proposition

This is an old idea that identified the need of a brand to have its own story to tell - some novel feature that anchor it in the consumer's mind.

Emotional Selling Proposition

This method recognises that the unique selling proposition dose not have to be tangible.

One, Two, Three or More Positions

How many postures can a brand assume? Fairy liquid claims both concentrated and gentle to hands. Could it be ecologically friendly too? Such bridging can render brand vulnerable.

Under Positioning

Leaves brand vulnerable because competing well-positioned brands can take away sales. Polo mints leaves them vulnerable to extra strong breath freshening or other functional confectionery.

Over Positioning

Can leave a brand in a declining market. Volvo positioning on practicality and safety left it vulnerable to attack by even more boxy 4X4's.

Confused Positioning

Can occur when brands swap their position time after time to find a viable platform or because of managerial ego. Most top brands' proposition are simple and constant.

Tip

Show how some firm have moved successfully from position to position; Lucozade went from being a drink for invalids to a pick me up for housewives and energy giving sports drink; Ribena from a carefully administered Vitamin C drink for children to a healthy family drink. Bran Flakes from a source of fibre to a great tasting cereal.

Notes for PM 10-6

Comments on Discussing the Issues

1. Many companies offer the customer what are essentially the same products or services. To try and ensure the customer chooses its products or services rather than those of its competitors, a company needs to differentiate. Basically a company differentiates its products or services by providing " something extra" not offered by its rivals and which the customer perceives as being beneficial. If the company is successful then it can charge a premium price for this difference - customers are often heard to admit to their friends that product A cost more than product B, but the extra price was worth it. There are four main tools of differentiation; product, service, personnel and image. Each of these can be further subdivided into several other factors. For instance, product covers design features such as performance, durability, reliability and style. IKEA for example sells self-assembly furniture but differs from other similar retailers by offering stylish, contemporary furniture at reasonable prices. Marks and Spencer are very successful in the highly competitive food sector by emphasising the quality and freshness of their products and their customers certainly do not seem to mind the fact that prices are generally much higher than in other supermarkets.

   Service incorporates factors such as delivery, installation, training, consultancy and repair. Computers are on sale in many shops but the specialist retailer can justify the fact that it charges more than the discount electrical stores because it can offer after sales service such as a helpline to sort out those faults that are not mentioned in the handbook.

   Personnel covers such factors as competence, courtesy, reliability and communication. For example the Disney shops only recently opened in the UK, have assistants placed at every door to greet shoppers as they arrive and leave. Although this very American approach is rather brash to the reserved Brits, it is certainly a vast improvement on those shops where the sales staff are so busy talking that the customer is made to feel guilty for being there!

   Image is concerned with how the company is identified to the consumer. One of the main factors involved here is advertising but it is not the only one. For instance the Body Shop rarely advertises nowadays but customers still flock to buy their toiletries there as they are seen as being environmentally and ethically sound products.

2. A company must be able to support the positioning chosen for a product but beyond this, perceptions of attributes may be more important than actual product attributes. In selling a perfume, for example, the perfume's image is at least as important as its scent. Successful positions may be based on attributes that are not unique to the product. Campbell makes the soup that is "good food", for example, even though other canned soups may be just as nutritious.

3. The term positioning was coined by two advertising executives Ries and Trout, to describe the placing of a product in the mind of the prospective buyer. They further argued that in an advertising saturated world, products tend to form into ladders in the consumer's mind and that people remember best the topmost product or firm on the ladder example Coca Cola, as the most popular soft drink, British Airways as the world's favourite airline and Microsoft as the best software house, etc. However, it should be emphasised that a company's position on the ladder depends on the consumer's perception which is usually obtained as a result of advertising. If a

company wants to change its position on the ladder i.e. reposition itself higher up the ladder, then it is obvious that it has to move its rivals lower down the ladder i.e. deposition them. This is not as simple as it sounds; in the UK, unlike the USA, it is against advertising standards to mention a rival's product by name, which is why laundry products, for example, have to make do with comparing their washing powder to brand X. Depositioning advertisements have to be more subtle. In the current advertisement for John Smith beer which starts off with singing, dancing penguins which later move off, leaving the message that while other beers may need gimmicks to promote them, John Smith beer does not. The current campaign for Orange, follows a similar tactic - Cellnet is offering a revival of a traditional idea, the Christmas bonus, which is worth up to £50 for the subscriber, but Orange claim they do not need to make such offers as their prices are low all the time.

Another strategy for depositioning is to change the product name and/or packaging, perhaps to mimic that of its rivals. Sainsbury successfully used this ploy when launching its brand of cola, copying the style of writing used by Coca Cola. The tactic of depositioning may also be employed by the top of the ladder, to prevent their own depositioning. Foe example Fairy Liquid uses almost the same two commercials on a rotational basis. The first claims to be mild and gentle on the hands in comparison with its rivals while the second seeks to prove that, while it may be a more expensive product, it lasts longer than other cheaper brands. Depositioning and repositioning therefore have similar intentions as differentiation but whereas differentiation merely seeks to have the consumer think of the product as distinct from its rivals, depositioning wants the product to be thought of as the best in its field.

4. Students need to come up with some examples of beer or lager brands. In Denmark for example, Heineken, the market leader is positioned as a premium brand. Targeted at people who enjoy life and are concerned about family and friends. Grolsch beer is positioned to attract the young adult, yuppie-like people. Bavaria beer is targeted and positioned to address the average person on the street. Some positioning themes are not as clear, for example some of the beer TV advertisements in the UK have the tendency to be very creative and artistic to the extent that it is difficult to say what their positions are and to whom they are targeting the product.

5. Benefits of perceptual mapping are ; (1) Enables the manager to obtain the customer's perception of the market; (2) Helps to understand competitors; (3) Powerful tool for analysing the product and market structure to identify possible market gaps, potential new product/brand opportunities; (4) Develops understanding of how relative strengths and weaknesses of products/brands are perceived; (5) Builds knowledge about (dis)similarities between products/brands; (6) Assists the process of (re)positioning a product/brand; (7) Assists the measurement of effectiveness of communication programmes and marketing actions; (8) Enables managers to identify areas where customers' needs are not met. Limitations are; (1) Requires marketing research skills and experience; (2) Assumes uniformity of perceptions; (3) Assumes that all customers in the survey are familiar with all the products/brands; (4) Requires that all benefits and attributes are known; (5) Does not always disclose all benefits because some subjective benefits are hard to measure; (6) Gives only 1,2 or 3 dimensional attribute comparisons. (D.W.Cravens (1994), Strategic Marketing; C.Fill (1995), Marketing Communications; J.P.Guiltinan et al (1994), Marketing Management)

6. Positioning is not only helpful but also vital to not-for-profit organisations as they are existing in an increasingly competitive environment. A charity should select a positioning strategy that is in coherent with its mission statement of the charitable organisation. This "position" will be communicated in all of their promotional tools to raise funds and increase membership.

Comments on Applying the Concepts

1. Students will say that most of the soft drinks are positioned based on lifestyle and personality and taste; some chocolate bars are positioned along the lines of a particular lifestyle, some on usage occasions and some on the contents of the chocolate bars. We could say that there is a close similarity in the positioning of confectionery and soft drinks. Students will say that chocolate bars, to some extent, are clearly positioned than soft drinks.

2. Some students may object to this question because it can imply that people are misrepresenting themselves for Machiavellian ends. These students would answer that they would not position themselves differently for anybody. Most people do attempt to represent themselves in a way that they feel others will appreciate. For a potential employer students are likely to emphasise such characteristics as intelligence, diligence, education and having a businesslike appearance and demeanour. For a potential romantic partner students are likely to mention attractiveness and appropriate dress, showing interest in similar activities and being empathic and charming. For a mother and father desirable qualities to exhibit might be politeness, good grooming, diligence, maturity and obedience. Clearly, these potential positionings differ. There is one key reason they differ; they are very different target markets, each with different wants and needs. The characteristics of an employer or parent values may be distasteful to a romantic partner. To be effective in positioning for an audience we must know what the audience appreciates.

Case 10
Cadburys Time Out:
Choc Around The Clock

Synopsis

Cadbury's TimeOut, a development of the management of Cadbury Ireland, is considered the most successful product ever developed and launched by Cadbury in Ireland. Its success is attributed to technological advances, strong markets and original positioning. In light of the restructuring of the industry and as a result of Ireland and Britain joining the EEC, there was a need for Cadbury Ireland to reshape its manufacturing so as to benefit from scale economies both internationally as well as domestically. Cadbury Ireland identified its core competencies in the form of three technological expertise which are extrusion, flake chocolate manufacture and wafer making and baking, which account for the development of a variety of successful products. Cadbury segmented the market on the basis of how consumers buy rather than on product attributes. This enabled the company to identify the growing take-home segment of the confectionery market and the competitors' positioning of their traditional chocolate bars being suitable to be eaten as snacks as well. This growth of the snack market is attributed mainly to culture and lifestyle habits, where there is a tendency towards less structured meals and increased snacking i.e. grazing tendency. The Irish and British are particularly large confectionery consumers. This is because of the snacking culture and the actual existence of snack breaks, in which people drink tea or coffee and have a snack. In light of the grazing tendency and the core competencies of the company, Cadbury saw an opportunity to bridge between the confectionery and the biscuit markets, and develop a product that will be suitable for different uses, but with roots at the break market. Cadbury had therefore developed its marketing mix including product, pricing, promotion and positioning strategies in an attempt to establish the intended position of TimeOut within the market.

Teaching Objectives

1. Demonstrate the need to identify target markets and to position a product clearly in the minds of the consumers.

2. Illustrate a typical market segmentation issue facing a specific company.

3. Apply principles in positioning and segmentation in relation to the European environment.

Study Questions

1. What criteria did Cadburys Ireland use in developing TimeOut? What role did they play in the positioning strategy of TimeOut?

Some students will highlight the following criteria that Cadbury Ireland used in developing TimeOut; (1) Core competencies - Cadbury assessed their strengths and competencies in the confectionery industry and identified three core technological competencies that could be capitalised upon in order to develop new products namely, extrusion, flake chocolate manufacture and wafer making and baking. The unique combination of technologies enabled them to produce a product that is suitable for various purposes and even more importantly to be perceived suitable for different purposes; (2) Market trends - Cadbury segments the market on the basis of how consumers buy (occasion, usage, etc.) rather than on product attributes. Recent trends towards take-home consumption have driven Cadbury to develop TimeOut in order to serve both the biscuit and confectionery markets, i.e. target the bridge brand. These markets' trends allowed Cadbury to identify the growth segments and establish their positioning strategy; (3) Culture and lifestyles - Cadbury identified the characteristics of the tea break habit of the marketplace in terms of the need for accompaniment product to the beverage. Based on this break culture and the trend towards unstructured eating lifestyle, Cadbury decided to bring the confectionery values to the biscuit market and vice versa. In order to capture "both worlds", Cadbury did not restrict TimeOut to be seen as simply a snack, but positioned it so that it was seen having many uses, in which it could also be used as a bar; (4) Competitors actions - Cadbury noticed the actions taken by competitors who were aiming to reposition their traditionally known bars to be perceived as snacks. This criterion was taken into account as Cadbury did not restrict the positioning of TimeOut to be merely within the snack market. They positioned it so that it was perceived to have multi-uses. Notice that the two parts to this question are interrelated.

2. TimeOut has adopted what it describes as a "bridge-brand" position. What are the risks of the "bridge-brand" position? Which marketing mix variables were most important in positioning TimeOut?

There are various arguments to this question. Some points students might highlight are; (1) The bridge-brand position may create confusion. On the one hand, snack consumers may not treat it as a snack because of its chocolate content is too rich, while on the other, confectionery consumers may claim the biscuit dilutes the taste of the chocolate. Hence, the market may not approve of this concept and may see it as not good enough for both uses; (2) There is a higher risk of damage to the company's brand name. Since the Cadbury logo exists on all of its products, failure of such a product can be regarded as failure in both markets and lead to damage for the company's name in both markets. This may affect other products not just in one market, but in two; (3) The introduction of such a product that is aimed at the bridge brand position may create competition between TimeOut and other product ranges in both sectors produced by the company; (5) Failure in one of the sectors may jeopardise possible success in the other due to bad word-of-mouth that may influence people who have not tried it yet, now may not try it at all; (6) Competition with established brand such as Kit Kat and Twix who are already strongly identified as bridge brands.

Students need to emphasise that all of the elements in the marketing mix have contributed in the positioning of TimeOut; (1) Product - the competitive advantage of the product is the composition of ingredients. It contains both biscuit and flake contents, where the wafer itself is already an ideal snack and the flake content makes it suitable as a bar of chocolate. Product design - the brand name "TimeOut" was chosen because it clearly communicated the desired position as a snack accompaniment and the time at which it was intended to be consumed i.e. during break time. The brand name objectives were supported by the use of a clock and a mug to reinforced the TimeOut beverage break accompaniment role. It is believed that the blue/red/yellow association is the colour scheme most easily associated with light biscuit bars. The company used these colours on the packaging to attract attention and create competitive distinction. Blue is the main colour used and it has a symbolic connotation as a peaceful and resting colour; (2) Price - TimeOut is launched at a price of 28p while a standard bar was priced at 30p. Pricing however does not form a major basis for differentiation as prices within standard-size chocolate bars are very similar; (3) Place - In order to meet the requirement of different segments, 4 types of formats were developed, with the aim to locate the product at different levels; (4) Promotion - Heavy TV and radio advertising emphasised the "TimeOut at any time" theme. Promotions included poster, balloon releases, a variety of street activities involving a national radio station and using branded characters and participation at the annual St. Patrick's Day parade in Dublin. Free samples were distributed at street activities and in-store promotions. The company also used family brand promotions and brand alliance promotion in its initial positioning. The family brand promotion with Lyons tea helped to establish the position of the product as a beverage accompaniment. Moreover, due to the high market share of Lyons it enabled the trial of the product by many consumers. Students may add that overall, all elements of the marketing mix were present during the launching of TimeOut. Nevertheless, some elements played major role in communicating the intended positioning to the market. Most students will say that the product and promotion elements were the most important elements but at the same time the importance of the remaining variables must be appreciated and considered. For example, the wrong choice of price or place can jeopardise the way in which people perceive the product and its position, as they may perceive it as belonging to a different category of products.

3. How did the positioning and marketing strategies of its main competitors influence TimeOut's positioning?

The main competitors who offer similar products to TimeOut are Kit Kat and Twix. Both of these products have moved into the "bridge brand" position from strong positions initially in the bar segment. They have been very successful by diversifying in terms of bar and pack size and selling in subtly different areas of supermarkets e.g. biscuit section. By launching TimeOut into a "bridge brand" position Cadbury have copied the strategies employed by their main competitors in terms of format and place of sale. Cadbury is selling TimeOut at a slightly cheaper price than a standard bar which matches the pricing policies of Kit Kat. Twix and Kit Kat are attempting to move from the confectionery market segment into the snack/biscuit segment whilst retaining their market share in the confectionery market whereas TimeOut is positioning itself in both segments from its inception. Some students might suggest that despite the fact that TimeOut is a new product, it may prove successful than its main competitors as it is more difficult to categorise as either a biscuit snack or a chocolate bar. Ask them justification for this answer.

4. Discuss the promotional strategy used to launch TimeOut. What are the cultural factors that account for the success of TimeOut? Could TimeOut be successful in other European countries?

TimeOut was launched amid vast publicity. The advertising included television, radio and poster campaigns. Cadbury also took part in street activities and in-store promotions where free samples of the product were given out. The blanket coverage ensured that the high level of product awareness was achieved. This was proven by the results collected by a research company 6-8 months after the launch which showed 86% awareness among adults and 100% awareness among 11-14 year old children. To facilitate a wider trial of the product and also to strengthen the perceived link between breaktime and TimeOut bars were given away with purchases of tea. The trial of TimeOut without any "risk" to the consumer served to create a positive attitude towards the product. Of the 69% of adults who tried the product

61% became repeat users, of the 97% children, 87% repeated. The promotional message of a new, friendly, modern beverage-break accompaniment that was suitable for use at any time coupled with the free trials resulted in a positive or neutral brand appeal to 93% adults and 99% of children.

The success of TimneOut particularly in Ireland and Great Britain can be attributed to the lifestyles of the people living in these countries. Irish people consume the largest amount of both chocolate and biscuits in the EU with Great Britain coming a close second. In both Ireland and Britain eating habits no longer centred around family meals once or twice a day. Less time is devoted to meals resulting in more prevalent snacking. The habit if taking breaks during the day for a cup of tea or coffee accompanied by biscuits, cake or chocolate provided ready-made niche for a new product such as TimeOut. As food consumption is dispersed throughout the day more opportunities for snacking occur which may account for the heavy consumption of confectionery in Ireland and Great Britain.

Time Out could be potentially successful in some European countries. By examining the table for European Union consumption of confectionery it is clear that none of the other European countries consume comparable quantities of either chocolate or biscuits to Ireland or Great Britain. The inhabitants of Belgium, Denmark, West Germany, France and the Netherlands may be suitable prospective customers as they consume a fair amount of chocolate. The lifestyles of these potential consumers should be closely examined. We are told that snacking is increasing in Europe but it is not clear whether breaks for beverages during the day are the norm, advertising and marketing techniques may have to be amended to match the consumers snacking habits.

Teaching Suggestions

Because students are fairly familiar with the products discussed here, it should generate lots of interest and involvement. The instructor may want to begin discussion by asking students to say one or two words the first thought they have when they hear the word TimeOut. They can then show how many of them snack on TimeOut or another brands. In what circumstances they eat the brands? Why do they eat one brand versus another? Students may want to visit local supermarkets and convenience stores to see what kinds of chocolate bars and bridge brands available and note their prices. Instructors can use this case with many other chapters. Because the products are so well known, the case can be used with Chapters 1,2 or 3. It goes well with the Consumer Behaviour Chapters (Chapters 7 and 8), the Promotion Chapters (Chapters 18, 19, and 20) and with the Global Chapter (Chapter 5). It also fits with both Product Chapters (Chapters 13 and 14) because of the interest in developing new products to target new markets.

Jokes and Quotes

Segmentation without position is like wetting your pants. It gives you a warm feeling at first but it is not a very good long term strategy.

You don't buy coal, you buy heat;
You don't buy circus tickets, you buy thrills;
You don't buy a paper, you buy news;
You don't buy spectacles, you buy vision;
You don't buy printing, you buy selling
ANON

If you want to persuade people, show the immediate relevance and value of what you're saying in terms of meeting their needs and desires.
HERB COHEN

The woman selling cosmetics door-to-door wasn't having much success when suddenly she had a bright idea. The next house she came to, when a woman opened the door, the saleswoman said, "I don't suppose you'd be interested in our new range of lipstick. The lady next door said it would be far too expensive for you."
JOKE

An ad on TV was for a mouthwash that guarantees to kill all known germs. But who wants a mouthful of dead germs?
JOKE

To be successful in business, be daring, be first, be different.
WILLIAM MARCHANT

Ice cream	70 cents
Pie (like Mother made)	50 cents
Pie (like Mother wished she could make)	$1.50

MENU

In the factory we make cosmetics.
In the store we sell hope
CHARLES REVSON

Milk from contented cows.
SLOGAN (CARNATION)

Heineken refreshes the parts other beers cannot reach.
SLOGAN

Often a bridesmaid, but never a bride.
SLOGAN (LISTERINE MOUTHWASH)

Her honeymoon - and it should have been mine.
SLOGAN (LISTERINE MOUTHWASH)

Even your best friends won't tell you.
SLOGAN (LISTERINE MOUTHWASH)

The taste you love to hate (twice a day).
SLOGAN (LISTERINE MOUTHWASH)

Say it with flowers.
SLOGAN

Two years ago I used your soap since when I have used no other!
SLOGAN (PEARS SOAP)

Since using Pears' soap for the hands and complexion I have discarded all others.
SLOGAN (PEARS SOAP)

At 60 miles an hour the loudest noise in this new Rolls-Royce comes from the electric clock.
SLOGANS (ROLLS-ROYCE)

The best car in the world.
SLOGANS (ROLLS-ROYCE)

The beer that made Milwaukee famous.
SLOGAN (SCHLITZ)

You know what comes between me and my Calvins? Nothing!
SLOGAN (CALVIN KLEIN JEANS)

Chapter 11

Building Customer Satisfaction Through Quality, Value, and Service

Chapter Objectives

After reading this chapter, you should be able to:

1. Define customer value and discuss its importance in creating customer satisfaction and company profitability.
2. Discuss the concepts of value chains and value delivery systems and explain how companies go about producing and delivering customer value.
3. Explain the importance of retaining current customers as well as attracting new ones.
4. Discuss customer relationship marketing and the main steps in establishing a customer relationship programme.
5. Define quality and explain the importance of total quality marketing in building value-laden, profitable relationships with customers.

Chapter Overview

This chapter reviews a key trend in marketing for the twenty-first century: the trend toward the use of *relationship marketing* to improve customer satisfaction. The chapter reinterprets the marketing concept, stressing the need to offer real *customer value* and *customer satisfaction* in order to compete effectively. The chapter discusses how companies deliver value and satisfaction through a *value chain* and a *value delivery system.* Discussion additionally focuses on the strategic need for marketers to retain current customers through relationship marketing programs versus how marketers attract new customers. The chapter concludes with an examination of *total quality marketing* by defining quality and discussing the importance of building value-laden, profitable relationships with customers.

Teaching Notes

Refer to the following pages for teaching notes.

Defining Customer Value

Transparency PM 11-1 relates to the material on customer-centred marketing, customer value, and satisfaction on pp.438-445 and Figure 11-1 on p.439. It previews the concepts that underlie the following discussion on Porter's Value Chain.

Elements of Customer Value

1. Customer-Centred

To win in today's marketplace, companies must excel at becoming more customer-centred in delivering superior value to their target customers. A key concept is market engineering - the process of designing the whole company system to deliver customer value at every level.

2. Customer Delivered Value

Delivered value is defined as the difference between total customer value and total customer cost. The text example emphasises the dollar value of customer costs. Consumers also weigh psychological costs such as image reputation, and decision-time.

3. Customer Satisfaction

Customer satisfaction with a purchase depends upon the product's performance relative to a buyer's expectations. Expectations are based upon the customer's past buying experiences, the opinions of friends and associates, and marketer and competitor information. Expectations may be realistic or unrealistic. Further, as the text observes, satisfaction alone does not retain customers. Total Customer Satisfaction aims at meeting, exceeding, and then continually raising customer expectations for product performance. To achieve this end, companies must track their customer's expectations, perceived company performance, and customer satisfaction. The goal is to create customer delight - an emotional affinity with a product or service, not just a rational preference. This kind of bond is required for obtaining high customer loyalty in an increasingly competitive marketplace.

Tip

Ask student to think of a commodity product, like sand or building bricks, and ask how a company could increase total customer value to such a dull item. Answer could include scheduling delivery, stock holding, spread of delivery, style of delivery. Fertiliser companies do not just sell fertiliser to the farmer they spread it and analyse the soil and recommend the best mix.

Notes for PM 11-1

Value Chain

Transparency PM 11-2 relates to the material on Michael Porter's Value Chain on pp.445-448 and Figure 11-2 on p.447.

The Generic Value Chain

Primary Activities:

1. Inbound Logistics

Inbound logistics consists of those activities and their co-ordination that bring needed materials into the business. Value is added in the choice of materials and their integration into the business operations in a timely manner.

2. Operations

Operations is the first step in developing materials into value-added products. Operations add value through manufacturing innovations and processes.

3. Outbound Logistics

Outbound logistics refers to the distributions stem set up by the business. As with inbound logistics, co-ordination and integration of the firm's products with the needs of retailers and customers creates value.

4. Marketing and Sales

Marketing and sales educate consumers and position the firm's products and image to create value.

5. Service

Service creates value both by keeping the product's performance in line with customer expectations and by demonstrating to the customer the firm's commitment to meeting customer needs.

Support Activities: (occur within each primary activity).

1. Firm Infrastructure

How the firm is set up permeates each primary activity and determines the parameters of action each activity can take.

2. Human Resource Management

Recruitment, training, and evaluation add value in relation to the competition's efforts.

3. Technology Development

All primary activities must develop and maintain technological advantages.

4. Procurement

Every primary activity procures inputs of both material and expertise.

Tip

Choose a product, say a PC, and ask how each part of the value chain can help add value (or take it away).

Notes for PM 11-2

Core Business Processes & Value Delivery Systems

Transparency PM 11-3 relates to the material on core business processes and value delivery systems on pp.447-448 that follows the discussion of Porter's Value Chain. You may wish to leave transparency PM 11-2 of Figure 11-2 showing while discussing this material or use this transparency as a separate transparency for discussion.

Core Business Processes

Product Development

This consists of all the activities involved in identifying, researching, and developing new products with speed, high quality, and reasonable cost.

Inventory Management

This consists of all the activities involved in developing and managing the right inventory levels of raw materials, semifinished materials, and finished goods so that adequate supplies are available while avoiding the costs of high overstocks.

Order to Payment

This consists of all the activities involved in receiving orders, approving them, shipping the goods on time, and collecting payment.

Customer Service

This consists of all the activities involved in making it easy for customers to ready the right parties within the company to obtain service, answers, and solutions to problems.

Value Delivery Systems

To enhance competitive advantage, firms look beyond their own value chains for ways of improving customer value. In linking the company's value chain with those of its suppliers and resellers, the company improves the performance of the entire customer value delivery system. A key concept of the value delivery system is partnering.

Partnering

Partnering involves merging key aspects of two or more companies in the delivery system to increase customer value. The text relates to the example of Marks and Spencer's employees working at suppliers' factories. Other examples include sharing sales information with suppliers by manufacturers and retailers, co-ordinating promotional activities throughout the chain, and sharing new technological developments in inventory and database ordering systems with other chain

Notes for PM 11-3

Relationship Marketing

Transparency PM 11-4 relates to the material on pp.449-450.

Retaining Customers

Getting New Customers Costs Money

Marketers need to think in terms of how much of each aspect of the promotion mix and marketing mix must be spent each time a new customer is recruited. Common sense tells us that current customers will need fewer of these expensive resources to make their buying decisions than will potential customers.

Cost of Lost Customers

Once marketers realise that losing customers is expensive, they need to determine how to identify why customers are lost to measure the actual cost of customer loss. Large companies should prepare frequency distribution indicating the percentage of customers who defect for different reasons.

Customer's Lifetime Value

When the revenues of each customer are factored in, it is possible to determine the customers lifetime value - the amount of profit generated each year for the company over the lifetime of that customer's business with the company.

Levels of Relationship Marketing

Relationship Marketing - involves creating, maintaining, and enhancing strong relationships with customers and other stakeholders. Levels of relationships with customers include:

Basic - The company salesperson sells the product but does not follow up in any way.

Reactive -The salesperson sells the product and encourages the customer to call whenever he or she has any questions or problems.

Accountable - The salesperson contacts the customer shortly after the, sale to check performance and seek the customer's suggestions for improvement.

Proactive - The salesperson contacts the customer from time to time with suggestions about improved product use or helpful new products.

Partnership - The company works continuously with the customer and with other customers to discover ways to deliver better value.

Tip

Question current loyalty programmes being run by firms. Ask if they are obtaining loyalty to producer or to the "sales promotion". Do such promotions distract from brands? Ask about good ways of establishing relationships.

Notes for PM 11-4

Relationship Marketing Programme

Transparency PM 11-5 relates to the material identifying the main steps in establishing a relationship marketing programme on pp.452-453.

Steps in Establishing Relationship Marketing

1. Identify the key customers meriting relationship management.

Choose the largest or best customers and designate them for relationships' management. Other customers can be added who show exceptional growth or who pioneer new industry developments.

2. Assign a skilled relationship manager to each key customer.

Relationship managers should have characteristics that match or appeal to the customer. Salespeople should be trained in relationship management techniques or be reassigned to non-relationship accounts.

3. Develop a clear job description for relationship managers.

Describe their reporting relationships, objectives, responsibilities, and evaluation criteria. The relationship manager should be the focus for all client contact and manage only one or a few key clients.

4. Have each relationship manager develop annual and long-range customer relationship plans.

Plans should state objectives, specific actions, and required resources. Further, plans should identify the evaluation criteria that will be used to evaluate performance. The criteria should be checked against company goals for assessment and possible revision before implementation.

5. Appoint an overall manager to supervise the relationship managers.

The overall manager develops the job descriptions, evaluation criteria, and resource support of the entire program to increase relationship manager effectiveness.

Tip

Ask whether college students should be targeted for relationship marketing programmes for such items as clothing, entertainment and sports products?

Notes for PM 11-5

Total Quality Marketing

These notes relate to the material on Implementing Total Quality Marketing and summarise the information in Marketing Highlight 11-4 on p.458.

Quality and Performance

Quality is defined as the totality of features and characteristics of a product or service bear on its ability to satisfy stated or implied needs.

Performance Quality refers to the level at which a product performs its functions.

Conformance Quality refers to the freedom from defects and the consistency with which a product delivers a specified level of performance.

Marketing Highlight 11-4: Pursuing a Total Quality Marketing Strategy

1. Quality is in the eyes of the customer. A quality programme must begin with the customer's needs and end with customer perceptions.

2. Quality must reflect every company activity. Each functional area and each company activity must understand and embody the total quality concept.

3. Quality requires total employee commitment. All company employees must be personally committed to the total quality programme

4. Quality requires high-quality partners. Value chain members of the customer delivery system must also embody total quality commitment.

5. A quality program cannot save a poor product. Companies must recognise that poor product cannot be "quality imaged" successfully.

6. Quality can always be improved. Nothing is ever perfect.

7. Quality improvement may require quantum leaps. Competitive conditions may demand vast and immediate improvements over small and incremental ones.

8. Quality does not cost more. Cost savings come from lower rejection rates, better customer satisfaction, and new technologies

9. Quality is necessary but may not be sufficient. More demanding buyers have even higher expectations for performance. Companies cannot assume that quality alone will be competitive.

10. Quality needs long-term commitment. Quality is not a one off quick fix. It is a commitment to continuous process of improvement.

> **Tip**
>
> Ask who defines quality? Is it a technical specification or a national or international standard? Does the achievement of total quality mean there is no longer need for improvement?

Comments on Discussing the Issues

1. All consumers have stories of personal dissatisfaction, and this topic can create a lively classroom discussion. You can highlight the idea that value is relative by probing answers. When a student recounts a problem, ask whether there were other customers receiving the same quality product or service who were satisfied, or even more dissatisfied than the student was. Stress the fact that following the marketing concept—meeting consumer needs—is really the key to quality.

2. Quality is a relative phenomenon. Once quality reaches acceptable levels for a particular customer, further improvements may be less noticeable and much more difficult or expensive to achieve. Service quality levels are often used as an example: changing customer service levels from 85 per cent to 95 per cent, a relatively small 10 per cent increase, may require a 60 per cent increase in inventory levels. This can be very costly, as working capital must be raised to buy the extra inventory, and physical space must be built to accommodate it. If customers do not require this extra service level, the extra costs may have been wasted.

   Students may be able to relate quality levels from past purchase experience. Certain levels of quality are clearly unacceptable: the sales representative totally ignoring the student. At a higher level of quality, the sales rep might ask if he or she could be of any help and subsequently show the students the different types of brands or alternatives the store carries. Some quality improvements may go completely unnoticed: a change in the decor and lighting in the store takes considerable effort on the part of the owner, but be imperceptible to the reader.

3. TQM for; (1) A packaged food company - price, taste, environment-friendly disposal methods, legal compliance on health of consumer, design and downsizing of package, and so on; (2) a restaurant meal - high standards of hygiene, good quality of service, variety in menu, relaxed comfortable seats; (3) a new car - good after sales service, safe, reliable, good performance, production processes use teamwork, quality circles, JIT in order to eliminate unnecessary cost and waste; (4) a family holiday - customer expects everything to be well prepared and organised so that he has nothing to worry about; (5) A university education - affordable fees, availability of grants, high achievements standards, accreditation from other bodies, facilities, quality instructors and so on.

4. Which department should define quality standards? Different departments have different values, and these affect how they define quality. Research and development typically seeks a high level of technical performance, engineering may look for a sophisticated design and processes of production, manufacturing wants ease, speed, and economy of manufacturing, and marketing attempts to satisfy end-user needs. Each of these viewpoints is legitimate, but they often conflict in practice. In general, the customer-centred view of quality advocated by marketing is a good starting point for quality standards. However, the views and experience of other departments are usually helpful and often critical in setting appropriate, affordable, and achievable quality goals.

5. Let us take health care for example. Quality in health care is a difficult and emotional topic. As national health care reform moves forward, we will be faced with the question of how much care we can afford, and how to allocate funds to maximise quality. Fortunately, some aspects of medical service quality are easily measured and improved: we can quantify how promptly patients are seen in a clinic, how often bills are over- or undercharged, the caesarean section rate for obstetrics wards, the level of preventable diseases such as measles, or the postoperative infection rate of a hospital. Researchers are also working on the difficult issue of defining how well people feel: did a given treatment make the patient feel any better? As this research moves forward, we will learn more about perceived quality in health care, and the true cost effectiveness of various treatments.

6. "Just-in-time" inventory management is a very demanding discipline: if inventory does not arrive properly, a whole factory can be shut down almost immediately. There is great value to the process, however: users of JIT cut their needs for working capital and warehouse space, and discover many ways to improve their manufacturing simply by paying closer attention to the processes.

   For a supplier selling products on a JIT basis, the value chain is an essential part of making the process work. *Outbound logistics*, *marketing and sales*, and *service* are all integral parts of maintaining a JIT partnership with a customer. These elements make up the core of the JIT relationship. The early parts of the supplier's value chain, managing *inbound logistics* and *operations*, must be managed with great care, or the latter parts of the chain cannot function.

Comments on Applying the Concepts

1. This question is based on an interesting article by Gary L. Clark, Peter F. Kaminski, and David R. Rink, "Consumer Complaints: Advice on How Companies Should Respond Based on an Empirical Study," published in the *Journal of Consumer Marketing,* 9:3, Summer 1992, pages 5-14. The authors had a group of business majors send letters to 166 companies complaining about 248 different branded products, and surveyed the students' attitudes about the companies involved before and after writing. They found that students who received a free product in response to their complaints had significantly improved images of the companies they had written to, regardless of whether the response was received promptly or late. Students who received a letter only showed little change in their images of the companies they had written to. Students who received no response developed significantly worse images of the companies they had written to, including perceptions that the company was uninterested in consumers and unfair in dealings with customers.

   This study looks at how companies work for *customer retention*. A company that sends a free product is responding in a careful, deliberate, and expensive way to enhance the customer relationship—and the study results show that customers respond very positively. A basic form letter reply, a simple *reactive* response by a company, gets essentially no response from the customer: it is just enough to maintain the current company image without damage. A company that does not respond at all clearly does not practice relationship marketing, and is very vulnerable to losing customers to a more responsive competitor.

2. This question explores the strongest sort of relationship marketing, instances where the product is *very* closely tied to the customer. A computer manager may say, "We're an IBM shop," showing that the brand of computers in use is a part of the organisation's identity. At the extreme, these relationships have been called "cult" marketing. Harley Davidson can attract Harley riders to ride from all over the world to a Milwaukee anniversary celebration for the company. Car owners such as the BMW car owners formed the BMW Car Club, and they rent race tracks for the weekend to allow members to drive at *autobahn*-like speeds.

   The values and satisfactions that these loyal customers receive vary widely. At their basic level, there is usually a strongly felt customer need that is exceptionally well satisfied by the product. Celebrities have often looked at customer needs, then made a concerted effort to market themselves, setting up organisations and using public-relations consultants and other marketing techniques. Princess Diana, for example, has made a commitment to speaking out for the homeless, John Major on the classless society and Tony Blair for those disgusted with Westminster insiders. They speak on the national stage with conviction and eloquence, and all inspire strong admiration among their constituents and strong disagreement from others. However we may feel about any or all of these people, there is clearly a strong relationship between each of them and their followers.

Case 11
Feinschmecker Saucen:
Pricey n' Spicey

Synopsis

Uncle Ben's Rice is the market leader in the Austrian market for parboiled rice. A survey has shown that the brand was very dominant and well known within the market. Uncle Ben's Rice gained competitive advantage through being perceived by consumers as; superior quality, superior taste, easy to prepare, modern, wholesome, nutritious, expensive (yet justifiable due to superior quality). Master Foods Austria (MFA) the owners of Uncle Ben's saw the strengths of the brand as an opportunity for brand extension. In view of the general trend towards international eating, MFA decided to extend the Uncle Ben's brand to ready-to-serve sauces with exotic tastes. The logic was that both the rice and the sauce were to be fast and easy to cook and thus be eaten together. This was to provide a good solution to people coming home late from work or in those occasions where they have no time to cook. To maintain the high quality and naturalness image of the brand the sauces were to contain whole pieces of vegetables and were named Uncle Ben's Feinschmecker sauce, to emphasise the quality. MFA identified the target market to be women between 20 to 40 years who were interested in food and variety, well educated, willing to try foreign tastes and have high income to consume the relatively expensive sauce. They decided to produce different sauces to suit different segments of the target market. Having conducted concept tests using the target market, MFA established that the reasons for purchasing the sauces would be quality, comfort (ease of use), confidence in the product and the unique foreign taste.

In September 1992 MFA launched six varieties of Uncle Ben's Feinschmecker sauce in Austria and two more were added later. The sauces were also launched in other European countries but using different recipes, brand names and varieties to suit the different markets. The advertising concentrated on creating awareness and interest, and emphasised the link to the highly reputable rice. Point-of-sale promotions allowed consumers to taste the new sauces. The launch of the Feinschmecker sauces was regarded as successful but the purchase frequency varied from group to group and the popularity of the sauces contrasted with the results of the concept test. The concept tests were performed based on the intended target market while the consumption survey used a random sample. The survey revealed that the main consumers of the sauces were not necessarily the targeted ones. People with medium to high income bought them for the purpose of preparing quick and easy meals due to their fast lifestyle rather than for the unique tastes. They mainly bought the Chinesisch sub sauer, a taste they were familiar with, rather than the more exotic sauces. The case also suggests that there were already dried and frozen alternatives of offering exotic tastes, as well as spices that enabled people to add seasoning to their liking. Nevertheless people still regarded the sauces to be of high quality, wholesome, secure and modern.

Teaching Objectives

1. Provide students with an opportunity to understand the close relationship between the buying process and customer satisfaction.

2. Challenge students to comment in the appropriateness of the marketing research that was carried out in the case study.

3. Demonstrate that the elements of a marketing strategy must fit with one another to ensure customer satisfaction.

Study Questions

1. **What internal and external stimuli may start the buyer decision process for Uncle Ben's Feinschmecker Sauce? Compare the buyer decision process of an initial purchase and a repeat purchase. What is the type of buying decision behaviour in each case? How does Uncle Ben's the brand name influence the decision?**

Some of the internal stimuli students should mention are; hunger - this is one of the basic needs of human beings and therefore a need that must be satisfied. Concerning Feinschmecker sauces, this need can be activated where a person returns home late from work and will seek something to satisfy his needs. He may decide to buy a type of Feinschmecker sauce to satisfy his need. The decision to buy the sauce may be based on past experience, external stimuli, etc.; past experience - the knowledge of a certain taste may activate the decision to buy a Feinschmecker sauce. Furthermore, a person may have bought a Feincshmecker sauce before and enjoyed it and therefore would like to satisfy the need with this sauce. External stimuli are such as; changed circumstances - for example a person who is promoted in work to a higher and more demanding job, may not have the time to cook and thus change his lifestyle and purchase brands that will suit his new needs i.e. to cook fast. Uncle Ben's sauces may provide the solution as they offer good quality and nutrition but do not require a long time to cook; marketing influences - marketers can activate the needs of the consumer through advertising, sales promotions and provide product attributes that appeal to the target market. (Use examples given in the case study)

A consumer considering buying a cook-in sauce for the first time will evaluate all the brands and varieties in the store where their food shopping normally takes place. There are several factors which will influence the final choice; product packaging and appearance of the sauce; if it is in a jar; amount of product in jar or tin; are the instructions easy to follow; price; brand name or name of the manufacturer; money saving promotions; guarantees of satisfaction. Initial purchase will be made by taking into account some or all of the above criteria. Repeat purchase decisions will miss out some or all of the above criteria. If the customer was satisfied with the product they initially purchased they may repeat the purchase without assessing any other brand or variety. Repeat purchasers will probably try different varieties in the same range produced by the manufacturer whose product met their initial expectations, thus brand loyalty has been created. If the product which was purchased initially was unsatisfactory but the consumer is still attracted to the notion of quick and convenient meals using sauce, they will probably try an alternative brand or variety.

Students should highlight that previous reluctance to buy cook-in sauces may be overcome by consumers' confidence in Uncle Ben's products, their rice in particular. Consumers are familiar with the quality of Uncle Ben's rice and they believe that it is a better product than other brands of rice. This perceived quality is associated with the brand name and therefore the new sauces are automatically perceived to be of better quality and more likely to be satisfactory than its competitors' products. Initial purchasers may therefore be influenced to try Uncle Ben's varieties in preference to other brands. The brand name Uncle Ben is associated with quality and easy to prepare foods such as their easy cook rice. This association will serve to reassure potential purchasers that the meal made with their sauces will be easy to prepare and of satisfactory quality.

2. Show the importance of the post-purchase behaviour for Uncle Ben's Feinschmecker Sauce? What figures in the case study indicate consumers' satisfaction with the product? How can MFA influence the level of customer satisfaction achieved? How does MFA's targeting help achieve customer satisfaction?

Once the consumer has purchased and tried Uncle Ben's Feinschmecker Sauce they will form an opinion of the product. If the product failed to meet their expectations the consumer will be disappointed and will not buy the product again. The consumer probably had high levels of expectation when the product was first purchased due to their perceived value of products carrying the Uncle Ben's name. The dissatisfied customer is not only unhappy with the sauce but may become disillusioned with all products carrying the Uncle Ben's name and be deterred from buying or continuing to buy those products. In addition to the personal dissatisfaction the consumer will convey their disappointment in the product to others. This is very damaging to the brand. On the other hand, if the product exceeded the customer's expectations they will be delighted and certainly make further purchases. Additionally, they will strongly recommend the product to other people which enhances the product's chance of penetrating the market further. The excellent experience with one product branded with Uncle Ben's name may persuade the consumer to try other product line bearing this brand name.

According to the case study by November 1993, 6% of Austrian households had bought the product once and 7% had bought it more often. During the first 3 months of the product's life, 1% of those consumers who bought the product initially had already repurchased signalling their satisfaction. The repurchase rate surveyed by the Gfk panel of households 9 months after the launch of the product was 32%. This level of repurchase signifies the high rate of product satisfaction.

Some students will suggest that customer would increase their level of satisfaction if marketers can differentiate their brands by developing relevant added values to the product, that is values over and above their commodity constituents. Instructors might want to discuss the product levels such as the generic level, expected level, augmented level and potential level. Ask students to give examples of the various levels in relation to the Feinschmecker sauce, in order to increase customer satisfaction. Other students will mention the importance of segmentation and targeting to ensure customer satisfaction.

In order for a product to be successful it must fulfil the customer's wants and needs. MFA recognised that the attributes of their product fitted a particular customer profile therefore Feinschmecker sauce has been deliberately marketed in order to capture that market segment. By fulfilling the customer's expectations of the benefits derived from using the product customer satisfaction follows automatically. The product attributes MFA identified were as follows; meals could be prepared quickly and easily, convenient to transport and store, jar is reclosable for later use, several varieties to satisfy diverse tastes. The product attributes were then matched to the market segment which MFA felt would derive the most benefits from the new product thus making them more likely to purchase it. The identified customer profile was as follows; two person households - jar large enough for two people, 20 - 40 year old - more likely to try new food types, interested in food and variety - adventurous enough to try different tastes, open-minded - willing to try something new, high income - able to afford product and career women- too busy for conventional cooking. In addition to the main target group MFA provided a variety of mild sauces which would appeal to other market segments thereby enlarging their customer base to include families and children.

3. Several stores sell the product below the recommended price of SCH 30. Why should they do that and could it harm Uncle Ben's reputation?

Students will highlight several reasons why some stores sell below the recommended price; (1) The target market originally identified by MFA was not responding as expected. It was found that other market segments purchased the product. These segments do not necessarily belong to the high income social class. This reason may have driven these stores to reduce the price in order to attract more people of the lower social classes; (2) Target market do not perceive the product as having a high value. Therefore the stores reduce the price to attract a higher proportion of this target market; (3) Stores may have decided to adopt a penetrative strategy and increase their volume of sales. By offering the same products at a lower price, they may attract more people to the stores and away from other stores selling the same products; (4) Possibly the store's customer base is the lower social classes. These stores know their customers and may have decided to lower the price accordingly. It may be that to those social classes, the recommended price is perceived as being too high.

Selling Uncle Ben's sauces at a reduced price may damage the reputation of the brand. (1) Consumers who have bought elsewhere at the full price may think that the quality of the product is declining. They may perceive the products as being of lower quality. This inference by consumers may be extended to the original products of the Uncle Ben's brands, namely the parboiled rice. Thus, the reduced price may lead the consumers to perceive the products and the entire brand possessing lower quality; (2) Because of the above Uncle Ben's brands may lose their position as market leaders especially in the parboiled rice market. Consumers that want high quality may switch to other brands. The positioning of Uncle Ben's brands in the eyes of the consumers may be changed; (3) The price reduction in some stores may present conflicts with other retailers and will establish a price war.

4. What explains the big difference between the concept test results and eventual buyer behaviour? Does the difference in the results matter?

The results of the concept test for Feinschmecker sauces were vastly different from eventual buyer behaviour. The test indicated that the more exotic sauces were likely to sell the best, with Karibisch being the most popular variety. In contrast, the best selling sauce turned out to be the non-spicy Chinesisch, with the least sales being attributed to Karibisch! There is insufficient information about the concept test to establish why this difference occurred, but there are several possibilities. (1) Consumer feedback at the concept test may have led the company to substantially modify the product or packaging before launching the sauces; alternatively the questions asked at the tests may have been badly phrased (e.g. leading or ambiguous). (2) Consumers involved in the test may not have been representative of the consumers who subsequently purchased the product, because whilst the spicier sauces were the most frequently purchased by Feinschmecker's target market, it was households with children (a group outside the target segment) who generally purchased the best selling Chinesisch sauce. Fortunately the brand was deemed to be successful anyway but the implications of the misleading test results could have been serious. By targeting the wrong market segment, MFA may have found that at best customer satisfaction with the product was low, and at worst it failed to take off completely. It is quite possible that the repurchase rate of Feinschmecker sauce would have been considerably higher if the company had more accurately identified and targeted the appropriate market segment.

5. How does this brand extension endanger the standing of Uncle Ben's rice? Was the brand extension worth the risk? Do you agree that Feinschmecker Sauce is a success?

Uncle Ben's rice is the market leader in the Austrian market for parboiled rice because of its superior quality and taste. MFA therefore decided to increase the potential of Uncle Ben's image by extending the brand - a strategy which accounts for approximately 40% of all new grocery launches. The introduction of a product which was complementary to the rice would potentially enable Feinschmecker sauces to benefit from Uncle Ben's strong image, without the risk of cannibalising the brand's rice sales. On the other hand, brand extensions that fail to meet expectations will often be rejected and even more seriously may undermine the consumer's perception of the entire brand name. The implications to MFA therefore are that rejection of Feinschmecker sauces could potentially result in the image of Uncle Ben's rice being undermined, thus reducing sales and jeopardising the brand's position as a market leader. The study indicates that MFA understood the risk and carefully considered the characteristics of the new sauce to ensure that it was compatible with brand image of Uncle Ben's rice. They therefore took a calculated risk which potentially could have been extremely successful.

Feinschmecker has proved successful although some fine tuning of the varieties on offer would seem appropriate. Market research may be helpful in pin-pointing how the tastes of certain varieties need to be altered in order to satisfy the customer. Some varieties which are not proving popular perhaps need a boost from specialised advertising i.e. advertisements, either television or magazines which feature a specific flavour of sauce to enhance customer awareness and create interest in that particular variety. The fact that 32% of the members of the panel which MFA are monitoring are still repurchasing after 6 months would indicate long-term brand loyalty and customer satisfaction.

Jokes and Quotes

Zero defects gives zero defections.

If you . . . our course "How to fly solo in six easy lessons". . . Send us your new address and we will send you the last chapter, "How to land your plane safely".
ADVERTISEMENT

Nothing is more satisfying than when timing and delivery occur in perfect sequence.
ANON

Be not slothful in business.
BIBLE

Those who most enjoy ads, already own the products.
EDMUND CARPENTER

A consumer is a shopper who is sore about something.
HAROLD COFFIN

Business neglected is business lost.
DANIE DEFOE

Those who enter to buy, support me. Those who come to flatter, please me. Those who complain, teach me how I may please others so that more will come. Only those hurt me who are displeased but do not complain. They refuse me permission to correct my errors and thus improve my service.
MARSHALL FIELD

Remember that time is money.
BENJAMIN FRANKLIN

One catches more flies with a spoonful of honey than with twenty casks of vinegar.
HENRY IV

Value is the most invisible and impalpable of ghosts, and comes and goes unthought of while the visible and dense matter remains as it was.
W. STANLEY JEVONS

A shopworker, tired of his job, gave it up and joined the police force. Several months later a friend asked him how he liked being a policeman. "Well", he replied, "The pay and the hours are good, but what I like best of all is that the customer is always wrong."
JOKE

Just give me a shave. I haven't got time to listen to a haircut.
JOKE

Barber: How was that lotion I gave you for your bald patch?
Customer: You remember telling me to rub it every night?
Barber: Yes
Customer: Well, my head's still bald but I have to shave my fingers twice a day.
JOKE

In the factory we make cosmetics. In the store we sell hope.
CHARLES REVSON

Warning - customers are perishable.
SIGN

The difference between failure and success is doing a thing nearly right and doing a thing exactly right.
EDWARD SIMMONS

Does she . . . or doesn't she/ Only her hairdresser knows for sure.
SLOGAN FOR CLAIROL HAIR COLOURING

Quality never goes out of style.
SLOGAN FOR LEVI JEANS

Once you've driven one, you're unlikely to drive another.
SLOGAN FOR MERCEDES BENZ

A railroad is 95 per cent men and 5 percent iron.
A. H. SMITH

I have been against commercial broadcasting ever since I heard a Toscanini radio concert in New York interrupted by the sponsor's slogan - "It may be December outside, but it is always August under your armpits."

JOHN SNAGGE

A well-informed employee is the best sales person a company can have.
E. J. THOMAS

Always do right. This will surprise some people and astonish the rest.
MARK TWAIN

Those who arrive early at the battlefield will be in a position to take the initiative.
SUN TZU

In the past human life was lived in a bullock cart; in the future it will be lived in an aeroplane and the change of speed amounts to a difference in quality.
ALFRED NORTH WHITEHEAD

R. J. Wrigley was on a flight when a friend asked why, with Wrigley's chewing gum far outselling all other brands, he still needed to advertise. He replied, "For the same reason that the pilot keeps this plane's engines running even though we're already in the air"
R. J. WRIGLEY

Chapter 12

Creating Competitive Advantage:

Competitor Analysis and Competitive Marketing Strategies

Chapter Objectives

After reading this chapter, you should be able to:

1. Explain the importance of developing competitive marketing strategies that position the company against competitors and give it the strongest possible competitive advantage.
2. Identify the steps companies go through in analysing competitors.
3. Discuss the competitive strategies that market leader use to expand the market and to protect and expand their market shares.
4. Describe the strategies market challengers and followers use to increase their market shares and profits.
5. Discuss how market nichers find and develop profitable corners of the market.

Chapter Overview

In order to prepare an effective marketing strategy, a company must consider its competitors as well as its actual and potential customers. Competitor analysis first involves identifying the company's major competitors, using both an industry and a market-based analysis. The company then gathers information on competitors' objectives, strategies, strengths and weaknesses, and reaction patterns. Which competitive marketing strategy makes the most sense depends on the company's industry position and its objectives, opportunities, and resources.

A market leader faces three challenges: expanding the total market, protecting market share, and expanding market share. The market leader is interested in finding ways to expand the total market because it will benefit most from any increased sales. To protect its existing market share, the market leader has several defences: position defence, flanking defence, pre-emptive defence, counteroffensive defence, mobile defence, and contraction defence. Leaders can also try to increase their market shares.

A market challenger is a firm that aggressively tries to expand its market share by attacking the leader, other runner-up firms, or smaller firms in the industry. The challenger can choose from a variety of attack strategies, including a frontal attack, flanking attack, encirclement attack, bypass attack, and guerrilla attack.

A market follower is a runner-up firm that chooses not to rock the boat, usually out of fear that it stands to lose more than it might gain.

A market nicher is a smaller firm that serves some part of the market that is not likely to attract the larger firms. Market nichers often become specialists in some end use, vertical level, customer size, specific customer, geographic area, product or product feature, or service.

A competitive orientation is important in today's markets, but companies should not overdo their focus on competitors. Companies are more likely to be hurt by emerging consumer needs and new competitors then by existing competitors.

Teaching Notes

Refer to the following pages for teaching notes.

Competitor Analysis

Transparency PM 12-1 corresponds to Figure 12.1 on p.469 and relates to the material on pp.468-477.

Competitor Analysis

1. Identifying Competitors

Competitors include those who make products that compete directly against those of the company and more broadly those that meet the same needs. Companies are more threatened by latent competitors than current ones. Competitors may be identified by industry or by markets.

2. Determining Competitors' Objectives

Competitors differ in the relative emphasis they put on variables such as technological innovation, cost leadership, quality, and market share.

3. Identifying Competitors' Strategies

A strategic group is a group of firms in an industry that follows the same or similar strategy in a given target market.

4. Assessing Competitors' Strengths and Weaknesses

Companies keep data records on competitors' performance to assess likely future moves and capabilities. Benchmarking involves identifying the top performance features of a given product and measuring company performance against that standard.

5. Estimating Competitors' Reaction Patterns

Beyond capability, competitors must be assessed in terms of how they respond to the company's strategies. Each competitor will have preferences based upon a combination of functional specialities, management preferences, and historical patterns.

6. Selecting Competitors to Attack and Avoid

Companies typically classify competitors for possible strategic action. Strong or Weak Competitors may be attacked. Weak competitors are easier targets but less profitable. Close or Distant Competitors may be targeted. Well-Behaved or Disruptive Competitors also provide different opportunities and pose different threats. A valuable tool for selecting competitors to attack and to avoid, Customer Value Analysis, is covered on the following transparency.

Tip

Relate the competitor analysis sequence to a team game such as soccer. Choose some well-known teams and evaluate them.

Notes for PM 12-1

Customer Value Analysis

Transparency PM 12-2 corresponds to the information in Marketing Highlight 12-2 on p.476.

Customer Value Analysis

1. Identify The Major Attributes That Customers Value

Use market research to verify which attributes customers value in products. Link attribute lists to distinct customer groups.

2. Assess The Importance Of Different Attributes

Market research should also identify attribute importance by ranking and rating each attribute.

3. Assess Company/Competitor Performance on Different Customer Values Against the Values Rated Importance

Research should have customers compare competitors' products against those of the company on attributes rated important.

4. Examine Specific Segment Company/Competitor Performance on an Attribute-by-Attribute Basis

Competitive advantages can be identified when the company evaluates ranking/rating measures in terms of key strategic attributes the company can exploit through product improvements and/or production improvements in quality.

5. Monitor Customer Values Over Time

Success in achieving competitive advantages both draws competitive response and changes the customers expectations for performance. As time passes, customer tastes will change as well as ranking-rating levels of identified important attributes.

> **Tip**
>
> Ask students to evaluate the growing market for small cars for young single people, particularly women. How do the competitors shape up to this segments' needs? Do they shape up differently up to the car market for young men?

Notes for PM 12-2

Competitive Strategies

Transparency PM 12-3 relates to the material on pp.477-480. You may wish to link this discussion to Porter's Value Chain Analysis covered in Chapter 11.

Competitive Positions

Cost-Leadership

Cost-leadership is gained by being the lowest-cost producer in the industry. This affords the company flexibility in responding to competitive moves by always being able to offer the lowest price to the consumer.

Differentiation

This strategy creates competitive advantage by offering products with unique customer benefits or features not available from competitive offerings. Here the company concentrates on creating a highly differentiated product line and marketing programme so that it comes across as the class leader in the industry. This image helps it to compete against lower cost rivals.

Focus

This narrow-focus strategy achieves competitive advantage by concentrating on a narrow segment of a larger market. Emphasis is often on quality or benefits in a tightly defined market subsegment.

Middle-of-the-Road

Firms that do not pursue one of the three general strategies above lack strategic focus. While they may survive, they are extremely vulnerable to more focused competitors and will be poorly positioned to react successfully to environmental changes such as economic downturns.

Tip

Ask students to identify dangers in each of the strategies. Ask what sort of manager an organisation need? Is there no difference?

Notes for PM 12-3

Market Leader Strategies

Transparency PM 12-4 relates to the material on pp.480-486 and Figure 12-4 on p.484. Leaders have the most influence on the market of all competitors and are often in a position to drive the market.

Expanding The Total Market

The leader gains the most when the market expands. New Users can be attracted from those who are still unaware of the product. New Uses can be discovered and marketed to increase purchase. More Usage strategies aim at convincing buyers to use the product more often and in greater amounts for each existing usage occasion.

Protecting Market Share

1. Position Defence

This strategy commits resources to maintaining the status quo of successful products. This strategy is seldom successful as consumer tastes and expectations change and competitors innovate.

2. Flanking Defence

Weaknesses in product lines, usually require flanking defences. Smart companies fill gaps to defend flanks.

3. Pre-emptive Defence

This strategy anticipates new competitive moves and repositions the company in advance of the introduction of the competitive offer.

4. Counteroffensive Defence

When a challenger makes a successful attack, the leader can sometimes counter the offer more successfully due to greater resources. Under these conditions, the leader essentially mimics the challenging product but with greater marketing clout.

5. Mobile Defence

Almost the opposite of "marketing myopia", the mobile defence focuses on broader underlying consumer needs versus current product form. A further extension of this defence involves market diversification where the company enters new markets as current markets or products lose their appeal or are successfully attacked.

6. Contraction Defence

As conditions change, some leaders restructure by reducing operations and refocusing exclusively on core businesses.

Tip

Ask how IBM could have defended itself from the attack from Japanese mainframe makers, mini computers, game machines and PC makers? Could they defend by sticking to the mainframe?

Notes for PM 12-4

Market Challenger Strategies

Transparency PM 12-5 relates to the material on pp.487-490 and Figure 12-5 on p.489.

Frontal Attack

Strong challengers sometimes match the market leader's product, advertising, price, and distribution efforts.

Flanking Attack

This strategy chooses weak ends of the competitor's existing product lines and launches new products to meet consumer needs. Alternatively, gaps within the competitor's lines may be filled by the challenger.

Encirclement Attack

When the challenger has superior resources, it can launch product offers against all of the competitors positions.

Bypass Attack

This strategy usually involves technological innovations that ignores the competitor's offers and offers the consumer new ways to meet needs.

Guerrilla Attack

Smaller and poorly financed challengers sometimes use sporadic marketing offers that probe competitors for weaknesses. These guerrilla attacks must be followed more substantial strategies to lead to long-lasting competitive advantage.

Tip

Ask how Japanese has successfully attacked markets such as watches, hi-fi, car, motorcycles, TV, etc. Is their mode of attack changing?

Notes for PM 12-5

Specialist Strategies

These notes relate to the material on pp.490-494.

Market-Follower Strategies

1. Cloner

Followers may choose to copy closely the leader's products, distribution, advertising, and other aspects of the marketing program.

2. Imitator

The imitator copies some things from the leader but maintains some differentiation in terms of packaging, advertising, pricing, and other factors.

3. Adapter

The adapter builds on the leader's products and marketing programs, often improving them.

Market-Nicher Strategies

1. End-Use Specialist

These firms specialise in one type of end use customer, such as criminal law.

2. Vertical-Level Specialist

These firms specialise in meeting the needs of a particular level in the production-distribution channel.

3. Customer-Size Specialist

These firms focus on meeting needs of organisation by size category.

4. Specific-Customer Specialist

These firms sell to one or only a few other firms.

5. Geographic Specialist

These firms specialise by location.

6. Product or Feature Specialist

These firms focus on supplying narrow needs of a single product or product feature, often very high-requirement products.

7. Quality-Price Specialist

These firms pick one end of the price-quality spectrum.

8. Service Specialist

These firms provide special services not usually offered by other firms.

> **Tip**
>
> Ask for examples of successful "cloners", "imitators" and "adapters".

Comments on Discussing the Issues

1. Competition is usually a positive force that can provide many benefits to the consumer. In general, competitive forces stimulate innovation, keep prices down, and spur companies to find new ways to satisfy consumer needs. The nature of a particular competition, however, can determine whether it is actually helpful in the long run.

   In the short run, a disruptive competitor is likely to drop prices sharply, providing an immediate benefit to the consumer. However, this may make the market unprofitable, and force innovative but well-behaved companies out of the market. This can result in a long-term loss for consumers.

   But this pattern can also reverse. If a larger competitor buys the smaller defeated companies, as happened after Bausch & Lomb disrupted the contact lens market, a higher level of competition among new and larger firms may result. In this case, disruption eventually resulted in more and better competition. Thus, consumers are served by competition, but it may not matter how well-behaved the firms are, as long as they compete.

2. Market leader has the largest market share and usually leads the other firms in price changes, new product introductions, distribution coverage and promotion spending. A leading firm's life is not easy. It must maintain a constant watch. Other firms keep challenging its strengths or trying to take advantage of its weaknesses. British Airways, Coke and the financial services for example should respond to Richard Branson's activities by continuously innovate their offering. As mentioned in the text, "the best defence is a good offence and the best response is continuous innovation". Ask students for more specific examples as to what British Airways had done to counteract Virgin's actions. What other possible market leader strategies that Coke, British Airways and the other financial institutions could do to challenge the pervasive nature of Virgin.

3. Manufacturers for athletic shoes such as Adidas, Nike and Puma can grow by increasing their market shares further. Studies have found that profitability rises with increasing market share. These manufacturers could for example expand their market by extending the product line to include athletic shoes that are not too expensive but retaining the same basic quality as the original shoes. Students will be very interested in this subject area because they know the product quite well. Ask them for more examples of expansion strategies.

4. Medium-sized firms occupy a difficult position: they are too large to gain the benefits of smaller, focused competitors, but too small to gain real economies of scale. Market-nicher strategies may help these firms out of this quandary. A mid-sized firm can develop multiple niches and do well in their served markets. The Limited, Inc. has six different divisions, totaling over 2,500 stores. Each division successfully concentrates on a different target audience.

   IBM is now attempting to follow a market-nicher strategy in personal computers, keeping its flagship PS/2 line, but introducing a range of other brands for different markets. In 1993, this line-up included PS/1, Valuepoint, and the new Ambra division selling through direct marketing channels.

5. A competitor-centred company has a goal of defeating its competitor. It bases most of its moves on competitors' actions and reactions. The company spends most of its time tracking its competitors' strategies and marketplace results, and trying to find ways to counter them.

The marketing concept is based on reacting to consumers wants and needs, not competitors' actions. Consumers do not care about competitors' strategies: they care about having their needs fulfilled. In general, a competitor-based company is in opposition to the marketing concept.

A company that concentrates on competitors may have similar results to a marketing-driven company - if the process of competitive action/reaction results in consumer needs being served. For example, if a competitor succeeds with a product and the competitor-centred company follows with its own version, it will probably succeed. Consumer needs are being met because the follower imitated a consumer-based success. Likewise, reacting by countering failure may result in consumer needs being served as well. These results are not controllable, however - they depend upon the competitors actions, followed by the company's own reactions, that happen to meet consumer needs. A marketing-centred company can succeed by reacting to the consumer directly, and responding to competition only as appropriate.

6. A market challenger must first define its strategic objective. For example the Number Two Brand can attack the market leader, a high-risk but potentially high-gain strategy that makes good sense if the market leader is not serving the market well. Number Two Brand must have substantitive competitive advantage over the leader. Another alternative is, Number Two Brand can avoid the leader but attack firms its size or smaller local or regional firms. Many of these companies are underfinanced and will not be serving their customers well. Ask students to give examples of the frontal attack, flanking attack, encirclement attack, bypass attack and the guerrilla attack.

Comments on Applying the Concepts

1. **(a)** Students can probably name many groups of competitors from memory. Competitors can be defined in different ways. At the industry level, we see all the firms competing to satisfy the broad need for personal transportation vehicles, including Ford, Rover, Nissan, Toyota, Honda, Vauxhall and several other firms. This is not a very helpful analysis, however: it tells us only who is in the market, but nothing of how they actually compete.

Looking at competitors from a market point of view offers a different type of analysis. In this approach, we look at companies or divisions that are trying to serve the same customer need or customer group. If we define the need as transportation, this might include public transportation such as buses or subways, airline companies, and even bicycles. This may appear improbable to some students, but local circumstances may offer consumers different options. In London, for example, there are millions of people who do not own cars, and find public transportation adequate for their needs. Many native Londoners have not even learned how to drive! Contrast this to life in a suburb, where almost everyone owns cars

The most useful form of analysis for mangers is probably product/market segmentation. As illustrated in Figure 12-2, this form of analysis looks at how customers are segmented, how product lines are segmented. The intersection of these two segments shows which products are positioned to compete for which group of consumers. One simple example is shown below. This same approach could be done at a finer level, with products segmented by company division or specific model, and consumers segmented in many different ways.

	Young Buyers	**Families**	**Empty Nesters**
True Sports Cars	Mazda, Nissan		Porsche, Ferrari
Sporty Cars	Ford, Volvo, Audi, Lexus, Mercedes	Ford, Volvo, Audi, Lexus, Mercedes	Ford, Volvo, Audi, Mercedes
Vans	Volkswagen	Ford, Nissan, Toyota	
Family Sedans	Ford, Nissan, Toyota	Ford, Volvo, Audi, Mercedes	Ford, Volvo, Audi, Lexus, Mercedes
Luxury Cars		Mercedes, Acura, Lexus, Volvo	Mercedes, Acura, Lexus

(b) The answer to this question depends upon how we define terms like leader and follower. A classic car competitive strategy was the divisional strategy pursued by Vauxhall. Each division competed for different consumers: Corsa for the single women, Vectra for the business executive, and a mix of divisions in between. The market is now far more complex, and consumer segments are less clear cut. Ask your students to define the competitive strategies used by firms they know such as Mazda or Nissan.

(c) Many strategic groups exist in the auto market, and they are easy to define. The luxury car strategic group includes BMW, Acura, Lexus, Mercedes, Jaguar, and Rolls Royce. Exotic sports cars include Ferrari, Maserati, Lamborghini, Porsche, and Acura. Students generally have a good understanding of this concept, and can easily list other groups and how they compete.

2. **(a)** Market leaders often attempt to spur total market demand. The rationale for this practice is that the leader will receive the largest share of the incremental sales. The way this strategy is executed varies. Advertising often has a generic message that could apply to any brand. Public relations efforts usually promote total market demand to a greater extent than brand-specific demand. Why? Media will give free space to public relations items on topics of general interest, but only if the brand selling message is subtle. If the brand sell message is too blatant, media will not run the story: it hurts their credibility and could reduce advertising spending.

(b) Students may find ads that have generic strategies that could apply to any product in the category. More likely, they will find recipes and other new uses for products. Ask students for some examples.

(c) Many marketers attempt to go after all three at once. Promoting Persil detergent as a crafts sculpture medium may attract new buyers, gain more consumption from current buyers, and give everyone a new use.

Case 12
BMW:
Putting the "Brrrrum" Back in Brum

Synopsis

The European car market has seen many changes in the last 50 years, not least in the UK, where the formation of British Motor Holdings in 1952 subsequently led to the formation of British Leyland and then to the Rover Group. Rover itself, has had several owners/partners. The latest change taken place recently with BAe selling its 80% stake in Rover to BMW. An action which completely and utterly bewildered Rover's other share holder, Honda. Through the clever acquisition of Rover, BMW has repositioned itself in the European car market. By gaining valuable market share and significantly broadening its product base, without affecting its core business and brand identity, it has become a major force to be reckoned with in the European car market. Consequently, this has left Honda to "lick its wound" and to ponder its future in the European car market.

Teaching Objectives

1. Allow students to apply ideas presented in the customer satisfaction and competitive analysis chapters.

2. Give students an opportunity to analyse a small-share competitor's marketing strategy and its attempt to revise that strategy.

3. Provide students with practice in developing marketing strategy recommendations.

Study Questions

1. Why did the combining of a large number of car makers to form British Leyland not help the country's "chief strategic industry?" Why did British Leyland's broad range of vehicles not allow it to defend its position in the world's markets?

In the UK, prior to British Leyland (BL) being nationalised the Labour government was very enthusiastic to merge companies. Their objective was to encourage the UK's chief strategic industry to become more internationally competitive. The basic philosophy was to merge companies together and then select the best managers to run them. Although on the face of it this was a viable proposition, previous evidence had shown that many company mergers have failed. However, this did not deter the government who in 1968, encouraged the formation of BL by combining British Motor Holding with Rover, Triumph and Leyland. Students should emphasise the failure of the BL merger, like many others, was due to the following reasons; (1) The appointment of Donald Stokes should be questioned. Although Stokes has been very successful in selling trucks and buses throughout the world, he had no experience in managing such a huge company in the car manufacturing industry; (2) As an organisation, BL was vast and consequently the company was fragmented and over diversified. Although BL was producing one million cars a year with over 30 factories, 13 brands and dozens of models, it was not producing high quality cars which the market demanded. The combination of increasing competition in Europe and the production of low quality cars, BL started to lose its market share and income; (3) The company lacked any investment. To succeed a company must invest into areas such as R & D, marketing, improvement in manufacturing techniques, etc. Without adequate investment into these areas BL struggled to compete with its rivals; (4) The nationalisation of BL in 1975 did not improve matters. Although BL absorbed £2 billion in government aid it accumulated £2.6 billion loses. The heavy losses may have been due to the fact that a nationalised company is more likely to be production orientated rather than profit based, i.e. relying on funds from the government BL did not have the incentive to maximise profits; (5) Some of the brands and products suffered due to the concentration of management and financial efforts on the weaker products/brands, for example, Morris took considerable amount of resource from Rover and Jaguar.

After the merger of the various British motor companies, BL was producing one million cars a year, had 30 factories, 13 brands, dozens of models but no synergy. Although the company was producing one million cars a year it was still not successful. The key factors which did not allow BL to defend itself against world markets are; (1) BL had no core marketing strategy. It did not have a core business mission and did not audit the environment and develop a strategic plan; (2) The portfolio of BL businesses comprised of mainly dogs i.e. low growth and low share products, that may generate enough cash to maintain themselves but do not promise to be large sources of cash; (3) BL had a wide product range and is not focusing on a particular area. Thus it is not possible to defend its position in the global market. As the saying goes, "Jack of all trades, master of none".

2. Attacking the US luxury car market forced Honda, Toyota and Nissan to move from making cars equivalent to American inexpensive "compacts" to large expensive luxury Acura, Infiniti and Lexus models. Why do you think they attacked these segments rather than the mass market for "regular" sized cars in the United States? Why did the Japanese attack the luxury car market in the USA rather than taking the battle to Europe?

Firstly, at that time, the recession in Europe, Japan and the USA brought car sales down in all of the worlds major markets. Hence Japanese car makers need to expand to new and fresh markets and the US luxury car market was the ideal opportunity since Japanese manufacturers had little presence in this type of car market. The Japanese had already established themselves in the small car market and had built excellent reputation for quality, reliability and being sporty. They had exploited the US car makers' reluctance to make small cars which in turn allowed Japanese car companies to form a beach head from which they swiftly achieved market-wide penetration. Hence by using the success in this market segment as a "spring board" it was able to launch itself more easily in to the US luxury car market - aimed at customers with similar needs, characteristics, an affluent market base which was commercially viable and highly profitable. Secondly, the Japanese's competitors in the US markets were more vulnerable than in other markets. The Japanese manufacturers created a differential advantage by exploiting its competitors' weakness i.e. providing a luxury car with many extras at no extra cost. BMW, for example, did not provide any extra facilities without adding to its basic price, even a simple radio was optional. The Japanese car makers saw this as a major weakness and accomplished a successful flanking attack.

There are many reasons why the Japanese attacked the luxury car market in the USA rather than Europe. Students should highlight the following reasons; (1) In the early 1900s, Europe's 13 million a year car industry had 2 million cars a year in excess capacity and too many manufacturers were making too many models. As a direct result, there was a 16%

decrease in the number of cars sold in Europe. Thus, it seemed quite rational that the Japanese car makers should attack the growing US market rather than the declining European market; (2) The US market as a whole, when compared with Europe is much larger in size. Thus, by successfully attacking the larger market the Japanese would accumulate greater profits which in turn could be used to further invest in their companies and thus attempt to increase market share in other segments of the industry; (3) With the US being a more free market economy, there would be less barriers to entry in comparison to the European markets. The US would be less resistant to new entrants into the car industry and would more easily accept new ideas and innovations, whereas the Europeans are more conservative and traditional and would resent new arrivals and would thus create higher barriers to entry. Hence, the Japanese would find the US easier and friendly to access.

3. What enabled Land Rover to hold its position in the market even though the Rover group could not? Why did Rover manage to increase sales when the rest of the world's car industry was in decline? Given Rover's much wider range, why were they not as successful as BMW who had a much smaller range of vehicles.

Prior to 1970 Land Rover had only made civilian and military off the road vehicles. In 1970 Land Rover decided to change direction and started to produce a luxury vehicle designed for the wealthy with polished wood trim and the capability to cross fields, streams, deserts and jungles. By doing this it has defined a new product class which is perceived as a fashion statement. The factors which enabled Land Rover to hold its position in the market it entered are as follows; (1) Land Rover had product differentiation. Land Rover's unique design enabled it to pursue a niche market segment which had not been served. Consequently, it avoided direct competition from other companies as there was no other car manufacturer which produces a car with a similar design. Thus, by creating a competitive advantage Land Rover was able to enjoy success within this small niche market; (2) Land Rover defined a new product class. Designed for the wealthy and country living class. Essentially it appeared wherever there was money; (3) By targeting the wealthy, Land Rover quickly became a fashion statement to the extreme that it became a piece of art which was even exhibited in Paris. Its popularity amongst the rich soared and many people who would not use the vehicle for its functional purpose liked the design as it allowed them to stare and look down on other road users, i.e. it portrayed a superior class brand image; (4) As a result of establishing links with Honda, Rover was able to use the manufacturing and development knowledge it acquired from Honda and thus was better prepared to defend its position at the top of the market. This was evident when Subaru realising Land Rover's complacency, introduced their cheaper, "fun" four wheel-drive vehicles. Land Rover responded to this challenge by developing the successful Discovery model; (5) The launch of the Discovery allowed Land Rover to move its new generation model, priced between £31,950 to &43,950, enabling it to compete with the top of the range BMW, Mercedes, Jaguar and Lexus.

Rover's link with Honda had clearly saved it from slow death ultimately extinction. This was evident in 1993 when Rover, in a declining market, was the only car manufacturer in Europe to increase its sales. This can be explained by the following reasons: (1) Rover had adopted superior Japanese manufacturing and development methods such as just-in-time, total quality, continuous improvement, etc. This resulted in Land Rover's sales increasing from 46,700 in 1988 to 79,527 in 1993, during a period when the rest of the world's car makers suffered declining sales; (2) Rover repositioned itself from producing low quality unreliable cars to good quality reliable cars. It was not only producing the cars effectively but also efficiently. It moved from a production based business to become a more market orientated company which provided the opportunity to compete against car manufacturers such as Mercedes, BMW and Jaguar etc.; (3) Rover's continuous improvement of its successful models (Land Rover) enabled them to keep customers interested and by being a brand leader in the market with a successful image and continually upgrade its products, Rover has managed to increase sales; (4) The market for the off the road vehicles was increasing. Sales increased from 50,000 in 1980 to 300,000 in 1990. It can be inferred that as a result of an overall increase in sales for off the road vehicles, Land Rover sales also increased accordingly.

Although it was true to say that Honda had saved Rover from extinction the deal which was struck was much more favourable to Honda than Rover and eventually it was the heavy restrictions of the deal which led to BAe selling its share of Rover to BMW. The main body of the deal was that Honda was entitled to a 20% stake in Rover, the other 80% being owned by BAe. In exchange BAe was allocated 20% share of Honda (UK). From the case study it can be deducted that Honda's dominant position in the partnership enabled them to have a strangle hold over Rover. Although Rover continued to exist it had to pay a heavy price. Rover was a company experiencing success but not making any profit. This was due to the fact that firstly, Rover had to pay Honda handsomely for the floor plan and engines it needed for its larger models. Secondly, Rover had to pay royalties to Honda for each jointly developed car Rover sold. Thirdly, a technology agreement barred Rover from selling Honda based models in markets Honda wanted for themselves such as the USA. It can be said that "the sumo held the recovery of Rover in a constricting embrace".

4. If BAe wanted to get rid of Rover and Honda did not want it, what good is it to BMW? What do you think explains Honda's reaction to the supposed contact with BMW? Would you recommend Honda to pull-the-plug on their deal with Rover?

The purchase by BMW of Rover can be explained by the following reasons; (1) The sale of Rover by BAe immediately doubled BMW's European market share to 6.4% and consequently made BMW a much stronger and more dominant force in the European car industry; (2) With the purchase of Rover, BMW was instantly able to extend its car range by acquiring models such as the Range Rover and the Mini. It was able to enter new market segments such as the small car market without the danger of losing its own identity as a high priced and high quality car maker. Thus, the fear of BMW damaging its own brand image and name was evident as BMW did not want to directly associate their distinguished trademark with Rover who produced cheaper cars, in the likely event Rover failed with its marketing activities pursued; (3) BMW obtained access into off-the-road vehicle market which rivalled its own luxury cars and simultaneously became the market leader in that particular segment i.e. BMW captured the brand which it feared the most, the Range Rover model. Thus, in a sense BMW eliminated its competition by buying into its competitors and using its success for itself; (4) BMW was able to gain access into Honda's, one of its main competitor, successful and profitable managerial expertise. Hence, the implication for BMW would be to utilise these methods and techniques and make itself more profitable than its rivals; (5) BMW's capture of Rover seemed to be the most cost effective and time saving approach of competing against Honda who at the time was BMW's main rival. For BMW to invest in the development of a new model to compete against one of Honda's models would have cost far in access of the DM2,000 it had paid to acquire an 80% share of Rover which included in the price 17 brands including Land Rover and Range Rover.

Prima facie, Honda's management was resentful and bewildered from the sale of Rover to BMW. As a result of its associate being captured by its competitor, BMW, Honda was forced to completely reassess and analyse it operation in Europe. The president of Honda, Mr Kawamoto expressed adamantly that he had no intention of collaborating with BMW in the UK. Mr Kawamoto stated that Honda had nothing to gain from such a collaboration. There are a number of reasons why the management of Honda reacted in this way; (1) As a result of the Rover sale to BMW, Honda's European strategy was wrecked. Honda had hoped that by adopting a similar strategic plan as it did in the US car market (i.e. by establishing itself in the small car segment, it could then use this success as a "spring board" to launch itself more effectively in other car market), it would enable them to be a greater force in the European car market; (2) At the time of Rover sale, Honda was concerned with the very depressed Japanese market and the US where Honda was losing share to the revitalised American car makers. It therefore saw Europe, with its alliance with Rover at its side, as a key growth market to attack in order to compensate for the depressed Japanese and US markets. However, now that BMW had bought an 80% share of Rover, Honda would find it very difficult to attack the European market as BMW would create many barriers of entry which Honda would not be able to overcome by using Rover as an attacking weapon; (3) Honda had lost a submissive partner and had obtained a more dominant competitor. In the Rover-Honda deal Rover had needed Honda more than Honda needed Rover and thus Honda was able to obtain a strangle hold over Rover and dictate its moves. The sale of Rover to BMW now meant that Honda would not be in a position to intimidate and dictate to BMW in a similar fashion as it did Rover. Therefore, the advantages that Honda had acquired from the original deal were lost.

Shortly after BMW captured Rover, Honda threatened not to honour their deal with BAe. The disadvantages of Honda pulling out of the deal are; (1) Honda would lose any competitive advantages it had gained from its alliance with Rover i.e. it would lose any ground it had made, via Rover, in the European market and thus its market share in Europe would increase; (2) Pulling out of the deal would mean that Honda would be left with no real source of direction. Without the alliance of BMW, Honda do not have an obvious source of entrant to make an impact in the European market. If they cannot combine with BMW, who else is there to form ally which will enable Honda to compete strongly in the European market. Thus, would Honda by themselves really have a future in the European market; (3) If Honda pulled out of the deal they would lose vast sums of money that they had invested into Rover. If Honda formed alliance with BMW it would mean that BMW would still have to honour the original deal between Rover-Honda and if BMW made a greater success of Rover it would mean that Honda's share would be worth a lot more in the future than it would now. Hence, a 20% share in Rover and access into Europe is better than nothing; (4) The combination of BMW and Honda may prove to be formidable force in the car industry. Without attempting to experiment and give each other a chance a great opportunity may be lost. If a strong alliance is formed between BMW and Honda, there would be potential to pull resources together and attempt to attack other market segments or even jointly enter a new market industry such as the motorcycle industry. The advantages of Honda pulling out of the deal are; (1) It would immediately generate a large cash flow which in turn could be invested into Honda itself and thus enable Honda to attempt conquering the European market on its own; (2) If Honda did decide to honour the original deal with BMW, Honda may incur the same disadvantages it inflicted on Rover but now BMW would be the more dominant company. Hence, in effect the tables would now be reversed and Honda would be in a similar position to that it had put Rover in. Thus, to avoid the potential difficulties it may be more wise for Honda not to honour the contract. On balance, for Honda to make a decision to pull out of the deal would be one that is made in retaliation and resentment due to the fact that BMW beat Honda to clinch the sale of Rover. The decision not to break the contract with BMW would be reached once Honda had time to rationally and systematically evaluate their circumstances which is their normal method of approach in other situations. Some students will say that Honda should cooperate with BMW for a few years in order to establish whether or not the German-Japanese alliance can be successful or otherwise. Looking at past evidence such alliances have succeeded for example Hoechst-Mitsubishi and Siemens-IBM-Toshiba. However, in order for such alliances to be successful compromises must be made to overcome difficulties and differences in such areas as the cultural environment, managerial styles and techniques, etc. If after a trial period of 3-5 years in which the alliance failed, Honda could then re-evaluate the situation and decide upon the merits of whether or not to sell their share of Rover. At the present time, Honda is repositioning itself by utilising the knowledge and experience it acquired from its alliance with Rover and has launched the new CR-V model to compete in the off the road four wheel drive vehicle market. Thus, evidence suggesting that Honda did not react impulsively by prematurely ending links with BMW but is attempting to form a successful alliance with BMW.

Teaching Suggestions

This case should generate lots of interest because students are familiar with the products and the companies involved. Student groups may want to visit local outlets and discuss the Honda strategy with them to get retailers' reactions. They may also discuss other companies and how they are doing.

This case goes well with the Strategic Planning Chapter (Chapter 3), with the Product Chapters (Chapters 13 and 14) and with the Positioning Chapter (Chapter 10).

Overview Case 4
A Cola Challenge:
Cola With Breakfast

Synopsis

The case opens with the scenario of Ron Watson, a tractor trailer driver, stopping at 7:00 A.M. for breakfast. Ron orders a Pepsi to go with his sunny-side-up eggs and pancakes--startling the waitress and a nearby customer. The waitress's reaction highlights the challenge facing both Coca-Cola and Pepsi as they make separate and different attempts to encourage people to drink cola in the mornings. The companies' moves are prompted by the continued decline of coffee consumption, which peaked in 1962, and the slow but steady increase in morning soft-drink consumption, which now accounts for 12 percent of soft-drink sales.

Coca-Cola has entered the morning competition by subtly repositioning its drinks with a promotional campaign it calls "Coke in the Morning." Pepsi, in contrast, has moved aggressively to attack coffee head-on. Pepsi has developed a new, higher-caffeine product, Pepsi A.M., to address this segment and is utilising advertising that takes direct aim at coffee and coffee drinkers.

Both companies face a significant challenge in over-coming the loyalty of coffee drinkers and the "yuck factor."

Teaching Objectives

1. Illustrate how target audience selection and buyer readiness states shape promotion strategy.

2. Show how the nature of the product and the goal of the company also shape the promotion strategy.

Study Questions

1. What is the target audience for Coca-Cola's "Coke in the Morning" campaign? What is the target for Pepsi A.M.? Are these audiences the same?

At first thought, the target audience for both firms would seem to be "morning coffee drinkers." However, more thoughtful examination indicates that Pepsi, with its more direct attack, has focused more narrowly on coffee drinkers, while Coca-Cola, with its more subtle approach, is really targeting a broader audience. Coke's targeted customers may very well have coffee with breakfast at home. Coca-Cola is trying to get these people, as well as those who drink orange juice or other beverages with breakfast, to consider Coca-Cola later in the morning, perhaps during their coffee break. Thus, Coca-Cola seems to be positioning its drink as another alternative for consumers in the morning, while Pepsi is positioning Pepsi A.M. as a direct substitute for coffee.

2. What buyer responses are Coca-Cola and Pepsi Cola trying to generate among their target customers?

Again, the subtle differences in the two target markets produce differences in the responses that the two companies are seeking. There is certainly *awareness* on the part of most consumers of both Coca-Cola and Pepsi Cola products. But where Coca Cola is merely repositioning its products to appeal to the morning segment, Pepsi Cola has set itself the more difficult job of creating *knowledge* on the part of its target audience that it has developed a product specifically for morning consumption. Further, the taste of Coca-Cola products is so well-known that it does not have to generate *liking* among its target audience, but Pepsi must generate this buyer response. Students who have read the case carefully will have noted that the Pepsi A.M. product has a higher level of caffeine but a lower level of carbonation--suggesting that the drink will be "flatter" than a traditional soda. Because the product is packaged as a traditional soft drink, this might create some customer confusion. Both companies must create *preference* for their products relative to the numerous alternatives from which consumers may select. Hopefully, this preference will lead to the *conviction* that soft drinks are as good or better than alternatives. Finally, Pepsi has a more difficult job in that Pepsi A.M. must be purchased specifically for morning consumption, whereas consumers may have lots of Coca-Cola around their house or available at work, which they simply may decide to drink in the morning.

3. What general message content and message structure decisions should the two companies make in setting their message strategies?

The text outlines three choices that firms may make in designing their message content: rational appeals, emotional appeals, and moral appeals. The scenario that opens the case illustrates the point that the companies will be dealing with consumers who will often have emotional reactions to the idea of drinking soft drinks in the morning. The companies would have a difficult time overcoming these emotional reactions with more emotional appeals, so they might consider rational appeals. Such appeals could play on the fact that many consumers really prefer cold to hot drinks all the time, so morning colas make sense as an alternative to coffee. Although Pepsi has promoted the higher caffeine level for Pepsi A.M., the case notes that the product has only about one-fourth the level of caffeine contained in regular coffee. Thus, for people concerned about caffeine, both companies could point out that colas offer a way to cut back on caffeine consumption. Further, because the companies are interested in generating awareness and knowledge, they might institute a "try it you'll like it" type of approach to encourage consumers to at least give the product a try.

Concerning message structure, the text suggests that the company must decide whether to draw a conclusion or leave it to the audience, whether to present one-sided or two-sided arguments, and when to present the strongest arguments.

It can be argued that in the face of the strong loyalty of many consumers to coffee, the companies would be better off asking questions and making suggestions in a way that would allow consumers to draw their own conclusions rather than trying to attack their beliefs by telling them what to do. Given the potentially negative disposition of the audience, the companies might also present two-sided arguments--for example: "Yes, you're used to that warm drink in the morning, but you're also concerned about caffeine." The companies could also save the strongest argument for the end of their promotional messages, capping a case they have made gradually in the message.

4. What promotion mixes should the companies use? Should the two companies use the same or different mixes? Why?

Personal selling should be used by both firms to get their distributors to participate in the promotional campaign, and both should use more advertising and sales promotion in their promotion mixes. However, because of the nature of its campaign, Coca-Cola would probably rely more heavily on advertising. It is repositioning its established product, so it needs to build consumer awareness. Coca-Cola would probably use more newspaper and radio advertising, which not only can be done on a small budget but which also tends to reach more consumers in the morning as they're having breakfast or driving to work. Pepsi, on the other hand, might be expected to concentrate more on sales promotion tools since it is introducing a new product. Coupons, money-off or 2 for 1 deals could be offered to encourage initial purchases. These offers could be tied in with the mass media advertising. Further, Pepsi has the ability to develop point-of-purchase displays that could be tied in with other products normally eaten at breakfast. Or it could encourage retailers to put its Pepsi A.M. near the area where coffee and other morning beverages are displayed.

Again, a basic problem faced by Pepsi stems from the fact that it is introducing a new product, whereas Coca-Cola is already widely available and within reach of many consumers, who must only be persuaded to drink it earlier in the day. Thus Pepsi would have to allocate a much larger proportion of its promotion budget for Pepsi A.M. than Coke would for its morning campaign.

5. Given the promotion mixes you recommend, what specific ads and other promotion ideas would you recommend to Pepsi Cola and Coca-Cola to help them win over the morning-cola market?

The case is deliberately vague as to what promotional steps the firms have taken in order to allow students to develop their own ideas.

The fact that Coca-Cola is not directly attacking the breakfast market suggests that its campaign should be aimed at commuters, whom it may be able to catch between home and the office. Students might propose radio jingles that would encourage people driving to work to think about having a Coke for morning refreshment. In fact, one advertisement in the campaign describes a person driving to work who needs "a cool, refreshing drink to make him come alive." The consumer then decides to stop on the highway and grab a Coke. Coca-Cola has also carried out in-store advertising, placing advertisements near breakfast foods--a marketing technique known as *cross-merchandising*. Students might suggest that point-of-purchase advertisements near the bakery or pastry areas of stores would catch people shopping in these areas in the morning. In larger cities, Coca-Cola might promote morning consumption on the mass transit systems (buses and subways). Breakfast restaurants and doughnut shops are other potential outlets where Coca-Cola could develop co-operative campaigns. So far, Coca-Cola has stayed away from television advertising.

Although Pepsi might do many of the things suggested for Coca-Cola, it could try some different tactics since it has a special product. In fact, Pepsi has already persuaded some grocery stores to stock Pepsi A.M. in the coffee aisle. Pepsi could also consider having representatives stationed in the stores during the morning hours to offer free samples of Pepsi A.M. to customers as they shop.

Another possibility for both Coca-Cola and Pepsi is to focus on convenience stores where many people stop to buy petrol or get coffee in the mornings. Point-of-purchase displays in these facilities could attract consumers' attention and encourage them to try a cola.

Students might identify one area of concern for both Pepsi Cola and Coca-Cola: Emphasising drinking cola in the morning might annoy mothers who are worried that their children are consuming too many caffeinated drinks already. Both firms would want to be careful not to create the impression that they are targeting children for their morning colas.

6. Should Coca-Cola and Pepsi-Cola be concerned about the ethical issue raised by encouraging consumers to have colas with breakfast, especially if its efforts encourage young children to drink colas with breakfast?

Some students will state that the companies should not show children drinking colas in the morning, but it is the parents' responsibility to decide what their children can and should drink with breakfast. Coffee companies don't specifically discourage or address the problem of kids drinking coffee with breakfast, and coffee has about four times more caffeine than colas.

Other students will argue that colas, unlike coffee, target young people. Pepsi has used the "drink of a new generation" theme and in 1993 uses the "be young, drink Pepsi" theme. Because they do target young people, it is not hard to imagine a very young person thinking of having a cola with breakfast. Thus the cola companies have a different problem. These students will suggest that the companies need to take a proactive approach and specifically say in their commercials that young children, say under 12 years old, should not drink colas with breakfast. Others will say that doing this only calls attention to the practice and will encourage young kids to drink colas. They will say that simply avoiding showing young kids drinking colas with breakfast is the best the companies can do. The companies should have a standby plan, however, if a problem were to develop.

This discussion should point out the difficulties involved in such ethical issues. The "right" answer often depends on one's viewpoint. It is often hard to see a clear "right" answer from all points of view. For how much do we hold companies responsible versus consumers (parents)?

Teaching Suggestions

Because of the nature of the challenge facing Pepsi Cola and Coca-Cola, this case lets students have some fun trying to decide how to overcome the "yuck factor." The instructor might begin the class discussion by asking if any students regularly drink colas with their breakfast or early in the morning. Those who do could be asked how they got into the habit and why they prefer colas to coffee or some other traditional morning drink. Then the instructor could ask students who are disgusted by the thought of having colas with their breakfast what it would take to get them to try a soft drink in the morning. This discussion will help the class develop strategies and promotional tactics aimed at overcoming this aversion.

Additional Information

The Pepsi Cola test markets mentioned in the case began in September 1989. Additional information on the test will be found in the *Wall Street Journal* article, "New Pepsi Soda Will Seek to Break the Coffee Habit," published on September 28, 1989.

A second *Wall Street Journal* article, "Test Shows That Pepsi's Rival to Coffee Hasn't Become Most People's Cup of Tea" (March 30, 1990), may be consulted for additional information on how the market test is progressing. As reported in that article, nearly six months into the test market, Pepsi A.M. was not making much headway against coffee. Consumer reactions indicate that a primary problem is the taste of Pepsi A.M. By reducing the carbonation, the drink not only tastes but *sounds* "flat" to many consumers. This information provides an excellent opportunity for the instructor to stress to students that the strongest promotion program cannot put over a product that is not satisfactory to the consumer.

Students often tend to think that more money or greater creativity with promotional tactics will solve marketing problems. However, the experience of Pepsi and many other firms shows other-wise.

On October 15, 1990, PepsiCo Inc. announced that it had discontinued its Pepsi A.M. test market. A spokeswoman indicated that Pepsi had no plans to bring the new soft drink back. The test market, she said, showed that "We don't need to introduce a reformulated [product] to encourage morning consumption" of regular Pepsi-Cola.

The company indicated that it plans to push morning consumption of regular Pepsi by running a "Pepsi in the Morning" promotion, which it would test in Fort Wayne, Indiana.

Jokes and Quotes

Question: How do you beat Mike Tyson?
Answer: At chess

Free competition is equivalent to a reward granted to those who furnish the best goods at the lowest price.
JEREMY BENTHAM

Merchants are occupied solely with crushing each other: such is the effect of free competition.
CHARLES FOURIER

The meek may inherit the earth, but not its mineral rights.
JOHN PAUL GETTY

No enemy bomber can reach the Ruler. If one reaches the Ruler, my name is not Goering.
GOERING

No guts, no glory.
GRAFFITI (STANFORD BUSINESS SCHOOL)

If you've got it. flaunt it. And if you haven't, wing it.
JONATHAN GREE

Bullets have little stopping power against the horse.
EARL HAIG

The Vietcong have no vehicles and no airplanes. How can they be mobile? How can they win?
GENERAL HARKINS

Planning and competition can be combined only by planning for competition, but not by planning against competition.
F. A. HAYEK

Potter is potter's enemy, and craftsman is craftsman's rival; tramp is jealous of tramp, and singer of singer
HESIOD

Business is a fight - a continual struggle - just as life is.
ELBERT HUBBARD

Competition...The life of trade and the death of the trader
FRANK MCKINNEY HUBBARD

It is an American characteristic not to stop running even after you have arrived.
CLIVE JAMES

There was this seven year old girl playing in a chess tournament in Moscow against twenty world champion chess players - all at the same time. And would you believe it - she lost every game.
JOKE

A nuclear war wiped out the planet. The only living things left alive were two monkeys in Africa. One turned to the other and said, 'OK, let's start again!'
JOKE

War is a relatively simple economic problem. The objective function has only one argument - winning.
C. P. KINDLEBERGER

Winning isn't everything - it's the only thing.
VINCE LOMBARDI

The meek shall inherit the world, but they'll never increase market share.
WILLIAM G. MCGOWAN

The Beatles will never last.
HENRY MANCINI

When you win, nothing hurts.
JOE NAMATH

Probably Mr. Marconi will succeed in signalling without wires to America from his laboratory at Poole (in England), but the cable companies have no fear, for the rate of transmission in aetheric telegraphy is much slower than where wires are employed.
NEWSPAPER ARTICLE (LONDON 1890)

Be first at the feast, and last at the fight.
INDIAN PROVERB

I don't meet competition, I create it.
CHARLES REVLON

Competition brings out the best in products and the worst in people.
DAVID SARNOFF

They couldn't hit an elephant at this dist...
GENERAL SEDGWICK (LAST WORDS)

A perambulator hasn't much choice of tactics against a furniture van.
GEORGE BERNARD SHAW

Avis: We try harder
SLOGAN

When you're only No. 2, you try harder. Or else.
SLOGAN (AVIS RENT A CAR (1963))

When an obstinate small force wants to fight a big power...It must succumb in the end to the greater force.
SUN TZU

The worst battle plan is to besiege the enemy's walled city!
SUN TZU

Armies at war usually fight in direct confrontation.
SUN TZU

A good strategy avoids the powerful but attacks the weak
SUN TZU

God is always on the side of the heaviest battalions.
VOLTAIRE

Sometimes it is more important to discover what one cannot do, than what one can do.
LIN YUTANG

Part V

Product

Chapter 13

Designing Products:

New Product Development and Product Life-Cycle Strategies

Chapter Objectives

After reading this chapter, you should be able to:

1. Describe the new-product development process.
2. Explain how companies find and develop new-product ideas.
3. Describe the stages of the product life cycle.
4. Explain how marketing strategy changes during a product's life cycle.

Chapter Overview

Organisations must develop new products and services. Their current products face limited life spans and must be replaced by newer products. New products can fail. The risks of innovation are as great as the rewards. The key to successful innovation is in a total-company effort, strong planning, and a systematic new-product development process. The new-product development process consists of eight stages: idea generation, idea screening, concept development and testing, marketing strategy development, business analysis, product development, test marketing, and commercialisation. Each product has a life cycle marked by a changing set of problems and opportunities. The five stages include the product-development stage, the introduction stage, the growth stage, the maturity stage, and the decline stage.

Teaching Notes

Refer to the following pages for teaching notes.

The New Product Development Process

Transparency PM 13-1 corresponds to Figure 13.1 on p.514 and relates to the material on pp.514-528.

Steps in New Product Development

1. Idea Generation

- The systematic search for new product ideas. Sources for new product ideas include internal sources, customers, competitor's products, distributors & suppliers, and other sources.

2. Screening

- Focuses on reducing the number of ideas by dropping poor ideas as soon as possible. This helps reduce costs and focus attention more productively.

3. Concept Development and Testing

- Involves translating ideas into product concepts or detailed versions of the ideas stated in meaningful consumer terms. Concepts are then tested on target consumers.

4. Marketing Strategy

- This stage consists of three parts. The first part describes the target market, the second part outlines the product's projected price, distribution, and budget for the first year, the third part describes long-run sales, profit goals, and marketing mix strategy.

5. Business Analysis

- Reviews the sales, costs, and profit projections for the product to find out if the satisfy overall company objectives.

6. Product Development

- Involves bringing the product concept into existence as a physical product to ensure that the idea is a workable product.

7. Test Marketing

- The stage at which the product and marketing program are implemented in one or more realistic market settings.

8. Commercialisation

- Involves actually introducing the new product into the competitive marketplace. In this stage, the company must make decisions involving when to introduce, where, to whom, and how.

Tip

Ask students why it is important to carry out the above steps in NPD.

Notes for PM 13-1

Speeding Up Development

Transparency PM 13-2 relates to the material on p.528.

Speeding Up New-Product Development

Sequential Product Development

Isolated groups in each stage work on the new product until the stage is completed. This completed stage is then passed to the next group or department to begin its stage in the process. This organisation brings control to complex development projects and reduces the risk associated with costly mistakes. But it is also extremely slow and subjects the company to greater competitive risk and potential lost sales while the process is completed.

Parallel Product Development

This approach organises new product development into a more flexible integration of each stage in the process. Parallel organisation features close communication and co-ordination of departments and groups working on different stages, more overlap of work on steps to save time and increase effectiveness. Co-ordination facilitates each stage benefiting from the developmental process of the other stages while still planning what the product should be and will become.

Notes for PM 13-2

The Product Life-Cycle

Transparency PM 13-3 corresponds to Figure 13.2 on p.532 and introduces the product life cycle concept.

Product Life Cycle Stages

Product Development

Development begins when the company finds and develops a new product idea. During development the product has costs but no sales. Development costs must be strategically weighed against the projected length of the product's PLC.

Introduction

During the introduction of new products initial sales growth is slow as the market is just becoming aware of the product. Profits are usually non-existent at this stage due to heavy promotion spending.

Growth

This stage is characterised by rapid market acceptance of the product and increasing profits.

Maturity

In maturity there is a slowdown in sales growth as the product has achieved acceptance by most potential customers. Profits may level off or decline as marketing costs increase to defend existing market share.

Decline

In this period sales begin to fall off and profits decline dramatically.

Tip

Discuss with students the PLC for products such as Coca-Cola, Sony Walkman, Pork Pies, Microsoft 95, etc.

Notes for PM 13-3

Product Life-Cycle Strategies

These notes relate to the material on pp.533-538.

Introduction

In this stage marketers spend heavily on promotions to inform the target market about the new product's benefits. Low or negative profits may encourage the company to price the product high to help offset expenses. Companies can concentrate on skimming strategies to generate high profits now or on penetration strategies to build market share and dominant the market for larger profits once the market stabilises.

Growth

In this stage the company experiences both increasing sales and competition. Promotion costs are spread over larger volume and strategic decisions focus on growth strategies. Strategies include adding new features, improving quality, increasing distribution, and entering new market segments.

Maturity

In this stage the company must manage slower growth over a longer period of time. Strategic decisions made in the growth stage may limit choices now. Marketing managers must proactively seek advantage by either market modification to increase consumption, product modification to attract new users (quality, feature, and style improvements), or marketing mix modification in an attempt to improve competitive position.

Decline

In this stage the costs of managing the product may eventually exceed profits. Rate of decline is a major factor in setting strategy. Management may maintain the brand as competitors drop out, harvest the brand by reducing costs of support for short term profit increases, or drop the product (divest) altogether.

Comments on Discussing the Issues

1. It is commonly understood by marketer that the development and introduction of new products are costly and risky activities. The costs of new product failure can be immense therefore the willingness to take risks is so important. For example, the financial costs associated with the development and launch processes, the marketing costs which include any damage to the organisation's relations with its distributors and customers, lost opportunities. Other costs are such as organisational costs, including any loss of confidence on the part of those involved with the development and launch of the product and a reduction of top management commitment to future new product development activity. These are some of the major costs involved. Students should mention other minor costs. Nowadays, buyers are increasingly demanding and discriminating, the expectations of distributors and dealers are increasing, the pace of technology becoming faster, the competition generally is increasing. In the light of these factors, it seems likely the pressure on the marketing strategists will increase and a dilemma will be created. While there is widespread agreement that new products are needed if the firm is to grow and create profit, the likelihood of success appears to be getting even smaller. In realising the risk and uncertainty in future returns, the willingness of top management to commit themselves in developing new products and services are ever so important.

   Technology is a useful and vital weapon in the new product development armoury that help the company to stand a better chance of success in this competitive market. However, technology alone is insufficient to claim a success in the market. Ask students to name some examples.

   In gaining success in commercialisation apart from advancing the technology, a good long run new product planning requires systematic research and development, matching the requirements of new product opportunity against company abilities, emphasis on consumers' perceived product attributes, sizeable expenditure of time and money. There is no guarantee for a new product or technology to succeed, but if the companies are willing to spend more time studying the needs of the target market and getting their reactions and suggestions as the product moved through the development process, then the chance of success will be greater.

2. The "find a need and fill it" philosophy does not say that needs can be identified only by asking customers. Customers may be unable to describe their needs, so suggesting new products or ways to fill their needs is even more difficult. Customers are often slow to accept really innovative new products. Even 3M's Post-It Notes, which are basically a minor modification of scratch paper, were resisted until 3M blitzed companies with samples and allowed secretaries to see their usefulness.

   Customer involvement is an integral part of concept testing. Concept tests may use sample sizes ranging from 100 to 400 consumers. Though customer participation may benefit product development at an earlier stage (after all, 28 per cent of new product ideas do come from watching and listening to customers), customer reactions to new product concepts become especially important at the stage of determining which concepts to develop and which ones to drop.

3. One basic issue in new product success is meeting consumer needs in an appropriate way. This requires that a company understand consumer needs intimately, and be able to link their product designs to these needs with an appropriate level of newness and

creativity. A product must be exciting and new, but also meet enough of the criteria for diffusion (relative advantage, compatibility, complexity, divisibility, communicability) so that it is adopted widely and quickly.

The difficulty with formalised new-product development systems is that they are formal systems, with established players and routines. These systems often produce lacklustre results. Formal organisations naturally tend to duplicate what has worked before, even if the environment has changed and adaptation is needed. Innovation is very hard to institutionalise.

Successful new product developers have three elements in common. First, different departments interact in unusual and more intense ways, developing a stronger sense of joint identity with the project. Second, successful product developers operate with a very simple view of the new product that made sense to people in all departments. Third, successful developers develop new ways to judge the new product - they do not judge a new idea with old criteria, because that can impose inappropriate answers.

Unsuccessful new product developers tended to follow set routines. This resulted in "more of the same" new products that ultimately were not successful in the marketplace. (Source: Deborah Doherty, "Interpretive Barriers to Successful Product Innovation," MSI Report No. 89-114, Marketing Science Institute, Cambridge, MA 1989.)

4. Essentially when product is tested in an actual market situation, the interdependence of the variables of the marketing mix can be determined. Several factors should be evaluated before deciding whether to test-market the product; (1) The company should compare the costs and risks of product failure with the profits and probability of success. If the costs and risks of product failure are low, commercialisation and national launching can proceed without a test market; (2) If the technology for the new product requires about the same investment whether the new product is nationally launched or market tested, the company has good reason to proceed directly to national launch. However, when this is not the case and a larger investment is required for a national launch, test marketing is frequently warranted; (3) The extra time that the competition has to develop a similar product must be assessed in terms of the benefits of the market test. The competition will usually monitor the test while simultaneously developing their version; (4) All other aspects of the new products must be examined. Advertising expenditure, effort by the sales force, and possible negative impact on the firm's reputation if the new product fails must be carefully weighted before deciding on a market test.

Test market results are often better than the same brand achieves after national launch. The key factor in this discrepancy is the careful attention that is paid to the test market. Every element in a test market is new and carefully planned. Management meets frequently with the salesforce. Sales management has special training sessions with their field representatives. The resellers are usually aware that this is a test market, and are often especially co-operative. Distribution, shelving, and displays are usually executed flawlessly. Promotion and advertising plans are followed with microscopic precision. In many cases, plans are modified during the test market to improve results.

The careful attention that the test market received cannot be duplicated on a national scale. The execution of all elements is usually less precise, and less effective. Other elements come into play as well. Test markets are often geographically isolated, and chosen for category usage and marketplace trends that are representative of the country as a whole. Often these trends are somewhat more favourable than those in the total country. Finally, the national launch takes place many months, or even years, after the test market. Other factors in the marketplace may have changed in the intervening time.

5. The concept of the PLC constitutes an important component of product strategy. The PLC is meant to serve as a conceptual base for examining product growth and development but every product does not necessarily fit all the elements of the theoretical curve. PLC allows companies to be aware of the fact that products evolve, die and new ones have to be developed to replace them PLC also emphasises the need to review marketing objectives and strategies as products pass through the various stages. The key to successful use of the PLC concept lies in the accurate determination of where each stage start and end. But the duration and determination of the PLC stages are most of the time unpredictable and difficult. So this limits its use as a forecasting tool. Another drawback relates to the fact that PLC concept is both a cause and result of the product life cycle. Is the life cycle for a particular product an inevitable independent force to which the companies must adapt their marketing effort or can the marketing strategies change the course of the life cycle? At least, the PLC represents a general tool but not all products follow the S-shaped curve. The PLC should not be viewed as a panacea to marketing thinking and decision-making but as an aid to managerial judgement. (G. Lancaster et al, 1988, Essentials of Marketing; D. Jobber, 1995, Principles and Practice of Marketing)

6. This question is meant to illustrate the fact that factors outside a company's control can affect the life cycles of its products. Growing public interest in reducing the risk of heart disease, the aging of the baby-boom generation, and scientific evidence that oatmeal consumption can reduce high cholesterol levels associated with heart attacks, all point to increased levels of oatmeal consumption in the future. To capitalise on this trend, Quaker Oats Co. has run ads linking oat consumption with cholesterol reduction, Kellogg has introduced an oat-bran cereal, and other companies have introduced other oat-based products.

Comments on Applying the Concepts

1. This question, listing new product ideas for favourite chocolate or candy bar, will attract fairly predictable responses from most students. Many of the ideas will be "channel transfer" concepts: take an idea that is known to work, and put it in a new context.

   If students are honest about rating their ideas, the percentage of potentially successful ideas should be fairly low. The reason for the anticipated successes are likely to centre on several factors: fulfils a real need, has a clear target audience, easy to understand, and has a good fit with the existing brands, positioning, and target audience of the chocolate.

2. Periodic assessments by such publications as *New Product News* have rated the innovativeness of most new products as extremely low, and this may help to explain the low new product success rate. Adding a small improvement or change to an existing brand is faster, easier, far cheaper and much less risky than investing in real innovation. This slow, incremental improvement is also boring for consumers, resulting in low acceptance rates overall: there is no new need being met.

   Student's findings are likely to mirror these results. Very few (if any) products will be rated a 10, and many are likely to be closer to a 1 or 2. Risk aversion in the marketplace is very clear. The reasons for such risk aversion are not as clear. In large part, it probably results from the high new product failure rate. Managers are very reluctant to place large bets when the risks appear so insurmountable. The result is many small bets being placed: they are not big ideas, but they cannot lead to big losses either.

Case 13
The Swatchmobile: Any Colour Combination, Including Black

Synopsis

In the existing and established world watch markets, Hayek developed, marketed and commercialised a new product - the Swatch watch. This watch captured and increased its country's share of world watch market from 15% to 50%. It became a fashion-oriented youth product and a collectable cult object. At a stage in the product life cycle, the sales and share price of the Swatch watch started levelling out; hence Hayek, being a marketer, realising the above fact, started looking into the car market to develop a new and innovative product. This is a diversification strategy in which they use the knowledge of their partner, Mercedes. In this case study students have to analyse factors such as; success factors, product development process, marketing research and name choice.

Teaching Objectives

1. Allow students to understand the importance of innovation and new product development.

2. Provide an opportunity to appreciate the importance of the various sources of ideas in generating new products for example in this case the role of Hayek.

3. Allow students to make recommendations for Swatchmobile's name and related strategies.

Study Questions

1. **How was Hayek able to make such a great success of Swatch and can those ideas be transferred to other products in other markets? Would the ideas transfer to hi-fi, pens, kitchen goods and so forth? How were Swatch able to beat the huge and established Japanese competitors?**

Hayek was able to make a great success of Swatch because he first of all identified a gap in the market and then exploited the opportunities opened up by that gap through the introduction of the Swatch watch and good use of the marketing mix. In the global market for watches, there are the two main markets. The luxury market dominated by Swiss brands like Blancpain, Audemas, Piguet and Rolex. The market for cheap but reliable products was dominated by the Japanese brands like Casio, Seiko, Pulsar and others. The main issue arising from the identified gap is the large difference in quality, price and perceived image of the watches, neither markets cater for the younger generation. Hayek identified that gap and produced a watch which mixed reliability, quality with fun and economy as well as some new qualities which captured a new youth market. In essence students should highlight some of these qualities such as; it was beautifully engineered, fashion led, plastic body, the ever changing range, quartz movements, Swiss reliability and quality, fun and economy. Swatch was aimed at the age range between mid teens to early twenties and on numerous continents. This market was chosen because during teenage years young adults are just becoming self aware, with a need to exert their own individuality and Swatch watch provided the variety in design and colour which teenagers could identify with and relate to. Essentially, Hayek had managed to revitalise and recreate the watch market.

Before answering this question let us first look at Swatch as a product. A watch is an accessory which is very personal in nature and it is constantly worn on the wrist and is considered to reflect the personality of the wearer in the way that clothing does. A watch is not purchased only for its basic function, but also for what it stands for. The product has both functional and psychological aspects. To answer whether Hayek ideas can be transferred to other products some students will say, YES, to a limited extent. This is the case because we must choose products which relate directly to individuals or the environment in which they exist. For example, we could choose a small item which is used on a day to day basis by an individual at work or at home, or a larger product used by the an individual at home which reflects their own sense of style and complements other accessories and furniture. Whilst this combining of functionality and individuality or style is possible, there are limitations in terms of the expense of doing so and the impact that adding style or individuality to a product may have on its functionality.

Students will give a variety of answers. Some will say that hi-fi is usually one off item purchased for the whole family and is more of an investment and a status product than a fun product. An individual purchasing a hi-fi is more concerned with practicality and the different features and quality of the product. The hi-fi market is a market where price is associated with quality. The main competitive advantage in this particular market is technology. The image of a brand is built on technology, innovation or price never on fashionable aspects. Therefore these ideas could not be transferred to hi-fi. Other students will suggest that hi-fi could have all of the characteristics of Swatch such as fashionable, reliable, quality, fun and economy. Ask them to justify their answers. As far as pens are concerned Hayek's ideas could be transferred more easily. Pens could be viewed as a type of accessory. Brands like Du Pont and Cross provided customers with expensive and luxurious pens and there are also many brands that provided customers with cheaper reliable products like Bic. There is a possible market for a company to produce pens in Hayek's manner. Famous designers like Gianni Versace and Pierre Cardin also extended their brand names and produced kitchen goods like plates and glasses and so forth. People who are brand conscious would be a possible target market for kitchen goods produced in Hayek's manner.

Swatch revolutionised the watch industry and market by making it design driven. There was a total rethinking of watch as a fashion product. Swatch competed in an area where the Japanese are not prepared for. People rushed to buy Swatch watches because no other company offered a similar well-designed product at a good price. The Japanese who are engineering driven have totally ignored the design and fashion side of the product.

2. What is Hayek's role in the new product development process? Why does he need the help of a partner?

Hayek can be see to fulfil the role of project leader, originator, champion or entrepreneur in the development process. He is the innovator behind the idea and has worked hard pushing the project forward. Hayek is core to the project, whilst being likely to be strongly supported by Mercedes Benz. He plays an important role trying to maintain the progress of the car especially assessing the major teams which he is working with, guiding them towards his vision. This is particularly important as both Swatch and Mercedes personnel are in new territory. Hayek with his marketing drive will develop relations with the market. He may not design the car but he is the controlling and motivating force behind it.

Students should understand that Hayek needs a partner to make this project a reality. The most obvious point to be made is Hayek's complete lack of experience in designing a car. Although Hayek employed engineers and designers to make his Swatch watches, it is not feasible for these people to do the same for Swatchmobile. It is better all round, especially financially, if Hayek teams up with a car manufacturer. In this way he can rely on the car company designing expertise built up over many years. Success requirements of this project include; (1) Having good relations with suppliers of the car parts; (2) Having the skill and resources to mass produce the car; (3) Having a strong distribution capacity to store, show and sell the car; (4) Having the skill base and capacity for after sales service and maintenance; (5) Having the confidence of buyers that the company is able to produce and distribute a quality car. Mercedes provided Hayek with all of the above. Hayek cannot hope to succeed without the input from Mercedes.

3. Is the Swatchmobile a market-driven idea? Is there now any justification for not basing new products on marketing research?

Students could present two points of view for this question. Some factors presented in the case study suggest that Swatchmobile is a market driven idea while other factors pointed to the opposite direction. Let us first look at the "for" arguments. New product ideas can come from many sources; customers, scientists, competitors, employees and also top management executives. But customers' needs and wants are the logical place to start. The idea is market driven due to the following factors; (1) In today's society people are becoming ever dependent on cars. For example, supermarkets are no longer predominantly located in city centres but on city edges. Therefore, we need a car to be able to do our shopping. The fact that supermarkets and indeed other shopping centres are located out of town reflects upon the fact that more people own cars. Younger generations are growing up with cars being fundamental part of their life. Surveys show that 80% of 13-16 year olds said that cars were indispensable. This is very encouraging for the Swatchmobile as this would be a large proportion of up and coming buyers of the car; (2) The increasing popularity of green issues is also a positive factor for the Swatchmobile. The car intends on being powered by petrol or electricity an is extremely energy efficient whilst giving the same performance as a basic Ford Escort. Thus, it has an attractiveness as a car for the future. However, evidence suggests that although consumers are aware of environmental conditions and thus want eco-friendly products, they are hesitant to pay more for these products. Even if the price is relatively similar they want performance to be of a high or matching quality. Thus, the quality will have to be comparable to that of other small cars in the market; (3) Safety and security are also factors which are very important to many drivers especially women and young people. The Swatchmobile would provide maximum safety and security without consumers having to upgrade their cars; (4) The Swatchmobile does provide many features which consumers want and are not at present provided. The reduction in the nuclear family and changing trends in what people want from a car means that the Swatchmobile could be a very desirable car in the future. Some factors which are "against"; (1)The Swatchmobile is not a market driven product. Hayek did not initially conduct any conclusive market research to say that Swatchmobile is in great demand. The Swatchmobile seems to be more a creation of Hayek needing to diversify his product mix; (2) Past experience in similar ventures show failure, Hayek partnership with Volkswagen ended in disaster in 1993 when Swatchmobile's economic viability was questioned; (3) At present there is overcapacity in the world car market, making it a very bad idea to develop such a high risk car. The recession in Europe also means that it is much cheaper to produce cars in Japan; (4) People feel that congested roads will soon be unable to cope with increasing traffic; (5) Many financial institutions publicly condemned the venture as a failure.

Most marketers would tell you that new products should definitely be researched before development and introduction to the market. Market orientated companies would not dream of introducing products without prior research. Without prior research you would not know who is going to buy your product, where, how and etc. Research can help determine whether a new product is going to be accepted in the market or not. However, it is sometimes pays to go against research and take a major risk based on gut instincts. Hayek is doing this by going against what banks and car manufacturers are saying about the Swatchmobile. With an innovative product such as this, comprehensive research cannot be conducted because nobody has commercially used the product. For example, before Sony introduced the Walkman to the market, research was conducted. When people were asked about the product, they were negative. The reason was because people were not accustomed to listening to music in private in public places. It was not socially acceptable at the time. When the product was introduced it was a huge success because people now has access to the technology and were seeing the benefits from the product. The need for a product was created. The creation of such products is very expensive and has a higher than normal risk factor. However, if successful, then Hayek will be a market leader and reap the benefits.

4. What market research would you conduct to test the market for the Swatchmobile and when would you do it?

Students will propose a wide array of market research activities. For example, Swatchmobile should carry out concept testing and test marketing at this stage of product development. Concept testing calls for testing new product concepts with a group of target consumers. Focus group discussion is a common technique to obtain such information. To evaluate the consumers' acceptance of the Micro Compact Car (MCC), different questions should be asked such as; do you understand the concept of a MCC?, what do you think are the benefits of a MCC?, would the MCC meet your automobile needs? and so on. Motor shows could also be used in concept testing. It must be emphasised that concept testing is used before large scale production of the new product. Such research should be conducted at the preliminary stage of the new product development process. However, if the marketer wants to evaluate the market in a more realistic sense, test marketing is essential. Test marketing should be conducted before commercialisation of the Swatchmobile. Test marketing is the stage in which the product and marketing programme are tested in more realistic market settings. It allows the marketer to measure how the product satisfies the expectations of the consumer and to measure his purchase intentions. Even though the new product has been thoroughly tested for performance during each of the earlier stages in the product planning and development process, it still needs to be evaluated by consumers in order to measure their satisfaction with the product's performance and their degree of interest in purchasing. Other students will emphasise the importance of competitor intelligence, environmental scanning and analysis, and primary research. Ask them to justify their choice of the research activity.

5. How should the Swatchmobile be branded? Should it be a Swatchmobile Eco-Speedster, Mercedes Eco-Speedster. Mercedes Swatch Eco-Speedster, Swatch Eco-Speedster, MCC Eco-Speedstern, or some other combination? What are the pros and cons of the alternative names? Does the name really matter if the product is right?

The choice of brand name is very important to the development of the product as it conveys an image. Some of the important criteria a good brand name should fulfil are; (1) Evoke a positive associations; (2) Easy to pronounce and remember; (3) Suggest product benefits; (4) Distinctive; (5) Use numerals when emphasising technology; (6) Not infringe on existing registered brand names. Students will suggest several merits and demerits of the various possible names for the car. The following table analyses each of the proposed names;

Name	**Pros**	**Cons**
Swatchmobile Eco-Speedster	Swatch - fashion image Mobile - vehicle Eco - ecological	Speed unimportant Mercedes - not associated Too long No compact car association
Mercedes Eco-Speedster	Mercedes - quality etc Eco - ecological	No Swatch image No compact car association Speed unimportant Too long
Mercedes Swatch Eco-Speedster	Swatch- fashion image Mercedes - reliability etc. Eco - ecological	Speed unimportant Too long No compact car association
Swatch Eco-Speedster	Swatch - fashion image Eco - ecological	Mercedes - not associated No compact car association Speed unimportant Too long
Micro Compact-Car Eco-Speedster	Eco - ecological Size advantage	No Swatch image No Mercedes image Speed unimportant Too long Micro sounds like Micra
MCC Eco-Speedster	Eco - ecological MCC -sporty/boy racer	No Swatch image No Mercedes image Speed unimportant Too long

Name does matter even if the product is right. The name of the product affect the way it is perceived. If properly chosen it will help create a positive image or conversely if poorly chosen can detract from the product. Thus, it is important that a good, appropriate and effective brand name is created, complimenting the quality of the product.

Teaching Suggestions

Instructors can use this case with the Product Chapter (Chapter 14) as well as with the Promotion Chapters (Chapters 18, 19 and 20).

Jokes and Quotes

Post Euphoric Trauma: What Archimedes felt after he jumped out of the bath, shouted Eureka and realised he was running through the middle of Syracuse, naked.

The freedom to make mistakes provides the best environment for creativity.
ANON

Exhilaration is that feeling you get just after a great idea hits you, and just before you realise what's wrong with it.
ANON

It takes genius and courage to originate, not imitate.
ANON

As the births of living creatures, at first, are ill-shapen: so are all Innovations, which are the births of time.
FRANCIS BACON

If it works, it's out of date.
STAFFORD BEER

If it's good, they'll stop making it.
HERBERT BLOCK

Basic research is when I'm doing what I don't know I'm doing.
WERNER VON BRAUN

Today every invention is received with a cry of triumph which soon turns into a cry of fear.
BERTOLT BRECHT

There is a correlation between the creative and the screwball. So we must suffer the screwball gladly.
KINGMAN BREWSTER

Henry Ford was a thinker; he wasn't a repeater.
W. J. CAMERON

I don't think necessity is the mother of invention - invention in my opinion arises directly from idleness, possibly also from laziness. To save oneself trouble.
AGATHA CHRISTIE

We must beware of needless innovations, especially when guided by logic.
SIR WINSTON CHURCHILL

Nothing that results from human progress has unanimous consent. Those that are enlightened before others pursue that flight in spite of others.
CHRISTOPHER COLUMBUS

For God's sake go down to reception and get rid of a lunatic who's down there. He says he has got a machine for seeing by wireless. Watch him - he may have a razor on him.
DAILY MAIL

Inventors and men of genius have almost always been regarded as fools at the beginning (and very often at the end) of their careers.
FYODOR MIKHAILOVICH DOSTOEVSKY

I think and think for months and years. Ninety-nine times, the conclusion is false. The hundredth time I am right.
ALBERT EINSTEIN

Young's Law: All great discoveries are made by mistake.
HAROLD FABER

Nothing recedes like success.
BRYAN FORBES

You don't have to destroy the city before you can build a new Jerusalem
LANE KIRKLAND

The history of every dead and decaying 'growth' industry shows a self declining cycle of bountiful expansion and undetected decay.
THEODORE LEVITT

He who builds a better mousetrap these days runs into material shortages, patent-infringement suits, work stoppages, collusive bidding, discount discrimination - and taxes.
H. E. MARTZ

The Wankel will eventually dwarf such major post war technological development as xerography, the Polaroid camera and colour TV.
GENERAL MOTOR

Enough research will tend to support your theory.
MURPHY'S LAW

If I have seen further it is by standing on the shoulders of giants.
SIR ISAAC NEWTON

Oh, I don't know. You cannot sink the boat.
MAJOR PEUCHEN

Technology or perish.
JOHN R. PIERCE

There are three ways of courting ruin - women, gambling and calling in technicians.
GOERGE POMPIDOU

The energy produced by the breaking down of the atom is a very poor kind of thing.
SIR ERNEST RUTHERFORD

I am not a management type. I am an inventor. I am awful at managing established businesses.
SIR CLIVE SINCLAIR

The greatest advertising campaign ever conceived.
SLOGAN (FORD EDSEL)

Looks right! Built right! Prices right!
SLOGAN (FORD EDSEL)

The reciprocal piston engine is as dead as a dodo.
SPORTS ILLUSTRATED

The man with a new idea is a Crank until the idea succeeds.
MARK TWAIN

If necessity is the mother of invention, what was Papa doing?
RUTH WEEKLEY

An idea that is not dangerous is unworthy of being called an idea at all.
OSCAR WILDE

The longer I live the more keenly I feel that whatever was good enough for our fathers is not good enough for us.
OSCAR WILDE

Ideas are like beards: men do not have them until they grow up.
FRANCOIS VOLTAIRE

Chapter 14

Designing Products:

Products, Brands, Packaging and Services

Chapter Objectives

After reading this chapter, you should be able to:

1. Define product and the main classifications of consumer and industrial products.
2. Explain why companies use brands and identify the chief branding strategies.
3. Describe the roles of product packaging and labelling.
4. Explain the decisions companies make when developing product lines and mixes.

Chapter Overview

Product is a complex concept that must be carefully defined. Product strategy calls for making co-ordinated decisions on product items, product lines, and the product mix. Each product item offered to customers can be viewed on three levels: the core product, the actual product, and the augmented product. All products can be classified according to their durability. Consumer goods are usually classified according to consumer shopping habits. Industrial goods are classified according to their cost and the way they enter the production process. Companies have to develop strategies for the items in their product lines. They must decide on product attributes, branding, packaging, labeling, and product-support services. Most companies produce a product line instead of a single product. Product mix describes the set of product lines and items offered to customers by a particular seller. The product mix can be described by its breadth, length, and consistency. The four dimensions of the product mix are the tools for developing the company's product strategy.

Teaching Notes

Refer to the following pages for teaching notes.

Product Levels

Transparency PM 14-1 corresponds to Figure 14.1 on p.546 and relates to the material on pp.545-547.

Product

A product is anything that can be offered to a market for attention, acquisition, use, or consumption and that might satisfy a want or need. Products can be physical objects, services, persons, places, organisations and ideas.

Product Levels

Core Product

This concept refers to the use-benefit, problem-solving service that the consumer is really buying when purchasing a product.

Actual Product

The actual product is the tangible product or intangible service that serves as the medium for receiving core product benefits. Five characteristics: Quality Level refers to product performance. Features include combinations of product attributes. Styling consists of design and aesthetic or ergonomic aspects of the product. Brand Name may help consumers position and identify the product. Packaging serves to both protect the product and to promote it to consumers.

Augmented Product

The augmented consists of the measures taken to help the consumer put the actual product to sustained use. Measures can include installation, delivery & credit, warranties, and after sale service.

> **Tip**
>
> Choose a product like toothpaste. Ask students to identify and discuss the product levels of toothpaste.

Notes for PM 14-1

Product Classifications

Transparency PM 14-2 corresponds to Figure 14.2 on p.548 and Figure 14.3 on p.550 and relates to the material on pp.547-551.

Consumer Goods

Convenience Goods

Purchased frequently with a minimum of comparison and buying effort. May be divided into staple, impulse, and emergency goods.

Shopping Goods

Compared on such bases as suitability, quality, price, and style. Consumers may distinguish between uniform and nonuniform shopping goods. Price negotiation is more common in uniform goods shopping.

Speciality Goods

Have unique characteristics or identification with buyers and are generally specifically sought by the consumer.

Unsought Goods

May be unknown to the buyer or not normally considered for purchase. Unsought goods require special marketing effort.

Industrial Goods

Materials & Parts (Raw materials & manufactured parts)

Enter the manufacturer's product in production.

Capital Items (installations and accessories)

Indirectly contribute to production.

Supplies & Services

Do not enter into production at all. Supplies include operating supplies and repair and maintenance items. Business services are often offered under contract to do the actual repair and maintenance. Many equipment manufacturers include repair and maintenance agreements in combination with installations.

Tip

Ask students examples of consumer goods and industrial goods.

Notes for PM 14-2

Individual Product Decisions

Transparency PM 14-3 relates to the material on pp.551-555.

Product Attribute Decisions

Product Quality

Product quality stands for the ability of a product to perform its functions. Quality includes the attributes of overall durability, reliability, precision, ease of operations, and quality consistency - the ability to maintain the targeted level of quality in delivering benefits to consumers. The importance of quality has lead to widespread adoption of Deming's Total Quality Management, first by the Japanese and now increasingly by US and European firms.

Product Features

The number and combination of product features offered consumers are assessed in terms of customer value versus company cost. Consumers seek value and need-satisfaction. Features irrelevant to consumers are undesirable. Also, additional features cost money to produce and higher quality features are more costly still. Product feature decisions must be carefully tied to consumer needs and consumer perceptions of received, affordable value.

Product Design

Product design combines attention to style (appearance) with enhanced performance. Style alone may attract attention but not improve performance.

> **Tip**
>
> You may wish to discuss how style may adversely affect perceptions of product performance. Good styling may inadvertently lead to higher performance expectations on the part of the interested consumer. For this reason, product attribute decisions incorporating a marketing perspective should focus on product design over style alone.

Notes for PM 14-3

Brands

Transparency PM 14-4 relates to the material on pp.555-559.

Definition

A brand is a name, term, sign, symbol, or design, or a combination of these intended to identify the goods or services of one seller or -group of sellers and to differentiate them from those of competitors. Powerful brand names have consumer franchise - they command consumer loyalty.

Levels of Brand Meaning

Attributes

A brand elicits certain product attributes in the minds of consumers. The company may use one or more of these attributes in its advertising to reinforce these perceptions in the consumer.

Benefits

Consumers buy benefits, not attributes. A key aspect of a successful marketing program is linking attribute perceptions to tangible product benefits. The benefits may produce objective need-satisfiers, such as increased safety, or psychological benefits, such as enhanced self-esteem. But in both cases, the actual benefit must be available in the product.

Values

Brands communicate information about the buyer's values. The benefits of the brand indicate that these things are important to the consumer who chooses them. Some consumers, especially those of luxury goods, often select a particular brand in part because of what it communicates to others about the owners' values.

Personality

Brands project a personality. People personify brands and products. Psychologists have pointed out that we tend to be attracted to those like us, those we aspire to be like, and those we want others to view us as being like. Brands can help people, almost literally, become the type of person they want to be.

Brand Equity

Brands are used to create awareness, build preference, and ultimately, to command loyaltv among consumers. Companies with strong brands often attempt to build brand portfolios by acquiring brands with strong brand equity from other companies.

Notes for PM 14-4

Major Branding Decisions

Transparency PM 14-5 corresponds to Figure 14.4 on p.560 and relates to the material on pp.559-569.

Brand Decision

At this stage, the company must decide whether or not to place a brand name on its product. Brands usually command higher profit margins than non-brands.

Brand Sponsor

Who sponsors the brand must also be decided. Manufacturer's or National brands are owned by the producer. Private brands are created and owned by a reseller. Mixed-brand strategies combine both approaches.

Family Brand

National brands may implement at least four brand-name strategies. Individual brand names for each product of the company. Blanket brand names for all company products. Separate family names for all related product categories (i.e. household, tools). Company trade name combined with individual product names.

Brand Extension

This strategy seeks to extend existing brand qualities to new products.

Multibrand

This strategy develops two or more products in the same product category. P& G and Unilever pioneered multibranding.

Brand Repositioning

Even successful brands must be constantly evaluated in relation to competitive and market changes. Repositioning can be challenging to marketers because the strengths of a brand's image may make altering its position difficult to communicate to the target market.

Notes for PM 14-5

Packaging Decisions

These notes relate to the material on pp.569-574.

Packaging Concept

Packaging

Packaging includes the activities of designing and producing the container or wrapper for a product. The package includes the immediate container (that holds the product for use), a secondary package that is discarded prior to use, and a shipping package necessary for storage and shipping.

The packaging concept states what the package should be or do for the product in support of marketing objectives.

Labeling Decisions

Labels perform several functions. Labels identify, describe, and promote the product. Also, labels must meet the demands of legal regulations.

Identifies

Especially in support of brand strategies, labels distinguish the product from others.

Describes

Labels can provide information about contents, production, freshness, and instructions on safe and effective use.

Promotes

Use of colour and graphics can stimulate and arouse consumer attention for the product.

Legal Regulation

Mis-use of labels has lead to regulation on product claims, the addition of unit prices, open dating, and nutritional labelling for processed foods. Including all required information is necessary to ward off governmental investigations.

> **Tip**
>
> Both environmentalists and consumer groups have complained about unnecessary packaging. Environmentalists point out the ecological costs of more packages to throw away. Many firms now recycle packages to reduce wastes and save money. Consumer groups express concern that unnecessary packaging costs consumers more.

Product Line Decisions

These notes relate to the material on pp.574-579.

Product Line Length

Refers to the number of products in the line. The line is too short if adding items increases profits; too long if dropping items increases profits. Company objective of full-line offerings may decrease strict profit criterion on length.

Product Line Stretching

Occurs when a company lengths is product line beyond its current range. Downward stretch offers items to lower end of the market. Upward stretch introduces items to high end of market. Two-way stretch extends the line both upward and downward.

Product Line Filling

Adds items within the existing product range of the line.

Product Line Featuring

Occurs when the line manager selects one or a few items to receive special marketing attention to either increase volume of the featured items or draw customers closer to other products in the line.

Product Mix Decisions

Mix Width

Refers to how many product lines the company carries.

Mix Length

Refers to the total number of products the company carries.

Mix Depth

Refers to how many versions are offered of each product in the line.

Mix Consistency

Refers to how closely related the various product lines are in end use, production requirements, distribution channels, or other ways.

Comments on Discussing the Issues

1. The distinction between core, tangible, and augmented products has important marketing implications. Organisations that consider only the tangible product are likely to overlook opportunities and misunderstand the benefits sought by consumers.

   The core product of a university is an education. The tangible product is the campus, library, faculty, course offerings, and so on. The augmented product typically includes such features as social and sporting events, job placement services, eating facilities, and medical centre.

2. A meal is obviously a nondurable good, but restaurants have many of the same features as a dentist's office, a beauty parlour, and other services. The decor, the location, the quality of the service, and other factors may all be more important to patrons than the quality of the food. Most areas contain some restaurants that succeed only because of the quality of their food and other restaurants that succeed *despite* the quality of their food.

3. After years of trying, US and European automakers have failed to convince the public that the quality of American and European cars has improved. Despite engineering improvements, better warranties, and advertising that emphasises quality claims, people believe the quality is the same as ever—"meaning lousy"—or improving, but no faster than the quality of foreign cars.

   One reason that perceptions are slow to change is that, for most people, there is a four or five year interval between car purchases. After buying a domestic lemon, it may be a decade before a person is ready to consider an American or European car again. During this time, this person may have no direct experience with American or European cars, and hence have no evidence of quality improvements made in the meantime.

   Another reason that perceptions have been slow to change is that US and European cars outsell foreign cars three to one. Given the same percentage of problem cars, there would be three times as many unhappy domestic-car owners to influence people's perceptions about American or European cars as about foreign ones. (One auto analyst says that one person's lemon can sour ten other people's attitudes toward the car.)

   In the US, perhaps the most important reason for Detroit's continuing bad image is that reports of quality problems continue to appear. *Consumer Reports*, for example, dropped the Ford Taurus from its "recommended" list, citing trouble-prone electrical and fuel systems.

   So what can Detroit do? Continued quality-oriented advertising and good guarantees should change perceptions—eventually. Getting people into the cars and letting them see the quality improvements for themselves is another step. But the most important step of all is to make the cars better.

4. The chapter discussion shows that branding benefits buyers, sellers, and society. Consumers pay more for branded products than for unbranded products because branding gives evidence of quality, but there may be even more fundamental psychological reasons. Taste tests consistently indicate that many people's taste perceptions are more influenced by a brand name than by the actual product, as the Coca-Cola Company's experience with its Coke reformulation clearly shows. In blind taste

tests, over half the participants preferred the new version; in the store, 14 times as many people reached for Coca-Cola Classic as chose Coke.

Also see the chapter annotations for an example of a court ruling recognising the greater value of a branded versus an otherwise identical unbranded product in the Borden case.

5. Brand extensions have become a very common way to launch a new product. For the manufacturer extending a successful brand has many advantages. It allows a new product to capitalise on the success of an established brand, as in the case of Coca-Cola. Both consumers and the trade are aware of the new product's heritage, so the manufacturer does not need to spend nearly as much to create brand-name awareness. This strategy also improves the chance of obtaining retail distribution for the new brand. If the brand fails, however, it can reflect poorly on other products carrying the same brand name.

Brand extensions are less attractive for retailers. While this strategy does improve the odds of a new brand succeeding, it may make shelf usage less efficient. If the new extension takes some of its sales from the older brand, sales per square foot may fall. Overall management of the number of items to stock becomes more difficult. In the US for example, Procter & Gamble introduced Unscented Bounce Fabric Softener in 3 sizes, added to the existing 4 sizes of scented Bounce—a 75 per cent increase in items. The brand extension was expected to add only 15 to 20 per cent in overall sales, however, making the change inefficient for retailers who stocked the entire line. This problem is likely to occur with Coke.

Brand extensions offer interesting trade-offs for consumers. An established brand name on a new product offers certain assurances of quality, but also expectations that may or may not be met. New Coke failed both as a new product and as a line extension because it did not meet consumers' expectations of what Coke should be.

6. Extending brand names has become a very common way for manufacturers to launch new products. Brand extending saves the high cost of promoting a new brand name, and allows the consumer to recognise the new product instantly. It offers a greater chance to gain distribution through resellers. The manufacturer has total control of its brand name, and can use it carefully and appropriately. Any failures, however, may reflect poorly on all items using this brand name.

A brand owner that licenses its brand name can achieve an attractive return with no investment at risk: the licensee provides the investment, and takes the risk of success or failure for the licensed product. The licensing process can extend the brand name into categories where the licenser company does not compete, and provide some of the profits from this expansion with little direct risk. If the licensee firms do well with their products, it can enhance the awareness and value of the brand name. However, the licenser has some control over how its brand name is used, but this control is limited. If the name is used on a product of poor quality, or one that fails, it can reduce the value of the brand name.

Licensing of brand names and related concepts, such as characters, is a very large business. Participants in this process range from Walt Disney to Harley Davidson. Many companies have been successful with licensing arrangements. When done properly, licensing offers greater profits for the licenser firm, enhancement of the brand name's value, and a business opportunity for the licensee firm.

Comments on Applying the Concepts

1. The answer to this question will depend upon the type of shopping centre that students assess. In general, however, most shopping centres concentrate on speciality and shopping goods. There are exceptions, of course. Most modern shopping centres have a "Food Court," consisting of fast-food outlets catering to convenience.

The commercial strip is likely to have fewer speciality goods retailers, far more convenience goods sellers, a mix of shopping goods and possibly stores and offices specialising in unsought goods.

Differences in the environments clearly exist. The reasons are fairly straightforward. Unsought goods sellers might like a shopping centre location, but probably cannot afford the high rents involved. Furthermore, the environment may not be conducive to selling, say, encyclopaedias. Convenience goods marketers are well-suited to a shopping precinct where customers can park at the door and easily toss their purchases in the back seat. In a shopping centre, impulse purchases need to be carried, possibly for some distance and perhaps for an hour-long shopping trip—hardly the way to encourage purchase of a 3 litre bottle of Coke. Finally, many speciality retailers would not want to be on the local shopping precinct: the sales of a House of Fraser department store would not be helped by locating next to a "Happy Shopper" convenience store.

2. Sainsbury has a broad product line for a grocery store. The line also has moderate depth. By comparison, Asda has a much narrower product line. There is somewhat even narrower depth to the line than Sainsbury offers. Either stores could stretch its lines downward slightly, or upward substantially. The downward stretch would require going to a very low unit price strategy like the Co-op. Either stores could stretch upward substantially, although there is a limit on how high upward would be plausible.

Case 14
Colgate: One Squeeze Too Many?

Synopsis

This case focuses on a Colgate test market conducted in late 1989 and early 1990 in which the company tested the strength of the Colgate brand name. Specifically, it wanted to determine if the Colgate name had enough "equity" to carry a range of new over-the-counter drug and cosmetic products. Colgate tested ten new products ranging from Colgate aspirin-free pain relievers to Colgate natural laxative and Colgate dandruff shampoo. The company positioned each product to compete directly with another major brand name in that category - for example, Colgate dandruff shampoo went up against Head and Shoulders. This excursion into brand-name extension represented a significant departure from the higher-margin, high-visibility household goods that Colgate traditionally markets. The firm used heavy couponing and other promotional practices to encourage trial of the products, and it priced them as much as 20 per cent below competitive products. Some marketers were concerned about Colgate's strategy, fearing that it would dilute the value of the brand name and increase the risk that dissatisfaction with one product would lead to dissatisfaction with all of Colgate's products.

Teaching Objectives

1. Introduce students to the issues involved in deciding to extend a brand name.

2. Allow students to think through branding strategy.

Study Questions

1. What core product is Colgate selling when it sells toothpaste or the products in its new line?

This question gets students to consider what Colgate is really selling. The concept of the core product suggests that, as Ted Levitt would say, Colgate sells promises: Colgate toothpaste is the promise that the consumer will have whiter teeth and fresher breath after using it. The new Colgate dandruff shampoo is the promise that the consumer will have clean hair without dandruff. Once students realise that promises are being sold, they will have an insight into why the brand name is so important. A promise from an unheard-of company or an unfamiliar brand name carries less value than one from a name consumers know and trust. As the text points out, although the brand name is part of the tangible product, it brings with it an intangible assurance that is as important as the core product.

2. How would you classify these new products? What implications does this classification have for marketing the new line?

Of the classes of goods suggested in the chapter, we would typically call Colgate's products "convenience goods." Convenience goods are goods that are purchased relatively frequently without a lot of involvement on the part of the consumer. Brand name is very important in these kinds of consumer decisions. If a consumer who has a positive image of Colgate looks at a shelf full of aspirin-type products and sees the name Colgate, that consumer may well select Colgate's product without much examination of the competing brands.

The implication for marketing convenience goods is that they must be available widely--for example, in drugstores, grocery stores, and convenience stores. This requires a strong distribution system, which Colgate has. In fact, its distribution system makes it possible for the company to consider launching a wide range of such products.

3. What brand decisions has Colgate made? What kinds of product-line decisions? Are these decisions consistent?

Colgate is stretching its brand name in order to test the equity that has been established in the brand. By equity, we mean the consumer franchise that has been built over the years - the value of the brand name. Colgate has made a brand-extension decision and has decided to extend the brand downward. However, Colgate would argue that whereas the text implies that a downward stretch involves lowering both price and quality, the company has only lowered price. Its new products are of the same quality as its other consumer products. Colgate has used a *blanket family name*--it is putting the same name on a number of different products. The text would also designate this as a *manufacturer's brand*.

Students should see one inconsistency here - the significantly lower price. Although Colgate would argue that it is simply using the lower price to generate awareness and trial in the test market, the instructor can point out that price is often associated with quality in the consumer's mind. Thus, although Colgate has a quality brand name, its pricing may communicate to consumers that these new products are of a lower quality--especially if the prices are significantly below established brand names in the various categories.

The instructor should also raise the issue of how valid a test market is if price is set significantly lower than the competition and heavy couponing results in even more discounting. Students should see the inherent conflict between trying to generate trial and awareness while also trying to determine "normal" consumer reactions to a new product. Test marketing would have to continue long enough to stop the discounting and evaluate repeat-purchase behaviour.

4. If you were the marketing manager for the extended Colgate line, how would you package the new products? What risks do you see in these packaging decisions?

After the discussion of the previous question, most students will argue that Colgate should adopt a uniform package that is easily recognisable to the consumer and makes the Colgate name readily apparent. They may suggest that Colgate put its name in the same form on each of the packages, and perhaps that the packages should look alike. That is, labels on the packages should all be traditional red-and-white Colgate colours and be uniform in appearance. Although this makes good sense, one marketing consultant who has commented on the Colgate strategy believes that if Colgate makes all the new products look like "a tube of toothpaste" by using its traditional red-and-white packaging, the company will run the risk of decreasing the perceived quality. When purchasing an aspirin-free product, for example, consumers might think that "medicines" are of higher quality and are more important than toothpaste. This is, or course, one of the issues that Colgate will have to explore in the test market.

This discussion should help students see the importance of the packaging decision even when a brand name is involved. There are no clear or easy answers in these kinds of decisions. If there were, we would not need test markets.

Teaching Suggestions

This case provides the opportunity for more field research by students. They can examine the various categories of goods that are mentioned in the case to determine what other competition Colgate faces in each one. What are the significant brand names in each category? Are there other brand names that are common across categories? What are the price ranges within the categories? Are there generic products in each category?

This case can also be used in conjunction with the Marketing Research Chapter (Chapter 6) and the Pricing Chapters (Chapters 16 and 17).

Additional Information

In June 1992, Colgate had completed its test market and was in the process of evaluating the results. The company made no statement about whether it intended to go forward with any or all of the brand extensions.

Jokes and Quotes

A rose by any other name may smell as sweet but what would the customer ask for?

If you call a spade a spade you won't last long in the advertising business.
ANON

I'm a man of rare gifts. I haven't given one in years!
ANON

Free competition is not war, but rivalry in mutual service.
EDWIN CANNON

Polished brass will pass upon more people than rough gold.
LORD CHESTERFIELD

A hamburger by any other name costs twice as much
EVAN ESAR

Names are but noise and smoke, obscuring heavenly light.
GOETHE

Business is usually good in a good store.
E.W. HOWE

Take an object. Do something to it. Do something else to it.
JASPER JOHNS

You can't sell something nobody wants, no matter how you package it.
GERALD KAUFMAN

If the package doesn't say "New" these days, it better say "Seven Cents Off"
SPENCER KLAW

Go, make my coarse commodities look sleek. With subtle art beguile the honest eye.
THOMAS MIDDLETON

Let advertisers spend the same amount of money improving their product that they do on advertising and they wouldn't have to advertise it.
WILL ROGERS

What's in a name? That which we call a rose / By any other name would smell as sweet.
SHAKESPEARE

An engineer is a man who can do for ten shillings what any food can do for a pound.
NEVIL SLUB

The desire of food is limited in every man by the narrow capacity of the human stomach; but the desire of the conveniences and ornaments of buildings, dress, equipage and household furniture seems to have no limit or certain boundary.
ADAM SMITH

What's in a name? A 35% mark-up
VINCE THURSTON

Chapter 15
Marketing Services

Chapter Objectives

After reading this chapter, you should be able to:

1. Define a service.
2. Describe the distinctive characteristics that affect the marketing of services.
3. Explain how service business can improve their differentiation, quality and productivity.

Chapter Overview

Marketing has been broadened in recent years to cover marketable entities other than products - namely, services, organisations, persons, places, and ideas. Services are activities or benefits that one party can offer to another that are essentially intangible and do not result in the ownership of anything. Services are intangible, inseparable, variable, and perishable. Organisations can also be marketed. Organisation marketing is done to create, maintain, or change the attitudes or behaviour of target audiences toward an organisation. Person marketing consists of activities undertaken to create, maintain, or change attitudes or behaviour toward particular persons. Place marketing involves activities undertaken to create, maintain, or change attitudes or behaviour toward particular places. Idea marketing involves efforts to market ideas.

Teaching Notes

Refer to the following pages for teaching notes.

Characteristics of a Service

Transparency PM 15-2 relates to the material on pp.588-593.

Service Defined

A service is any activity or benefit that one party can offer to another that is essentially intangible and does not result in the ownership of anything.

Characteristics of a Service

1. Intangibility

Services are intangible. They have no prior sensory appeal before purchase. Buyers look for signs of service quality and sellers seek to provide surrogate measures of tangibility to reassure the buyer. Thus financial services are housed in solid buildings; life insurance may be sold by well-groomed salespersons.

2. Inseparability

Services are inseparable from their providers. The provider-client interaction is especially important in services and sometimes is the distinct feature of the service sought by the buyer.

3. Variability

Services are highly variable. Especially in large service organisations, standardising service across locations and many employees is very difficult. Yet reducing and controlling the amount of variability is a key part successful service business growth.

4. Perishability

Services are perishable and cannot be inventoried or stocked for later sale. For personal services, matching demand to supply often involves innovations in distribution - odd shop hours, weekends, even nights.

Notes for PM 15-1

Strategies for Service Firms

Transparency PM 15-2 corresponds to Figure 15-1 on p.593 and relates to the material on pp.593-605.

Marketing Strategies for Service Firms

Internal Marketing

Internal marketing means that the service firm must effectively train and motivate its customer-contact employees and all the supporting service people to work as a team to provide customer satisfaction.

Interactive Marketing

Interactive marketing means that perceived service quality depends heavily on the quality of the buyer-seller interaction. Customers judge both technical quality and functional quality (interpersonal interaction and evaluation).

Managing Differentiation

Provider differences become less important as consumers see services as essentially similar. Service firms can seek to add innovative features to differentiate. Service delivery can also be used to differentiate the offer based on differences in people, physical environment, and the service process.

Managing Service Quality

Because of the characteristics of services, standardising quality is particularly difficult. A key component of managing service quality is to identify customer expectations for service performance and linking the delivery of that quality to specific tasks whenever possible.

Managing Productivity

Productivity can be managed by "industrialising" the service or designing more effective service offers.

International Services Marketing

For global service firms, marketers must balance both the different cultural and environmental forces in each market with the different needs and expectations of employees in each international market who provide the service.

Tip

Ask students to discuss the above strategies in relation to their college or university.

Notes for PM 15-2

Comments on Discussing the Issues

1. Demand for services are growing because of changes in some basic cultural, demographic trends. In addition, the growing number of double-income households means that families have more money and less free time. Therefore they require many type of services to satisfy their needs for example, home delivery of fast foods like Pizza. People are spending less time in the kitchen, so they are looking for alternatives to home-cooked meals - fancy frozen dinners, fast foods and restaurant meals. A factor that will stimulate more marketers to emphasise the service element of a product in the future is the growing number of older people who may not have the desire or ability to go out shopping. Companies should try to identify (or stimulate) customer desires for increased services, then provide services that competitors do not. Examples could be suggested for almost any industry - car dealers (pickup and delivery for car service), cinema and videotape stores (letting customers order tickets or tapes by phone) and so on.

2. Cinemas are good examples of services, characterised by intangibility, inseparability, variability, and perishability.

   Intangibility—There is not much that a cinema can do to make a film tangible, though a few films are promoted with posters or other souvenir objects that viewers can keep. The cinema itself is tangible, and it should be made attractive, comfortable, and clean. Films must start on time, and the snack bar should be run efficiently with fresh, tasty food and good service.

   Inseparability—When people see a bad film, they blame the film, not the cinema. When the cinema is too cold or the popcorn stale, though, they may decide not to patronise it in the future, even if that means driving farther to another cinema or missing a film they might otherwise watch. Therefore, cinema managers must recognise that the surroundings and the employees are important parts of the film-going experience, and ensure that the experience is as enjoyable as possible.

   Variability—Employee training is important for maintaining service quality. Cinema must offer the same service whether there are three people or three hundred in the audience.

   Perishability—Film time is highly perishable. To smooth out demand, many cinema charge different prices at different times of day or have bargain prices on particular days of the week. They also adjust employee schedules or duties to have the appropriate number of workers for different levels of demand. Cinemas could be more creative in this area than they have been. For example, selling film passes good for unlimited admission to nonblockbuster films at off-peak times would be a way of increasing income at no real marginal cost, because the expense to the cinema of showing a film is the same whether a seat is empty or taken.

3. Airlines use a variety of ways to solve the perishability of unsold seats. The most direct way is offering a lower standby fare for those passengers willing to trade off uncertainty in their plans for a lower fare. A standby passenger will fill a seat if needed, but not cost anything if the plane is full. Overbooking is another way to address the problem. This practice assures full planes so that no seats perish—at a cost of paying incentives to bumped travellers and risking goodwill. Special promotional fares during off-peak hours attract vacationers to otherwise empty seats. Other promotions such as

military fares, free frequent flyer trips, and the like assure that the airlines run as close to capacity as possible.

Other examples of perishability occur in all service businesses. Restaurants offer lower-priced senior citizen specials during off-peak hours. Cinemas have lower-priced matinees. Resorts offer lower off-season accomodation rates. Video stores offer mid-week two-for-one rental specials. Students can find many additional examples.

5. Several types of exchange occur with non-profit organisations. A museum-goer exchanges an admission fee for an afternoon of recreation and education. A volunteer board member for the museum exchanges time and effort in exchange for the prestige of a board appointment. All volunteers exchange their efforts for psychological benefits: the satisfaction of helping a good cause, higher self-esteem from being altruistic, and the fun of working with a group. Donating blood has a similar exchange profile: donors trade a pint of blood and a small amount of pain for the knowledge that they have helped others in a very intimate way. Many blood donors and other volunteers feel a moral duty to continue helping others.

Those who donate money exchange their funds for psychological satisfaction similar to other volunteers. Very large donors many also receive substantial prestige, or even immortality, by having a building or institution named after them. In the US many business schools have received large donations from living donors in exchange for the school's being named after them. Marketers for non-profit organisations must be keenly aware of the exchanges they offer, and position their benefits to attract their target audience.

6. Refer to question 1 of Comments on Applying the Concepts for some examples.

Comments on Applying the Concepts

1. Students should answer the question by using an example of a college or university. First they should discuss the "product" aspect of the college such as the product consists of the courses provided by the institution. The price element will be course or tuition fee that students have to pay to be enrolled in the respective courses. Place element will be things such as the location of the institution. For example, near an underground or bus station, in a rural setting, etc. The promotion element should discuss the various tools and techniques being employed by the institution to promote themselves to the target audience. As far as the people element is concerned the institution should take into account the human resources aspect of the organisation. The institution should consider the method of recruiting, training, motivating and rewarding staff to ensure quality staff is employed to provide quality service for its customers. Physical evidence relates to the physical appearance of the buildings, offices, whether they are clean or otherwise; computer facilities; well-stocked and well-equipped library, are some examples. Process is connected to, for example the efficient service of the inter-library loans, several electives that can be chosen that are of interest to the students and several and different times in the week students could take a particular module to fulfil their credit requirements. These are just some examples that can affect the effectiveness and efficiency of any educational institutions.

2. **(a)** With the exception of certain sales, airline fares have a standard structure for purchasing tickets in advance. The lowest fares are available for purchase two weeks or more in advance, the next level of fares are available one week in advance, and the highest fares are available for purchase until moments before departure. Travel restrictions also influence fares. The differences are potentially huge for similar flights.

   (b) Most perishable goods are sold at a discount as their expiration date approaches. Airlines are doing exactly the opposite: as expiration date approaches (the day the flight leaves), prices go up dramatically. Furthermore, flying standby at reduced rates has been dropped. You can still fly standby, but only at full fare.

   This pricing strategy would seem to be counterproductive, but airlines are still flying heavily-loaded planes. There are reasons that this counter intuitive strategy works. First, business travellers, the mainstay of the industry, often do not know their schedules two weeks in advance. Even if they do, they often cannot stay over a Sunday night, which is required to get the lowest fares. Because these travellers need to travel anyway, they will pay whatever is necessary to go. Another factor is the increased demand for air travel, combined with the loss of several carriers to bankruptcies. This means that demand for seats is higher, regardless of fares.

   The current strategy probably comes close to maximising revenues. Small increases could be achieved by attracting incremental passengers onto flights that have empty seats. This might be done by allowing standby travel at low fares. Another approach is to sell low fares on short notice with restrictions that would make them good for vacationers (who would not buy a full-fare ticket) but not attractive to businesspeople (who do fly full-fare). This attracts incremental passengers without cannibalising full-fare revenues.

Case 15
Tribigarden: Is There Life After EuroDisney

Synopsis

The failure of Disney - the "king" of entertainment services - to make a success of EuroDisney, its first venture in Europe, has cast doubts on the viability of the theme park concept. Investors, the French government and management alike expected much from the project which opened in the spring of 1992; share prices reached an all-time high and predictions showed EuroDisney would break even in its first year of operation. Although the number of visitors was only half a million below the 11 million target in the first year, this dropped considerably the following year, leading to a financial loss of approximately Ffr 5.5 billion by the end of 1993. The bad publicity which resulted from EuroDisney troubles compounded their problems as potential customers stayed away. While the fortunes of the Disney operation were flailing, Grand Peninsula was developing its plans to build a theme park on the Spanish Mediterranean coast, to be called Tribigarden. This would be a more modest venture, aimed at attracting some 2.7 million visitors in its first year of operation, but was, nevertheless, a conventional theme park like the Paris EuroDisney. The question now being asked is whether Tribigarden stands any chance of succeeding when such an experienced, world famous organisation as Disney has apparently misread the market for theme parks in Europe and most of France's other theme parks are struggling.

Teaching Objectives

1. Demonstrate the application of marketing principles in the service sector.

2. Consider the differences between marketing services and marketing products.

3. Provide a vehicle for the discussion of services in a global environment.

Study Questions

1. What accounts for EuroDisney's failure to date? Would EuroDisney have worked if located elsewhere in Europe?

There are many factors students should highlight. Some of them are; (1) Huge financial outlay; (2) Debts from construction overruns and trading difficulties; (3) Over ambitious throughput targets of visitors i.e. 11 million required in the first year to break even and this figure will need to increase annually; (4) Inclement Parisian weather; (5) Food, drinks and goods are expensive; (6) Strong French franc deterred visitors from Italy and UK; (7) Financial troubles caused bad publicity; (7) Large fees commanded by Walt Disney i.e. 3% management fees, 10% royalty fee on admissions and 5% on food and merchandise sales; (8) Anti US culture amongst French, i.e. why build fake castles when we have the real thing?; (9) Other Europeans say why go EuroDisney when you can go to Disney World more cheaply, with better accommodation and where good weather is virtually guaranteed; (10) Guests stopping for one day instead of three leaving the hotel with just 55% occupancy.

Some students will say "yes". EuroDisney would probably have worked better if located in a part of Europe with a better climate such as Spain. Others will say that there would be a much smaller cultural gap to bridge if it had been located in the UK (London

Docklands was one of the original proposed locations). Some will say in terms of favourable local economies, there are many countries within Europe that have currencies weaker than the French franc, thus making them more attractive to foreign holiday makers and foreign investors alike. Some students will say that many of factors which have been responsible for EuroDisney's failure to date would have occurred wherever the park was located; the recession was Europe-wide, the management and royalty fees levied by the parent company would be the same, but most importantly the same unacceptably high cost of admission, refreshments and hotels would have prevailed.

2. Were EuroDisney problems foreseeable? If so, why were they not seen? Are they solvable now? Will changing the name to Disneyland Paris help?

Yes, some omens would have already been evident. For example (1) The European economy was already in recession at this point. The national unemployment level was starting to rise in France; (2) France had already established itself as a bad place to open a theme park. All but one of France's other theme parks were struggling; (3) French intellectuals were expressing their objections to the US culture and therefore vetoing EuroDisney; (4) Significantly, the singular most important question, in terms of consumer choice had not been addressed by the Disney marketers, prior to the EuroDisney launch, "Why got to Paris rather than the real thing in Florida". The Orlando alternative is no more expensive per night, has better hotels, has sunshine and simply more fun!

These problems were not seen possibly because Disney was such a successful company. At home in the USA, Walt Disney World in Florida was the world's greatest attraction. Abroad, Tokyo Disneyland had ten million visitors in its first year of opening. It soon became a financial success. As one of America's most successful businesses, Disney probably believed that they could not fail. They had a winning formula and that no mountain was too high enough to climb, so to speak. Despite the unfavourable economic and cultural omens, the "Disney Marketing Machine" took over and the venture went ahead anyway.

Most of EuroDisney's problems are solvable but management must move quickly in order to prevent further damage to its reputation from continued adverse publicity. Students could mention some actions to consider; (1) Lowering the prices charged in entrance fees, with perhaps special discounts at off-peak periods; (2) Lowering costs is a priority. This can be achieved by introducing productivity measures to reduce labour costs and Disney should waive all management royalty fees; (3) Raising the quality of service. EuroDisney must adjust its service to a level which is consistent with the expectations of its target market. They may not be able to provide the sunshine but a friendly and helpful atmosphere would go a long way to matching the reputation of the US parks that are "more fun"; (4) Differentiating themselves from the other theme parks in France. They are biggest but are they the best? People go to Disneyland for fun and thrills - introducing/publicising a more daring ride may be seen as having only a short-term advantage but would attract customers who will hopefully be won over by the friendly staff, quality of service and value for money they find at the park, and will return; (5) Urge the government to open the promised TGV terminal to provide alternative quick and easy access to the site. However, EuroDisney's financial situation is so dire that this overrides all other internal problems which the company can correct itself. The loss of confidence by investors resulted in share prices diving from the euphoric Ffr 164 immediately prior to the park's opening, to the catastrophic Ffr 30 less than two years later. Efforts would have to be made to obtain further financial backing from for example the French government, who were responsible for enticing Disney to build near Paris in the first place.

A name change could improve the park's image. Some students will say "Euro" sounds a little dull with its connotations of governments, currencies and so on. Combining "Disneyland", synonymous with fun and magic, and Paris, probably the most internationally known capital on the continent, with its reputation for culture and *bonhomie*, evokes a positive image. Additionally, by standardising the name, Disneyland Paris should gain from the reputation and success of the Californian Disneyland and the more recently established and successful Tokyo Disneyland. Also, it may have more appeal to the French if it has the name of their capital city its title!

3. Contrast the Tribigarden proposal with EuroDisney? What are the differences and does any give Tribigarden an advantage over EuroDisney?

Tibigarden is planned to be the third largest theme park in Europe, but is nevertheless a much more modest scheme than the extensive EuroDisney complex. Major differences are;

EuroDisney	**Tribigarden**
Ffr 20.8 bn development costs	Pta 41bn development costs
Break-even point: 10.5 million visitors/year	Break-even point: 2.7 million visitors/year
Sited 32 km east of Paris	Sited near Spain's Mediterranean coasts
Climate cold and damp	Climate warm and sunny
Large hotel complex on site	No hotels on site
Open all year round	Open 156 days - April to October
Royalties/ management fees 30% of operating income and set to rise annually	Design/management fees 12.4% of income and schedule to decline

Advantages of Tribigarden over EuroDisney are; (1) There is not a huge debt to service; (2) The smaller operation means that less visitors are needed in order for the venture to break even; (3) Plenty of hotels exist nearby but the cost of empty rooms is not borne by operators of the park; (4) Situated in the most popular tourist areas of Europe, particularly for families with young children; (5) Only operating in the months when the maximum number of tourists visit the area; (6) Visitors will not be deterred by adverse weather conditions.

4. Is the European theme park market already over-subscribed? Will Tribigarden succeed despite the failure of EuroDisney and the other theme parks in France?

There are only a hand full of parks at present, far fewer than the American market, for example. It is true to say however, that the European market is very unforgiving to those organisations who misinterpret their target markets and position their service inappropriately. In light of the EuroDisney's problems, other potential market entrants may be reluctant to try the European theme park market.

Tribigarden will be the third largest conventional theme park in Europe and the tenth largest world-wide. Apart from Disneyland, its nearest rivals of a comparative size are situated on the northern periphery of the European Union, in Denmark and Sweden, a less popular holiday destination with a completely contrasting climate. Smaller successful parks, for example, Futurescope in France, are operating in niche markets and are thus not competing directly with the mass market which the conventional theme park is targeting. There would seem to be room for another large theme park to be situated in southern Europe. Positioned in the warmer south, Tribigarden is far enough away not to be vying for the same customers as its Scandinavian rivals, nor is it competing directly with EuroDisney which aims to attract customers who take their holiday in the park rather than merely visit it for the day. Factors in favour of a successful venture for the Tribigarden investors are; (1) Among their investors are experienced operators of successful smaller venture in both the USA and UK; (2) The Tribigarden management have the additional advantage of learning from the mistakes of their EuroDisney rival. They know that the prices they charge must not deter customers; (3) Visitors will be attracted by the novelty of a new theme park.

Teaching Suggestions

Instructors might open a discussion of this case by asking if any of the students have been to Euro Disney, Disney World or Disneyland. If some have, the instructor may ask them to describe their experiences. There may be students in the class who plan to go to one of the three major theme parks. They may be willing to share their decision-making process in reaching such a conclusion.

In addition to using this case with the Services Marketing Chapter (Chapter 15), instructors may use it with chapters 1,3, 5, or 6.

Overview Case 5
Mapanza Breweries

Synopsis

Brewed by Mapanza, Kafue beer has been the most popular and well-known lager in Zambia for over 30 years. Mapanza was once the sole supplier to the Zambian lager market, enjoying a monopoly situation. In October 1992 a new democratic government came to power and introduced a large scale privatisation and liberalisation programmes. The new government favoured free trade and offered less protection for local industry from foreign competition, and tariff barriers came crashing down. As a consequence, Mapanza was suddenly faced with international competition from brands produced under license in Zimbabwe and South Africa such as Heineken and Carling Black Label. In addition, competition from other native African brews increased. Kafue still enjoys 60% market share, but this is being eaten away. In a recent survey when asked to compare Kafue with imported lagers a large percentage criticised the taste, alcohol content, price and packaging. Previously, Mapanza operated from two sites but the plants were poorly maintained and operated at only 40% efficiency. A South African brewer has bought the Lusaka plant with the promise of investing. The Mapanza name will be retained. Zambia itself is a relatively well developed and stable country when compared with its neighbours with a growing economy, with COMESA and GATT membership. Fifty-three per cent of its population live in urban areas, and the economy depends more and more on mineral excavation. In terms of Zambian drinking habits, bars represent the predominant outlet for Kafue, while hotels tend to sell more imported lagers. The government has offered local brewers some respite in the form of 20% duty on imported lager, meaning that Kafue is roughly 60% cheaper than its counterparts. However the fact remains that Kafue is rapidly losing market share and the Mapanza marketing team need to take swift action if they are to remain the market leader.

Teaching Objectives

1. Allow students to appreciate the need to change from a product-driven organisation to a market-driven corporation.

2. Expose to students the importance of the micro and macroenvironment in positioning old product and development of a new product.

3. Allow students to make recommendations for Mapanza's new marketing strategy.

Study Questions

1. What are the problems facing Mapanza Breweries in the marketplace? What are the brewer's main weaknesses and main strengths?

Question 1 could be answered by using the SWOT analysis. The strengths are; (1) Mapanza has over 30 years of brewing experience; (2) Mapanza has established distribution links; (3) There is still some level of protection for local brewers in the form of import duties; (4) Kafue is the best known and most popular Zambian lager brand; (5) Kafue is the market leader with a 60% market share; (6) Kafue is now sold in new dumpy bottles in line with competition; (7) Kafue is highly available; (8) Imported lagers are higher priced and availability is low, rendering supply inaccessible for low income groups; (9) Mapanza has first hand knowledge of local culture, customs and consumer behaviour. The weaknesses are ; (1) Mapanza is stuck in its protectionist past; (2) Failure to invest in its plants means poor efficiency; (3) Failure to invest in research and development means it is losing share to younger, leaner, meaner competition; (4) Kafue has a poor taste perception; (5) Kafue has a poor quality perception; (6) Kafue is under promoted; (7) Kafue has dated packaging; (8) Kafue has a relatively short shelf life; (9) Kafue is not available in cans; (10) Kafue has a comparatively low alcohol content compared to imported lagers. The opportunities are; (1) Zambia has a growing economy; (2) Zambia has a growing urban population; (3) Zambia has a growing middle class; (4) Export potential exists as trade agreements are drawn up with other African countries (COMESA) and countries affiliated to GATT; (5) There is a growing trend in the Western world toward ethnic products and rediscovering roots, further export potential; (6) Legislation banning the advertising of alcohol has been lifted; (6) Faced with privatisation and external competition Mapanza, the sleeping and cumbersome dragon is being forced to react and restructure. An opportunity which should be seized; (7) Tourism is growing in Zambia which is famous for the Victoria Falls and its national parks and nature reserves; (8) To counter large multinationals Mapanza now has the backing of a South African brewery, which promises large investment and potential for product development; (9) The Zambian government has introduced duties on imported lagers; (10) A growing preference for canned drinks, an opportunity to poach customers by changing packaging; (11) Inspite of the fact that lager is drunk all over the world, its promotion varies immensely and in this respect it is not a standardised product and local producers have the advantage of knowing which media works best; (12) Zambia has a growing trade union movement and "working men" associations and bars are starting to appear. The threats are; (1) A sudden influx of lager brands produced under license in neighbouring countries; (2) Increased African lager competition i.e. new "Opaque"; (3) Increased mining and poaching is ruining the environment and threatening the potential tourist market; (4) Hotels tend to sell more imported lagers, are tourists looking for brand familiarity?; (5) Imported lagers are becoming status product; (6) Competition in the shape of Carling Black Label and Heineken, has the backing of large multinationals and therefore increased resources are available in the form of price subsidies, promotion budgets etc.

2. How should Mapanza Breweries respond to the threat from imported lagers? Should it change Kafue lager so that it competes with them more directly or seek to avoid competition?

Students will highlight that Mapanza has been idle and complacent for too long. Having once enjoyed monopolistic market the company has become lazy, uncreative, inefficient, archaic, outmoded, out of touch with its changing customer base and laden with dead wood. The organisation has to change and become market oriented if it is to maintain its current position and share. The acid test of any marketing oriented organisation is its ability to change its behaviour when faced with the threat of competition. One thing is certain it cannot ignore this threat, it has to react. Mapanza requires a new marketing strategy if it is to regain its competitive advantage. Kafue is competing against a new enemy in the shape of imported multinational brands who possess all the latest consumer weaponry to annihilate Mapanza with its primitive marketing tools. Mapanza has to re-examine its marketing strategy. It needs to reposition Kafue in the market place and be more selective in its target marketing. More comprehensive research needs to be done if Mapanza is to fully understand its customers. Marketing audit should be carried out if it is to effectively assess its competitive advantages.

Mapanza's strengths should be exploited and tied with market opportunities, its weaknesses should be overcome. Kafue's greatest advantage lies in its low price and Mapanza should play on this in certain target markets. At this point some students will feel that Mapanza could also fight the competition head-on by modifying its standard product, to combat the smoother international competition by introducing Kafue Elite (possible name). This should recapture the status seeking middle and upper class market. Possible new marketing mix to combat imported lagers are as follows;

Original Kafue

Product
For its target market of shanty town dwelling miners and land workers Standard Kafue need very little change in terms of formula and taste because price is the important factor. Shelf life could perhaps be improved upon as in more isolated areas without modern refrigerators, bulk purchases may be necessary. Labels could be made more appealing and brought in line with current design trends. Thus making the product fashionable. They could play on national roots and emphasise "made in Zambia". The label should also have a very masculine look. The stubby bottles are good and can perhaps form part of packed lunch. Tins may also be a good idea due to their resilience. Flip tops could be introduced as bottle openers are not always on hand.

Price
The price should certainly not go up but incentives to buy should be offered i.e. returnable deposits for bottles and tins. Price promotions such as "buy 4 get one free" could be introduced.

Place
Kafue's widespread availability and Mapanza's excellent distribution network should be exploited to the maximum. Kafue should be made available in all local bars and working men's clubs and sold in shanty town shops and supermarkets.

Promotion
Very few working class Zambians own TV sets and illiteracy is also a problem. Consequently, TV and printed media are poor choices for this market segment. Billboard pictures with few words would work, portraying the Original Kafue drinker as a strong attractive, muscly, "man's" man, employed as a miner or land labourer depending on geographic location. Radio is another important media for Zambians. Radio commercials could be used here. Promotional gimmicks such as lighters, beer mats, playing cards, sun hats, T-shirts would also increase sales and heighten public awareness.

Kafue Elite
Product
The aim is to capture a growing middle class who see imported lager as a novelty and a status symbol. Therefore it is important that Kafue can compete with imported lagers on taste and quality. A smoother brew needs to be concocted. Packaging needs to have a trendy, rich, cultured, artistic and educated look to it. Again the new bottle shape should be made more appeal. Tins may have novelty effect. Brand image is all important for this target market,

Price

Price should be slightly below imported lagers but much higher than the original Kafue. This is a premium product and demands premium prices, thus this should be reflected in its superior taste and quality which will probably give the brand a certain snob value.

Place
This is a brand which will be targeted at tourists, so hotels are an obvious outlet. Incentives should be offered to hoteliers to promote Kafue Elite for example fidelity bonuses for selling Kafue exclusively, etc. Middle/Upper class bars, suburb shops, high class restaurants, should be targeted. Souvenir shops at airport, national airlines also offer potential.

Promotion
TV is an accessible media to the middle and upper class Zambians. Newspapers and printed media are also a good bet. The Kafue drinker should be portrayed as trendy, smooth, handsome, intelligent and above all sophisticated and rich! Promotional gifts would be perceived as tacky and therefore out of place for a high class lager.

The above outline are just some possible examples that students will highlight. Ask students to give their own examples.

3. Mapanza Breweries have many ways they could develop Kafue but it is unlikely that they could do them all at once. What changes would you advise and how would you prioritise them? Which changes are likely to increase Kafue's sales most, and which are likely to cost most to implement?

Students will give many variation of answers. Some will mention; (1) Improve the taste; (2) Increase the alcohol content; (3) Increase the shelf life; (4) Introduce Kafue in cans; (5) Introduce bottle tops that can be removed by hand; (6) Create a trendier image i.e. packaging and labelling; (7) Introduce Kafue Elite - high quality, high taste product; (8) Total diversification - move into hotel and restaurant business; (9) Improve advertising.

Kafue is still a very workable product in certain target markets because of its cheap price and high availability. It may be however be an idea to improve on label design to give the product a more up-beat image. This would be the principle change for Kafue at this stage of its product life cycle. This is also the cheapest solution. An improved shelf life and higher alcohol content could also potentially improve sales but at a greater research cost. For this particular product cans may be a good idea or flip tops but having to invest in a canning plant would be a very expensive product development.

The introduction of a premium lager to appeal to the straying middle and upper classes would improve Mapanza's share position and sales. This would require research into improving taste and quality of the brand. Again a new labelling would need to be developed to help Kafue Elite stand out from imported brews. This task also require a large promotion budget to publicise the product launch. Although the investment may be high the dividends would pay in the end. Kafue Elite should be targeted at the tourist market and Mapanza could make a move into the hotel and restaurant chain to ensure that Kafue lager gets top billing although at this stage this would be an extreme, expensive and foolish move.

4. Should Mapanza Breweries increase their product range? If so, what products should they introduce and how should they be positioned? What is the most important dimension in the beer market: the product, its taste, its strength, its packaging, its distribution or its image?

As mentioned previously, some students suggested that the Kafue Elite be introduced to fight imported competition. Kafue Elite should be targeted at the upper and middle class Zambians who perceive imported expensive lager to be a status symbol. This is the ground that Mapanza is losing. Kafue Elite is still slightly lower priced than imported lagers but expensive enough to justify its superior taste and quality. It has nationalistic connotations yet sophisticated. Other students will suggest a canned Kafue lager with a better shelf life and fresh image aimed at the existing low income market and priced accordingly. Kafue Ice is also a possibility.

It is important not to generalise about the important reasons for purchase, after all one man's lager is another man's champagne! Consumers will rank all these dimensions differently dependent on age, income, etc. For example; (1) Product - important for the thinking drinker for example the real ale buffs; (2) Taste - as the above but also younger drinkers will look for a cleaner taste; (3) Strength - the case study shows a clear demand for stronger lagers especially amongst the younger drinkers; (4) Packaging - in a country where drinking is done out of the package this is very important, in this instance it is closely linked to image; (5) Distribution - important for consumers who live in rural areas and villages - making the product available at the right places at the right time; (6) Image - especially important for younger drinkers and fashionable drinkers. These are just some examples. Students should come up with different examples and reasons.

Teaching Suggestions

Instructors can use this case with the Product Chapter (Chapter 7) as well as with the Promotion Chapters (Chapters 18, 19 and 20).

Jokes and Quotes

The aim of fast food marketing is to minimise the time and distance between a man and his meal.
ANON

A little bit of quality
  Will always make 'em smile;
A little bit of courtesy
  Will bring 'em in a mile;
A little bit of friendliness
  Will tickle 'em 'tis plain-
And a little bit of service
  Will bring 'em back again.
ANON

A banker is a pawnbroker with a manicure.
ANON

Economic competition is not war, but rivalry in mutual service.
EDWIN CANNAN

Everything comes to him who hustles while he waits.
THOMAS E EDISON

Human service is the highest form of self-interest for the person who serves.
ELBERT HUBBARD

The money raised tonight will go towards a charity. It may not get there, but it will be going towards it. . .
JOKE

I stayed in a hotel that was so smart even the room service was ex-directory.
JOKE

We went to a holiday camp one year for a couple of weeks. Actually we were only there for seven days. They gave us a week off for good behaviour!
JOKE

The aim of legitimate business is service, for profit, at a risk.

BENJAMIN C. LEEMING

The showmanship idea of yesterday was to give the public what they wanted. This is a fallacy. You don't know what they want and they don't know what they want.
S. L. ROTHAFEL

It's a hectic crazy life. You're not like a shoe salesman, who can get rid of his wares. You're stuck with a product - yourself.
NANCY SINATRA

In this bank, "No" is a complete sentence.
SIGN (ABOVE A BANK PRESIDENT'S DESK)

They laughed what I sat down at the piano, but when I started to play.
SLOGAN (US SCHOOL OF MUSIC)

Passenger: You're one of the stupidest people I've met
Stewardess: And you're one of the nicest gentlemen I've ever come across. But perhaps we're both mistaken.
SWISSAIR

Part VI

Price

Chapter 16

Pricing Products:

Pricing Considerations and Approaches

Chapter Objectives

After reading this chapter, you should be able to:

1. Understand the internal and external factors affecting price.
2. Explain the impact of cost on price.
3. See how market structures influence price setting.
4. Compare and evaluate the general approaches to price setting.

Chapter Overview

Despite the increased role of nonprice factors in the modern marketing process, price remains an important element in the marketing mix. Many internal and external factors influence the company's pricing decision. Internal factors include the firm's marketing objectives, marketing mix strategy, and organisation for pricing. External factors that influence pricing decisions include the nature of the market and demand, competitors' prices and offers, and factors like the economy, reseller needs, and government actions. In the end, the consumer decides whether the company has set the right price. The consumer weighs the price against the perceived value of using the product. If the price exceeds the sum of the value, consumers will not buy the product. Consumers differ in the values they assign to different product features and marketers often vary their pricing strategies for different price segments. The company can select one or a combination of three general pricing approaches. These include: cost-based approach, the buyer-based approach, and the competition-based approach.

Teaching Notes

Refer to the following pages for teaching notes.

Internal Factors Affecting Price

Transparency PM 16-1 relates to the material on pp.622-629 and Figure 16-1.

Internal Factors Affecting Price

1. Marketing Objectives

Survival

Survival can be the primary factor in setting price especially in marginal businesses or industries. Price is used to stay in business in hopes of making profits when conditions improve.

Current Profit Maximisation

Means the company is emphasising short term results over long-run performance.

Market-Share Leadership

Affects price when the company seeks the dominant market share. Low prices increase demand so that later volume creates profit.

Product-Quality Leadership

Tends to push prices high. This pricing strategy may be linked to niching strategy in other discussions.

2. Marketing Mix Strategy

Price must be considered in light of its role in support of the overall marketing mix. Price is one kind of information the consumer receives about the product. Price should consistently support the overall positioning strategy targeted by the marketing mix.

3. Costs

Costs set the pricing floor that the company can charge for its product. Fixed Costs (or overhead) are costs that do not vary much with production or sales levels. Variable Costs vary directly with the level of production. Total Costs are the sum of the fixed and variable costs for any given level of production.

4. Organisation for Pricing

How the organisation delegates the pricing function affects price. Pricing is also linked to overall company goals.

Tip

Many firms are now trying to cover their fixed costs with variable costs. Ask students how they do that and why do they do it.

Notes for PM 16-1

External Factors Affecting Price

Transparency PM 16-2 relates to the material on pp.629-635 and Figure 16-1 on p.622.

The Market and Demand

1. Types of Markets

Pure Competition - is characterised by many buyers and sellers so that no one agent affects pricing. Going rate pricing is the rule.

Monopolistic Competition - consists of many buyers and sellers trading over a range of prices. Products can be differentiated in quality, features, or styles.

Oligopolistic Competition - consists of few sellers each sensitive to the other's pricing and marketing strategies. Barriers to entry prohibit new sellers from entering the market

Pure Monopoly - consists of a single seller. The seller may by a government/private regulated monopoly, or unregulated monopoly. Pricing may be linked to other than cost or profit factors, including fear of competition entering or regulation.

2. Consumer Perceptions of Price and Value

Buyers ultimately decide prices. Marketers must combine technical expertise with creative judgement and an awareness of buyers' motivations.

3. Price Demand Relationship

A demand curve show the number of units the market will buy in a given time period at various prices. The price elasticity of demand illustrates how responsive demand will be to a change in price. If demand hardly changes with a small change in price, demand is inelastic. If a small change in prices changes demand greatly, demand is elastic.

4. Competitors Prices and Offers

How the competition prices its products in relation to consumer reactions can affect company pricing strategies. Some companies have standing policies to match price changes of their competition. Other respond with nonprice changes in the marketing mix such as increased features or performance.

5. Other Environmental Forces

Other factors include general economic conditions that affect buying power of the market and/or the company's ability to meet demand. The role of resellers in the channel of distribution may affect pricing. Government's role can also be a consideration as are social concerns.

Tip

The aim of marketing is to drive, not be a slave to the demand curve. How can marketers shift their demand curve from "elastic" to "inelastic", or from being "pure competition" to "pure monopoly"?

Notes for PM 16-2

General Pricing Approaches

Transparency PM 16-3 relates to the material on pp.635-645 and Figure 16-5 on p.636.

1. Cost-Based Pricing

Cost-Plus Pricing

Consists of adding a standard mark-up to the cost of the product. Mark-ups vary widely across different industries. Cost-plus simplifies pricing strategy and covers costs but ignores market demand factors.

Break-even Analysis

Utilises an analysis of the company's costs in relation to units of the product produced and sold. This approach identifies the minimum pricing level the company's activities can support.

Target Profit Pricing

A variation on break-even analysis that links price to profit objectives above total costs. Target profit pricing is mathematically appealing but fails to accommodate the fact that increased prices decrease demand.

2. Buyer-Based Approach

Also called Perceived Value Pricing, this approach uses the buyer's perception of value as the key to pricing. Strategy under this approach utilises non price mix variables to help set perceived value in the buyer's mind.

3. Competition-Based Approach.

Going-Rate Pricing

Bases price largely on what competitors charge for their products. This approach is popular in markets where demand elasticity is difficult to measure.

Sealed-Bid Pricing

Involves competition between sellers attempting to underprice each other while still covering costs. Winning a sealed bid contract requires careful estimation of competitor's costs and likely profit margins to bid successfully.

Tip

Ask students why surveys show that "cost-plus" and "going-rate" pricing are the most common forms of pricing used. Ask which approach is most market oriented.

Notes for PM 16-3

Comments on Discussing the Issues

1. Sellers of high price, low cost products should try to convince potential customers to think about long-term costs rather than short-term expenditures. An example of a product whose cost is much higher than its price is the ordinary rock salt that is used by the US highway departments on roads to prevent icing. The price of this salt is only 1 or 2 cents a pound, but its cost is estimated to be as much as 80 cents a pound because it corrodes cars, bridges, and underground cables, pollutes ground water, and destroys vegetation. Calcium magnesium acetate (CMA) de-ices like salt but does not have salt's harmful effects. Companies that manufacture CMA, could use information on the cost of rock salt to make CMA's price of 25 cents a pound look like a bargain.

   According to the National Tooling & Machining Assn., there are many hidden costs to buying parts and components from foreign vendors. Foreign sourcing "typically adds 5% to 15% to the bid price for shipping, 3% or more for additional paperwork and for overseas communications, 5% to 10% for added inventory, and up to 35% for unanticipated design changes." The association is publicising these hidden costs to make domestic suppliers' prices appear more competitive. (Mimi Bluestone, "Machine Parts: It Really Pays to Buy American," *Business Week*, May 30, 1988, p. 101).

   A college degree provides another example of costs that are higher than prices. According to a letter to *The Chronicle of Higher Education* by Stephen T. Riley, the monetary costs of attending college average about $60 a day, but the foregone income of the jobs that students might have if they were not in college may add another $75 daily to the true cost of a college education. This is a pricing issue that colleges facing declining enrolments definitely do *not* want prospective students to consider.

2. Malaysia's Proton Saga is a low cost, value-for-money car with a low price. The Proton Saga's pricing strategy strategy falls into the "good-value" strategy category where the low price of the car is complemented by a medium quality product specification. With this pricing strategy, complemented with a good product, distribution network and promotional mix, Proton is obviously hoping for high volume sales. Their objectives appear to be maximum market penetration and sales growth rather than, for example, maximum current profit. Here the low price will be the major selling point of the car. The key factors that the company must be aware of when taking this pricing approach include; (1) Awareness of the relationship between price and quality of the product; (2) Total cost must be covered in the long term; (3) Awareness of what the competitors are charging for their products; (4) The Proton Saga must not be positioned so as to cannibalise any other Proton cars; (5) Perceived value of the car to the customer is high. Some internal factors are; (1) The marketing mix strategy; (2) Costs. These are just some examples of factors. Students could highlight other factors that might affect pricing decisions.

3. A change in the malt whisky increased sales were apparently due to the price boost. This suggests that the demand curve for the product was upward sloping and that the elasticity of demand was positive. With alcoholic beverages, and other products such as cosmetics, clothing, and fine restaurants, price helps to create perceived values. In these product categories, price may be determined first in order to establish the positioning of the product, and other marketing mix elements - advertising, packaging, and distribution—are designed to support the chosen positioning. Heavy advertising

may be required to support a high-price, prestige positioning. For example a company could spend 20 per cent of its sales on advertising. It successfully persuades people to spend £10,000 or more for a Piaget watch that tells time no better than a £50quartz watch - and performs fewer functions to boot.

4. Genentech is a young company based on recombinant DNA technology. Its purpose is to create unique pharmaceuticals, many based on substances the human body itself produces to fight illness. TPA is its first major product, a clot-dissolving drug that can halt a heart attack in progress. Genentech has priced the drug at $2,200 per dose. Analysts believe that Genentech's gross profit on this drug is over 90 per cent, even higher than the 80 per cent level commonly seen in pharmaceutical products.

Genentech is clearly using a perceived value approach in pricing TPA. There are many factors that create a very high value for this drug. It minimises hospital stays and rehabilitation expenses, which can be easily calculated. Even more important in creating value for the drug are factors that cannot be evaluated in monetary terms: TPA saves lives, and reduces damage to the heart so that quality of life is improved for the survivors of heart attacks. The cost of $2,200 seems reasonable given the potential benefits, and is not large compared to the total cost of hospitalisation for a heart attack.

TPA is unlikely to be elastic with price. The drug will be given only on an emergency basis. The decision maker, the patient's physician, will be concerned only with using the best therapy to save the patient's life. Price will not be considered if it is the appropriate treatment. Furthermore, most administrations will be paid for by health insurance. Insurance companies are unlikely to complain about the cost of this drug if it causes other savings in the total bill through reduced hospital stays.

5. The pricing strategy followed by the Japanese firms wanting to enter the global market was one of penetration pricing with a strong emphasis on maximum sales growth. The Japanese set a relatively low price in order to gain the maximum penetration of the market as quickly as possible. This meant that large scale of economies were eventually enjoyed from the high levels of production. This in turn leads to higher long term profits. This type of penetration pricing also had the effect of making the low end market less attractive to potential competitors. It was only later, once the Japanese were established, that the lower priced cars and cameras started to enter the markets. Prime examples are Skoda cars and Practica cameras who both undercut the Japanese on price. The Japanese greatly benefited from the ongoing experience of the market. Japanese pricing strategies changed and evolved over time. Generally speaking the relative pricing of the Japanese cars and cameras is far higher now than when they first entered the markets. The successful but painful experience of the Japanese car giant Toyota is a good example.

6. Students will come up with all sorts of examples of personal care or cosmetic products. This question is essentially an opinion-based question therefore ask students to give clear answers in relation to the questions. They also need to know the materials in this chapter before they can attempt to answer some of the sub questions.

Comments on Applying the Concepts

1. There are usually clear patterns to the pricing of petrol in a given area, and students can often discuss this question from memory. Competition and convenience are the driving factors that explain much of the pricing difference. In general, stations that are located at a major highway exit ramp or in a central business district will have the highest prices. Small stations with no nearby competitors are also able to maintain higher prices. Studies have shown that petrol costs about 5p per gallon more in a small town than the same brand in a nearby suburban area. The lowest prices will be found at convenience stores and petrol stations in shopping areas.

   Proximity to competitors will also affect pricing. If there are three high-priced petrol stations located at the same highway exit ramp, it is likely that all three will have nearly identical prices. Likewise, two stations on opposite corners will probably have prices that are within 1p to 2p of each other. Brand names do make a difference: Esso petrol will usually cost more than the local no-name product.

   In general, petrol stations do not use cost-based pricing. A given grade of petrol from Shell Oil costs the same to the station owner whether it is delivered to the cut-price station on the strip or the price-gouging monopolist station at an isolated motorway ramp. The pricing difference is explained by a combination of buyer-based and going-rate pricing.

   Buyer-based pricing, in this case, assumes that drivers will pay for convenience. Long-distance drivers usually know that driving a mile or two away from the motorway will result in finding petrol stations with lower prices. Most of these drivers simply make the choice that it is not worth the time, trouble, and uncertainty of wandering around in order to save a few pence per gallon. Some drivers may not have the option of driving around—if the petrol gauge has been hovering below "Empty" for the past twenty miles, the closest station is the only option, regardless of price.

   The other factor that moderates buyer-based pricing is the going-rate effect. Stations must provide a reasonable value relative to their close competitors. A BP outlet that is located next to a low-priced Burmah Castrol station must be price-competitive, even if BP unleaded sells for 15p more down by the motorway.

2. £50,000 (fixed costs) divided by £0.50 (profit margin per car) indicates a break-even volume of 100,000 cars per year. Reducing the price to £.75 doubles break-even volume to 200,000 cars; charging £1.50 cuts break-even to 50,000 cars per year; charging £2.50 cuts break-even to 25,000 cars per year. An estimate of the demand schedule for this car wash and its capacity would greatly improve the chances of choosing the best price.

   Stringent efforts to reduce variable costs would have some impact on the break-even volume. Cutting variable costs in half would reduce the break-even volume at £1.00 per car by one-third, to 66,667 cars. Reducing fixed costs has a much more direct impact on the break-even volume—a 10% reduction in fixed costs would reduce the break-even volume 10% at every price level. Alternatively, a strong promotional campaign might increase demand for washes, reduce price sensitivity, and allow a higher mark-up.

   This question can be discussed at several levels of complexity. If the £2.50 price is assumed, it can be used to calculate a single break-even volume. Break-even volumes at several prices can be calculated, as shown above. Alternative fixed and variable costs can be considered to see their effects on break-even volumes. Actual demand at different prices can be estimated and used to calculate expected profits (or losses). Most complex—and probably rather tedious—would be to combine all of these variations.

Case 16
Proton MPi:
Malaysian Styling, Japanese Engineering and European Pricing

Synopsis

Proton, a Malaysian car producer is seeking entry into the European market. This requires a well thought marketing strategy since the European car market is highly competitive. Using the UK as the entry to the European market, Proton's success in the UK is very important as it will influence Proton's survival in the European market. The small car market is price sensitive and the price varies significantly between the European Union (EU) countries. With cost advantages on its side, the current situation gives Proton a few pricing options to consider. The pricing policies should not only allow Proton to gain market share, but also to maintain and expand in the near future. Therefore, Proton's pricing considerations and approaches must take into account the short-term and long-term impacts of these underlying implications. Proton's success hinges on its "value for money" approach to pricing as reflected by its TV advertisement campaign - "Japanese Technology, Malaysian Styling".

Teaching Objectives

1. Show how managers need to understand the reality of the pan-European pricing strategy.

2. Highlight the need to consider factors other than product cost in establishing selling price.

3. Illustrate a situation in which customers perceive a strong price-quality relationship.

Study Questions

1. **Clearly there is currently no pan-European pricing policy, but should that ever exist across the EU? Should the car companies continue with what are essentially national policies? Who is benefiting from the European Commission's intervention?**

The aim of creating a single market was to form one big new market with more customers, more competitors, more choice and lower prices. Particularly, lower prices was one of the major targets that was thought to be achievable by lowering of trade barriers, by deterring price fixing and raising production capacity across Europe.

Most students will emphasise the need to continue with the national policies. There are different legal regulations in different European countries, for example yellow headlights in France and car emission standards in Germany. There are also differences in the driving culture, for example the UK practice left hand driving while other European nations are right hand driving. Consumers in the car market of the different European countries have different views about attributes in a car that are important, for example in Germany consumers placed more importance on performance while in Spain the market stated fuel economy as the main criteria in buying a car. Other reasons are such as the variation in production costs, wage differences and currency differences.

The car manufacturers are the parties benefiting from the European Commission's intervention. The benefits they earned through the Block Exemption Regulation are as follows; (1) They have control over supply and pricing; (2) They have control over discounts; (3) They have control over advertising their products; (4) They control over their dealers and restrict their dealers from selling other than their own products through exclusive dealerships in EU countries; (5) They have control over the sales of their products sold by the dealers (through percentage of sales per year); (6) They have monopoly control over the retailers in the geographical area under their territory.

2. Is Shem justified in his concern about being charged too much for new cars? What explains the big difference between EU and US car prices? Does the price demand function vary from country to country in Europe and is that in the United States completely different?

Students will highlight that Shem is justified in his concern about being charged too much for new cars in the UK for the following reasons; (1) Private buyers like himself have to pay the price that subsidises the discount, free servicing and other inducements given to fleet buyers; (2) New car prices across Europe vary up to 70%. The same new car cost more in the UK than in other EU countries for example Denmark; (3) The high specification equipment in new cars is more than what Shem wants and can afford but it fits the requirements of fleet buyers. The cost incurred is too much for him as a private buyer.

The reasons for a big difference between EU and US car prices are as follows; (1) In the US the same legislation and common pricing policies applied. However, EU countries have different legislation and therefore do not have standardised pricing policies; (2) US dollar is used throughout the US. In the EU each country has their own currency. Unless ECU is introduced as a standard currency, EU countries have to account for currency fluctuations within the trading block; (3) In the US , there are no subsidies given to fleet car buyers. Therefore, car companies can charge lower price on average compare to their EU counterparts; (4) Cars in the EU have different specifications in different EU countries. This raise production costs. In the US a standard specification can be applied in the production of cars for the common US market.

The price demand function differs from one European country to another. The demand for cars does not depend only on price. There are other variables that distort the demand function and price elasticity such as; (1) Availability of adequate public transport; (2) Availability of car parking spaces in town centres; (3) Maintenance and costs of having a car; (4) Number of fleet buyers; (5) Number of dealership; (6) Competition within one country; (7) Number of manufacturers in one country. In the US the situation is rather different. The price demand function is quite stable. As indicated in the case study, car prices in the US are much lower than those in the EU. The US operates as a one big car market, thus there are no distortions in terms of tax, etc. The prices are fairly stable across the different states. As there are no dealership restrictions as in Europe, the US market is very competitive as people can purchase cars from different regions. The high competition lead to a high price sensitivity and quick response. Dealers are not restricted to selling a given number of cars within a period of time. They can try and sell as many cars as possible by, for example lowering the price. There are the same number of manufacturers competing in one large market as opposed to the EU where a very high number of companies compete in relatively small individual markets. Moreover, in the EU companies need to develop a different marketing mix for each country to cater for differences in culture, economic wealth and the limitations imposed by the different languages, all of which present barriers to pan-European marketing. These factors increase the costs of advertising, etc. On the other hand, in the US, companies operate in one big market, and have less costs of advertising etc. (Although they also need to account for different lifestyles, etc.).

3. How should Proton price their cars? Should they keep their list prices high, reduce them or give big discounts to buyer? Why might giving discounts be better than lowering the list price?

As the case indicates, Proton is a low cost supplier to the EU and is not targeting the fleet buyers. It is rather concerned with the private customers. Proton can either cut the prices in an attempt to gain market share or charge moderate prices, enjoy comfortable margins and offer discounts on these prices. As suggested by the case, present prices are moderate and the cars can be assumed to be of medium quality (Japanese engineering). Proton currently is charging moderate prices for a medium quality car. Lowering the prices would initially take the company to the good value position. The perceived quality may then drop and the company may then be positioned in the economy category. Offering discounts would also put the company to the good value category but is less likely to affect the perceived quality. Proton must also take into account the competitors' actions and their abilities to match its prices. Should proton decide to cut down price, there will be certain implications. Lowering the price would draw customer awareness and attention. Customers who like to drive new cars and enjoy the smell of a new car but cannot afford to buy other cars or perceive the prices to be too high, may well decide to try this low price car. On the other hand, customers may perceive the low price as an indicator of a low quality car.

If Proton was to decide to keep its current price and offer discounts, then the results may be more beneficial to the company. By offering discounts, people may perceive the cars of being good value for money and thus decide to purchase the car. This strategy is preferable to price lowering as it does not harm the quality perceived by customers and increases market share. The increase in market share will also benefit the company as there will be more cars to be serviced. The discounts are unlikely to change the market price and thus would not stimulate negative attitudes. Furthermore, offering discounts involved a smaller degree of price sensitivity than lowering prices. The discounts may prevent dragging competitors into a price war situation that is more likely to occur is the price is reduced.

4. What is likely to happen if Proton cuts its prices to gain market share? Is the differential pricing policy across Europe and between private and fleet buyers a way for car makers to maximise profits or is it forced upon them by differences in EU governments and customers?

Lowering of prices will affect buyers, competitors, distributors and suppliers. Proton might be able to gain market share by cutting the price provided that the customers are having positive attitude towards the Proton car. However, customers might perceived the price cuts in several ways; (1) Current model are about to be replaced by newer models; (2) Cars have some faults or are defective; (3) Quality has been reduced; (4) Price will come down even further and that it will pay to wait and see. In the above case Proton may fail to increase market share by implementing a price cutting policy. Competitors may have different reaction towards Proton's price cutting policy. Actions depend on whether competitor products are being built, held or harvested. Where a competitor has a build or hold strategic objective, price cutting is likely to be followed. In such circumstances a price war will be provoked. Such competitors are likely to fight back, reduce their prices as well and hence not allow

Proton to gain market share. This is also dependent on their ability to respond. Where companies are harvesting, they are more likely to ignore the price cuts, price cuts are also likely to be ignored in conditions of rising costs, excess demand and when servicing price is insensitive to customers. Premium price positioners may be reluctant to follow competitors' price cuts for to do so would be incompatible with brand image. Companies that are aiming at the fleet buyer rather than the private buyer are more likely to ignore Proton's action. The European commission may also intervene. Should Proton increase market share at the expense of European car manufacturers, then the European Commission may decide to restrict car imports through quotas, etc. so that the Gross European Product will not be reduced and the European cars will not suffer from decline in sales. Some distributors may not be willing to launch or promote their car because of the low return from the profit margin. They may better off selling another type of car which can provide them a higher return. Suppliers on the other hand may be happy to see if Proton manages to gain the market share and may offer a better deal to Proton for example by giving discount for bulk purchase on engines or parts in order to support them maintaining a lower pricing policy and thus attract more sales.

The differential pricing policy across Europe can be seen as both a way for the car manufacturers to maximise profits as well as resultant reaction on the differences in EU governments and customers. The regional dealership's agreement in the EU are being exploited by the companies to maximise their profits as they restrict the competition between dealers and therefore are able to maintain high prices. In addition, the agreements between the manufacturers and the dealers restrict the dealers to selling a maximum quantity of cars in a given period. Due to the limited supply from the manufacturers, the dealers are more likely to sell the limited amount of cars at the list price to maximise profit. Different countries have different consumption power and demand. In those countries where there is excess demand or high consumption power, the manufacturers may raise up their price to achieve more profit return. It shows that countries like Germany, Italy, United Kingdom and Netherlands have a high percentage of senior managers provided with company cars. On the one hand, the manufacturers offer better discounts to fleet buyers whilst on the other they charge private buyers with premium prices, in order to maintain their profits. The price difference amongst countries can also be created by the different tax systems, exchange rate variation and different car specifications required by customers. In some countries, the government encourage citizens to use public service transport and therefore they charge high car tax and road tax to discourage people buying cars. The rise of imports tax can lead to the rise of the cost of the car. The expectations of the customers can also affect the price setting. For example, Rover 400 costs less to manufacture than the Rover 200, however, market research has shown that because the Rover 400 is a bigger car with a larger boot, customers expect to pay more for that model. So manufacturer price the two models in line with customer expectations, not costs. In addition, perception of customers can alter the manufacturers' price setting policy. To some people high price means high quality or high performance and thus an expensive car reflects on the status of the owner. Hence some people are quite prepared to pay high prices. If the manufacturer sets the price too low, those customers may not be interested or consider to buy the car due to their beliefs. Advertising costs, production costs, maintenance costs, dealer discounts, location of the manufacturing plant and labour costs in various countries vary. There are far too many variables that could differ the selling price on an identical product across European countries.

Teaching Suggestions

Although quite simple, this case can stimulate much lively and fruitful discussion. Students can be asked about their own or their parents' experiences in buying a car and other products about which they do not have much knowledge. The instructor might list selected products for which students probably use price as a quality cue.

In addition to the discussion of pricing issues, this case is useful in the context of consumer behaviour and retailing. In discussing Chapter 5, Consumer Markets, students can describe the buyer decision processes

Jokes and Quotes

The three most common ways of pricing are cost plus, competitive rates and historical rates. Cost plus means you don't know how to price. Competitive rates means you don't know how to price but your competition must do. Historical rates means you don't know how to price but someone once did.

A fair price for oil is whatever you can get plus ten per cent.
DR. ALI AHMED ATTIGA

Our pricing policy: to charge like a wounded bull.
ANON

Price, n. Value plus a reasonable sum for the wear and tear of conscience in demanding it.
AMBROSE BIERCE

That which cost little is less valued.
MIGUEL DE CERVANTES

Q. What's two and two?
A. Buying or selling?
LORD GRADE

In the same open market, at any moment, there cannot be two prices for the same kind of article.
W. STANLEY JEVONS

That's a great tan. Did you get it in the Caribbean?
You bet. It cost me £23.50 per square inch.
JOKE

I drive a '75 Chevy. That's not the year - it's the resale value!
JOKE

There are two fools in every market; one asks too little, one asks too much.
RUSSIAN PROVERB

Costs merely register competing attractions.
FRANK H. KNIGHT

Natural price is only another name for cost of production
DAVID RICARDO

Cost [is] of two kinds, either (1) the endurance of pain, discomfort, or something else undesirable, or (2) the sacrifice of something desirable, either as an end or a means.
HENRY SIDGWICK

Cost of production... in the sense of the historical and irrevocable fact that resources have been devoted to this or that special purpose, has no influence on the value of the thing produced, and therefore does not affect its price.
PHILIP H. WICKSTEED

What is a cynic?... A man who knows the price of everything and the value of nothing... And a sentimentalist... is a man who sees an absurd value in everything, and doesn't know the market price of any single thing.
OSCAR WILDE

I have never heard of a circumstance in which competition did not mean lower price.
LORD YOUNG

Chapter 17

Pricing Products: Pricing Strategies

Chapter Objectives

After reading this chapter, you should be able to:

1. Understand alternate new-product pricing strategies and know when to use them.
2. Explain how pricing decisions are influenced by the product mix.
3. Appreciate price adjustment strategies and how to make changes.
4. Differentiate between alternate geographical pricing strategies and know their implications.

Chapter Overview

Pricing is a dynamic process. Companies design a pricing structure that covers all their products. They change this structure over time and adjust it to account for different customers and situations. Pricing strategies usually change as a product passes through its life cycle. Some pricing strategies include: skimming policy and penetration pricing. When the product is part of a product mix, the firm searches for a set of prices that will maximise the profits from the total mix. The company decides on price zones for items in its product line and on the pricing of optional products, captive products, and by-products. Companies apply a variety of price-adjustment strategies to account for differences in consumer segments and situations. When a firm is considering a price change, it must consider customers' and competitors' reactions. The firm that faces a price change initiated by a competitor must try to understand the competitor's intent as well as the likely duration and impact of the change.

Teaching Notes

Refer to the following pages for teaching notes.

New Product Pricing Strategies

Transparency PM 17-1 relates to the material on pp.657-658.

Pricing Innovative Products

1. Market Skimming Pricing

Market skimming pricing is the strategy of setting high initial prices to skim maximum profits from each successive layer of the target market. Skimming strategies typically set a price as high as some segments will bear. Once all customers within this segment have purchased, prices are lowered only so far as the next segment needs to be persuaded to buy. Skimming usually works well only when product quality, image, and innovation are sufficiently distinct to support a high price and costs of producing small volume are not prohibitive.

2. Market Penetration Pricing

Some innovations are priced low upon introduction in order to capture large market share quickly thus penetrating the market. Penetration pricing works well in highly price-sensitive markets with very large volume potential. Penetration pricing may also accelerate overall market adoption rates thus supporting low price continuance that may discourage competitors from entering the market.

Tip

Ask students why some firms launch with a "skimming" price then switch to "penetration" pricing. What are the financial implications of the two approaches? How do they relate to promotional strategies?

Notes for PM 17-1

Product-Mix Pricing Strategies

Transparency PM 17-2 corresponds to Table 17-1 on p.658 and relates to the material on pp.658-660.

Product Line Pricing

Companies usually develop product lines rather than single products. In product line pricing, management must decide on the price steps to set between each product in the line. Companies often use price points to target distinctive combinations of product features and value represented by a particular price.

Optional-Product Pricing

Under this strategy, the company offers a base product and prices differently for each combination of additional features or options added to the base product as desired by the customer. Automobile pricing is famous - or infamous - for this practice. But many manufacturers use optional-product pricing, such as personal computer makers.

Captive-Product Pricing

Under this strategy, producers price products that must be used with a main product. The text describes razor blades as an example. The razor is priced low while high mark-ups are attached to the price of the blades.

By-Product Pricing

Waste from production and distribution may be marketable as by-products. Selling by-products allows producers to lower prices and costs on their main products. Otherwise, the prices of main products must cover the disposable or storage of by- products.

Product-Bundle Pricing

This strategy combines several products and offers them at a reduced price from the cost of each product purchased separately. Season tickets and group rates are examples.

Tip

Ask students to distinguish captive pricing from optional pricing on the basis of need versus convenience. When Apple Computer prices its keyboards separately from its computers, is it practicing captive-product pricing? When it offers additional RAM beyond the included board memory, it is practicing optional-product pricing.

Notes for PM 17-2

Price Adjustment Strategies

Transparency PM 17-3 corresponds to Table 17-2 on p.660 and relates to the material on pp.660-668.

Price Adjustment Strategies

1. Discount Pricing

Cash Discounts - are price reductions to buyers who pay bills promptly.

Quantity Discounts - refer to price reductions per unit on large volumes.

Functional Discounts - are granted to channel members who perform various marketing functions.

2. Seasonal Discounts

Are granted to buyers who purchase merchandise out of season.

3. Allowances

Such as trade-ins for turning in old items on new purchases or promotional allowances for participating in seller sponsored advertising can also lower buyer prices.

4. Discriminatory Pricing

Refers to pricing differences not based on costs and takes several forms:

Customer-segment pricing such as senior citizen discounts.

Product-form pricing varies costs on versions of a product by features but not production costs.

Location pricing stems from preferences such as seating in a theatre.

Time pricing refers to price breaks given at times of lower demand.

5. Psychological Pricing

A key component in psychological pricing is the reference price consumers carry in their mind when considering sellers prices.

6. Promotional Pricing

Promotional prices are temporary reductions used to attract customers.

Loss leaders may be offered below costs to attract attention to an entire line.

Special event pricing may be used during slow seasons.

Cash rebates or low financing may be offered.

Notes for PM 17-3

7. Value Pricing

This strategy offers a desired combination of features and prices to identified target markets.

8. Geographical Pricing

FOB-Origin - Free On Board has customer pay freight.
Uniform Delivered - company charges the same price to all.
Zone - different areas pay different prices on freight but all customers within the same area pay the same freight charges.
Basing-Point - all customers charged freight from a specified billing location.
Freight-Absorption - the seller pays all shipping costs to get the desired business.

9. International Pricing

Firms may charge the same price throughout the world, especially for high-ticket, high-tech products like jetliners. Or it may offer different prices based upon differing taxes, tariffs, distribution, and promotion costs.

Tip

Ask students to explain the huge difference in prices of air fares, first class vs. "budget shop" prices or why air fare purchased in the US are lower than in the EU?

Notes for PM 17-3 (contd.)

Price Changes

These notes relate to the material on pp.668-673.

Initiating Price Changes

1. Price Cuts

Reasons for cutting prices may stem from overcapacity, falling market share, or attempts to dominate the market through lower costs.

2. Price Increases

Inflation is a major source of price increases but so is the tendency to speculate on inflationary trends and raise prices beyond the rate of inflation. Over demand may also cause prices to rise. Higher prices can also increase profit margins.

3. Buyer Reactions to Price Changes

Buyer reactions usually respond directly to price changes but not always. Usually lower prices please consumers, higher prices do not. But sometimes higher prices support quality improvements and lower prices mean company or product problems. Whether the buyer is correct or not in these perceptions will not immediately change their inclination to act on them.

4. Competitor Reactions to Price Changes

Competitors most often react in industries with a small number of firms, uniform products in the market, and buyers are well informed. Competitive reactions may be similar price changes or increased non price competition. Companies should anticipate probable competitive moves prior to initiating price changes.

Tip

Ask students why price cuts rarely lead to increase in market share. If long term gains rarely come from price cuts, why are price promotions so popular?

Comments on Discussing the Issues

1. **(a)** Ariel Future uses a skimming strategy in the sense that it tries to attract the cream of the laundry detergent market to its high-priced, high-quality detergent. It tends to maintain its high prices, rather than following a strategy of lowering its prices over time to skim successive market segments.
(b) Reebok is normally a high-priced seller in the sport shoes industry, and its price cuts generally appear to be in response to competitors' actions or unexpectedly low sales rather than part of a planned market-expansion strategy.
(c) The new American Diner introduces itself with promotional pricing in order to induce trial. Eventually it ends the promotion and sells the product at its higher regular price.

None of these companies have any apparent reason to change their pricing strategies. Their strategies fit their images, customers know what to expect, and as long as they are making a reasonable profit, the risks involved in a pricing change seem to outweigh any potential benefits.

2. Salespeople could emphasise the improvement in the cards moving from the £100 card to the £300 card, while noting that the £100 card is a bargain compared with the higher-priced card. (For a discussion of various reasons underlying an increase in the sales, see Joel Huber, John W. Payne, and Christopher Puto, "Adding Asymmetrically Dominated Alternatives: Violations of Regularity and the Similarity Hypothesis," *Journal of Consumer Research*, June 1982, pp. 90-98.). We could probably assume that the platinum card follows the premium strategy, the gold card is the high-value strategy and the green card relates to the average strategy.

An issue worth discussing with this question is the "contrast principle." This principle states that when two things are compared, if the second item is fairly different from the first, people will perceive the difference as being greater than it actually is.

3. This discount pricing was a good fit with Brand B image as an inexpensive product. Brand B reaped large benefits from its penetration pricing strategy: the brand quickly became the largest brand in the product category. After the brand was established, Brand B prices could be raised by resizing to a smaller box at a lower retail price, which yielded a substantially higher cost per ounce.

4. Brand names are a major element in the pricing for most products. Companies invest heavily in advertising and promotion to build value for a brand name. If this marketing is successful, the company can charge a higher price for its product than a non-branded equivalent.

Clorox is an excellent example of a premium-priced product with no real differentiating factor aside from brand name. Clorox has good quality control, but no product-based differences are perceivable by the consumer. However, Clorox has steadily advertised and promoted its name, and it is the only significant brand name in the liquid bleach category. Consumers use the product for important purposes: they trust their clothes to its efficacy and safety, and they use it to disinfect during housecleaning. The reassurance of a known brand name is worth the small amount extra that consumers pay.

There can be ethical issues when branded products offer little real value to consumers for their premium price. Clorox, however, appears to offer excellent value to the consumer, even though it is more expensive than similar products. Clorox has many uses, and consumers appreciate the confidence of a known brand name in a product used for important purposes. Value perceptions are also helped by the fact that Clorox, while expensive for a liquid bleach, is still a fairly cheap product, especially when compared to other cleaning and laundry products. Ultimately, however, consumers vote with their dollars, and brands that do not offer a perceived value will not be purchased.

5. Let us take tennis balls for example. Tennis-ball manufacturers could set a discount price on "dead" balls and try to sell them as practice balls or balls for beginning players. The manufacturers appeared to have found a more ingenious strategy for pricing this manufacturing by-product: They sell them in high-altitude markets (where the lower air pressure makes the balls livelier) at a *premium* price.

6. As exporters to Singapore, Bodum must cope with the additional costs of modifying the product, higher shipping and insurance costs, import tariffs and taxes, cost associated with exchange rate fluctuations and higher channel and physical distribution costs.

Comments on Applying the Concepts

1. This is a question that cannot be discussed in the abstract: students must take the trouble to look at prices and write them down. The examples that they find will vary from store to store. One good category to examine is coffee, where there is often a mix of 11.5, 13 and 16 ounce packages. The sugar section will sometimes carry a 4 pound size in addition to the 5 pound standard. Items measured by count rather than volume also follow this strategy. Students may find pain relievers in 80 and 100 count sizes, or beer (and even expensive soft drinks) in 4-packs instead of 6-packs.

   Unit pricing labels can undercut this strategy, but they do not defeat it entirely. Many people may prefer a smaller package or a lower dollar outlay even if they know that the unit costs are higher. One interesting question to explore is whether the unit pricing labels in your local supermarkets are usable. In some cases, stores will use unit pricing labels with differing units, making comparison impossible without doing the required math. Ask if anyone noted a section where the unit pricing for one brand mentioned *X¢* per ounce, while a comparable brand was listed as *X$* per pound.

2. Students will say that the major reason for the "end of season" sales is that the retailers want to clear the stock of the season so that they have enough space for the new season's collection. Shelf space for the high street retailers is particularly expensive. By holding these type of sales consumers might be persuaded to buy something because it is a bargain. Discounts in general terms is something that all organisations, not just high street retailers, want to avoid, because per unit price discounting has a considerable effect on the overall revenue. In addition, discounts might lead to price wars with competitors where they chances of everybody losing (except the customers) is heightened. In some instances retailers "co-operate" and decide collectively when to start the "sales". Some students will say that if a retailer decides to offer discounts outside conventional "sale periods", would definitely be more effective than during conventional "sale periods", in terms of sale volume. Nevertheless, you might lose revenue from those customers who would buy anyway whether there is a sale or not. In addition, the unconventional sale time period might lead customers to think that the products are discounted because of theor poor quality.

Case 17
Stena Sealink Versus Le Shuttle, Eurostar and the Rest

Synopsis

The subject of this case study is the reaction of ferry companies to the drastic change in the cross-channel travel market caused by the opening of the Channel Tunnel between Folkestone and Calais. Much of the case study is concerned with the burgeoning price war started by P & O heavy discounting strategy and how Stena Sealink should position itself to survive in the shrinking and increasingly competitive ferry market.

Teaching Objectives

1. Allow students to apply the pricing concepts and principles presented in the chapter.

2. Provide insight into European competitors' strategies in the transportation market.

3. Give the students an opportunity to make some pricing decisions.

Study Questions

1. Explain P & O heavy discounting strategy? Explain Eurostar's pricing? is Brittany Ferries right in saying the fares make profits impossible? Should prices be fixed on cross-channel routes to prevent unprofitable price wars?

In reaction to competition from Eurostar trains on the Folkestone, Calais "short route", P & O was looking to gain market share on the "long route" luxury crossings such as Cherbourg Le Harve through heavy price discounting. P & O would then cross subsidise from profits made on food, drink and souvenirs by the increased number of travellers. The aim of the incentive is to fill the less attractive long route voyages, which are less threatened by the tunnel and attract customers from Sally Lines and Brittany Ferries who at present dominate this segment. One victim in this segment Olau Lines a subsidiary of the German TT Line who stopped trading in May 1994. Implementing this strategy would result in P & O survival but result in the possible failure of Sally Lines and Brittany Ferries. Brittany Ferries described P & O 's discounting strategy as "predatory pricing" which they believe breaks French law if it proved to be intentionally aimed at eliminating rivals.

Eurostar's pricing is targeted at business passengers travelling between London and Paris which are Europe's busiest air routes. Eurostar's first class fare between the two capitals is £195 which drastically undercuts British Airways and Air France's £318 business class fare. The pricing strategy used by Eurostar suggests they are targeting the business passenger segment which currently appears to be dominated by the airliners. Eurostar also has the advantage of capital to capital transfer eliminating any need for secondary or tertiary travel which passengers are exposed to using airports. However, Eurostar, British Airways and Air France's fares are substantially higher than £79 first class passenger fare for using British Rail, Stena Sealink and SNCF to travel the same route. This may indicate that Eurostar are not trying to compete in this market. The lowest Eurostar fare (£95) is more expensive than both the cheapest fare (£85) and the lowest price for the rail-sea-rail or hire car-sea-hire car costing £62. Again it appears that Eurostar are not trying to compete in this area.

Brittany Ferries complained that the "massive price cut to 75% off normal tariffs throughout the peak summer season made profits impossible". This is not necessarily the case as industry experts say that low fares can be cross subsidised by increased profits on food, drink and souvenirs sold on-board the ferries as a result of increased passenger numbers. In 1993 P & O made £77 million operating profits on sales of £615 million, one third of which (£25 million) came from Duty and tax free sales.

Most students will say that competition is healthy. The case study tells us that fares are down, on average 20%. However the quality of their offering and frequency of service they present is up. This is a function of competition and the efforts of competing companies to differentiate themselves on quality and service and not just price. Competition forces inefficient companies out of business such as the German TT Olau Line, leaving their customers to be served by more efficient remaining companies, thus getting better value for their money. Some students will say that in a free market it is contradictory to impose prices on cross channel routes to prevent unprofitable price wars. One should question whether ferry prices have been too high in the past. Also, it is difficult to impose minimum fares as the ferry service offered by the different ferry operators is not the same. Other students will say that price fixing is more of a political rather than a marketing decision. Fixing price could increase the number of operators across channel transportation but service...?

2. Should Stena Sealink follow P & O's price cutting? What else could they do? Can Stena Sealink get away with charging more than P & O at any time, any place, any way?

Stena Sealink has to decide whether to follow P & O's price cutting or not. In the short term they will probably have to address price cutting in some form, perhaps with special promotions such as targeting the frequent traveller (like Sally Line's extension of its nautical miles-frequent-traveller programme). They would be advised that initially they should follow P & O's lead so that they do not lose market share, but they must develop some form of differential advantage so that they are not drawn into a suicidal downward spiral of price cutting. Another argument students could present is the fact that Stena Sealink does not have the margin of P & O. Stena Sealink's margin is smaller thus very dangerous to enter complete price war with P & O.

Options open to them highlighted in the case study are as follows; refurbish ships to provide luxury service, get passengers to spend more whilst on board, concentrate on running a basic efficient service like Le Shuttle, invest in new terminals to help them serve the long channel crossings and invest in radically new ships.

Stena Sealink could get away with charging more than P & O in the following instances; (1) If the quality of service exceeds P & O's, especially their borrowed Club Class idea; (2) If there is an increase in demand, exceeding supply during the summer period; (3) If Stena purchase and use high speed catamarans as stated in the text.

3. Is P & O discounting consistent with their luxury "cruise" positioning? What prevents Le Shuttle driving the ferries out by cutting prices? Does Le Shuttle's speed advantage make its victory over the ferries inevitable?

Technically price discounting should never be associated with any kind of "luxury" positioning. This sends contradictory messages to the consumer and devalues the image of the product. Hence perfume companies' reluctance to allow their prestige products to be sold in Superdrug outlets. Some students will say that cross channel crossings are not considered conspicuously prestigious. Passengers will appreciate and seek out the superior services that P & O refer to as the "cruise" experience. Price discounting in this case will actually affect the image of the product.

The case quotes Wendy Wang, Smith New Court analyst as saying "Euro tunnel has to be careful with any price cutting. It has some anxious (and very long suffering) shareholders to consider. The Eurotunnel took longer to complete than was expected. This time delay resulted in extra funding requirements from major shareholders who saw share values dropped. If Eurotunnel reduce prices, shareholders will have to wait yet longer to see a return on their investment which may result in very angry shareholders. Secondly, the rail network is still not complete to offer the rail interlink between large cities that was planned. When the interlink is up and running they will be in a position to offer their full service, gain market share and reduce fares.

Le Shuttle's speed advantage does not make its victory over the ferries inevitable for the following reasons; (1) Ferries will still be required for most of the long routes which include Ireland, Scandinavia, South of France, Spain/Mediterranean; (2) A survey amongst 102 senior transport executives found that 62% of transport companies believed that their drivers would prefer to stick with the ferries while 84% thought that the ferries would offer better facilities than the tunnel, which they do; (3) Le Shuttle has yet to compete on price with the ferries for haulage business, which again is a sensitive issue with customers; (4) Car, truck and bus drivers enjoy the rest period provided during the ferry voyage, especially when the drivers have endured a long road journey to the terminals. This is more important when considering bus and truck drivers who rely on the long channel crossing journey to catch up on sleep, eat and enjoy a rest period. This is a legal requirement for drivers whose vehicles are fitted with tachograph; (5) People enjoy the excitement of an ocean voyage; (6) The speed advantage Le Shuttle has will be reduced if ferry companies switch to high speed catamarans.

4. Since the cross-channel ferry market will decline, explain their investment in gaining market share by price cutting, operating new routes, refurbishing vessels and buying expensive sea cats? What strategy should Stena Sealink follow? Should they follow all P & O's moves, follow some, do something completely different or like Olau Line, get out?

The ferry market will decline as a result of the entry of Eurotunnel but the magnitude of that decline is not established. Eurotunnel aims to capture a considerable market share of the existing business but also expects to create new demand. Ferry companies are operating new routes, investing in expensive seacats, etc. because they need to reposition themselves in the new marketing environment i.e. responding to changes in demand and technology. The crucial factor here is service and speed. There is no reason to doubt that with these efforts they can relaunch the ferry business into a new life cycle with Eurotunnel as another competitor just as they have coexisted with the airlines.

Stena Sealink should aim to gain market share and eliminate competition which may withdraw like Olau Line. To do this Stena should; (1) Invest in high speed catamarans for the short journeys with the aim of competing with the tunnel on speed and gaining market share from P & O; (2) Refurbish the current ferries (replaced by the catamarans) and used them on the longer routes. When the rail interlinks are complete then use catamarans on the longer routes and sell the excess ferries off to Third World countries; (3) Make sure the overheads are covered by filling the seats on both the outbound and return journeys. To accomplish this they should improve their timetabling method to suit seasonal changes and offer discounts for pre-bookings where a deposit is given. This will improve Stena's short term cash flow and guarantees filled seats; (4) Use direct marketing to attract new customers, target markets - businesses, groups, organisations e.g. Caravan Club, schools and colleges, AA and RAC members/customers; (5) Increase the number of duty free facilities on board the vessels to gain greater advantage from duty and tax free sales; (6) Offer discounts and free travel to frequent customers to gain greater customer loyalty and repeat business.

Stena should not follow all of P & O's moves, they should devise a strategy with the objective of gaining market share in the medium term. P & O has tried to gain market share in the short term by reducing their tariffs. P & O will not be able to sustain this for a long period of time as it will start to have substantial effects on their profitability. Stena cannot afford to compete with P & O on price and should therefore consider a cost focused approach. This would be offering a fast, moderately priced ferry service for ferry users by providing high speed well-equipped catamarans for travellers on short routes. This would provide Stena with a significant advantage over P & O who will not be able to react immediately due to lack of short term cash available as result of their heavy discount strategy. Stena will then be able to enjoy economies of scale after increasing their market share and hopefully reduces their tariffs to prevent the competition from catching up. Stena should not adopt Olau Lines approach and get out, this would enable P & O to gain instant market share and create a potential monopoly, Stena still has the resources to put up a fight.

Teaching Suggestions

This case can be used with the other Pricing Case (Chapter 16), with the Place Chapter (Chapter 21), with the Promotion Chapters (Chapters 18, 19 and 20), and with the Global Chapter (Chapter 5).

Additional Information

One issue which is likely to damage the long term strategy of Eurostar and Le Shuttle is the axing of the high speed TGV lines in France due to the lack of money (The European, 13/12/95).

Stena has introduced several measures; (1) Introduced new routes in the Baltic sea; (2) Introduced a new long route service from Stranraer to their new port in Belfast; (3) Planning to release the Stena HSS catamaran in 1996, which is five times bigger than the Lynx and travels at forty knots; (4) Have introduced a faster checking system; (5) Have introduced a 20% early booking discount offer. (Stena Sealink Autumn brochure)

Overview Case 6
Amaizer:
It Tastes Awful, But We're Working On It

Synopsis

Amaizer is a new savoury snack made from maize. Its method of manufacture is similar to cornflakes breakfast cereal but it is to be sold as a savoury snack. Amaizer is sweeter than potato crisps but can be flavoured. Unfortunately consumer trials showed that the Amaizer versions of popular crisp flavours - salt and vinegar, cheese and onion and so on - "taste awful". Research and development were still working on the taste of these flavours. The brand manager asked three different managers to come up with the price of Amaizer. The brand manager's confidence crashed when the sales, finance and market research managers each came up with different recommendations. The finance officer demanded that the price be set to cover the usual 100 per cent overhead charge plus a 20 per cent margin. The sales manager wanted the price to be £100 per tonne below potato crisps. He claimed that only with a price advantage could they achieve the target sales against the established competition. The marketing researcher's contribution to the pricing debate confused the brand manager even more. Rather than giving a price, the researcher gave a string of prices and sales and to the annoyance of the financial officer, some financial information.

Teaching Objectives

1. Introduce to students the importance of the numerical dimension in marketing.

2. Allow students to make decisions based on their findings.

3. Highlight to students that the other 3 Ps must be taken into account in setting price for any product or service.

Study Questions

1. Evaluate the pricing suggestions of the sales, finance and market research officers. What criteria should be used to select the best price?

The finance officer is utilising the cost based pricing strategy - where a company adds a standard mark-up to the cost of a product. The premise of this strategy lies in the company's historical approach in price setting. The financial officer is following the company's method of pricing which is 100 per cent overhead charge plus 20 per cent profit margin. Some students will present the following advantages; (1) Safety net - tried and trusted method (assumption); (2) Company's knowledge of existing markets can in many cases be transferred to potential markets, hence a pricing strategy used in an existing market can be transferred to other FMCG products; (3) All costs are catered for, hence a profit will be realised, assuming the level of sales are reached. The disadvantages are: (1) The sales figure is assumed. No prior research has been carried out to see if that level of demand can be met at that price; (2) Views the customer as reactive rather than proactive. The finance officer's theory ignores the customers importance in the buying/selling process; (3) Does not take into account external prices for substitutes, over/under pricing may occur. The approach taken by the sales manager was that of penetration pricing also known as competition based pricing. Encompassed in this strategy is the notion that by selling at a lower price than the nearest competitor, the producing company can gain market share and therefore has a foothold in the new market. Advantages; (1) Competitors give an outline of the present situation in the market; (2) Buyers have the ability to directly compare the new offering with that of competitor offerings on the basis of price; (3) The economic theory of demand and supply suggests that the lower the price the higher the demand. Some disadvantages; (1) No first mover advantages, as the firm is a market follower, not a leader. Everything is based upon competitor's movements; (2) Lower price may imply lower quality, unless marketed effectively; (3) Selling at lower than market price will reduce profits. The market researcher is using a strategy known as demand or marketing orientated pricing, where figures are calculated using all available data to map price to demand at differing levels. Following this theory the optimal mix of price/demand will give maximum profitability. Some advantages are; (1) Allows the decision maker to see the optimum point of profitability; (2) Accuracy of pricing structures can be maximised using this theory; (3) Varying marketing strategies can be adopted from the same pricing strategy. This means that given the figures of demand/price the decision maker can decides if the marketing strategy will be penetration, skimming, etc. Disadvantages; (1) The optimum point may conflict with the original marketing strategy i.e. if the company wants to go for market penetration this theory may suggest that the best use of resources i.e. maximum profit return lies in market skimming. Most students will be partial towards the market researcher's recommendations.

Most students will suggest that the main criterion for choosing this theory is the accuracy of the model relative to the others and the substantial rate of return made it more attractive than the higher rate of return associated with the higher risk in relation to the finance officer's theory. They will add; (1) The best pricing strategy would be the one that takes into account the organisational goals; (2) The price of competitive goods must be looked at to see what effect there is on sales and what strategy would be possible for Amaizer; (3) The impact of complementary or substitute products must be considered. Complementary goods such as Coca Cola and other drinks could have an impact on sale of Amaizer; (4) The demand of the product must be analysed closely; (5) Market research must be carried out in order to make the final decision e.g. test marketing.

2. How could the price elasticities provided by the marketing researcher be estimated?

Price elasticity of demand shows the responsiveness of quantity demanded to a change in prices. The formula to work this out is as follows:

$$\text{Price Elasticity of Demand} = \frac{\text{Percentage Change in Quality Demanded}}{\text{Percentage Change in Price}}$$

The price elasticities for each of the four changes are as follows:

Change	1	2	3	4
% Change in Quantity Demanded	-12.5	-20	-28.57	-50
%Change in Price	20	16.67	14.28	12.5
Price Elasticity of Demand	-0.625	-1.2	-2	-4

What this table tells us is that at change 1 where the price has increased from 2.5 to 3 that is a change in price of 20% and where demand has fallen by 50 tonnes thus giving a change in demand of -12.5%. The price elasticity of demand equals -0.625. Demand is therefore said to be inelastic that is where the quantity demanded changes proportionately less than the price change. At change 1 a price change will lead to an increase in total revenue. Therefore, if the company wants to increase its revenue it will need to increase its price. But for change 3 and 4 we can see that the price elasticity is -2 and -4 respectively. This implies that demand is elastic that is where the quantity demanded changes more in relation to the price. With changes 3 and 4 the increase in price will lead to decrease in total revenue. Therefore, in this situation if the firm wants to increase its total revenue it will have to decrease its price. Change 2 gives a price elasticity of -1.2 which means that at this situation a change in price will only give a small change in quantity demanded which is not as large as change 3 or 4. With change 2 as the figure is near one, this will show that a change in price will have a low impact and will result in a relatively small fall in total revenue. The negative figures show us that there is an inverse relationship in terms of quantity demanded and price, that is a change in price will lead to a fall in quantity demanded.

3. What prices give the highest gross margins, return on investment, capital cost covered (C^3), economic value added(EVA), net contribution, sales value and sales volume? What price would you choose and why? What do you notice about the room to manoeuvre around the optimum prices?

The table below shows the effect of changing prices on the different variables. The optimum value for each of the variables is shown in bold type. From the table you can see that the optimum sales volume occurs at a price of £2500 per tonne. However the optimum sales value or revenue could be achieved at a price of £3000 per tonne. The price of £3500 per tonne results in the greatest profits both gross and net and also gives the greatest return on sales. At a price of $4000 per tonne the product adds the greatest EVA to the company and the cost of capital is well covered at this price level. Finally, no optimum values are obtained at a price level of £4500 per tonne.

Price (£000's)	2.5	3.0	3.5	4.0	4.5
Volume	**400**	350	280	200	100
Revenue (£000's)	1000	**1050**	980	800	450
Gross Profit (£000's)	400	525	**560**	500	300
Gross Profit Margin	40%	50%	**57%**	62.5%	67%
Net Profit (£000's)	100	225	**260**	200	0
Return on Sales	10%	21.4%	**26.5%**	25%	0
Return on Investment	4.44%	11.25%	15.76%	**16.67%**	0
C^3	0.296	0.75	1.051	**1.111**	0
EVA (£000's)	-237.5	-75	12.5	**20**	-90

Students will come up with several options. They need to justify why they have chosen that particular option. The price range will be between £3500 per tonne to £4000 per tonne. By looking at the above table some students might decide to sell Amaizer at £3500 per tonne. This conclusion is made by using information provided by the market researcher. At this price level the company will not achieve the greatest sales volume or revenue but will make the greatest gross profit, net profit and return on sales. In addition to this the company would have covered the cost of capital by achieving a C^3 figure of 1.051, while not being the largest would still mean that the profits were covering the cost of capital and adding economic value to the business. Also, at this price the company is achieving sales which are close to the targeted figure of 300 tones per year. However, it should be noted that the price is based on the assumption that the company wants to maximise its profits from this new product. If, the company had other objectives when first launching this product a different price may be chosen.

If for example it was the company's objective to penetrate the market and achieve high levels of sales regardless of the profits made, then the company would price the product at £2500 per tonne. At this lower price the company is still making a profit of £100000 but its net profits do not cover the cost of capital it will need to employ. This leads to the economic value being added at -£237500. What this means to the company is that it will have to eat into reserves or other capital sources in order to finance the production and capital of this new product.

If on the other hand the new products success was established by its return on investment then a price of £4000 per tonne would achieve the best ROI figure of 16.67%. At this price the company is making sales much lower than its targeted 300 tonnes per year and also making less profits. But because the capital investment needed is significantly lower the ROI, C^3 and EVA figures are highest at this price level.

With regard to the question about room to manoeuvre the optimum prices it is obvious that the different price levels have different advantages and disadvantages related to them. For example, moving from £3500 per tonne to a price of £4000 per tonne the company will reduce the amount of profits made and the sales volume generated but simultaneously increase the return on investment and also cover the cost of capital at a better rate. Another noticeable fact is that the effect on sales and profits decrease in proportion to the increase in the price after the initial move from £2500 to £3000 per tonne. Moving from £2500 to £3000 i.e. an increase of 20% gives an increase of only 5% in revenue but a large increase of 125% on the net profit. However if we then move from £3000 to £3500 per tonne, you find that the sales revenue decreases by 6% but the net profit increases by 15%. Therefore, the size of increase in the profits has reduced compared to the increase in the profits by the first change in price.

4. Assuming the price of £3500 per tonne, what would be the best advertising strategy, given the following advertising response?

Some students will suggest that an amount of £200000 should be spend on advertising. The following table shows the reason:

Group	A	B	C	D	E
Sales (£000's) Advertising (£000's)	630 25	735 50	980 100	1260 200	1470 400
Capital Investment (£000's)	165	187.5	247.5	308	345
Contribution (£000's)	440	497.5	632.5	**752**	725

From the above table advertising strategy group D gives the best contribution. We can also observe that the incremental advertising expenditure was not proportionally matched with the increase in sales . Other students will take into account net profit (NP), capital cost covered (C^3), economic value added (EVA) and return on capital employed (ROCE), and suggest that £100000 is the optimum amount that should be spent on advertising.

Assumptions:

1. Price per tonne = £3500
2. Revenue = Price per tonne x sales
3. Direct cost = Cost of goods sold x sales
4. NP = Revenue - direct cost - fixed cost - advertising
5. Cost of capital = capital investment x 15%
6. Capital cost covered = $\frac{\text{Net profit}}{\text{Cost of capital}}$
7. EVA = Net profit - cost of capital
8. ROCE = $\frac{\text{Net Profit}}{\text{Assets}}$

Students should show a table as follows:

Advertising	25	50	100	200	400
Sales (tonnes)	180	210	280	360	420
capital Investment (£000's)	1100	1250	1650	2050	2300
Revenue (£000's)	630	735	980	1260	1470
Direct Cost (£000's)	270	315	420	540	630
Fixed Cost (£000's)	300	300	300	300	300
Net profit (£000)	35	70	**160**	220	240
Capital Cost Covered	0.212	0.373	0.646	**0.715**	0.696
EVA (£000)	-130	-117	**-87**	**-87**	-205
ROCE (%)	3.18	5.6	9.7	**10.73**	10.4

Spending £100000 on advertising would be the best strategy because it offers the optimum net profit. This is also the point at which EVA is at its highest. The return over capital employed is not at its highest at this point however the difference with the optimum figure is very small. An adequate amount of advertising is needed because the product is new. If the advertising is effective then its benefits will be seen now and in the future. Capital investment seems to be quite high in the beginning. However the benefits will be spread over time even though the cost is being incurred now.

5. How does the optimum advertising agency strategy change with alternative manufacturing processes: one with a fixed cost of £300000 and a variable cost of £1500 per tonne and the other a fixed cost of £50000 and a variable cost of £2500 per tonne? What d o these results tell you about the interaction between price (margin) and the other elements of the marketing mix?

Let us take for example:

Price	£3500
Advertising	£100000
Sales	280 tonnes
Capital Investment	£1650000

Manufacturing process A:

Fixed Cost	£300000
Variable Cost	£1500

Net profit = Sales - Variable Cost - Fixed Cost - Advertising Cost
= (£3500x280) - (£1500x280) - £300000 - £100000
= £160000

Capital Cost Covered = NP x Sales x Assets

Sales Assets Cost of Capital

$$= \frac{NP}{\text{Cost of Capital}}$$

$$= \frac{£160000}{£1650000 \times 15\%}$$

$$= \frac{£160000}{£247500}$$

$$= 0.646$$

$$ROI = \frac{NP}{\text{Assets}}$$

$$= \frac{£160000}{£1650000}$$

$$= 0.097$$

EVA = NP - Cost of Capital
= £160000 - (£1650000x15%)
= -£87500

Manufacturing process B:

Fixed Cost £50000
Variable Cost £2500

NP = 130000
C^3 = 0.525
ROI = 0.079
EVA = -£137500

Considering manufacturing process A, where we have a high fixed cost and a low variable cost the company will not suffer financially since the fixed cost has been spread over the 280 tonnes that have been produced, with a result of each tonne bearing a smaller cost. If the company decides to increase production, costs per tonne will decrease. This will in turn increase profits, enabling them to spend extra on other elements of the marketing mix. The product itself could be improved with better packaging. Extra promotional activity can be carried out e.g. increasing advertising spend and the use of sales promotions to encourage customers to try their product. However with Manufacturing process B, the greater the production the more expensive it will be for the company. This is because the variable costs are high and they vary directly with the level of production. Since a price of £3500 has already been decided, the company will need to cut costs across the rest of the elements of the marketing mix in order to maintain good profit. They could cut costs by using cheaper packaging, reducing weight of packets, etc. Cheaper channels of distribution could also be used e.g. avoiding use of vending machines which are a more costly channel. Also, cheaper methods of promoting the product could also be used.

Jokes and Quotes

Bargain: A thing you never wanted at a price you never expected.

A bargain is something you cannot use at a price you cannot resist.
ANON

Our pricing policy: to charge like a wounded bull.
ANON

Anybody can cut prices, but it takes brains to make a better article.
PHILIP ARMOUR

Price, n. Value plus a reasonable sum for the wear and tear of conscience in demanding it.
AMBROSE BIERCE

The lower Manhattan branch of Brook Brothers was robbed. The thieves escaped with clothes valued at $200,000. One clerk complained: "If they had come during our sale two weeks ago, we could have saved 20 per cent".
BOOK OF BUSINESS ANECDOTES

Pile it high and sell it cheap.
SIR JOHN COHEN

If this is the revolution, why are the drinks so expensive?
GRAFFITI

Unfair competition: selling cheaper than someone else.
RALPH HARRIS

"After you've fitted the eyeglasses the customer usually asks, 'How much?' You say: '£20' Then if the customer says nothing, you add 'for the frames'. The lenses are £10'. If the customer still says nothing, say 'each'.
JOKE

Customer: 'Five francs each, the store across the road is only asking four.
Shopkeeper: 'So go across the road then'
Customer: 'But they are sold out'
Shopkeeper: 'When I have sold out, I will charge only three francs'

JOKE

Receptionist: Do you want a thirty-five pound room or a fifty pound room?
Customer: What's the difference?
Receptionist: The fifty pound room has a free TV.
JOKE

Landlady: Rooms overlooking the sea are five pounds extra.
Lodger: How much if I do not look?
JOKE

Mechanic to worried motorist: You can have my guess for £10 or a computerised diagnosis for £50?
JOKE

After telling the customer about the gadgets on a new car, the salesman asked: Is there anything else I can explain? Yes, said the customer. Why is the £10,000 price you're asking for the car modest when the £100 discount is substantial?
JOKE

If the package doesn't say 'New' these days, it better say 'Seven Cents off'.
SPENCER KLAW

Buy low, sell high, collect early, and pay late.
DICK LEVIN

To our foreign guests: A 10 per cent discount is given if you do not attempt to order in French.
MENU (IN PARIS)

Buy sheep, sell deer.
PROVERB

There is hardly anything in the world that some men cannot make a little worse and sell a little cheaper.
JOHN RUSKIN

Part VII

Promotions

Chapter 18

Promoting Products:

Communication and Promotion Strategy

Chapter Objectives

After reading this chapter, you should be able to:

1. Name and define the four tools of the promotion mix.
2. Discuss the elements of the marketing communication process.
3. Explain the methods for setting the promotion budget.
4. Discuss the factors that affect the design of the promotion mix.

Chapter Overview

Promotion is one of the four major elements of the company's marketing mix. The main promotion tools are advertising, sales promotion, public relations, and personal selling. They all work together to achieve the company's communication objectives. In preparing marketing communication, the communicator has to understand the nine elements of any communication process: sender, receiver, encoding, decoding, messages, media, response, feedback, and noise. The company also has to decide how much to spend for promotion. Finally, the company has to divide the promotion budget among the major tools to create the promotion mix. Companies are guided by the characteristics of each promotion tool, the type of product/market, the desirability of a push or pull strategy, the buyer's readiness state, and the product life-cycle stage. The different promotion activities require strong co-ordination for maximum impact.

Teaching Notes

Refer to the following pages for teaching notes.

The Promotion Mix

Transparency PM 18-1 relates to the material on pp.686-687.

Tools of The Promotion Mix

1. Advertising

Advertising is any paid form of nonpersonal presentation and promotion of ideas, goods, or services by an identified sponsor. Advertising often utilises mass media and may be adapted to take advantages of a given medium's strengths to convey information.

2. Sales Promotion

Sales promotions consist of short-term incentives to encourage purchase of sales of a product or service. Limited time offers or dated coupons are common sales promotions.

3. Public Relations

Public relations is an on-going process of building good relations with the various publics of the company. Key elements in the process are obtaining favourable publicity, building and projecting a good "corporate image", and designing an information support and response team to respond proactively to unfavourable rumours, stories, or events.

4. Personal Selling

Personal selling describes the use of oral presentations in a conversation with one or more prospective buyers for the purposes of making a sale. Personal selling combines product information and benefits with the interpersonal dynamics of the sales person. Good interpersonal relationship skills and effective oral communication skills are needed for personal selling.

Tip

Ask students which element of the promotion mix is the most important. Answer; They are all important. Instructors should emphasise the concept of integrated marketing communications.

Notes for PM 18-1

The Communication Process

Transparency PM 18-2 corresponds to Figure 18-2 on p.688 and relates to the material on pp.687-688.

The Communication Process

Sender

The sender is one of two major parties in communication. It is the sender who decides how to encode a message aimed at a particular target market or receiver. Senders need to anticipate what information receivers need and how receivers will interpret different kinds of information.

Receiver

The receiver in marketing communication is the target market or audience. Receivers not only "accept" information; they process and act on it according to their own needs.

Message

The message is the information content about product benefits transmitted by the sender as a set of symbols whose meaning is generally understood by other senders and receivers.

Media

The media are the means by which messages move from senders to receivers. Mass media such as television and radio are examples. These are also called communication channels.

Encoding

Encoding is the process of putting the sender's message into a symbolic form capable of being carried by the selected media of transmission.

Decoding

Decoding is the process by which the receiver assigns meaning to the transmitted message. Marketers must remember that this is an interpretative activity and may use different ways of assigning meaning than the sender used in encoding the message.

Response

Responses are reactions and can include behavioural changes, attitude changes, or no indications of change.

Feedback

Feedback consists of the part of the consumer's response that is communicated back to the sender. Feedback is a valuable but incomplete picture of the consumer's response to the marketing communication.

Noise

Noise is any distortion during the transmission process and is always present to some degree. Noise also occurs in the feedback stage.

Notes for PM 18-2

Buyer Readiness States

Transparency PM 18-3 corresponds to Figure 18.3 on p.689 and relates to the material on pp.689-691.

Buyer Readiness States

Awareness

Buyers vary in the relative awareness of a product. Marketers must first establish in the customer an awareness that the product exists. Awareness is usually required before the target market can be motivated to learn more about the product.

Knowledge

After awareness, the marketing communicator seeks to provide knowledge about the product's benefits and link these to the consumer's needs. Information about product performance and use increases consumer knowledge.

Liking

Knowledge and awareness may not say much about consumer's affective reactions. Information alone usually will not differentiate the product in the mind of the consumer. Marketers must link information to positive affect so that consumers feel good about the product.

Preference

Marketers attempt to turn liking into preference so that the product will achieve hierarchical superiority over other competing and also liked products.

Conviction

This state helps link information and feelings to a need for action. In this state marketers help encourage consumers that product use is a necessary action step to satisfy a demand for the product's benefits.

Purchase

It is important that the marketer not abandon marketing communication efforts at conviction. Many target consumers may still need encouragement from additional promotions to actually make the purchase. Effective promotion management will integrate tools of the mix to facilitate the continuing movement of the target market through each of the readiness states.

Tip

Ask students for current advertising examples that emphasise each of the six buyer readiness states.

Notes for PM 18-3

Choosing A Message and Choosing Media

Transparency PM 18-4 relates to the material on pp.691-699.

Choosing a Message

Message Content

Rational appeals relate to the audience's self-interest. Rational appeals are grounded in objective, logical reasons for purchasing a product such as improved performance, increased quality, better reliability and increased productivity: Emotional appeals attempt to elicit either positive or negative feelings that will facilitate a purchase. Moral appeals are directed to the consumer's sense of right and wrong and are often used in conjunction with the marketing of social causes.

Message Structure

Marketers deal with three message structure issues. First, marketers must decide whether or not to draw a conclusion in the message. Effectiveness depends upon both the nature of the information being communicated and the relative level of experience with the product concept on the part of the audience. Second, marketers must decide on the type of argument to be used. One-sided arguments work best when the audience is unlikely to examine the information critically. Two-sided arguments are useful if the audience is likely to be exposed to other information not under control of the marketer that may refute some of the product claims. Third, argument order must be decided. When many arguments are being used, placing the strongest argument either first or last can affect persuasiveness.

Message Format

Format issues involve sensory qualities, colour in visual ads, sound in radio, and effective use of novelty and contrast in the message.

Choosing Media

Personal Communication Channels

Personal channels involve two or more people in direct communication. Word of mouth is especially credible to consumers - either positive or negative.

Nonpersonal Communication Channels

Major media include print, broadcast and display. Atmospheres are designed environments that create or reinforce the buyer's leanings to buy a product. Events are occurrences staged to communicate messages to target audience.

Notes for PM 18-4

The Total Promotion Budget

Transparency PM 18-5 relates to the material on pp.699-700.

Setting the Total Promotion Budget

1. Affordable Method

This method involves setting a promotion budget based upon what management thinks the company can afford. This method often places promotion budget decisions in the hands of managers unfamiliar with what promotion does for the product. It also ignores the effect of promotion on sales volume and/or possible value-added to the product in the mind of the consumer by the promotion effort.

2. Percentage-of-Sales Method

This method sets promotion budgets at a certain percentage of current or projected sales or price of the product. While it does link sales and promotion together it tends to make promotion an effect of sales rather than a positive influence on it. Also, failing sales under this method will decrease promotional expenditures which might need to be increased to halt the sales decline.

3. Competitive-Parity Method

This method sets promotion budgets in line with what the competition spends on promotion. This "collective wisdom" philosophy suggests that management is unwilling or unable to decide what level of spending is needed to promote the product to the consumer.

4. Objective-Task Method

This method sets budgets by defining specific objectives, determining what tasks are necessary to meet them, estimates the cost of performing the tasks, and sets the promotion budget according to the estimates. This approach assumes that promotion is a resource to be allocated to meet company goals and managed proactively to compete successfully.

Notes for PM 18-5

Promotion Tools

These notes relate to the material on pp.701-703.

The Nature of Each Promotion Tool

Advertising

Advertising's public nature helps legitimise the product. It also allows marketers to repeat the message to a wide audience. Large-scale campaigns communicate something positive about the seller's size, popularity, and success. Advertising is also very expressive and can make use of powerful symbols and sensory appeals. Its shortcoming include expense, one-way communication, being impersonal, and lack of control over situational reception.

Personal Selling

Personal selling is the most effective promotion tool at certain stages in the buying process, especially in building preferences, convictions, and actions. The personal contact is two-way and allows adaptation to buyer reactions and the establishment of relationships. Personal selling is also the most expensive promotion tool and requires a long-term commitment to build an effective salesforce.

Sales Promotion

Sales promotion includes coupons, contests, cents-off deals, premiums, rebates, and other techniques designed to elicit a quick response. Sales promotions usually influence the timing of a purchase rather than the decision to purchase.

Public Relations

Public relations includes news stories, features, and reporting on company activities from objective and credible third-party sources. These events are perceived as more believable than company-controlled promotions. Difficulties include the lack of message content, format, and structure control over the public relations event. Further, public relations are generally underused by marketers both strategically and tactically.

> **Tip**
> Ask students to give some examples of services/products/brands that emphasise one promotion tool more than the others.

Factors in Setting the Promotion Mix

These notes relate to the material on pp.703-707.

Factors in Setting the Promotion Mix

1. Type of Market

The type market, consumer or industrial, varies the importance of the promotion tools available to marketers. Advertising weighs heavily in consumer markets whereas personal selling plays the greatest role in industrial markets.

2. Push or Pull Strategy

The promotion mix is also affected by the company's decision on either a push or pull strategy. Push strategies rely on personal selling and sales promotions to encourage intermediaries to take the product and promote, thus "pushing" it through the channel. Pull strategies rely on advertising and consumer promotions to build up demand in the target market of ultimate consumer whose behaviour effectively "pulls" the product through the channel.

3. Buyer Readiness State

The buyer will be more receptive to some promotion tools than others depending upon their particular buyer readiness state. Advertising and public relations help create awareness and increase knowledge. Liking and preference are more affected by personal selling and advertising together. Conviction and purchase come first from advertising and then personal selling to close depending upon the kind of product being considered.

4. Product Life Cycle Stage

The stage in the product life cycle also describes different appropriate promotion mix variations. Introduction utilises advertising and public relations to build awareness and personal selling to facilitate motivate channel members to carry it. In growth, the need for personal selling diminishes. In maturity, personal selling helps differentiate it again in distribution. In decline, sales promotion may be the most emphasised of the promotion mix tools.

Comments on Discussing the Issues

1. It is surprisingly difficult to develop a definition of marketing communications that includes all the things that people think of as marketing communications and excludes things that people think are not marketing communications. Given the difficulty of defining marketing communication, the form of communication represented by (a) is at least partly a matter of opinion: An advertising message on a T-shirt might be considered to be an advertisement, or it might be considered a form of sales promotion, or simply a noncommercial expression of speech. The other parts of the question are more straightforward: (b) is a form of public relations, (c) is sales promotion.

2. Linda McCartney has been a very effective spokesperson for reduced calorie, health-food products. The factors that contribute to her credibility, McCartney probably rates highest on likeability. Her long history of concern for health and naturalness in foods makes her an expert and trustworthy spokesperson for the company. Another possible reason is that she is married to a well-known artist, Paul McCartney, where people can easily recognise and remember the name.

3. The text discusses a variety of methods that companies can use to get feedback on the effects of their communication (specifically, advertising) efforts. Various research firms measure how many people remember seeing an ad in a magazine or newspaper or recall a commercial they were exposed to on TV. Other firms expose people to commercials in cinemas and measure their liking of the advertisements and their subsequent purchase behaviour. Still other firms measure physiological responses to a communication or conduct surveys of audience members. Other forms of feedback come from customer or media comments on the organisation's communications and in terms of sales and other behavioural responses.

   Some organisations prefer to spend funds on charitable causes rather than on research. Thus, the RSPCA is likely to treat contributions as its most important form of feedback, despite the fact that changes in the economy or in the fund-raising efforts of other organisations also affect contributions to charities. Unilever uses many forms of research to obtain feedback on its communications, and also makes it easy for consumers to volunteer their responses.

4. The purpose of this question is to have students consider the differences between advertising and sales promotion. These two tools are the most visible forms of product promotion. Advertising is usually viewed as a long-term tool that builds a brand's image. It encourages consumer purchases by taking them from no knowledge of the product through the steps of awareness, knowledge, liking, preference, conviction, and, hopefully, purchase. Advertising suggests a quality image for a brand by displaying it as standard and legitimate, and pointing out its advantages. Advertising encourages purchase because a brand is special and of high quality.

   Sales promotion, on the other hand, is designed to encourage quick purchase. Usually this involves offering a discount such as a coupon, a cents-off label, or a rebate. Manufacturers are, in many cases, undercutting their advertising by overemphasising price promotion. The advertisement says "buy because it's good," while the promotions say "buy because it's cheap." Because sales promotion has a quicker and sharper impact on sales, however, it has become increasingly used with the extra expenses covered by reducing advertising.

Advertisement and promotion can be synergistic. The Procter & Gamble "Special Olympics" is a good example of synergy. This program sponsors the Special Olympics for retarded children, offering a donation for each coupon redeemed. Ivory Soap has run image-building commercials in which the main character works in the Special Olympics. The promotion interacts in a positive way with the advertising, without undercutting it.

5. Currently the company is setting the advertising budget as a percentage in relation to its anticipated sales. This is a common way of determining how much to spend. This method encourages management to understand the relationship between promotion costs and selling price and profit per unit. Some disadvantages are; does not consider market opportunities, dependent on year to year sales fluctuations therefore interferes with long range planning. Other methods are such as; (1) Affordable method - setting the budget to what the company can afford. It completely ignores the role of advertising as an investment and the immediate impact of advertising on sales volume and market opportunities; (2) Competitive parity method - involves matching their budget with the competitors budget or to allocate the same percentage of sales for advertising as them. This method assumes that competition has arrived at the correct level of expenditure and ignores that market opportunities and competitors objectives; (3) Objective task method - setting advertising budget based on the company's objectives and the cost of the tasks required to achieve them. Company will initially determine the objectives that a campaign is to achieve then list the tasks required to achieve them. The costs of the tasks are then calculated to arrive at the amount of the total budget. This method encourages management to think about the firms objectives, media exposure levels and the resulting costs. Students need to select the preferred method and justify their answers.

6. It is best for students to use the steps in developing effective communication as outlined in this chapter in answering this question. They need to specify the target audience, objectives of the communication (given in the question), designing the message, choosing media and measurement. Answers to each of the component must relate to the Charity Projects

Comments on Applying the Concepts

1. This question, on the objectives and consistency of advertising over time, is really a project question. Addressing these issues requires that specific advertisements be studied in some detail. It can make a good assignment for a medium-length paper. This question can be discussed in class if the instructor is willing to do the preparation and prepare transparencies for the class to view.

   Students have been exposed to so much advertising that they make good analysts and critics. They may focus on the appeal of advertising rather than the effectiveness at creating sales. Try to turn their attention to the more objective list of desired responses: awareness, knowledge, liking, preference, conviction, or purchase.

2. As with Question 1, this question requires some homework to find and assemble information. Students may need some guidance in determining how to proceed. Suggest that they look at a distinctively-positioned car, such as a sports or luxury car. A trip to a dealership, while not strictly required, is very helpful.

   Lexus is a good example of a make that co-ordinates all elements of the marketing mix. Lexus set up exclusive dealerships so they could control quality and customer service. The advertising message is always stressing fit, finish, quality and luxury. Even the finest details are co-ordinated: Lexus designed a custom typeface for its logo, and this same typeface is used the spell out the dealership name all buildings.

Case 18
Absolut Vodka: Absolutely Successful

Synopsis

Absolut Vodka is the US brand name of Absolutely Pure Vodka, a product of Vin & Spirit the Swedish state-owned alcohol monopoly. In 1979 the 100th anniversary of the product was approaching and Vin and Spirit decided to export their vodka to the US. Since then the product has become the world's leading premium vodka. This case study discuss the reasons for its success, the product, the advertising, current and future markets and the possibility of extending into new brands.

Teaching Objectives

1. Highlight to students the importance of the "integrated" approach in designing marketing communication campaigns.

2. Show how the nature of the product and the goal of the company also shape the promotion strategy.

3. Illustrate how target audience affect communication strategy.

Study Questions

1. What is the foundation of Absolut Vodka's success? Is it the vodka, the bottle, the distribution or the promotion? Do Vin and Spirit's low profits suggest that Absolut is not a commercial success but one bought at the expense of losing their monopolistic powers elsewhere?

Students should highlight that the vodka, design of the bottle, the advertising and distribution have all been recognised as playing crucial roles in the success of Absolut Vodka. Nevertheless, the creative positioning of the product has led to its success. In the first instance, the company used market research in the form of a survey of the US spirits market which found that "a clearly discernible consumer trend towards "white" spirits", "white spirits are seen as being purer and healthier". These results showed the potential of exporting into the US market, especially with the company's exceptionally pure vodka. The competitive advantage of Absolut Vodka is the historical purity of the product emphasised by the bottle design, clarity of the product and an advertising strategy which emphasised its purity and exclusivity. The marketing teams have managed to generate a significant augmented product by emphasising the purity of the vodka and pandering to the public perception of white spirits being inherently healthier. They clearly began with an exceptional product as a foundation, distilled using a new method which produced no unhealthy by-products. The marketing teams then built a successful brand on the uniqueness and exclusivity of the vodka. The bottle is based upon an 18th century medicine bottle and is made from exceptional clear glass to reflect the "purity and clarity" of the product. The shape of the bottle also portrays a difference and an elegance which is partly due to its link with history. This link with history has echoed in the long history of the vodka itself. The innovative and award winning marketing has used the bottle design with its timeless shape, fine lines and exceptional clear glass, which distinguishes Absolut from other premium vodka brands. The early advertising strategy centred on the bottle and the word Absolut in short distinctive captions. This was in complete contrast to previous spirits advertising in the US and gave the brand a competitive edge which it maintained with hundreds of different advertisements. A further development was to emphasise the exclusivity of the product and improve its credibility through third party interest, by tying up with the arts world. Famous contemporary artist and designers have been commissioned to produce works of art which highlight the exclusivity of the product, reflected in the high price. The marketing has proved to be successful that the product receives free media exposure even in markets that did not allow alcohol advertising and an induction into Marketing Hall of Fame along with Coke and Nike. The company had also developed an internal marketing magazine, Absolut Reflexions, which publishes instructions on how the public and professional audiences should be introduced to Absolut Vodka. The well blended communications have positioned the brands in the minds of the target audience with the brand personality (of purity and clarity) projected and the favourable attitude of a healthy spirit reinforced. All of the above have proved to be successful that Absolut has now outgrown Carillion, its long standing international distributor. Therefore, in order to maintain and increase market penetration in its existing markets and expand in to new markets, Vin and Spirit has chosen Seagram, the world's leading alcohol distributor as its new distribution partner. In conclusion, all components have played a part in Absolut Vodka's success. The purity of the vodka has been emphasised in the bottle design which influenced the marketing.

To answer the second part students should note that Absolut Vodka contributes 25% of the total turnover of the Vin and Spirit company. The sales growth in the US of 38% in 1993 would suggest a success for the Vodka. As a monopolistic company one would expect there are opportunities to make abnormal profits. Vin and Spirit, however, is a state-owned monopoly and the sole supplier to the state retail company. A reason for the low profits maybe due to the inefficiencies and low productivity often associated with state-owned industry. This would explain the substantial restructuring that the company is going through in order to compete in their home market after losing the monopoly status in both production and retail. Although Absolut Vodka has been a sales success in the US the revenues may have been eaten up by inefficient production. Another explanation for the low profits may be lack of funds for the expansion into the US market, causing a drain on early profits. Students should note that brand building is a long term activity requiring significant investment to establish a brand in the marketplace. Vin and Spirit has clearly invested heavily in penetrating the US market and establishing Absolut Vodka as an exclusive brand. There is nothing to indicate a link between successful marketing of Absolut Vodka in the US and the decision of the Swedish government to open the home vodka market to other producers.

2. Absolut's successful advertising has benefited greatly from the publicity it generated. Can advertising campaigns be designed to create such media attention or is the success of Wonderbra, Benetton and their like, just good fortune? Compare the approaches of Absolut, Wonderbra, Nescafe Gold Blend, Boddingtons and others in creating publicity-efficient campaigns. Is all such coverage good publicity? Does it involve the advertiser losing control of the brand?

Vin and Spirit used market research to identify their target audience and inform the audience various aspects of Absolut's marketing mix. In the development of a promotional strategy advertising had played a key role. Part of Absolut Vodka's advertising objective is to create an awareness of the product in the minds of the potential consumers in the US. This is done by highlighting the aforementioned differential advantage of the product over competing brands. Other advertising sought to position the product by product characteristics and product class. The dramatic difference between the advertising for Absolut Vodka and other spirits helped to generate media interests. In particular the credibility arising by involving celebrity artists elevated the status of both the brand and the advertising campaigns.

In recent times the Benetton poster advertising has attracted substantial amount of media coverage. Most recently the poster featuring a new born baby. It would be hard to believe that this advertising and other Benetton's advertising campaigns were not deliberately designed to shock and disturb the consumer, provoking a high level of media coverage. This is clearly a case of a campaign designed to attract the media attention. The intention of any advertising is to give the product as much coverage as possible to the intended target group within the resources available. In considering other successful campaigns, who have received such media attention, it is very difficult to say whether this was "designed" or it was good fortune. Obviously, the advertiser would claim it was very clever and subtle approach, however, to the outside observer it is hard to believe that a certain amount of luck is not involved.

Absolut Vodka's exclusivity is linked to celebrity artists. Media attention is inevitable. Wonderbra "Hello Boys" advertisement uses sex. Who will buy the bra, the girl or her partner? Generated media interest because of the risqué approach. It has managed to get additional publicity and position Wonderbra as an essential fashion item. Benetton used shock tactics in the "United Colours of Bennetton" campaigns. Disturbing advertising which linked the products to ordinary people (anyone can wear Benetton). The shocking images succeeded in getting Benetton onto front pages and TV screens, across Europe and other parts of the world. Nescafe Gold Blend uses romance and intrigue very much soap opera style. Intended to become a talking point, especially by trailing an upcoming advertisement, with some limited success but the advertiser lost control of the campaign. Boddingtons uses "Cream of Manchester". Quirky advertising or an attempt to move into female beer drinking market. It has not generated heavy media coverage. Students should realise that there must be some level of risk associated with this type of advertising. The initial effect of the media coverage of the Benetton baby poster in the short term may have been adverse. However, all media coverage serves to heighten the profile of the product in the long run, any publicity of the name of a product is good publicity (e.g. sales of Nike footwear went up when Eric Cantona, their major endorser in the UK, was banned from playing).

The level of media coverage could result in the advertiser losing control of the brand because it overtakes the image of the product. Advertiser can avoid this problem by maintaining a flow of differing advertisements (e.g. Guinness). Although in many cases the media coverage colludes with advertiser by constantly naming the product and/or company. Advertisers should use a feedback loop to ensure the receivers (customers and potential customers) are decoding the message correctly. If the customers are not receiving the right message then the advertising strategy should be reconsidered.

3. How does Absolut's marketing build upon American trends in the late 1980's and early 1990's? Is Absolut a fashion product that will decline with the trends? Since Absolut Vodka is a such lifestyle product, would you recommend that Vin and Spirit should extend the brand into other markets in the same way as Virgin has extended into video games, PCs, cola and vodka?

Fashion trends in America in the late 1980's and early 1990's were built around clean and healthy lifestyles. This may have resulted in the consumer's trend moving away from brown spirits and towards white spirits, which are seen as being healthier.

The marketing approach adopted by Absolut emphasises the purity and clarity of the product and attempts to present a healthier image, i.e. in the bottle design and the association with white spirits being seen as healthier. This fashion trend has almost certainly had an effect on the popularity of Absolut. However, Absolut is aimed at the more exclusive market which may not be as affected by fashion trends. Although they may expect to see a fall in sales due to a swing back to brown spirits, they should be able to maintain their market share by building upon the success of the advertising campaign. Clearly in 1993 Absolut Vodka in the US is still in the growth phase of the product life cycle. Eventually sales will peak and level off. Vin and Spirit need to take steps to reinforce the brand or develop associate brands.

Vin and Spirit was the state-owned alcohol monopoly and presumably already produces a number of other alcoholic beverages i.e. beer and liquor. Their distinctive competencies are in the distilling and brewing industry. Their expansion plans may depend upon how Vin and Spirit class themselves in that industry. Do they want the Absolut brand name, a premium and exclusive product being associated with down-market and commonplace products. Virgin may class themselves in the general entertainment industry and therefore see no limit to expansion within that industry i.e. vodka, PCs, etc. Virgin vodka is obviously a product in direct competition with Absolut Vodka. Vin and Spirit already extend their product range of the Absolut brand into Absolut Citron and Absolut Pepper which are vodka based drinks (at least in the UK). Other markets and products could be; other spirits e.g. Absolut Gin, Absolut Rum; premixed cocktails, which are vodka based eg. Absolut Cocktail; the retail market, investing in exclusive cocktail bars; soft drinks, to be mixed with vodka e.g. Absolut Lemonade. The latter three ideas may not be considered sensible as they may taint the pure image of Absolut Vodka. If they decide to extend the brand they must maintain and build upon the exclusiveness of the product which they have worked hard to achieve and in doing so concentrate on upmarket products.

4. Do you believe that Absolut Vodka "is an idea whose time has come" and that nothing can stop its success? In what way are the conditions in Russian, European and Far Eastern markets different from those in the US? Vin and spirit's European campaign uses advertisements in the same style that has been successful in the US. Do you think the US approaches will work in other regions?

To some degree the success of Absolut is based upon fashion trends, hence, its demand may fluctuate. The potential world market for vodka is huge, 21% of Americans drink vodka, the European market is underdeveloped and there are new markets in the Far East. In Europe there may be opportunity to reduce costs by developing pan European advertising which has had some success with other products (e.g. Levi Strauss and United Colours of Benetton). In Russia, vodka is the national drink and there is a huge market. However, there is probably a high degree of brand loyalty for the home product and the average Russian income is very low making it very difficult to market a non-Russian premium vodka. In Europe, the market is slowly growing, fragmented and conservative with well-established traditions varying from region to region e.g. UK - whisky and beer; Germany - schnapps and beer; France and Italy - wine. However, there are a few home produced vodkas to compete with but by maintaining the upmarket exclusiveness, Absolut Vodka could increase its market share. In the Far East, there is no known national drink although there must be some e.g. Japan - saki. There is a certain degree of prestige associated with a particular brand. High priced, established brand like Remy Martin is considered the acceptable drink among the business elite. This market is large and therefore huge market potential.

The Russian market would be the most difficult, if not impossible to break into. Some students will suggest one approach could be to build upon the exclusiveness by supplying upmarket hotels, restaurants and bars only. This would associate Absolut with the top of the market establishments with promotion limited to personal selling. However, since vodka is their national drink there may be no real hope in gaining a significant market share. Recently in the UK there has been a trend towards white spirits. If this has been repeated elsewhere in Europe, then Absolut could use a similar advertising campaign used in the US. They could segment the market based upon region i.e. high profile in the UK and Germany where there is a tradition of spirit drinking, but low in France and Italy where spirits generally may not be so popular. A slightly more conservative approach may be adopted to reflect that of the European market. The European market should be approached with the view if gaining a significant market share in the long term. The Far Eastern market appears to be very fashion conscious. The same advertising campaign used in the US would probably work well in this type of market but using Asian models.

Teaching Suggestions

This case can also be used with the chapter on Consumer Behaviour and Decision Processes (Chapter 7).

Jokes and Quotes

If you've got it, flaunt it.
If you've not got it, sing it.

When business is good it pays to advertise: when business is bad you've got to advertise.
ANON

The business that believes that advertising is not necessary may find that customers take the same attitude about the business.
ANON

The advertisements in a newspaper are more full of knowledge in respect to what is going on in a state or community than the editorial columns are.
HENRY WARD BEECHER

We read advertisements... to discover and enlarge our desires. We are always ready - even eager - to discover, from the announcement of a new product, what we have all along wanted without really knowing it.
DANIEL J. BOORSTIN

Doing business without advertising is like winking at a girl in the dark. You know what you are doing, but nobody else does.
STEWARD HENDERSON BRITT

There is no such thing as 'soft sell' and 'hard sell'. There is only 'smart sell' and 'stupid sell'.
CHARLES BROWER

Advertising is what you do when you can't go to see somebody, that's all it is.
FAIRFAX CONE

Television is more interesting that people. If it were not, we should have people standing in the corners of our rooms.
ALAN COREN

I do not know any reading more easy, more fascinating, more delightful than a catalogue.
ANATOLE FRANCE

I read part of it all the way through.

SAMUEL GOLDWIN

Dyslexia Rules - K.O.?
GRAFFITI

I never read a patent medicine advertisement without being impelled to the conclusion that I am suffering from the particular disease therein dealt with in its most virulent form.
JEROME K. JEROME

Promise, large promise, is the soul of an advertisement.
SAMUEL JOHNSON

The longest word in the English Language is the one that follows 'And now a word from our sponsors...'
JOKE

Memo sent by the Managing Director to staff: We must avoid all unnecessary duplication of communication. I cannot repeat this too many times.
JOKE

Advertising is a valuable economic factor because it is the cheapest way of selling goods, especially if the goods are worthless.
SINCLAIR LEWIS

Advertising is the greatest art form of the twentieth century.
MARSHALL MCLUHAN

Consumption never needs encouragement.
JOHN STUART MILL

A lady is known by the product she endorses.
OGDEN NASH

Beat your gong and sell your candies.
CHINESE PROVERB

In baiting a mouse-trap with cheese, always leave room for the mouse.
SAKI

Lipsmackin thirst quenchin (ace tastin motivatin good buzzing cool talkin high walkin fast livin ever givin cool fizzin)
SLOGAN (PEPSI 1974)

Make your Armpit Your Charm Pit.
SLOGAN (1950's)

Often A Bridesmaid, But Never A Bride.
SLOGAN (LISTERINE MOUTHWASH)

Advertising is the whip which hustles humanity up the road to the Better Mousetrap. It is the vision which reproaches man for the paucity of his desires.
E.S. TURNER

Chapter 19
Promoting Products:
Advertising, Sales Promotion and Public Relations

Chapter Objectives

After reading this chapter, you should be able to:

1. Define the roles of advertising, sales promotion and public relations in the promotion mix.
2. Describe the main decisions involved in developing an advertising programme.
3. Explain how sales promotion campaigns are developed and implemented.
4. Explain how companies use public relations to communicate with their publics.

Chapter Overview

Three major tools of mass promotion are advertising, sales promotion, and public relations. They are mass marketing tools as opposed to personal selling, which targets specific buyers. Advertising is a strong promotion tool. European Union countries spend around 45.4 billion each year on advertising. Advertising decision making is a five step process consisting of setting objectives, budget decisions, message decisions, media decisions, and evaluation. Sales promotion covers a wide variety of short-term incentive tools such as coupons, premiums, contests and buying allowances designed to stimulate consumers, the trade, and the company's own salesforce. Public relations is gaining favourable publicity and creating a favourable company image. It is the least used of the major promotion tools, although it has great potential for building awareness and preference.

Teaching Notes

Refer to the following pages for teaching notes.

Major Decisions in Advertising

Transparency PM 19-1 corresponds to Figure 19.1 on p.716 and relates to the material on pp.716-732.

Major Decisions in Advertising

1. Setting Objectives

Advertising objectives are specific communications tasks to be accomplished for a specific target audience during a specified time period. Advertising objectives can be to inform (build primary demand), persuade (selective demand), or remind (brand loyalty). Advertising objectives are often linked to specific sales objectives.

2. Budget Decisions

Advertising budgets are set for each product consist with the advertising objectives. To implement objectives, budgets must be set in consideration of the products position in terms of; stage in the product life cycle, market share, competition and clutter, advertising frequency, and product differentiation.

3. Message Decisions

Advertisers must construct their messages carefully to reach target markets. Message generation consists of creative brainstorming to generate several alternative ways of communicating to the target market. Message evaluation and selection ranks and then chooses among message on the how meaningful, distinctive, and believable they are. Message execution involves determining how to best communicate with the target market including tone, style, word choice, and format for the ads.

4. Media Decisions

In selecting media for ads, advertisers must consider the reach (% exposed), frequency (number of times), and impact (qualitative effect) of the various media types, then specify which media vehicles to be used at what time (media timing).

5. Campaign Evaluation

Measures of communication effects and sales effects should be employed.

> **Tip**
>
> Ask students to comment on the importance of these steps in developing an advertising campaign.

Notes for PM 19-1

Sales Promotion

Transparency PM 19-2 relates to the material on pp.738-745.

Sales promotion consists of short term incentives to encourage purchase or sales of a product or service.

Growth of Sales Promotion

Key factors contributing to the use of sales promotion include: Top management acceptance of sales promotion as an effective element in the marketing mix. Increased competition and decreased differentiation. Decreased advertising effectiveness has also put pressure on companies to shift more emphasis to sales promotion.

Sales Promotion Objectives

The overall goal of sales promotion is to contribute to consumer franchise building - helping to effect a long term relationship with customers.

Consumer Promotion Tools

Samples offer a trial amount of a product.

Coupons give buyers a savings on specified products.

Rebates consist of cash back after the purchase.

Price packs offer reductions in price for special combinations of products or quantities of the product.

Premiums are goods offered free or at low cost as an incentive to buy the product.

Advertising specialities are useful items imprinted with the advertiser's name or logo.

Patronage rewards are cash or prizes offered for the regular use of the product or service.

Point-of-purchase promotions include displays and demonstrations at the retail level.

Contests, sweepstakes, and games give consumers a chance to win something and draw attention to the product.

Trade Promotion Tools

A discount is a reduction in the price from the manufacturer to a member of the channel of distribution.

An allowance is an authorised reduction in the amount paid to the manufacturer in return for performing one or more marketing channel functions.

Business Promotion Tools

Conventions and trade shows provide a stage for showing products and meeting the salesforce.

Sales contests provide the salesforce with incentives for performance over a given period.

Notes for PM 19-2

Developing the Sales Promotion Programme

Transparency PM 19-3 relates to the material on pp.745-750.

Developing the Programme

Incentives

All sales promotions must recognise that a certain minimum level of incentive is needed to have any effect.

Conditions of Participation

May be both legally mandated in some areas and/or linked to specific goals. Sweepstakes may restrict some participants or be linked to other behaviours such as prior purchases or bulk buys. How to inform participants must also be considered, for example, direct mailing of coupons or placing them on the package.

Length of Time

Considerations must be weighed between too short to have much effect or penetration of the market versus too long so as to lose any sense of immediacy to "act now."

Budget

Sales promotion budgeting suffers from the same organisational problems faced by marketers in other areas. Percentage of sales approaches are not linked to promotion as generating new sales. Objective based budgeting often fails to consider cost effectiveness.

Pretesting and Implementation

Sales promotion tools benefit from pretesting their effectiveness prior to implementation. Unfortunately, pretesting is seldom done. Implementation requires co-ordinating effective lead time and sell off time resources to manage the sales promotion effectively.

Evaluating the Results

A key part of evaluation is determining whether the promotion affected the total demand for the product or only its timing. Consumers may be surveyed or experiments conducted to ascertain the long-term impact of the promotion.

> **Tip**
>
> You may challenge students to come up with suggestions about how to do a "mini pretest" that managers might use within the time constraints of sales promotion deadlines.

Notes for PM 19-3

Public Relations

These notes relate to the material on pp.750-754.

Public Relations Tools

Press Relations

An on-going process of establishing and maintaining good relations with the news media reporters and editors to help place newsworthy information about company products or objectives in their vehicles.

Product Publicity

Seeks news coverage of specific products usually in conjunction with other promotional efforts.

Corporate Communications

Involves creating and managing internal and external communications promoting understanding of the company and its objectives.

Lobbying

Involves dealing with legislators and government administrators.

Materials

Include written information for reporters, and audio-visual information such as slide, sound programs, and videos on corporate identity.

Public Service Activities

Include contributions of time and money for community projects and programs.

Special Events

Consist of public service activities sponsored and controlled by public relations in-house.

Public Relations Decisions

1. Objectives

The first order of public relations business. PR must determine what it wants to accomplish and how these objectives support the overall promotion objectives.

2. Messages

Require that the PR department creates the "story" it wants to tell about the company and finds the appropriate media for transmitting it.

3. Implementation

Relies as much on the personal working relationships the PR people have with media editors as the content of the stories themselves.

4. Evaluation

Difficult because so much PR is designed to support other promotion efforts. Traditional evaluation includes clippings books counting the number of media exposures.

Comments on Discussing the Issues

1. The basic advantage of comparison advertising (often called "comparative advertising") is that it provides information that potentially helps consumers make better purchase decisions. This saves consumers the effort of finding the information from other sources, and helps producers of innovative products to position their products on the basis of competitive superiority.

   Comparison advertising has several disadvantages. One is misleading comparisons. By carefully selecting the grounds for comparison, most products on the market could describe themselves as superior to the competition. Another problem is confusion—consumers may not remember which product had which features in the comparison. The market leader has little reason to run comparison advertising—the competitor's product is as likely to benefit from the extra advertising exposure as it is to suffer from the comparison. Another disadvantage is the potential for consumer resentment at what they think of as irrelevant, unfair, or annoying comparisons. A 1983 survey by the Roper Organisation found that 51% of the respondents said that they did not like comparative advertising, for example. Yet another disadvantage is the potential for competitor retaliation. Competitors who feel they have been wronged are likely to challenge the comparison through the advertising industry self-regulatory process or in the courts, and with potentially painful results for the advertiser.

2. This question is designed to have students consider the credibility of advertising. The discussion may be quite animated—every student can relate examples of ads which make dubious claims. There is no quick and easy answer to the problem of building credibility for advertising. In general, it requires that advertisers make only claims that are true, and express them in a believable fashion. Advertising style is also a related issue. Consumers react negatively to fear appeals or ads which intrude by being irritating, for example, and this can also reduce the credibility of advertising as a source of information. Many quality advertisers already follow these guidelines, of course. Credibility will be difficult to increase unless nearly all advertisers act responsibly—which may not happen in the near future.

3. Some researchers suggest emphasising reach when a product is being introduced, when it has a large target market, and when implementing a pull strategy. Frequency should be emphasised when products are in the decline stage of their life cycles, when products are purchased frequently, when brand loyalty is not high, when the target market is small, and when the product message is difficult to explain. By sacrificing continuity, reach and frequency can be increased in a given time period without increasing expenditures. They also describe two forms of uneven ad scheduling: Flighting involves periods of advertising interspersed with periods of no advertising (useful for such products as vacation travel and many industrial goods), whereas pulsing involves continuous advertising supplemented by periods of heavier spending (useful for products where demand is seasonal, but off-season demand is still important, as with cars and beer).

4. If the advertisement had stated that Brand Y cookies were moister, chewier, and more perfectly baked than another brand of cookies, the competitor could have gone to court to force Brand Y to prove these claims or else discontinue them (and possibly pay damages). As a universal statement, though, most people would be expected to

recognise the claims as exaggerated and not meant to be taken literally. Regulators and media organisations are generally not concerned with these exaggerated advertising claims, or "puffery," because the claims are subjective and not capable of disproof and because they are not thought to affect behaviour. (For an argument that puffery is *not* a trivial matter, see Ivan L. Preston, *The Great American Blow-Up*, Madison: The University of Wisconsin Press, 1975.)

5. Most marketing mix elements interact, and it is often difficult to tease apart their effects. A new trier for a brand may have been triggered by advertising, sales promotion, or even public relations efforts—or a combination of these and other marketing mix elements. Ultimately, it is rarely possible to attribute specific business results to one single element of the marketing mix. However, it is possible to gauge the effectiveness of each element in different ways.

Advertising can be measured with survey research. Brand awareness can be checked before and after advertising, for example, to see what effects the ad has had. Similarly, the advertiser can measure attitudes about the brand, whether specific advertising claims are remembered, and so forth.

Sales promotion can be evaluated more directly. Trade promotions can be measured by how much product was sold to the reseller during the promotion. Consumer response can be calculated by examining sales before, during, and after the promotion to assess incremental sales. Other measures, such as the number of coupons redeemed, rebates submitted, or displays built can be helpful as part of the evaluation.

Public relations programs are quite difficult to evaluate. Most companies look at an output measure—how many mentions were received on television, how many articles covered the public relations topic, and the like. This can be converted to a rough estimate of how much this amount of media space and time might have cost if purchased outright. Going beyond output measures to assessing sales achieved is generally not possible.

Ultimately, the business results achieved are a result of all marketing efforts together. Evaluation can rarely attribute specific results to one program, but it can readily indicate which programs appear more effective overall.

6. Many advertising commentators have decried the trend toward increased sales promotion, saying that marketers are sacrificing long-run consumer loyalty for short-term sales. (They have been pointing out the perils of excessive dealing since the 1950s.) Sales promotion is being increasingly used because it does stimulate sales; unfortunately for the marketer, it also stimulates regular brand switching and an emphasis on buying from whoever is currently offering the best deal.

New products are being introduced at such a rapid pace that manufacturers have difficulty getting them into their channels of distribution. Heavy trade promotion is often necessary to convince wholesalers or retailers to carry a product.

These are marketing problems without any easy solutions. Marketers who try to cut back on sales promotions may lose market share to competitors who continue their promotions; marketers who continue to maintain sales through heavy promotions may sacrifice profits and any chance of having customer loyalty. Probably the best strategy marketers can take is to offer products with such obvious consumer value that they can be sold at a fair price without a suicidal amount of sales promotion.

Comments on Applying the Concepts

1. **(a)** This question can make a good short paper assignment. As with other application questions, students must actually do the assignment for it to be meaningful. The answer to whether multiple tools is more effective depends upon the circumstances. In general, a co-ordinated campaign using advertising, public relations, sales promotion and in-store displays can be very successful. Easter Sales and Special Olympics serve as platforms for many manufacturers to build a campaign. Commercial enterprises, such as Publisher's Clearing House, also distribute coupons and attempt to generate a great deal of consumer awareness and tie-ins from other manufacturers.

   (b) Imitation in marketing is very common. Competitors often conduct similar market research, target similar consumer needs, sell through the same channels, run similar advertising, promote at similar times, and even use the same value for their cents-off coupons.

2. This question can be used as an in-class discussion if the instructor picks the ads and brings videotapes to class. A useful comparison is a straightforward and effective (but boring) ad being compared to a beautiful, humorous, or otherwise distinctive ad that misses the mark. Students should remember that the purpose of an ad is to increase sales, not necessarily to provide entertainment.

Case 19
Diesel and Jeans & Workwear

Synopsis

Diesel Jeans and Workwear was the idea of one man, Renzo Rosso. The son of an Italian farmer who during the oil crisis in 1978 came up with the idea of Diesel as a trademark. He felt Diesel represented something that everyone need and in 1985 he created the company that has become second only to Levi in the European market. The goal is to become the world's number one jeans manufacturer. The case study considers the growth of the designer jean market and in particular Renzo Rosso's company. Diesel Jeans and Workwear. The strong image of the company lies with its concept or "mission", the trend-setting and often controversial advertising and its leader "the Renzo Rosso style". The company is represented in 69 countries, all of its 10 to 15 per cent is reinvested in the company and Renzo Rosso owns 100% of the shares. The company's largest market is in Germany but all advertising is sourced from Paradiset, a Swedish agency based in Stockholm, where one of their only two shops is located, the other being in Berlin. More shops are planned for Paris, Rome and New York.

Teaching Objectives

1. Allow students to study promotion ideas presented in the chapter.

2. Help students see how promotion mix decisions represent trade offs.

3. Show that elements of the promotion mix must support each other and fit with the total marketing mix.

Study Questions

1. Since jeans are street-led fashions, do jeans companies have to follow, not create, the demand for their products? Are sociologists correct in their perception of the cultural significance of jeans or are they merely inexpensive, practical clothes? How and why have Europeans jean producers been able to edge into the traditionally American jeans market?

Jeans are considered to be the "uniform of the street culture" and they lead the fashion market. Designers who understand the market are able to use their knowledge and create a "pull strategy" effect in promoting and selling their product. If a company understands what creates the perceived need for a pair of jeans, then they have the opportunity to correctly position a new pair of jeans to meet the perceived need of the market. Designers' companies have successfully brought in new types and styles of jeans. They set new trends which very quickly become a fashion statement and a necessity in the "street-wise" wardrobe. Other less fashionable labels will then copy the designer labels. Consequently, it is a matter of design, image, price and retail outlet which determine whether a particular brand is a leader or a follower in the market.

It is evident from the case study that jeans are perceived as significant items of clothing. When sociologist John Fiske asked 125 students their feelings about jeans, 118 of them used the word "freedom" , and expressed the idea that jeans allowed them the "freedom to be oneself'. This clearly demonstrates the cultural and sub-cultural significance of the product. Whilst practical in the generic form, jeans can be far from practical and extremely expensive under a designer tag. The designer label companies command very high prices, as any sought after products such as Nike trainers, Swatch watches, where a buyer will pay far more than the intrinsic value of the product, to obtain the lifestyle image that such product portrays. Since their original launch as hardwearing trousers for cattle ranchers it is clear that they have achieved a high level of cultural significance among young people.

The European designer jean companies have a very different product from the traditional generic American jeans. Traditionally, the jeans market has been dominated by American companies such as Levi and Wrangler and their designer companies such as Calvin Klein and Donna Karan. The new European market is much more design-led. The haute couture designer fashion industry is still based firmly in Europe especially in Paris and Milan. It is from this background that the new wave of designer ranges have been created. Another reason could be that the European companies are headed by dynamic and strong figures which have been able to move their products into a new up-market and socially distinctive sector.

2. How does the advertising for generic and designer jeans differ? Can one brand and advertising campaign straddle both markets? Explain Joe Bloggs' choice of Lara and the £150,000 jeans in a way of promoting the brand? Are twelve ranges a year really necessary?

There are various presentation of advertising for the generic jeans such as Levi's, Lee and Wrangler. For example some show young people in situations where there are elements of being tough, working class and so on. Other advertisements focus on tradition of the jeans. The latest Levi's advertisement still portrays a group of cowboys. It plays with the idea of inserting red hot rivets into jeans. The advertisement is very American and position the product as an historical object not as a wearable fashion statement. The Joe Bloggs range is linked to a high profile cricketeer. Advertising for designer jeans use celebrities, women, fashion orientated and normally in a sensual surrounding. Again the advertisement will try to project the elements of class and designer-led. The Diesel jeans brand is promoted by Paradiset, a local advertising agency in Sweden, which created advertisements that are conspicuous and directed at fashionable and modern intelligent people.

Generally, it would be very difficult to straddle both market. But Levi's, some years ago used universally known song/music and a "pin-up" type male undressing in a laundrette. This had wide appeal and subsequently led to the record being re-released. The campaign created a phenomena which crossed the market as a whole. It enhanced the Levi brand and was followed by other advertisements in a similar vein. It is possibly more difficult for the designer collections to straddle both markets. The main aim of many types of these companies, in particular, Diesel Jeans, is to be different and separate. The company's campaign is designed to appeal to a particular target group. Therefore, it would be inappropriate to develop advertising to attract the mass market when the product is clearly not aimed at them.

Brian Lara is a modern day hero who is easily identified and appeals to a wide range of people. Sporting figures have always been successfully used in promotions and Brian Lara is an obvious choice for the youth market. For a company that promotes an exclusive image and sells expensive items, there may be a need to have a continually changing range. This creates the idea of an ongoing need in the mind of the consumer. However, if the brand is continually stretched in this way, it can lead to confusion in the consumer's mind as to whether they really are buying an exclusive product or not. Conversely, an ever increasing product range helps to capture differing segments of the already highly targeted market and will satisfy needs of all customers. Some students will mention that the 12 range is necessary because that was their selling proposition. It is a strategy that they have adopted, "differentiation, trial and error in terms of variation".

3. What explains Rosso's choice of Sweden, rather than Italy, as the base for his international marketing activity? Why choose an agency and location outside the London and New York heartlands of modern global advertising? Can "the Renzo Rosso style" be separated from the brand identity and the advertising used? Are such organisational issues separate from the marketing of the products? How well does "the Renzo Rosso style" fit the needs of the jeans market and why.

Sweden was chosen as a base for all international marketing activity as it is seen as a wealthy market and receptive to new fashions as well as useful for test-marketing. The case study also states that Johan Lindeberg is a Swede and is the head of international marketing. The Diesel product is also avant garde and the market in Italy whilst very fashion orientated is much more traditional in nature.

The reason for this is in part similar to the reason for choosing Sweden. However, as the case study explains "Paradiset claim that their marketing success derives from a lack of respect for marketing strategies and their trend-setting advertising". With an avant garde product and a desire to set new trends and attack new markets, perhaps Rosso felt that to use an established British or American agency would dull the innovative nature of the company and brand.

Renzo Rosso style is Diesel and Diesel is Renzo Rosso. The company and the man are inextricably linked. Employees of the company have to understand the Diesel concept, wear Diesel clothes and devote their life to the company. His leadership is fundamental to the company's success and cannot be separated from the brand identity or the company's advertising.

In a company which has a successful marketing strategy, the organisational structure is linked with the marketing of products through the mission statement, the corporate and business goals down to the functional marketing strategy. If the head of any organisation has a strong message which they are able to communicate across the company then this must be linked eventually to the marketing of the company products.

"The Renzo Rosso style" fits perfectly with the jeans market. He is a dynamic entrepreneur with a flair for unconventional business practise which has an undeniable appeal to the target market who can readily identify with this somewhat "rebellious " style. Jeans as we have already seen are a "sign of freedom of constraints on behaviour and of class membership". This image is epitomised by Renzo Rosso and his Diesel company.

4. What is the controversial style of Diesel's advertising trying to achieve? Do you think it is effective? Ethical? Appropriate for all markets? How does the centralised nature of Diesel's advertising fit the entrepreneurial style of the company? How can the advertising be linked in with the rest of the marketing mix in the many markets and distributors that Diesel serves?

Diesel's advertising aims to be conspicuous and therefore remembered. It is aimed at a particular target group who want to be entertained by something ironic and controversial.

The effectiveness of the advertising is proved by the success of the company and its place in the world-wide jeans market. The advertisement which the case study highlights could be considered by some unethical. However it is only one advertisement from a company and it could be said that whilst we still allow advertisements for cigarettes, an advertisement which uses cigarette smoking as a joke is not a cause for a debate about ethics. Also, the advertisement was disliked in the USA in particular and not in Europe. This indicates that advertising is probably not appropriate for all markets. Cultural issues are viewed differently in the different countries and continents. However, Diesel is clearly successful in advertising in a pan-European market.

The strength of Diesel lies in the dynamic leadership of Renzo Rosso. One of his main concerns is the company's organisational structure, which he considers is more important than advertising. His strong leadership and 100% ownership mean he has total control. The role works well with the centralised advertising. By controlling the advertising he is able to maintain the strong company concept and image.

The promotion portion of the marketing mix is centrally distributed within the company as a whole and is linked with the other marketing mix elements by a strong and well-communicated company message. Diesel Jeans have a philosophy of using "strong collaborators". The strong marketing strategy and organisational structure mean that every aspect of the marketing mix is understood by company employees. Diesel products are sold only through "hand picked agents, licensees and subsidiaries". Franchising is not considered an option as this would relinquish some of the control of the company profile. Retailers are trained, they have to understand the Diesel concept and have to stock complementary clothes to Diesel products. There are strong point-of-sale items in shops so that the place element links in all aspects of promotion. The price and product elements are controlled, designed and made centrally so that the marketing mix is a harmonious package.

Teaching Suggestions

A good way to start the class is to ask if anyone owns or recently bought a pair of Diesel jeans. Students may want to discuss what they know about Diesel and their images of the company. They may want to contact Diesel focusing on its efforts in Europe and other international markets. Students can also search the business literature to learn how Diesel's strategy is progressing.

The case can also be used with the International Chapter (Chapter 5) if the instructor wants to emphasise the international marketing aspects. The case also goes with the Promotion Chapters (Chapter 18 and 19). It can be used with the Marketing Environment Chapter (Chapter 4) to emphasise how changes in the environment affect marketing strategies.

Jokes and Quotes

Advertising is not the world's second oldest profession, it must have been the first.

When business is good it pays to advertise;
When business is bad you've got to advertise.
ANON

An advertising agency - 85 per cent confusion and 15 per cent commission.
FRED ALLEN

The truth alone is not commonly selected as a medium for advertising
A. S. BISTOW

Some are born great, some achieve greatness and some hire public relations officers.
DANEIL BOORSTIN

Chess is as elaborate a waste of human intelligence as you can find outside an advertising agency.
RAYMOND CHANDLER

PR is like Christianity. If you don't believe in it, it won't work.
ALAN COMPTON-BATT

We predict that advertising expenditure will be a function of sales as the previous time period at least as much as the reverse is true.
R. M. CYERT AND MARCH

The more facts you tell, the more you sell. An advertisement's chance for success invariably increases as the number of pertinent merchandise facts included in the advertisement increases.
DR. CHARLES EDWARDS

Advertising is the most fun you can have with your clothes on
JERRY DELLA FEMINA

Overheard in the Jungle:
'Advertising is a people business. So is cannibalism'.
MARTYN FORRESTER

Overheard in Account Executive's Office:
'What's all the fuss about? It's going to be fish and chip paper tomorrow'.
MARTYN FORRESTER

That is the kind of ad I like. Facts, facts, facts.
SAMUEL GOLDWYN

The advertisement is one of the most interesting and difficult of modern literary forms.
ALDOUS HUXLEY

It is far easier to write ten passable effective sonnets than to write an advertisement that will take in a few thousand of the uncritical buying public.
ALDOUS HUXLEY

Advertising may be described as the science of arresting the human intelligence long enough to get money from it.
STEPHEN LEACOCK

There are two kinds of artists left: those who endorse Pepsi and those who simply won't.
ANNIE LENNOX

Most advertising is absolutely awful, easily forgotten, invisible garbage. That's why most advertising is ignored.
GEORGE LOIS

You can fool all of the people all of the time if the advertising is right and the budget big enough.
JOSEPH E. LAVINE

Advertising is the rattling of a stick in a swill bucket.
GEORGE ORWELL

The number of agency people required to shoot a commercial on location is in direct proportion to the mean temperatures of the location.
SHELBY PAGE

Puffing [advertising] is of various sorts, the puff direct, the puff preliminary, the puff collateral, the puff collusive and the puff oblique or puff by implication.

RICHARD SHERIDAN

Advertising is the art of making whole lies out of half truths.
EDGAR SHOAFF

In an Equadorian election, a producer of a deodarant, Pulvapis, ran an ad saying, "Vote for any candidate. But if you want well being or hydiene - vote for Pulvapi". On the day before the election they put out a flyer looking like a voting ship saying, "For Mayor - Honourable Pulvapi". In the town of Picoaza, Honourable Pulvapi won a landslide victory.
TRUE STORY

It has been said that Public Relations is the art of winning friends and getting people under the influence.
JEREMY TUNSTALL

The only truly bad publicity is no publicity.
E. M. WELLINGS

Chapter 20

Promoting Products:

Personal Selling and Sales Management

Chapter Objectives

After reading this chapter, you should be able to:

1. Discuss the role of a company's salespeople.
2. Identify the six main salesforce management steps.
3. Explain how companies set salesforce objectives and strategy.
4. Explain how companies recruit, select and train salesforce.
5. Describe how companies supervise salespeople and evaluate their effectiveness.

Chapter Overview

Most companies use salespeople and many companies assign them the key role in the marketing mix. The high cost of the salesforce calls for an effective sales management process consisting of six steps: setting salesforce objectives; designing salesforce strategy, structure, size, and compensation; recruiting and selecting; training; supervising; and evaluating. As an element of the marketing mix, the salesforce is very effective in achieving certain marketing objectives and carrying out such activities as prospecting, communicating, selling and servicing, and information gathering. A market-oriented salesforce needs skills in marketing analysis and planning in addition to the traditional selling skills. The art of selling involves a seven-step selling process: prospecting and qualifying, preapproach, approach, presentation and demonstration, handling objections, closing, and follow-up. However, a seller's dealings with customers should be guided by the larger concept of relationship marketing - the company's salesforce should work to develop long-term relationships with key accounts.

Teaching Notes

Refer to the following pages for teaching notes.

Major Steps in Salesforce

Transparency PM 20-1 corresponds to Figure 20.1 on p.762 and relates to the material on pp.762-763. This transparency provides an overview of the salesforce management process with following transparencies covering each key area in greater detail.

Major Steps Salesforce Management

1. Setting Objectives

Objectives can be general rules for guiding salespeople or more specific expectations for behaviour. Regardless, the sales objectives should address the relationship between sales, customer satisfaction, and company profit.

2. Designing Strategy

Strategy requires decisions on salesforce structure, size, and compensation. Variations in this mixture are appropriate for differing industries, markets and sales objectives.

3. Recruiting and Selecting

Knowing in advance what characteristics will always produce good salespeople is very difficult. Selecting procedures should attempt to screen candidates for both ability and retention-related issues.

4. Training Salespeople

Issues in training centre on skills such as order taking and order getting, seeing customers as unwilling to seeing them as people needing problem solutions.

5. Supervising Salespeople

Supervision addresses problems in directing and co-ordinating salespeople's organisation, time management, motivation, and customer relationships.

6. Evaluating Salespeople

Evaluation requires both qualitative and quantitative measures of salesforce performance.

Notes for PM 20-1

Setting Objectives and Strategy

Transparency PM 20-2 relates to the material on pp.763-766.

Setting Objectives

Objectives can be general rules for guiding salespeople such as "develop, sell, and protect" account or they can be more specific allocations of time such as 85% selling and 15% servicing. Salespeople must also understand that making a sale is only one part of the selling process. Customer satisfaction and confidence must be provided in the sales encounter and service to help build a strong base for repeat customers and company profits. Objectives should address the relationship between sales, customer satisfaction, and company profit so that each salesperson embodies a market-oriented rather than a sales-oriented approach.

Designing Strategy

Designing strategy requires decisions on salesforce structure, size, and compensation.

1. Structure

Territorial salesforce structure

Appropriate for single product lines in one industry and many customers.

Product line structure

Organises separate salesforces for each line.

Customer salesforce structure

Organises salespeople by customer levels for large, medium, and small companies.

2. Salesforce size

May be determined by workload estimates.

3. Compensation

Can be by salary, commission or bonus, and benefits. Variations in this mixture are appropriate for differing industries, markets and sales objectives.

Notes for PM 20-2

Recruiting, Selecting, and Training

Transparency PM 20-3 relates to the material on pp.767-769.

Recruiting and Selecting

The traits of effective salespeople are not easy to identify. Focusing on behavioural job duties may help set priorities. By linking traits to specific tasks, recruiters can more readily identify and screen potential employees. Recruitment must also address images of selling as a job versus a professional and legal requirements. College students especially often have unrealistic expectations about selling and their initial role in the company. The demands of many customers for integrated performance-based knowledge about products often require the skills of a college educated salesperson. Many companies also face legal oversight in hiring and recruitment and/or they have their own agenda to match salesforce backgrounds to changing customer markets such as emerging minority and foreign owned businesses.

Training

Training issues involve teaching recruits good selling principles and instilling in them a good philosophical orientation on selling. The selling process is detailed on a following transparency. Orientations usually centre on either a sales-oriented approach or a customer-oriented approach. Sales-orientations use stereotypically high-pressure selling tactics and view the customer as an adversary to be overcome to make the sale. Customer-orientations train salespeople in customer problem solving. Customer needs are seen as problems that salespeople attempt to solve creatively with the company's products and services. This builds both satisfied customers and confidence and trust in the salesperson by the customer.

Notes for PM 20-3

Supervising and Evaluating

Transparency PM 20-4 relates to the material on pp.769-777.

Supervising Salespeople

1. Developing Customer Targets and Call Norms

Companies often specify how much time their salesforce should spend prospecting for new accounts. Calls to accounts are often a function of how large or important the account is.

2. Using Sales Time Efficiently

The annual call schedule is a tool that shows which customers and prospects to call on in which months. The time-and-duty analysis helps salespeople identify when they are selling versus waiting, travelling, eating and doing administrative work.

Motivating Salespeople

1. Organisational Climate

Climate describes the feeling that salespeople have about their opportunities, value, and rewards for a good performance within the company.

2. Sales Quotas

Quotas are the standards stating the amount salespeople should sell and how sales should be divided among the company's products.

3. Positive Incentives

a. Sales meetings

Provide social occasions, breaks from routine, and chances to meet and talk with others.

b. Sales contests

Spur the salesforce to make a selling effort about what is normally expected.

Notes for PM 20-4

Evaluating Salespeople

1. Sources of Information

a. Sales report
The most important source of information managers have on their salesforce.

b. Work plan
Submitted by salespeople and describes the calls and routing for the coming week or month.

c. Annual territory marketing plans
Are outlines for building new accounts and increasing sales.

d. Call reports
Log sales calls and expense reports provide information on activity and expenses to be reimbursed.

2. Company Salespeople's Performance
Comparisons are helpful although many other factors influence performance such as differing conditions in each territory.

a. Comparing Current Sales with Past Sales
Past sales help identify trends. Interpretation is needed to evaluate trends with company expectations.

b. Qualitative Evaluation of Salespeople
These subjective evaluations look at a salesperson's knowledge of the company, products, customers, competitors, territory, and tasks.

Notes for PM 20- 4 (contd.)

The Selling Process

These notes correspond to Figure 20.2 on p.778 and relate to the material on pp.778-781.

Steps in the Selling Process

1. Prospecting and Qualifying

This step involves identifying qualified potential customers. Sales people must always contact more people than will end up becoming a customer. Prospecting is the process of obtaining good sources of information on who might be interested in or need the product. Qualifying seeks to improve that list by separating more likely leads from poor ones.

2. Preapproach

This step consists of doing the background research and preparation needed to understand the needs of the potential customer. Salespeople should set specific call objectives to accomplish when contacting the prospect.

3. Approach

In this step consists of the first contact with the buyer and seeks to establish a good working relationship. The salesperson must be aware of the effect of his or her appearance, opening remarks, listening style, and closing comments.

4. Presentation and Demonstration

In this stage the salesperson presents the product "story" to the buyer. Three styles for sales presentation are common. The canned approach uses a memorised script that covers the information carefully but sometimes lacks spontaneity. The formula approach matches one of many rehearsed outlined presentations to needs and attitudes identified in the opening. The need satisfaction approach has the customer discuss what they want and seeks innovative problem solving in response to their individual needs. All approaches are improved by audio-visual aids and demonstrations.

5. Handling Objections

This requires seeking out and resolving concerns that would stop a customer from purchasing.

6. Closing

Closing the sale means the salesperson may have to provide extra incentives to motivate the customer to take action now.

7. Follow-up

Follow-up is a necessary part of good selling to ensure satisfaction and repeat business.

Comments on Discussing the Issues

1. It is always important for salespeople to meet their customers' needs. In the case of the grocery trade, shelf maintenance is considered a service that is included as part of the sale. The salesforce must meet these expectations to assure future orders. In addition, shelves must be properly maintained to hold a brand's shelf position and prominence. Without careful attention, competitors will rearrange shelves to their own advantage.

   Maintaining shelves has benefits for the manufacturer, but it is very costly. A sales representative costs hundreds of pounds per average sales call, which is a very expensive resource to spend on shelf-stocking. Furthermore, shelf-stocking keeps salespeople away from revenue-producing sales calls. Many manufacturers have found ways to use lower-paid workers to provide the shelf maintenance services. Some companies hire part-time workers specifically as "merchandisers" whose duty is to stock, arrange, and dust the shelves. Other companies contract with a merchandising firm to provide these services for them. These solutions allow the salesforce to concentrate on selling, while still meeting customer needs.

2. Salespeople who are worried about whether or not they will be able to feed their family or make the mortgage payment are not likely to be at their best in their selling efforts. A regular salary allows a salesperson to concentrate on his or her job and also smoothes out the fluctuations in income resulting from commissions on sales that may take months to complete. It also compensates salespeople for nonselling aspects of their jobs—paperwork, orienting new salespeople, and so on.

   Straight salary may be appropriate for noncreative sales positions, where the salesperson's activities are less directly focused on making sales. In creative selling, commissions and bonuses help relate compensation to results and give more incentive for above-average performance. Typical compensation is about 75 per cent fixed, 25 per cent variable, but the ratio varies across companies and industries. For example, magazine sales representatives average about 30 per cent commission.

   Bonuses may be based on overall company performance, achieving a specified sales volume, accomplishing some specified task, or on anything else that the company thinks will encourage performance. Advantages to the company are that the bonus can be specifically tied to actions (as opposed to giving a large commission for a "windfall" sale, say), and it can be increased or decreased depending on overall company performance and resources. Disadvantages are the potential complexity of bonus systems and the fact that they may give little incentive if the bonus is seen as a "Christmas gift" rather than a direct result of performance. Typically, bonuses are a smaller part of total compensation than commissions are. *Sales & Marketing Management* frequently has useful articles related to salesforce compensation.

3. Many of the people who feel that they would not be good at sales probably have a sales-oriented view of selling rather than a customer-oriented view. When they realise that professional selling involves identifying customer needs and finding solutions for them, they may be more inclined to consider sales as a career.

   They may also be less reluctant when they realise that training can improve performance in any selling position, whether the task is asking customers if they would like fries with their hamburger, or selling £3 billion worth of aircraft. Selling skills can be taught—one survey found that 7 of 8 marketing executives feel that good salespeople are made, not born, and another showed that 30 per cent of companies' salesforce training programs are spent on sales techniques. Even experienced salespeople would like more training in general selling skills, especially in overcoming objections. An unproductive salesperson is very expensive in terms of lost sales, which is one reason that companies are willing to spend so much time and money training salespeople to be more effective.

4. Automatic reordering is highly efficient for both reseller and supplier. Similar systems are also very useful in implementing "just-in-time" inventory controls. It is clear that these systems will greatly expand in the future.

This innovation will have both positive and negative impacts on the role of the salesperson. It will free the salesforce to concentrate on creative selling rather than order-taking, and may allow more time to cultivate new accounts. On the other hand, it will reduce the interactions that the salesforce has with its customers. This may mean that interpersonal relationships between vendor and buyer become less intimate, reducing an important form of influence that salespeople use. It may also result in efficiencies for the buyer at the expense of the seller. For example, buyers may choose to reduce inventories and buy in smaller lots. With personal order-taking, the salesperson can push for a larger order. The machine, however, will simply respond to what is requested.

Overall, this innovation will mean that the salesforce will spend a greater proportion of its time on high-level selling tasks. Salespeople who are simply order-takers will become obsolete. The role of the salesperson will become less routine, and more time will be spent discussing innovations and programs available to the buyer.

5. Many companies assume that the best salespeople will be the best sales managers, but selling and managing are different skills. Top salespeople *may* be able to select, teach, supervise, and evaluate other salespeople—but then again, they may not. Salespeople have reason to believe that a sales manager who has been an outstanding salesperson knows what he or she is talking about, and may work harder for the rather than for someone who has never been especially productive. But before promoting someone to a sales management position, the company should look for evidence that the person can manage, not just sell.

Promotion to sales management is almost always rewarded with a higher salary. But for an outstanding salesperson, the higher salary could mean a cut in pay. Because a manager spends time managing, not just selling, there is less opportunity to make money from commissions. Managers generally earn commissions on sales by the salespeople that they supervise, but this may not be enough to make up for the lost commissions on their own sales.

6. In the Far East there is a variety of religions, cultures, subcultures, level of education, wealth, racial and other characteristics that must be considered prior to selling any products to the local inhabitants. Sales representative need to know about both factual and interpretative cultural knowledge to increase their understanding of the local culture and adapt their selling process accordingly. Prospecting and Evaluating - in order to find prospective buyers sales reps could for example find out and attend appropriate seminars, workshops and conferences in the UK and Far East to establish contact and relationship with potential buyers. Preparation - here sales reps need to know the prospect's background from education to language and so on. Approaching the Customer - once a company has decided to sell in the Far East they have to be prepared to stay for quite some time. Prospects will not make any decision immediately. They will take time before any decisions are made. Speak simple English where possible. To establish a warm personal relationship sales reps are advised to bring a gift. Their presentation - must be sincere and honest. To obtain credibility they must show information in print that supports the presentation. When using visual aids care must be taken that no offensive pictures, languages or symbols are used which can be interpreted in the wrong way. On closing - attention should be paid to cultural innuendoes and non verbal communication. Sales reps must follow up the sale to make sure everything was delivered in time. This shows sincerity and being concerned; a valuable asset in the Far East.

Comments on Applying the Concepts

1. This question, if assigned, may bring groans from your class. Salespeople have long been considered villains in the Western psyche, and being assigned to listen to one may be considered both unusual and cruel. For this reason, it may be an enlightening experience.

   (a) This part of the question requires that students take an objective and detached look at salespeople and their techniques. In discussing the experience, ask your students to describe the initial approach the salesperson used, including tone of voice, amount of eye contact, and the level of formality or informality. Was the approach a hard sell or a soft sell? Did this seem appropriate? Was the salesperson knowledgeable about the product being sold? Could he or she demonstrate it properly? How did the salesperson attempt to close the sale?

   (b) Most students will probably say they did not enjoy the experience, perhaps experiencing anxiety, irritation, or dismay. In truth, a well-done sales presentation can be a thing of beauty. Ask if anyone enjoyed or appreciated the pitch they experienced.

2. Question 2 expands on Question 1 by examining sales techniques in categories that have complex and expensive products. In theory, personal selling should be ideal for these types of categories. A good salesperson can explain the benefits of a product, how the product features support these benefits, and the advantages and disadvantages of different models. In fact, salespersons are often poorly informed, highly biased, or influenced more by commission rates than consumer needs.

   Parts (a) and (b) ask students to judge the salesperson's expertise, and decide whether he or she added value to the product (or detracted from it). Part (c) addresses an issue related to ethics and channel conflict. Some consumers window shop in full service stores to decide what they want, then purchase by mail to save on selling price and sales tax. This part of the question asks bluntly: do the salespeople add enough service and value to the basic product to make it worthwhile to buy from them?

Case 20
Britcraft Jetprop :
Whose Sale Is It Anyway?

Synopsis

This case reports the attempted sale of a small fleet of HS.748 (mentioned in the case study as Britcraft Jetprop) which is a medium-sized civil transport aircraft to a European air force. The customer is disguised throughout the case as the National Air Force (NAF). The case contains background information on Hawker Siddeley Aviation Ltd (HSA) and its products, the HSA Manchester divisions, the HS.748 and the sales organisation. A sales campaign is followed from initial contact through several stages of negotiation to what appears to be an impasse. The customer's government demands that an offset arrangement be made to cover a large part of the final contracts value.

The HS.748 sales operation from HSA Manchester is truly international. The product was designed for a geographically widely-dispersed segment of the world market and the sales effort is global. This case provides a basis for discussion of the problems facing companies like HSA who are world wide marketers of expensive capital equipment. The case is left open for discussion by leaving out details of the final bartering. Information concerning the close of the sale is presented at the end of this note.

Teaching Objectives

1. Illustrate that sales negotiations cover a wide range of technical and commercial issues, and involved many people with specialist skills from both the seller's and buyer's organisation.

2. Expose to students that bartering is becoming an increasing important part of deals in which it is expensive to organise, difficult to cost and even more difficult to expedite.

3. Explain that product such as this is seen as prestigious and strategic by the government of the buying nation and frequently in receipt of financial support from them.

Study Questions

1. Trace the stages in the buying process and how the Country's interests changed from one stage to the next. Why were the Country's interests changing and was Britcraft keeping pace with the changes? How well did the strengths of the Jetprop match the needs of the NAF?

The reader and student will be struck by the complexity of the negotiations described in the case. This complexity is easily underlined during a case discussion by asking students at the beginning of a session to give key issues and personnel from the case. A considerable list is usually forthcoming. It has been found that the sale is best analysed by using some model of the buying process. To trace the buying process and how the Country's interests changed from one stage to the next it is best to look at the "buyphases" from the buygrid model and their description: (1) Problem recognition - anticipation or recognition of a problem (need) and a general solution; (2) Characteristics determination - determination of characteristics and quantity of needed items; (3) Sanctioning - not included in the original buygrid model but included by the author to denote the sanctioning of the proposed purchase at a concept stage and the allocation of funds to it; (4) Characteristics description - description of characteristics and quantities of items needed; (5) Vendor search - search for and qualification of potential sources; (6) Proposal analysis - acquisition and analysis of proposals from vendors; (7) Vendor selection - evaluation of proposals and selection of supplier; (8) Contract negotiation - "selection of an order routine" in the original buygrid model. This was changed by the author to reflect the detailed contract negotiations common with expensive capital equipment; (9) Performance feedback - feedback of performance of product and supplier and evaluation by users of product. It will be noted that two changes have been made to the buyphases of the buygrid. These were thought necessary to reflect more accurately the stages in the buying process that occurred in the case. It is realised that the buying process does not follow a discrete sequence of phases. The decision process flows from one stage to another with continuous backtracking and overlapping of activities.

Superficially the Jetprop has few advantages over the Fokker as a utility transport aircraft for the NAF. The aircraft's outstanding performance out of "hot and high" airfields is unlikely to be of use to a European nation with modern airfields. The potential operator is also familiar with having aircraft of far greater sophistication than the contenders in this market so ease of maintenance is unlikely to be a critical factor. Ironically it is also likely that a military operator will evaluate an aircraft commercially in terms of typical peace-time operations, where high potential utilisation and the ability to take battle damage are of little consequence. Low fuel may be more important than the virtues of the Jetprop.

2. Identify the players in the buying centre and gauge their role and influence? How well did Britcraft manage the complexity of the buying centre and their diverse needs?

The players are; Users - the individuals who will eventually work with the purchase. In many cases the users may be the group that initiate a purchase. They are also the group most likely to resist a new product; Influencers - organisational members who directly or indirectly influence buying or usage decisions. They can exert influence by defining usage criteria which constrains choice or by providing information with which to evaluate alternative choices; Buyers - buyers are the organisational members with formal authority for the selection of suppliers and arranging the terms of purchase. Although buyers may have formal authority for negotiating with suppliers and for committing organisations to supply contracts, the choices available to them may be significantly limited by the formal and informal influences of others; Deciders - deciders are those members of the organisation who can make available funds for a purchase and who have either formal or informal power to determine the final selection of suppliers; gatekeepers - buying centre members who control the flow of information into the group. In extreme cases it can be a secretary to an executive or a receptionist who will not give a salesman access to key individuals. Usually it is a purchasing agent or buyer who has responsibility and authority for managing relationships with vendors.

It is evident that only two sections of the sales team have contact in depth with the buying centre, the agent and the sales executives. Although others from the sales team may frequently be working on the prospect, they are generally only involved with a few people in the buying centre and for short periods. It is also noticeable that direct contact with deciders (the Ministerial level) were few. Throughout the case, contact with the Department of Economic Affairs and the NAF was far below the decider level. As with the buying centre there is considerable movement of desirable involvement through the sales team as the sale progresses. Comparing desirable sales team involvement with actual through the buyphases shows Britcraft late entry into the buying process. According to Robinson, Faris and Wind "as buyphases are completed moving from phase 1 through phase 8 (9 in the author's modification) the process of "creeping commitment" occurs and there is a diminishing likelihood of new vendors gaining access to the buying situation". By the time Britcraft sales effort was in full swing, competitors aircraft had already been demonstrated to the NAF and several NAF personnel had become Fokker oriented. Also Fokker had been able to specify conditions for the "paper comparison" of the aircraft. The conditions specified inevitably favoured Fokker.

3. Discriminate between the sales roles of the people in Britcraft. Did Britcraft's structure help or hinder their sales campaign? How could it be changed for the better?

The sales roles played by the various parties shows weaknesses in the sales campaign and sales organisation. Britcraft entered negotiations late in the buying process. They did not directly influence the NAF's decision to re-equip nor did they find out about the prospect through their own channels. Similarly Britcraft did not initiate contact. Noticeably there is no Britcraft Regional Sales Executive for Europe as the region is the responsibility of the home office. Besides monitoring developments in a country and locating sales opportunities the agent should act as a source of detailed information on prospective customers and a means of contact with key individuals. In terms of contacts with the NAF, Air Commander Netherton seems a good choice and his work was definitely fundamental to the achievements of the company in the later stages of the buying process. However, the late appointment of an "active" agent could easily have excluded Britcraft from the race before they even knew it was being run. It is also evident that the agent's contacts outside the NAF were limited, giving Britcraft access to "buyers" and "influencers" within the buying centre but not the critical "deciders".

Britcraft's structure actually hinder their sales campaign. The complexity of negotiations, commercially, technically and in terms of number of people involved, demands close central control and supervision of the sales team. There are only two groups that are likely to have consistent contact in depth with the buying centre. These are the agents and the sales executives. As the agent is not an employee of the company and is geographically remote from the sales team, the continuity must be provided by the sales executive. During the NAF sales campaign several sales executives became involved in the sale. This is likely to have confused communications with the buying centre and within the sales team. The re-occurring confusion concerning off-set is probably as much due to the changes in Britcraft personnel as the Country's seemingly inconsistent demands. The confusion of sales executive control and involvement is partly due to the "creeping commitment" of senior sales management to the sale. As the sales campaign develops increasingly senior sales managers become involved in the sale to such an extent that the original Area Sales manager responsible for the prospect is relegated to a minor role. There are a number of rational and less rational personal reasons why the "creeping commitment" of senior management may occur.

It is sensible to use the most able executive in a critical sales campaign. Presumably the senior management is the most able and can draw upon more experience than junior colleagues and as such are more likely to be able to close a sale. As a sale progresses decisions may be demanded that junior executives are not able to take. The opening stages of a sales campaign are more likely to involve getting information, technical issues and developing contacts. Later financial and commercial issues are likely to be paramount. As a sale progresses senior people may be playing increasingly active roles in the buying centre. It is logical to match senior executives in the buying centre with sales team members of similar status. Senior management may feel it necessary that they keep tabs on their subordinates to make sure that they keep on the right track.

4. What characterises the sale described in the case? What were Britcraft's main failings and strengths? Do you think they will win the sale or are they too out of touch with the needs of the NAF and the Country's government? What could they do at this late stage? Is it still "Britain's turn"?

The sale is characterised by the importance of negotiating skills. Throughout, NAF shows considerable negotiating skills. Even though NAF personnel seem to favour quickly the Jetprop they continue to apply pressure concerning price, performance and multi-role capability of the aircraft. Also the rapid conversion of the NAF personnel to being "Jetprop oriented" shows the products own strengths and the technical sales ability of the sales team. The extent to which price haggling is of minor importance during the later stages of the buying process is shown by NAF's rapid acceptance of the large price increase made necessary by the aircraft being supplied from a later, more expensive batch. A primary lesson that has to be learned when selling expensive capital equipment is the need to be able to give a series of concessions to buying-centre participants. It is necessary to give concessions to the right people at the right time and to keep something in reserve. The seeming impasse at the end of the case relates to the level of offset agreed. Offset arrangements are becoming an increasingly common part of large international contracts. At the time of the case such deals were not as common as they were later to become and Britcraft had no mechanism for dealing with them. Offset cost money to negotiate, arrange, monitor and control. They also frequently necessitate non-optimum purchasing and manufacturing. Given the high cost of arranging offset it is likely that offsets will force a small contract like the one proposed for the NAF to be unprofitable.

Britcraft's main failings are; the lack of an active agent in the Country at the beginning of the case; a lack of continuity of sales executive involvement; lack of co-ordination between the groups of Britcraft personnel operating in the Country simultaneously; confusion concerning the offset. Britcraft's strengths are; continuity of high level contact; military sales team; selection of a suitable agent; demonstration of aircraft; gaining NAF support for aircraft; teamwork in Britcraft; British Embassy support.

Although it looks at the end of the case as though the sale was slipping away, the NAF did eventually purchase a fleet of aircraft from Britcraft. The hitch in the buying process was at the Ministerial level and well out of reach of the sales team's contacts. One can imagine the Minister for Defence whose experts had recommended the Jetprop on technical grounds being at loggerheads with the Minister for Economic Affairs who preferred the Fokker for national economic reasons. Aid eventually came from the HM Government who fought for existing contracts placed by themselves and Rolls-Royce in the Nation's aerospace and defence industries being accepted as part of the offset. This, together with further concessions on price and an agreement to train NAF operations personnel on a long-term basis, finally secured success.

Teaching Suggestions

On first reading, this case may appear rather complicated to students. Thus, it is important to help them sort through the information and organise key issues. Of course, an understanding of the product is also critical to the salesforce discussion, so the instructor should spend some time clarifying the product and its uses. Because the case involves an industrial product, it is also suited to Chapter 8, Business Markets and Business Buyer Behaviour.

Overview Case VII
Bang & Olufsen: Different By Design

Synopsis

In 1983 Bang & Olufsen, a Danish manufacturer of stylish consumer electronics were experiencing major problems in penetrating the huge German market. They need to decide whether to further penetrate or get out from the German market. Their sales have grown by less than 3 per cent over the last 5 years. As their turnover was so small, dealers were not too concerned with Bang & Olufsen. The small turnover also resulted in the German market not being of particular interest to the Danish parent company. The US, Canada and Japan showed growth and in light of the high value of the dollar, US looked profitable and more appealing. Bang & Olufsen had to decide whether to concentrate on these markets or re-establish itself in the German market. In Europe, specialised dealerships were becoming less popular. The trend was towards highly competitive, hard selling mass distributors. Bang & Olufsen were using a push strategy where they try to get dealers to stock their products and put them on display. In 1984 a new management team started analysing the situation and decided that Germany had to be a healthy market since it part of the EU and one of the world's largest markets for consumer electronics. The company realised that a new marketing strategy was needed, the target market had to be redefined and a new organisation was required.

Bang & Olufsen used the ACE pan-European segmentation of 10 sociocultural groups and selected those groups which were curious, open-minded and had the desire to learn new things. Bang & Olufsen also thought that these people are more likely to pay high prices for consumer electronics. In order to target the segments, Bang & Olufsen developed a new promotion strategy, realising the importance of creating public awareness of the company. They took into account the media and the quality of the medium and also analysed the target group purchase motives. Bang & Olufsen also understood that the relationships with the dealer base needed to be revised. Rather than basing the relationship on historical experience, the new strategy contended that dealers would be assessed by performance. The company now concentrated on pulling demand from consumers through creating awareness as well as emphasising the importance of decent display areas to increase turnover. Dealers were to have new partnership agreements with Bang & Olufsen to ensure commitment and loyalty. It was important that dealers would project high quality to match the quality of the company's products.

Teaching Objectives

1. Provide the student with an opportunity to distinguish between the pull and push strategy in action.

2. Provide the student with an opportunity to determine how they would turn around an existing marketing strategy.

3. Allow the student to deal with changes in the cultural environment and understand how those changes affect promotion strategies.

Study Questions

1. Distinguish between the old push and the new pull policies followed by Bang & Olufsen. Why do you think the push strategy was not working? Is it likely that the pull strategy will increase sales significantly without making Bang & Olufsen's products more attractive to German consumers?

Bang & Olufsen had been employing a push strategy prior to 1984. This strategy focused on pushing the products onto independent dealers with the aid of special offers and reduced prices. It was then the responsibility of the dealer to sell the products to potential customers who entered their stores at whatever price they saw it. The lack of direct marketing and advertising support made the sale of Bang & Olufsen's products difficult for the retailers due to low consumer awareness. This was further impended by their own low level of product knowledge. The small number of sales of Bang & Olufsen's products made the retailers reluctant to allocate showroom space. The new pull strategy concentrated on raising consumer awareness by targeted advertising campaigns and forming partnerships with dealers to ensure display space, staff training to guarantee good product knowledge and external identification to further raise consumer awareness in the high street. By giving dealers an incentive to make their products the focus of attention in these outlets, the target group of potential customers would be more likely to buy Bang & Olufsen's products in preference to the other brands available in these stores.

Studenst should mention that the failure of Bang & Olufsen's push strategy may be due to the following reasons; (1) The company's German operation is far too remote from the sales network. The dealers do not get enough support from the company in terms of technical support, availability of goods, advertising tools, training and promotion techniques; (2) The channel members may not have adequate knowledge of Bang & Olufsen's products. They may also lack confidence in the company's products; (3) There may have been conflicting marketing, pricing and service strategies between dealers that resulted in customer confusion and lack of trust. In addition there was emphasis on the transaction rather than on customer relations; (4) The retailers were free to interpret end-user or consumer needs. They may have not been able to recognise the need or even misinterpret it; (5) Due to the push strategy, there was low awareness of the company and therefore no demand for its products. This has led the company's products only account a very small percentage of dealers turnover, who therefore did not care whether they stocked the products or not; (6) The company did not promote the products in order to create awareness. The marketing strategies were dependent on the individual dealers. However, it may have been easier for dealers to attract consumers through promoting well-known brands; (7) It was not enough to get products on the shelves. In a highly competitive German market there was a need to create public awareness of the products and earn people's trust and confidence. Such products may involve a relatively high risk as they are expected to be fairly durable and reliable. It is unlikely that people would pay high prices for unknown brands of which the reliability may not be clear; (8) Bang & Olufsen may have failed to motivate their distributors. They were not providing up-to-date product or company information. The company failed to appreciate and understand the distributors' problems. There were no attractive financial incentives and insufficient salespeople to provide support for the distributors' sales force. The lack of control and communication between the company and the distribution channels, the unidentified target customer group and lack of direction and goal setting of the company, all led to the failure of using the push policy within the company.

In the short term, consecutive advertising or promotion campaigns under the new pull strategy may generate increased but limited sales, especially from the more innovative consumers which are classified as constantly trying to bring pleasure and new experience into their lives. However, as the Germans are relatively conservative in nature, it may not be easy to persuade them to buy the products especially those people who have knowledge of the products and realise the products have already been in the market for some time. In order to generate long term increased market share, it is essential for Bang & Olufsen to keep innovating and employ the latest technology. Significant long term increase in sales can only be achieved if the company could gain success in the following buyer readiness states; (1) Awareness; (2) Knowledge; (3) Liking; (4) Preference; (5) Conviction; (6) Purchase. Ask students to explain what these states are and then ask them to give some examples what Bang & Olufsen can do in each of the state.

2. How is the new pull strategy being funded? In what way is the new strategy attractive or not attractive to distributors? What compensates the retailers for having a lower margin and investing more in Bang & Olufsen's stock and display area?

Based on the case, the new pull strategy is being partly funded by cutting dealers' margin from 38% to 33%. In addition, it is indicated that dealers would be required to participate in promotional activities and would be obliged to stock a certain range of products and produce a minimum turnover. Yet the increase in sales should more than cover the cutting of margins and absorption of promotion costs. In addition, the increased sales would cover the costs of employing more staff at Bang & Olufsen Germany.

Some students might say the new strategy looks attractive to the distributors due to the fact that the company is more committed. Since the company is involved in the promotion and advertising they will understand the market situation better and therefore be able to appreciate the situation or the difficulties of the distributors. They can work together to solve the problems and could also speed up the process of responding to market changes. The new partnership agreement offered a better assurance to the distributors in terms of the supply, service/installation provision, etc. The partnership approach calls for frequent interaction between the producer and the distributors to develop a spirit of mutual understanding and co-operation. The anticipated increase in sales will increase the dealers' turnover. In addition, the selling and identification with Bang & Olufsen will make the dealers to be perceived as up market stores. Dealing with Bang & Olufsen means dealing with the latest technology and exclusive products. Comprehensive marketing in co-operation with dealers will also promote the dealers' stores themselves. In contrast the new strategy has some aspects that may not be appealing to the dealers. The cutting of the dealers' margins by 5 per cent is less attractive especially to those distributors who used to have high rewards from the company due to their historical relationships. In addition, they will not be judged by performance in terms of turnover and profits they generate. This may be pressurising and uncomfortable. The reward by performance means that they need to put a lot of effort in order to deal with Bang & Olufsen. The new strategy requires dealers to sacrifice more time and effort than in the past. This may mean that they need to employ more staff or cut down their efforts on other brands. In addition, according to the new strategy dealers will have partnership agreements under which more commitment is required in terms of presentation, display, training, exterior identification, stocking a minimum range of products and having a minimum turnover. This requires the dealers to carefully evaluate the attractiveness of the new strategy in terms of benefits and drawbacks. Conflicts may arise between the dealers and the company. The company may think a particular promotional mix should be used to promote the products, while it may not be suitable for the dealers. In addition, dealers may also have agreements with other companies, that may have different image and perception.

The lower margin and the required investment in Bang & Olufsen's stock and display are by the retailer can be compensated by the following factors; (1) Selling and identifying with Bang & Olufsen's products "makes you an up-market store", thus contributing to the better perception of the store by the public; (2) Anticipated increase in sales will compensate reduced margins. The anticipated capturing of the market share would justify the increased display and stock holding. Moreover, as the company will earn consumers' trust and will become highly reputable, the large display area and exterior identification with Bang & Olufsen will contribute to the dealers' image; (3) Joint promotion means that the dealers are also being promoted at the same time. The dealers do not need to promote themselves as much thus reducing the cost of advertising on their own; (4) Even if customers do not buy Bang & Olufsen products they may purchase a competitor's product thus increasing overall sales for the outlet; (5) The company will be more involved. The company's staff will be more externally oriented and will assist in technical and sales training. The company will be actively promoting the quality and loyalty with the dealers; (6) The binding partnership agreement provides assurance of a long-term commitment of the company to the retailers.

3. How does the target market influence Bang & Olufsen's promotional strategy? Since there are so few of the target customers in Germany, would it pay Bang & Olufsen to target other groups in that market? Does it seem likely that the European market segments into ten equally sized groups that are similar across all European culture?

Bang & Olufsen have selected the target market to be the northern sociocultural groups identified by the ACE research. These groups have attitudes and interests harmonic with Bang & Olufsen's philosophy; they influence public opinion, more frequent buyers and are likely to pay high prices for these products. They are generally curious, open-minded and have a strong desire to learn new things. They welcome change and are innovative. The target market's influence on Bang & Olufsen's promotional strategy is apparent in the choice of media. The company has therefore initiated a two pronged attack. One advertising campaign seeks to increase consumer awareness, this is achieved by advertising in high-profile, general interest magazines which are read by the majority of the population. More specific advertising appears in special interest publications most likely to be read by the target groups they are hoping to reach. By combining these two separate medium, brand awareness can be built and the target segment stimulated.

By advertising in general interest magazines, Bang & Olufsen have raised consumer awareness and by introducing designated dealers in the high street they have made their product range available to the whole market. It would be pointless for them to specifically target any other segment of the market as they have established the most likely purchasers and are targeting them directly. Other groups in the market have easy access to Bang & Olufsen's product range through their distribution network. The trained staff in these stores should be able to give any necessary information required by potential customers in order for them to decide whether to purchase or not.

Whilst the ten, equally sized market segments identified through market research may provide a picture of the overall population across Europe, it is highly unlikely that they are similar across European countries. For example, the case suggests that the percentage of Bang & Olufsen's target market (A, B1 & B2) varies across the different countries. The European average is 30% while the percentage in the individual country varies. In Germany the target market only accounts for 17% of the population. In France for 35% while Italy for 37%. Some countries may not comprise all of the groups while others may comprise more groups. In addition, due to inherent cultural differences and the existing socio-economic differences between the various European countries, it is unlikely that all the countries can be divided into the same groups or classified into the same groups. It may be that people of a certain economic class in Germany do not possess the same characteristics of people in the same economic class in France or Spain. Moreover, a high economic class in the UK for example may not be considered as such in Germany. Furthermore, the population of the different countries in Europe is also different. Thus it is not likely that there will be the same sized groups in all countries.

4. Would you "double or quit" the German market? Why were Bang & Olufsen more attracted to the United States and other markets than to Germany, and were they right in being so? What is the rationale behind Bang & Olufsen's new marketing and distribution strategy for Europe? Do you think it will work in Germany?

Students will highlight differing angles to the first question. Some will say that before deciding to double or quit they need to consider the company's objectives and resources. Others will say that the "double or quit" phrase is a very rigid statement. Time scale has been omitted. It is felt that a time scale of between three and five years should be allowed for the pull strategy to be developed. More specifically some will mention that it would be unwise for Bang & Olufsen to quit the German market for several reasons; (1) Germany is one of the world's largest markets for consumer electronics and the size of the economy, population and purchasing power means that the German market should have great potential for the future; (2) As a key member of the European community Germany may well be essential to the company's long term development and success; (3) The tendency of German consumers to be more conservative than many other Europeans may also means that Bang & Olufsen have a greater opportunity to build greater brand loyalty in Germany than elsewhere; (4) The country's close geographical proximity to Denmark means that distribution, marketing and shipping costs will be lower than for many other markets. Be prepared for some very differing viewpoints for this section.

Bang & Olufsen were more attracted to the US, Canada and Japan because of the high growth in consumer electronics in these countries and the high value of the dollar. These markets appeared to be potentially profitable, the German market accounted for only 3% of the parent company's turnover and was therefore deemed to be insignificant and unprofitable. Bang & Olufsen initially failed to realise that the German market was small and unprofitable because of the selling methods it had employed there. The outlets operated in many of the countries around the world had been acquired as bankrupt agents. These had been specialised distribution outlets which could no longer compete with the volume retailers. Some students will suggest that in order for Bang & Olufsen to compete in a country with a growing consumer electronics industry it would have to adopt similar strategies to their mass distribution competitors.

The rationale behind Bang & Olufsen new marketing and distribution strategy for Europe is that the company needs to adapt to a changing environment, including changes in both the electronics market and in consumer behaviour. More specifically they have adopted a new strategy of marketing their products to the target market which they have identified as the most likely to buy their products coupled with a programme to enhance consumer awareness. They have also opened dedicated high street retail outlets which further increase brand awareness, provide information and service as well as facilitate product sales. The whole aim of this strategy is to build brand strength and form relationships with their customers, it is hoped that satisfaction with the product, its quality and exclusivity and also their service in the store, will encourage customers to purchase more products from their range both now and in the future. Bang & Olufsen aim to meet the needs of those people seeking an alternative to the mass-produced products currently available in the trade.

Again differing viewpoints will be presented by students. Some possible views; (1) If the above strategy is applied in Germany, an effective and efficient promotion tactics together with the strong distribution network could most probably have a significant effect on the market. However, there is a hindrance as far as the German market is concerned. According to the statistics only 17 per cent of the population will be the company's target group. It is comparatively low in volume in relation to other countries such as 35 per cent in France and 37 per cent in Italy. The company might want to consider widening its target group in Germany, through another marketing mix. Also it may be worthwhile to consider groups C1,C2,C3 and C4 in Germany and study their characteristics and interests; (2) It will work in Germany but it is wise to research the market first and make any necessary modifications accordingly; (3) It will work in Germany but follow-up is salient; (4) Yes, provided that Bang & Olufsen can maintain their standards of quality, innovation and customer service it should be possible to foster relationships with customers which will prove beneficial to the company.

Teaching Suggestions

This case study could be used with the Product Chapter (Chapter 13), Promotion Chapter (Chapter 18) and Global Chapter (Chapter 5).

Jokes and Quotes

The three golden rules of selling are: make lots of calls, know. your products and know how to miss a one metre put by 5 cm.

Sales resistance is the triumph of mind over patter.
ANON

Sure I lie, but it's more like...tinting. It's all just negotiating theatrics.
IRVING AZOFF

It is nought, it is nought saith the buyer but when he is gone his way, then he will boasteth.
THE BIBLE

I detest life insurance agents; they always argue that some day I shall die, which is not so.
STEPHEN BUTLER-LEACOCK

It's a well-known proposition that you know who's going to win a negotiation: it's he who pauses the longest.
ROBERT HOLMES A COURT

If A is a success in life then *A* equals *x* plus *y* plus *z*. Work is *x*; *y* is play and *z* is keeping your mouth shut.
ALBERT EINSTEIN

Understanding is the beginning of approving.
ANDREW GIDE

Inequality of knowledge is the key to the sale.
DEIL O. GUSTAFSON

It's a salesman on the phone', the secretary told the boss. I'm busy, said the boss 'Put him on hold with the Muzak tape for about ten minutes, and then if he's still there, I'll talk to him'.
JOKE

Salesman: I only got three orders this week. Get out, stay out and don't come back!
JOKE

What a salesman - he could sell underarm deodorant to the Venus de Milo!
JOKE

A rep stranded by torrential rain and unable to continue his round of calls. He wired head office, "Trapped by floods. Send instructions".
The reply came "Annual leave granted, commencing today".
JOKE

When a man is trying to sell you something, don't imagine he is that polite all the time.
EDGAR WATSON HOWE

A salesman with bad breath is dear at any price.
ELBERT HUBBARD

Salesmen are decent, but buyers do not have to be. Buyers are inhuman, without bounds, passion or a sense of humour. Happily they never reproduce...all buyers go to hell.
ELBERT HUBBARD

Many a man has lost a sale because his necktie did not match his socks
FRANK MCKINNEY HUBBARD

Look out for the fellow who lets you do all the talking.
FRANK MCKINNEY HUBBARD

Whenever you're sitting across from some important person, always picture him sitting there in a suit of long red underwear. That's the way I always operated in business.
JOSEPH P. KENNEDY

Ours is the country where, in order to sell your product, you don't so much point out its merits as you first work like hell to sell yourself.
LOUIS KRONENBERGER

Nobody can blame this man... For a salesman, there is no rock bottom to the life. He don't put a bolt to a nut, he don't tell you the law or give you medicine. He's a man way out there in the blue, riding on a smile and a shoeshine. And when they start not smiling back - that's an earthquake. And then you get yourself a couple of spots on your hat, and you're finished. Nobody dast blame this man. A salesman is got to dream, boy. It comes with the territory.
ARTHUR MILLER

Appearances count; get a sun lamp... maintain an elegant address even if you live in the attic; patronise posh watering holes even if you have to nurse your drink. Never niggle when you're short of cash.
ARISTOTLE ONASSIS

He who findeth fault, meaneth to buy.
PROVERB

How to win friends and influence people.
SLOGAN

Everyone lives by selling something.
ROBERT LOUIS STEVENSON

If you can't convince 'em, confuse 'em.
HARRY S. TRUMAN

Part VIII

Place

Chapter 21

Placing Products:

Distribution Channels and Logistics Management

Chapter Objectives

After reading this chapter, you should be able to:

1. Explain why companies use distribution channels and the functions these channels perform.
2. Discuss how channel members interact and how they organise to carry out the work of the channel.
3. Identify the main distribution channel options open to an organisation.
4. Explain how businesses select, motivate and evaluate channel members.
5. Isolate the key issues managers face when setting up physical distribution systems.

Chapter Overview

Distribution channel decisions are among the most complex and challenging decisions facing a firm. Each channel system creates a different level of sales and costs. Once a distribution channel has been chosen, the firm must usually stick with it for a long time. The chosen channel strongly affects, and is affected by, the other elements in the marketing mix. Each firm needs to identify alternative ways to reach its market. Available means vary from direct selling to using one, two, three, or more intermediary channel levels. Channel design begins with assessing customer channel-service needs and company channel objectives and constraints. The company then identifies the major channel alternatives in terms of the types of intermediaries, the number of intermediaries, and the channel responsibilities of each. Just as the marketing concept is receiving increased recognition, more business firms are paying attention to the physical distribution concept. The task is to design physical distribution systems that minimise the total cost of providing a desired level of customer services.

Teaching Notes

Refer to the following pages for teaching notes.

Distribution Channel Functions

Transparency PM 21-1 relates to the material on p.810

Distribution Channels

A distribution channel is a set of interdependent organisations involved in the process of making a product or service available for use or consumption by the consumer or industrial user.

Distribution Channel Functions

1. Information

This function involves gathering and distributing marketing research and intelligence about the environment for planning purposes.

2. Promotion

This involves developing and spreading persuasive communications about an offer.

3. Contact

Contact involves finding and communicating with prospective buyers.

4. Matching

This function consists of shaping and fitting the offer to the buyer's needs by manufacturing, grading, assembling, and packaging.

5. Negotiation

This involves reaching an agreement on price and other terms.

6. Physical Distribution

This function consists of the transporting and storing of goods.

7. Financing

This function addresses the acquiring and using of funds to cover the costs of channel work.

8. Risk Taking

This function assumes the risk of carrying out the channel work.

Tip

The use of scanner technology has dramatically changed this function in the last few years. Ask students its impact on information management.

Notes for PM 21-1

Channel Behaviour and Organisation

Transparency PM 21-2 relates to the material on pp.812-820.

Channel Conflict

Horizontal conflict occurs between firms at the same level of the channel. Dealers and franchises of the same firm within the same market may argue about each other's competitive practices. Vertical conflict refers to problems between firms at different levels in the channel.

Channel Organisation

Channel organisation as traditional channel organisation lacks a specified controlling authority, new approaches have been developed.

Vertical Marketing Systems

Consist of producers, wholesalers, and retailer acting in as a unified system. Three main types of VMS are:

1. Corporate VMS

Combines successive stages of production and distribution under a single ownership.

2. Contractual VMS

Consists of independent firms at different levels of production and distribution to obtain more economies and sales than members could achieve alone. Three types of contractual VMS are wholesaler-sponsored chain, retailer co-operative, franchise organisation.

3. Administered VMS

Co-ordinates distribution by the power of one of its member not by contract or ownership.

Innovations in Channel Organisation

Horizontal Marketing Systems

Formed when two or more companies at one level join to pursue a new marketing opportunity. These may be temporary arrangements such as a joint promotion or more permanent distribution agreements.

Multichannel Marketing Systems

Utilised more than one channel to reach customers more effectively and with greater flexibility.

Notes for PM 21-2

Channel Alternatives

Transparency PM 21-3 relates to the material on pp.824-826.

Types of Middlemen

1. Company Salesforce

This approach expands the company's presence in the market by assigning its own people territories to sell the products.

2. Manufacturer's Agency

This approach hires independent firms whose salesforce markets related products from many companies. Agents seeking to best satisfy their customers can honestly represent each product well.

3. Industrial Distributors

This approach contracts with existing distributors in different regions who will buy and resell a product line.

Number of Middlemen

1. Intensive Distribution

Utilises as many outlets as possible and is especially appropriate for convenience goods and common raw materials.

2. Exclusive Distribution

Consists of a very limited number of outlets hold all the rights to distribute a product line. This strategy is appropriate for many high prestige goods. Distributor selling effort is usually very strong.

3. Selective Distribution

Uses more than one outlet per market but less than all available outlets. This strategy gains good market coverage and gains better than average selling effort.

Responsibilities of Channel Members

Channel members need to agree on price policies, conditions of sale, territory rights, and the specific services to be performed by each party.

Tip

Ask students to name some examples of products that fall in the categories of intensive, exclusive and selective distribution.

Notes for PM 21-3

Channel Management

Transparency PM 21-4 relates to the material on pp.829-831.

Channel Management Decisions

1. Selecting Channel Members

Choosing middlemen will vary in difficulty by product and producer. Very large and well-known companies often have more qualified middlemen seeking to carry their products than the company can effectively use. Some new products will be resisted by existing channels and may require adopting new channel members to carry the line.

2. Motivating Channel Members

Channel members must be motivated to perform. Positive motivators come from high margins, special deals, premiums, co-operative advertising allowances, display allowances, and sales contests. Negative motivators may include threatening margins, delaying delivery, or ending the relationship. Long term co-operation is enhanced by distribution programming which involves building a planned, professionally managed, VMS that meets all channel member needs.

3. Evaluating Channel Members

Assessing channel members requires regular measurement of performance against established criteria such as sales quotas, inventory levels, customer delivery time, training, and overall customer service for each channel member. Effective channel management rewards superior performance and seeks to improve substandard performance in a co-operative professional partnership. Channel member replacement should be used as a last resort when sincere efforts to improve performance have not succeeded.

Notes for PM 21-4

Physical Distribution Decisions

These notes relate to the material on pp.831-836.

Note to Instructor - Transportation is covered separately on the following transparency.

Nature of Distribution

Costs

In distribution stem from factors other than just size. How products are transported, stored, sorted, inventoried, ordered, and tracked can all affect distribution costs over and above the sheer volume being distributed. Modern facilities utilising technology to help innovate what it means to physically distribute goods both save on costs and become a viable promotional tool in providing customer service.

Objectives

A key operational problem is balancing customer service and distribution costs. Distribution must be co-ordinated with delivering customer service throughout the entire distribution system.

Order Processing

Processing orders is an area of distribution that benefits from the application of computer technology. Innovative applications of hardware and software can streamline order processing by connecting the salesperson with dispatchers and warehouses.

Warehousing

Storage of products to best meet demand requires decisions on stocking locations, estimation of time to be stored and distinguishing between storage warehouse needs and distribution centres utilising automation to move goods quickly.

Inventory

The cost of holding inventory requires developing accurate knowledge on when to order and how much to order to meet demand but not overburden inventory processing capacity.

Transportation

These notes relate to the material on pp.836-839.

Rail

Rail is the largest carrier mode with 37% of the total cargo shipped. Rail is especially cost effective for large amounts of bulk products shipped over long distances.

Truck

Trucks account for some 25% of the total cargo shipped. Trucks are the largest movers of within city shipping. Trucks are highly flexible in routing and scheduling. Trucks are an efficient short-haul mode.

Water

Water is very inexpensive for shipping high bulk nonperishable goods but is also the slowest transportation mode.

Pipeline

Pipelines are specialised modes for such goods as oil and natural gas. Pipelines are usually owned by companies that also own the raw materials being piped.

Air

Air is the most expensive mode of transportation but also the quickest. Extremely perishable goods, high-value, low-bulk, and time-sensitive goods often require air transport.

Choosing Transportation Modes

Deregulation

Deregulation in the 1970s of the transportation industry has made each mode more flexible, competitive, and responsive to customer needs. In choosing transportation mode, shippers consider up to five criteria:

1. Speed- measured in door-to-door delivery time.
2. Dependability- meeting schedules on time.
3. Capability - the ability to handle various products.
4. Availability- the number of geographic points served.
5. Cost- usually in per ton-mile.

Containerisation

Containerisation consists of putting goods in boxes or trailers that are designed for easy transfer between two transportation modes.

1. Piggyback describes the use of rail and trucks.
2. Fishyback refers to the use of water and trucks.
3. Tranship involves water and rail.
4. Airtruck combines air and trucks.

Comments on Discussing the Issues

1. Any one publisher would have more difficulty than the Book-of-the-Month Club (BOMC) in directly marketing its books to the public, because it would not have the economies of scale that the BOMC derives from offering the books of many different publishers. The BOMC performs such functions as finding customers, promoting its services, and distributing the books, more efficiently than a publisher could.

   BOMC members get book reviews, discounts on purchases, credits toward large discounts on selected books, and occasional gifts with purchases, in addition to the convenience of home delivery. The BOMC is part of a distribution channel that is able to compete with the large bookselling chains because it serves at least some customers' needs better than the chains do.

2. Franchising is growing so rapidly because it has so much to offer. Many people want to be their own boss, but they do not have the resources or know-how to build a business from the ground up. By becoming franchisees, they are able to work for themselves while benefiting from the guidance and experience of the franchiser. Franchising also allows economies of scale in purchasing and in promoting the total chain, to the benefit of each franchisee. Financially, franchising offers potentially high returns on investment: The median ROI in the second year of operations among *Venture's* Franchise 100 was 44.6 per cent; among service industry franchises the average return was 91.5 per cent.

   Franchising works only when franchisers and franchisees deal with each other in good faith. The franchiser has many forms of power over its affiliates, and franchisee groups have been formed in an effort to balance the power and support possible litigation. (In the US, One Burger Chef franchisee was awarded $14 million in a lawsuit claiming that parent company General Foods had forced a modernisation plan on franchisees to make it easier to sell the Burger Chef chain to Hardee's.) But at its best, when the expertise and national visibility of the franchiser are combined with the entrepreneurial spirit of the franchisee, franchising is a very successful form of vertical marketing system.

3. Varadarajan and Rajaratnam discuss a variety of environmental and organisational factors stimulating the emergence of "symbiotic" marketing arrangements: advances in and convergence of current technologies, emerging technologies, regulation and deregulation, complementary and compensatory strengths and weaknesses among partners, risk pooling, resource considerations, and complementary asset deployment/redeployment decisions. This article gives many examples of symbiotic relationships, and more can be found in practically every issue of such publications as *Business Week* and *Advertising Age*.

   In thinking of opportunities for companies to work together symbiotically, students should look for logical connections between the independent companies that allow both to benefit from the partnership. In the US when McDonald's works with Sears to market "McKids" clothing, for example, both firms benefit. But when Oldsmobile sponsored a $30 million tie-in with McDonald's $110 million Monopoly game, the promotion was a flop because it appealed to McDonald's customers who were not in Oldsmobile's target audience. The promotion drew 750,000 people to Oldsmobile showrooms, but "the calibre of people who keep coming into the showroom couldn't buy a bumper off one of these cars," according to a general manager of a dealership. "They have no intention of buying a car; they just want the game pieces" (quoted in "Olds, Big Mac Tie Falls Flat," *Advertising Age*, June 13, 1988, p. 8).

4. These personal-computer customers have different lot size needs, different attitudes toward market decentralisation and waiting time, and different demands for product variety and service backup. At one time, IBM sold to all three groups: to consumers through its own retail outlets, and to retailers and industrial buyers through its own salesforce. It later decided that operating its own retail outlets was impractical and chose to concentrate on the other groups.

5. **(a)** Piaget watches are priced as high as £1500,000, so they require exclusive distribution in order to support the image and customer service required.

(b) Lexus and most other car dealers use selective distribution to ensure that dealers will put a strong effort into selling the car.

(c) KitKat chocolate bars are sold in stores everywhere.

(d) Haagen Daz ice cream are sold at a premium price in selected stores

6. The consequences of stock-outs can be considerable. The best that can happen is that a sale is delayed; at worst, a customer can be lost forever due to adoption of a competing product bought at the time of the stockout. Other possible consequences include customer resentment at the inconvenience of not being able to buy the desired product and the effort of writing and redeeming a rain check for a later purchase.

Despite these problems, few companies would aim to maintain enough inventory to avoid all stock-outs. Costs rise at an increasing rate as service levels approach 100%, so companies must attempt to find a good balance between inventory carrying costs and the costs of running out of stock.

Comments on Applying the Concepts

1. Factory outlet stores are an increasingly popular channel of distribution. Many manufacturers have begun to operate their own stores, which serve as a way to liquidate overstocks of slow-moving items, discontinued styles, and second-quality goods. These stores pose minimal competition to the manufacturer's normal retailers for several reasons. First, they stock only less desirable items—old styles, damaged goods, and the like. Second, their range of stock is limited to what needs to be liquidated—a shopper looking for a specific item is unlikely to find it. Third, the stores are limited in number and often inconveniently located.

   These stores have two main reasons that support their operation. First, they allow a manufacturer to profitably liquidate merchandise that would otherwise have very limited value. Second, they allow a manufacturer to control the selection, pricing and merchandising of these liquidated goods.

   There are few disadvantages to operating these stores. They do cause some minor channel conflict from retailers who see the factory stores as competitors. Operating stores is generally not a part of the manufacturer's mission, yet it requires investment and development of skills which do not contribute directly to the corporation's main business.

2. This is an interesting exercise which requires some "reading between the lines." Authorised dealers often advertise the fact that they are authorised, and the legitimate importers help with this. The legitimate European Nikon importer, for example, has developed two names, complete with logos and promotional materials, for their authorised dealers. Thus, legitimate dealers can advertise that they are a "Nikon Advanced Systems Dealer" or a "Nikon Consumer Products Dealer." Other brands have similar programs, such as "Mamiya UK."

   Gray market goods may specifically note that they do not have a service warranty available. One other tip-off may be a price that is much lower than a legitimate dealer, with no claims made about being an authorised dealer. Typically there are significant price differences between legitimate goods (higher priced) and gray market goods (lower priced). The products are often identical, so consumers must decide the value of buying through a legitimate channel that can offer full service and support.

Case 21
Freixenet Cava:
Bubbles Down A New Way

Synopsis

Freixenet SA is an independent family run business and is owned by Jose Ferrer Sala who is both the chairman and president of the company. The company, based in Saint Sadurni d'Anoia, Spain, is the world's largest producer and exporter of cava (sparkling wine). Freixenet SA exports cava to over 100 countries world-wide and has a share of 70% of the total world exports. Cava is the generic name given to sparkling wine which is produced using a traditional brewing method known as "Methode Campenoise". Freixenet produces five cavas; Carta Nevada, Cordon Negro, Brut Nature, Brut Barroca and Brut Rose. Sales of cava have doubled in the last five years. Spain is now the second largest producer of sparkling wines, after Italy.

Freixenet began its international expansion at the end of World War II. The company targeted the United Kingdom first as part of its export strategy. The British company was called Direct Wine Supply (DWS). The international expansion involved three main phases. The first phase lasted over thirty years during which time DWS exported to several European countries. Freixenet also began to export to the United States following the same distribution system used in Europe. The second phase of expansion established two branches, one in the United States and the other in Germany. The third phase involved the setting up of two production facilities, one in the United States and the second in Mexico.

Teaching Objectives

1. Provide a vehicle for the discussion and analysis of direct and indirect channels of distribution.

2. Highlight the importance of channel decisions in development of the marketing mix.

3. Allow students to evaluate the proposed distribution systems.

Study Questions

1. Contrast Freixenet's entry into the US and UK markets. What went wrong in the UK market?

Students should compare and contrast entry into the US and UK markets. For the UK markets students should highlight the following. Following Jose Ferrer's initial market research which involved visiting several European countries, the UK market was the first to be targeted for export. This was mainly because of two reasons; (a) The UK's high consumption of Champagne; (b) The need to import because of lack of vineyards and local brands. Freixenet's initial distribution strategy involved an alliance with a sole channel intermediary in the shape of a UK distributor who would distribute all of their products. The rationale behind Freixenet's channel selection was based on an assumption that no one would buy from a Spanish distributor. This is quite an important market factor, as buyer behaviour dictates that British customers would not deal with a Spanish distributor, hence the company avoided possible conflict. Once the association with the first British distributor failed, another partnership was formed with two other associates, which also failed. As a result, Freixenet decided to take over the whole operation and established a new British company called Direct Wine Supply (DWS) to handle its entire UK distribution. For the US market students have to mention that Freixenet's entry into the US market followed the same strategy used in the UK market and involved a sole channel intermediary to distribute its product throughout the US. A national distributor was hired in New Jersey who would import their products and market them nationally. After a short period, due mainly to slow growth in the US market, Freixenet realised that a single representative could not adequately cover the whole country because of diverse regional markets. Having established a bridgehead in the market the sole importer was dropped in favour of the subsidiary company, Freixenet USA, Inc. The new approach emphasised decentralisation and allocated one import-distributor per state. As a result, the company's market presence intensified through a more concentrated market focus through each distributor.

There are several reasons why Freixenet did not do so well in the UK; (1) There was a bias towards French products by British consumers and Spanish products already had a poor image. Freixenet were trying to sell brand loyalty but this was bound to fail since the overall image and message did not emphasise Spanish products equal good products; (2) Freixenet's initial foray into the UK market failed due to disinterest shown by the UK distributor and hence they lost money. Instead of reanalysing their marketing strategy at this stage, Freixenet went down the same path with another two UK distributors. When this also failed for the same reasons Freixenet once again adopted the same channel of distribution but this time with their own distribution company. The company failed to change their marketing strategy quickly enough and went on the premise that one day it will work. In contrast, they did change their marketing strategy in the US after they had realised that there was a problem; (3) The company's entry into the UK market was based in the knowledge that the British consume large quantities of champagne. Cava really is not a substitute for champagne so selling into this market was likely to be difficult; (4) DWS was seen as a dead weight and would not work until a more creative and dynamic style of management was introduced; (5) The initial two channel intermediaries may have lost interest in the product due to bad channel management by Freixenet. The distributors lost interest in the product thus making loses. Most resellers try to maximise their own profits and if they cannot achieve this there is no motivation for them to continue selling the product. The producer must therefore take some action to improve product sales performance by either repositioning its price, image or promotion or provide the intermediary with incentives to continue selling the product.

2. Identify the different sorts of distribution and relationships Freixenet used in the US market? What are the advantages of each? How do Freixenet's control and investment change in each case?

This question requires students to outline the different distribution methods used by Freixenet in the US, analyse their respective advantages, control and investment. The first type is; Producer to national distributor to wholesalers/retailers. The advantages are; (1) Established distribution channels; (2) Importer is specialist in area of distribution. With regard to control, very little or no control of marketing, distribution, etc. In terms of investment, fixed percentage of landed price, marketing and distribution costs are the distributor's responsibility. The second type is; Producer to own distribution to import distributor to wholesalers/retailers. The advantages are: (1) More concentrated market focus therefore better market penetration; (2) Help given to importers; (3) More in tune with market requirements through market focus and communication with importers. Better control of product marketing. As far as investment is concerned, overhead of $600,000 to run office and no agent handling fee. The third type is Producer to producer (Paul Cheneau brand). The advantages are: (1) No marketing effort; (2) Use of excess production capacity. Here Freixenet will experience total loss of control of their customers. In terms of investment, they will incur production (plant and machinery) costs but little or no marketing costs. The fourth and last type is; Producer/Producer (Joint venture). The advantages are; (1) Share risk, investment and profits; (2) Combine marketing resources and share knowledge and expertise; (3) Increase market penetration. Control is shared equally between partners. Investment wise, all aspects of production and marketing investment are shared equally between partners.

3. Does the distribution system change with the segments serve? Does the different only apply to retailers used?

There are clearly four distinct price segments in the US market: (1) Below $4 - mostly wine produced using the granvas method and dominated by American and Italian brands; (2) $4 - $9 - dominated by Spanish and Italian wines; (3) $9 - $15 - dominated by Californian and Italian wines; (4) $15 plus - dominated by French champagnes. All of Freixenet products including those in the high price segment (Gloria Ferrer brand) are distributed through the same import distributors.

The difference is in the retailers that are supplied by the importers. There are three categories of retailers of wines in the US; (1) Retailers who specialise in wines and liquors; (2) Supermarkets and small retails shops; (3) "Clubs" patronised by wine connoisseurs. Freixenet's mid-range product, Cordon Negro will most likely to be sold in (1) and (2). Whereas, Gloria Ferrer may only be sold in (1) or (3), or just (3) dependent on the exclusivity/prestige associated with the product.

4. Is it wise for Freixenet to change its distribution system? What is the case for and against the existing and proposed distribution systems. How do Freixenet's relationship and controls change with the move from the existing to the proposed system?

A point students need to highlight is the fact that the new distribution system proposes a network of primary importers across the US who would not only be distributors but would also act as representatives of the company. Freixenet USA would look after all the advertising, ordering and public relation aspects for all the primary importers and assist in local advertising and promotional campaigns. The new system would eliminate a layer of management and promote a "family" approach with the primary importers. The new system will have a significant impact on current operations. One of the most significant of these is that the physical distribution system will become more complex. Freixenet USA will have to co-ordinate the transportation of its products to any of the fifty-two states. In the short term it probably would not be wise to change the existing system mainly because the company does not have the management experience necessary to implement the system. Also the risk here is, if the system fails, it could have disastrous effects on Freixenet's market share in the US. However, the benefits to be gained from the proposed system outweigh its disadvantages and would benefit the company overall long term growth and prosperity in the US market.

Case for and against the existing system. Case for the existing system: (1) Already established network of distribution channels; (2) Market already established and costs known - no risk; (3) Physical distribution is simpler. Case against the existing system; (1) Advertising not focused enough in terms of locality and product segmentation; (2) Advertising budget too low for current requirements; (3) Differences in goals - individual importers will have their own set of goals and may conflict with Freixenet's pricing, distribution and product imaging; (4) Distributors have little or no incentive to deliver the best service for Freixenet products. Case for and against the new system. Case for the new system; (1) Eliminate layer of management; (2) National wholesale network in favour of change; (3) Better strategy than competitors; (4) Share strategies and local expertise throughout importers network; (5) Reduce costs; (6) Importers could feedback information to Freixenet on sales and alert of ant problems; (7) Encourage importers to promote company and brand loyalty; (8) Help future growth and speed up expansion in the US market; (9) Increase control to Freixenet. Case against the new system; (1) Complex physical distribution required; (2) Management will need to be trained to implement new system; (3) Risk of failure could permanently damage the US market; (4) No financial benefit - money saved would be spent in organising Freixenet USA; (5) Would not be well received by the "old boy" network; (6) Increased administrative work i.e. processing orders, distribution, marketing etc.

Freixenet will have much more control over its distributors than with the existing system. The contract that each importer must sign includes several causes which "tie" the importer closer with Freixenet. Importers thus become the company's representatives and are made to feel part of the family.

Teaching Suggestions

To begin discussion, the instructor may wish to ask if any students in the class consider themselves to be in Freixenet's target market - sparkling wine. If so, the instructor can question the students about their buying decision processes. How do they buy their wines or beer? Where? How price sensitive are they? How often do they buy new brands? Such a discussion will give other students good insights for discussion of the case.

The instructor may also wish to ask other students if they simply buy name-brand wines or beer and ask them similar questions.

The instructor may also wish to have a group of students survey local wine dealers to see what brands they carry, price ranges, services offered, and so forth.

This case can also be used with the Pricing Chapters (16 and 17) and with the Promotion Chapters (18, 19 and 20).

Additional Information

In the UK, Freixenet DWS deals directly with both off and on customers; multiple grocers, multiple specialists, cash and carries, national and regional wholesalers and independent specialist and grocers. Customers buy either on a direct basis i.e. in containers directly from Spain or from UK stocks held by DWS with a national carrier, Cert Plc. This turnaround is largely due to hard selling and Cordon Negro is the company's best selling brand (and also the second largest selling sparkling wine in the UK) and receives above the line support with customer advertising in the national daily tabloid press.

Jokes and Quotes

Passenger to cab driver, "Why did they put the airport terminal so far out of town?"
Cab driver "I guess they thought it was a good idea to put it close to the runway".

It is well known what a middleman is: he is a man who bamboozles one party and plunders the other.
BENJAMIN DISRAELI

Entrepreneur: I've got a terrific new project. I'm going to open a bar in the middle of the Sahara Desert'.
Banker: That's a terrible idea. Nobody crosses the Sahara. You'll be lucky to get a single customer.'
Entrepreneur: Possibly, but if one does turn up, just think how thirsty he'll be!
JOKE

Good merchandise, even hidden, soon finds buyers.
TITUS MACIUS PLAUTUS

Game is cheaper in the market, than in the fields and woods.
PROVERB

Buy at a market and sell at home.
PROVERB

Fuel is not sold in a forest, nor fish on a lake.
CHINESE PROVERB

Creation comes before distribution - or there will be nothing to distribute!
AYN RAND

Stop me and buy one.
SLOGAN - WALL'S ICE CREAM VENDORS TRICYCLE

A speeding food salesman explained to the court "I was exceeding the speed limit because the hot puddings in the car for delivery had steamed up the speedometer".
TRUE STORY

Chapter 22

Placing Products:
Retailing and Wholesaling

Chapter Objectives

After reading this chapter, you should be able to:

1. Explain the roles of retailers and wholesalers in the distribution channel.
2. Describe the main types of retailers and give examples of each.
3. Identify the main types of wholesalers and give examples of these.
4. Explain the marketing decisions facing retailers and wholesalers.

Chapter Overview

Retailing and wholesaling consist of many organisations bringing goods and services from the point of production to the point of use. Retailers can be classified as store retailers and nonstore retailers. Store retailers can be further classified by the amount of service they provide, the product line sold, relative prices, control of outlets, and type of store cluster. Nonstore retailing consists of direct marketing, door-to-door selling, and automatic vending. Each retailer must make decisions about its target markets, product assortment and services, price, promotion, and place. Retailers need to choose target markets carefully and position themselves strongly. Wholesalers perform many functions including selling and promoting, buying and assortment building, bulk-breaking, warehousing, transporting, financing, risk bearing, supplying market information, and providing management services and advice. Wholesalers fall into three groups: merchant wholesalers, agents and brokers, and manufacturers' sales branches.

Teaching Notes

Refer to the following pages for teaching notes.

Retailing

Transparency PM 22-1 corresponds to Table 22.1 on p.857 and relates to the material on pp.856-877.

Definition

Retailing is all the activities in selling goods or services directly to final consumers for their personal, nonbusiness use. Retailers may be divided into two types: store retailing and non store retailing. Store retailing accounts for most retail business.

Store Retailing Classifications

Amount of Service

a. Self-service retailing

Used by convenience goods sellers and most discounters.

b. Limited-service retailers

Provide sales service to support shopping goods lines carried and may offer additional services such as credit.

c. Full-service retailers

Speciality stores with narrow product lines with deep assortment and knowledgeable salespeople.

Product Line Sold

a. Speciality stores

Carry narrow product lines.

b. Department stores

Carry a wide variety of lines.

c. Supermarkets

Feature low-cost, high-volume, self-service on food, laundry, and household items.

d. Convenience stores

Small units that carry a limited line of high turnover items.

e. Superstores, Combination Stores, and Hypermarkets

Variations on much larger versions of supermarkets also offering other lines and/or services.

Notes for PM 22-1

Relative Prices

a. Discount stores

Sell standard merchandise at lower prices by accepting lower margins and selling higher volumes.

b. Off-price retailers

Buy at lower than regular wholesale and sell under regular retail. The three major off-price retailers are: Factory outlets that are owned & operated by manufacturers; Independents owned by entrepreneurs or divisions of larger corporations; and Wholesale Clubs selling deeply discounted merchandise to paying members.

c. Catalogue Showrooms

Sell high-markup, fast-moving brand names at discount prices.

Control of Outlets

80% of retail operations are independents.

a. Corporate Chains

Two or more outlets that are commonly owned and controlled, employ central buying, and sell similar lines.

b. Voluntary Chains

Wholesaler sponsored

c. Retailer Co-operatives

Jointly own wholesale operations.

d. Franchise

A contractual association between a manufacturer, wholesaler, or service organisation and independent businesspeople.

e. Merchandising Conglomerates

Corporations that combine several different retailing forms under central ownership and share distribution and management functions.

Type of Store Cluster

Retailers can be classified as central business districts and shopping centres.

Notes for PM 22-1 (contd.)

NonStore Retailing

Transparency PM 22-2 relates to the material on pp.877-886.

Direct Marketing

Direct marketing provides a means of retailing that allows greater selectivity than store retailing. Messages can be personalised and customised to individual customers. Contacts can be timed to interested prospects leading to higher response rates. Promotions effectiveness is also more readily measured. Types of direct marketing include:

1. Direct Mail

Direct-mail marketing involves single mailings that include letters, ads, samples, foldouts, and other contact messages. Mailing lists are obtained for identified groups of people. Within the EU, direct mail is worth over ECU 12 bn.

2. Catalogue Marketing

Catalogue marketing involves selling through catalogues mailed to a select list of customers or made available in stores. The average household receives 50 catalogues annually.

3. Telemarketing

Telemarketing involves using the telephone to sell directly to consumers. In the US consumer marketers spend $41 billion in telephone charges each year. Business marketers sold over $115 billion worth of products last year.

4. Television Marketing

Direct-response advertising features television advertisements that provide a toll-free number for consumers to call immediately to purchase the product. Ads can be 60 second spots or half-hour informercials, often featuring celebrity spokespersons. Home Shopping Channels operate 24-hour a day product live product demonstrations and also feature toll-free numbers to operators, often on-site.

5. Electronic Shopping

The major form of electronic shopping is videotex, a two-way system that links consumers with sellers over telephone lines. Videotex can connect specially equipped television sets for interactive exchange or link marketers to home computers via modems to such services as CompuServe, Prodigy, and America-On-line.

Notes for PM 22-2

Retailer Marketing Decisions

Transparency PM 22-3 relates to the material on pp.887-895.

Retailer Marketing Decisions

1. Target Market Decision

These decisions require that the retailer carefully consider exactly what kind of customer they want to serve. Store image should support the needs and expectations of the target market in every respect.

2. Product Assortment and Services Decision

These decisions include matching product assortment width and depth and quality levels to shopper expectations. Variations in service mixed offerings can help retailers differentiate. Store atmosphere should be considered an assortment/service mix variable.

3. Price Decision

These decisions revolve around high margin/low volume vs. low margin/high volume approaches. May include traffic builders or loss leader tactics.

4. Promotion Decision

Promotions tools available to retailers include all elements of the promotional mix. Major decisions may include tie-ins with producer promotions.

5. Place

Key place decisions remain three: location, location, location!

The Future of Retailing

The wheel of retailing concept states that new retailing forms begin as low-margin, low-price, high volume, low status operations that slow evolve and upgrade their facilities over time. The advent of category killers and inventory tracking using high technology may signal a new development whereby value pricing retailers stay on the low-margin, high-volume end of the retailing scale while constantly improving product quality and consumer value.

Notes for PM 22-3

Wholesaling

Transparency PM 22-4 relates to the material on pp.895-896.

Definition

Wholesaling includes all activities involved in selling goods and services to those buying for resale or business use.

Wholesaler Functions

1. Selling and Promoting

Contacts and small retailer connections help wholesalers reach more buyers than distant manufacturers.

2. Buying and Assortment Building

Wholesalers can select items and build assortments needed by their customers better than manufacturers.

3. Bulk-Breaking

Wholesalers save customers money by buying large quantities and lots and breaking them into smaller lots.

4. Warehousing

Wholesalers hold inventories, reducing inventory costs and risks to suppliers and customers.

5. Transportation

Wholesalers provide quicker transport of orders to customers than do producers.

6. Financing

Wholesalers extend credit.

7. Risk Bearing

Wholesalers take title and absorb risks for loss, damage, or theft.

8. Market Information

Wholesalers provide information to suppliers and customers about competitors, new products, and price developments.

9. Management Services and Advice

Wholesalers provide training to retailers on sales, improved store layouts, displays, and accounting and inventory control procedures.

Notes for PM 22-4

Types of Wholesalers

These notes relate to the material on pp.896-900.

Classifications of Wholesalers

Merchant wholesalers

Independently owned and take title to merchandise. Two broad types are full service-wholesales and limited-service wholesalers:

1. Full-service Wholesalers

Provide a full set of services such as inventorying, salesforce, credit, delivery, and management assistance. Wholesaler merchants mostly sell to retailers while industrial distributors to producers.

2. Limited-service Wholesalers

Provide more specialised services.

a. Cash and Carry Wholesalers

Have a limited line of fast-moving goods and do not deliver.

b. Truck Jobbers

Perform selling and delivery.

c. Drop Shippers

Take title to bulk materials and find producers to ship them. Drop shippers do not carry inventory.

d. Rack Jobbers

Take title and deliver, shelf, inventory, and finance.

e. Producers co-operative

Owned by farmer-members and brand farm produce for local sale.

f. Mail-order wholesalers

Sell by catalogue.

Brokers and Agents

a. Brokers

Assist in bringing buyers and sellers together. The do not carry inventory, assume risk or title, or do financing. Brokers help in negotiation and are paid by the party hiring them.

b. Agents

Represent buyers and sellers more permanently.

c. Manufactures agents

Sell related lines of two or more producers.

d. Selling agents

Sell the producer's entire output.

e. Purchasing agents

Represent buyers.

f. Commission merchants

Take possession and negotiate sales.

Manufacturer's Sales Branches & Offices

These are owned by buyers or sellers. For manufacturers:

a. Sales branches carry inventory.
b. Sales offices do not carry inventory.
c. Purchasing offices are buyer owned versions of brokers and agents.

Comments on Discussing the Issues

1. Some convenience stores have expanded the breadth that they offer to include ready-to-eat cold and hot foods and have even provided financial services through automatic cash point machines, but their fundamental focus is on convenience rather than selection. By expanding length or breadth, stores would be larger, desired items would be harder to find, and prices might have to increase to support the slower-moving goods.

   If 7-Eleven were committed to expanding either the length or breadth of its product mix, it would probably choose to offer a wider variety of product lines (breadth) rather than more items within a line (depth). People in a hurry or who need to make an emergency purchase are going to buy the product they need, even if it is not the brand that they would choose under other circumstances, so extra depth would not contribute much to incremental sales. By expanding breadth, though, 7-Eleven could appeal to people who have an emergency need for a non-food purchase (for example, washers to repair leaky faucets).

2. Warehouse clubs such as Costco and Makro's Wholesale appear to be hybrids, with aspects of both wholesalers and retailers. Retailing is defined as selling goods or services directly to final consumers for their personal, nonbusiness use. Wholesaling is selling to those buying for resale or business use.

   The warehouse clubs have many aspects of wholesalers. They allow only members to enter, and memberships are restricted primarily to small businesspeople and those who purchase for larger businesses. They stock institutional products in addition to consumer goods. Clearly, much of the warehouse clubs' business is traditional wholesaling. Businesses do buy for their internal use, and smaller grocers do buy for resale.

   But much of the clubs' business comes from selling items for members' personal use. In this respect, the clubs are retailers, much like a gigantic discount store. Items intended for personal use can easily be seen in their merchandise offerings. Gourmet foods and windsurfing boards, which are unlikely to be offered for resale or business use, are stocked by Costco.

   The warehouse clubs are both retailers and wholesalers: it is impossible to make a distinction. In the future, other forms of hybrid businesses may also evolve.

3. In the US, a Supreme Court ruling has upheld manufacturers' rights to end relationships with discounters after receiving complaints from full-price distributors, indicating that large retailers may be able to pressure manufacturers to stop supplying to off-price retailers at below wholesale prices. Discounters and off-price retailers are such important outlets for many producers, though, that they may have more clout than conventional retailers. Manufacturers' willingness to deal with discounters will depend in part on which type of retailer they need most; in general, the Supreme Court ruling is not expected to block the flow of merchandise to discounters.

   Because electronics technology advances so quickly, off-price retailers selling outdated equipment probably appeal to different customers than those targeted by Sony's usual distributors. Sony's decision to sell or not sell to off-price retailers depends on many factors—potential profits from these sales, the impact on relationships with Sony's full-price dealers, the retailer support needed to sell and service Sony products, the fit between the image of discounters and Sony's image, and so on. The

Supreme Court's ruling permits Sony to quit selling to discounters if other distributors complain, so Sony could choose to sell to off-price retailers on a trial basis to see how consumers and channel members react.

4. Demand for postal services is largely price inelastic. During the 1980s postal rates rose 50 per cent, but the volume of third-class ("junk") mail doubled nonetheless. In 1988, a 25 per cent hike in the cost of third-class postage rates drew threats of lawsuits to force the exemption of some forms of mail from the Postal Service's monopoly. It also stimulated mailers to use lighter-weight paper, mail less often, screen mailing lists more carefully, and look for alternative ways of delivering messages—in short, to operate more efficiently. But as long as direct mail and catalogue marketing allows marketers to effectively reach likely customers, these forms of direct marketing will thrive in spite of postal rate hikes.

5. An independent retailer in a village community often sells a surprising variety of items. Because of the breadth of the product line and the different turnover rates of the items sold, a country store may obtain hardware from wholesale merchants, produce from cash-and-carry wholesalers, food items from truck wholesalers, and miscellaneous items from rack jobbers. Supermarkets, whether chain stores or members of retailer co-operatives, will deal with many of the same types of suppliers, though in much larger quantities and with the ability to demand more services.

6. Retailers, wholesalers, and manufacturers all make decisions about their target markets, their product assortments and services, pricing strategies, their promotional mix, and their channels of distribution. How they make their decisions can vary considerably—a manufacturer might perform detailed analyses of costs, competitors' prices, and test market results to determine the price that a retailer or wholesaler automatically marks up a fixed percent. But fundamentally, the decisions that they make are all intended to help them make a profit by satisfying customers' needs better than competing firms.

Comments on Applying the Concepts

1. **(a)** Students can probably discuss this issue without actually sorting their mail. It is likely that catalogues fall into one or two primary interest areas, such as clothing or outdoor equipment.

   (b) Students should already know that direct mail marketers buy and sell their mailing lists. Often, a person who has bought a certain type of product by mail becomes a prime target for similar direct marketers.

   (c) Buying habits can be effectively described in various terms including product categories of interest, price range, and frequency of purchase.

2. **(a)** Home shopping channels have become more sophisticated marketers recently. In the past, they often looked like a strange on-air flea market. Now, they target much more effectively.

   (b) Most of the products currently sold over the air are closeouts, overstocks, or promotional items. Often the narrator will describe the item as a closeout, or available in limited quantities, or as last year's model. This situation will change dramatically as cable systems upgrade to 500 channel capability. This will allow much more sophisticated marketing by traditional firms.

Case 22
Pieta Luxury Chocolates

Synopsis

Peter Abel was pleased with the way he had revitalised the firm after he took over in 1985. Since formed in 1923, Pieta had sold its luxury Belgian chocolates through its own small shops. It had a high reputation within the trade and many devoted customers. Peter felt that Pieta should be more like other leading firms such as Cadbury, Ferrero and Mars. When he took over he had launched the company into new ventures. Some examples are franchising, own labels, direct mailing and exporting. There were some new Pieta shops and 20 per cent of the old ones were refurbished. The product range was now wider. The outlets also carried a range of greeting cards and Pieta gift vouchers. As a result of his efforts Peter was able to present a dynamic set of results to his family shareholders. He was angry that some shareholders were not supportive as they had been. He thought it odd that the strategy they had supported and backed financially two years ago was now in question. He had just introduced a new tier of senior people to manage the day-to-day operations of the company. These were not family members but were bright, very well qualified and had broad experience within the industry. With them in place he would have more time to think about and initiate other ways of developing the company.

Teaching Objectives

1. Highlight to students the importance in considering the most cost effective channel performance.

2. Allow students to become more familiar with the calculations of C^3 and EVA.

Study Questions

1. Comment on Abel's expansion strategy and Pieta's performance since he took over?

Strategy is the pattern or plan that integrates an organisation's major goals, policies and action sequences into a cohesive whole. Abel made the claim that "Pieta should be more like other family corporations such as Cadbury and Mars" by this Abel is defining his goals for the company i.e. the mission statement. To accomplish the goals several strategies were carried out by Abel. Let us now examine the various aspects of the strategy. Abel's major strategy since he took over in 1985 has been to increase sales outlets, this has been done via a number of ways:

Own shops

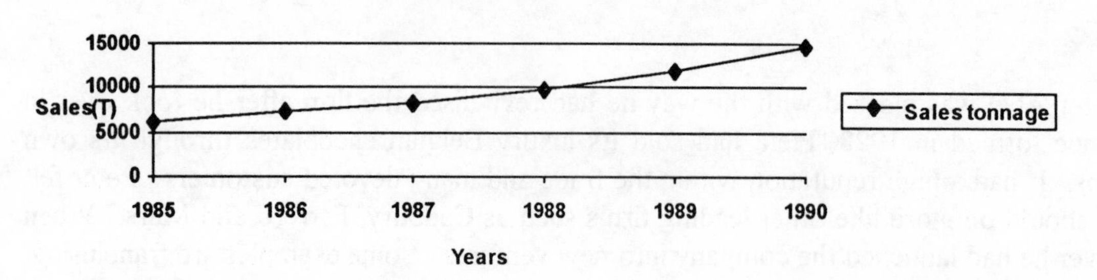

It can be seen from the above graph, sales for this type of distribution outlet has steadily increased. Pieta's strategy therefore seems to be working. Abel has managed to increase the number of own shops, at the same time upgrade a small number of existing shops. The aim was to become more like Mars, and it appears he has succeeded via this strategy. However despite the sales increase operating costs are far too high (discussed later).

Franchise

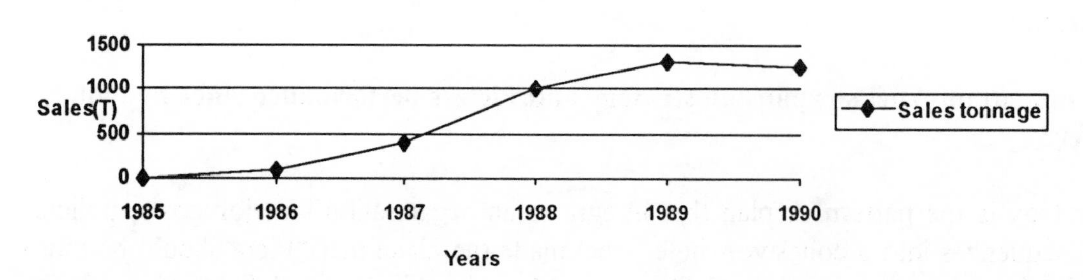

As the graph shows, a sharp increase in sales in the launching years was apparent. However, a slight decrease occurred in the last accounting period. The strategies such as increasing the number of outlets, making Pieta more known to the public, and invading Mars and Cadbury's market, without a doubt are working quite well.. The graph however seems to show a levelling effect possibly because of inefficiencies internally (will be discussed later).

M&S own labels

Sales tonnage against time.

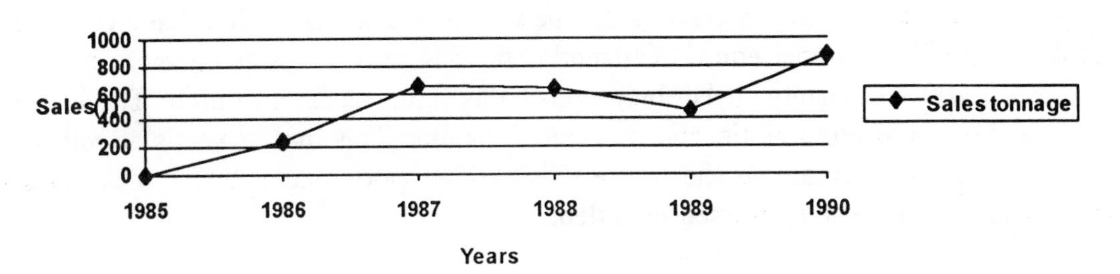

The graph shows an overall increase in sales. Abel's aim was to combat Cadbury and Mars, by direct competition in the market place. Pieta is becoming more like them hence strategy is working.

Direct Mail

Sales tonnage against time.

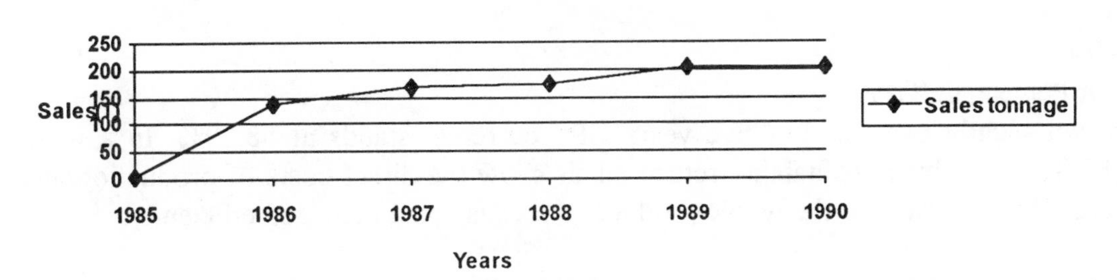

The graph shows a very steady increase in sales, again a levelling effect seems to be occurring. This strategy seems to be working.

Export.

Sales tonnage against time.

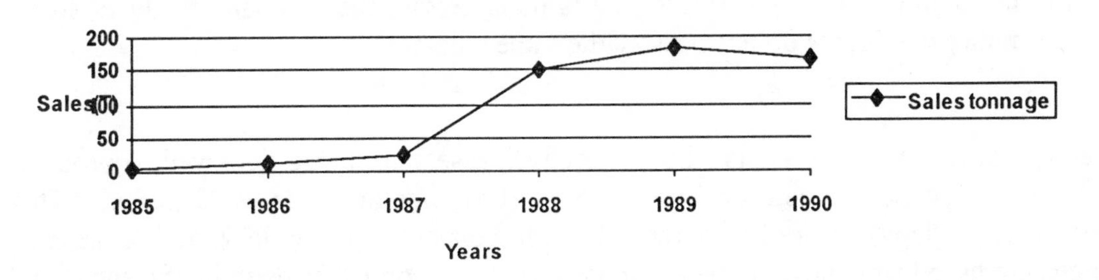

This particular graph seems to have peaked and is now falling. The fact remains that Pieta is becoming more like the other leading family confectioners because it is adopting their distribution channels. Therefore, this strategy is working.

Overall, despite the financial stability of Pieta (discussed later), Pieta is becoming more like Cadbury and Mars and because this was defined as their goal, all of the above strategies seemed to be working.

Financial performance of Pieta (refer to Appendix 1)

Liquidity

Debt/Equity ratio has steadily increased, this can be interpreted as more debt has been taken on instead of acquiring additional equity. Currently standing at 1.41 meaning there is 141% debt compared to 100% of equity. It is obvious that this figure is far too high. The interest payments alone must consume a noticeable amount of profits. This matter needs attention as there is a trend for it to increase in the future. This shows poor management techniques - allowing a company to become engrossed with debt.

Gearing ratio which shows how much total debt there is in the company. Gearing ratio currently stands at 0.59 meaning 59% of the company is all debt. Again the interest charge must take a sizeable amount of the profits. Gearing is far to high and shows the company's reliance on debt. The question, "why is there so much debt?", has to be asked. Possibly due to the refurbishment and expansion strategy to compete with Cadbury and Mars. The next question is, "was the strategy based upon economic and financial forecasting or was it just a whim? Either way if the company went bankrupt it would not be able to meet its debts, so very poor performance by Abel with regard to debt.

Profitability

Gross Profit Percentage(GPP)

Having grown slightly over the last five years GPP currently stands at 58.29%. In a word EXCELLENT, a very high profitability return. This show the direct costs of production and materials are relatively low and the whole production area is being managed efficiently.

Net Profit Percentage (NPP)

A steady decline except a minuscule increase in the last year can be seen from 13.78 to 8.82 over a period of five years. This shows that costs outside of production are relatively high. Interest is taking a large portion of the profits and other costs such as administration and distribution are all relatively high. Another cost to bear in mind is the wages for the newly appointed executives. As a result of these high costs, NPP has dwindled to 8.82% thus the whole question of staying in business must be answered. For a multi-million dollar company the NPP is rather pitiful. Although Abel suggests he is getting the company ready to surge forward in the future the figures do not portray the same message.

Efficiency

The percentage of return to net assets, shows how well assets are being deployed to produce profits. A steady decline can be seen from 27% to 18% over the 1985-1990 period. This shows inefficiency in deployment of resources. Pieta has expanded too quickly and because of that management have lost control of their company. Loss of control leads to inefficiency.

In conclusion, although Pieta's expansion looks impressive, the engine behind it is failing and needs urgent attention. Pieta has serious flaws in its accounts, these matters need urgent attention, otherwise the whole existence of the company may be threatened.

2. Argue the case for further expansion wanted by Abel.

Abel wants to expand so as to compete with the likes of Cadburys and Mars. He proposes to do this via an invasion of the market by developing more Pieta's own shops. The idea behind the strategy is a viable one but the company do not have the financial backing to do it. Abel feels that the company is not reaching its full potential and he aims to achieve this via his expansion strategy. However due to lack of funds he is now asking stakeholders for the much needed capital, but due to diminishing returns over the last few years, the stakeholders "are losing their faith" with Abel and his plans. "The best form of defence is attack" Abel strongly believes this. He wants to avoid being pushed into a corner by the larger companies. Abel holds the luxury market in Belgium but what he wants and where the real profits lie is in the faster-selling main-street-type confectionery, which the likes of Mars and Cadbury currently dominate. "To get a piece of a larger pie, than have a whole small pie" this is Abel's reasoning. To an extent this is true, if he makes more profits, more dividends, everybody will be happy. At the end of the day Abel has the company in mind. Further expansion is necessary for any business to succeed in this competitive world. One cannot just sit on one's laurels and expect everything to materialise, one needs vision and passion to make things happen. In conclusion expansion is necessary, but Pieta do not have the financial stability to afford it so quickly.

3. Practice the case of the shareholders against Abel. How is Pieta's strategy endangering Pieta's future performance and brand image? What if anything has Abel been neglecting?

Shareholders are primarily interested in profits and dividends. Gross profits are increasing whereas net profits are decreasing. Efficiency is falling at a marketable rate. No dividend payment has been given. Judging by the gap between gross and net profits (where dividends fit in the profit and loss account) we can assume that dividend payments are increasing due to the large fall between gross and net profits therefore costs (such as dividends) must have increased. Assuming dividends have increased and profitability of the company is very poor, shareholders will perceive the company as not doing so well. Subsequently, they will not be too interested in any expansion strategy, etc. Basically, they want to know how much profit they are getting on their investment. If this payment is less than the interest given by a bank, then shareholders will withdraw their monies. Falling profitability and decreasing efficiency are alarm bells for the shareholders. These alarms are telling them to withdraw before it is too late. Pieta should tell them at the Annual General Meeting or via a letter of falling levels of profitability due to expansion and try to paint a rosy picture for the future (see Appendix 1).

Future performance is being damaged due to the fact that Pieta is ignoring its core market. Instead of focusing and developing the market, Pieta places more emphasis on expansion. The future is also being compromised because:-

- Resources are being deployed now, these resources will not be available for the future.
- The long-term cost of debt also compromises future profitability.
- Repositioning of the company, may cause repercussions in the future because the core market is being ignored, thus in the future this segment may be open for attack by competitors.

The brand image is being endangered because:

- Exclusivity is being distroyed
- Quality is being compromised.
- A wider product portfolio with easier access is repositioning the brand name.
- By copying Cadbury and Mars, the high street retailers to chocolates, Pieta current brand associated with prestige, etc. will change

Pieta is associated with quality, indulgence and exclusivity. By having a wider product range selling in as many outlets as possible the brand image may be tarnished. The exclusivity is associated with products that are regarded as high quality. In addition to quality, the availability of the chocolates is important. High price is commonly associated with exclusivity. Usually for products that are available with difficulty a premium price is added. As it will be easier for everybody to buy the chocolate the exclusivity aspect of the product will disappear too. Only if the price is at a premium, will some level of exclusivity remain. By having so many retail outlets Abel has failed to notice that the level of quality of the product and service may deteriorate. There must be constant checks to make sure standards are maintained. The cost implication of the strategy may make the move not viable. This may mean an increase in price of the goods to cover the costs. Customers may not feel that they are getting value for money with the new inflated price and may stop purchasing, causing market failure. The increase in the product portfolio may not be a prudent move. If the ice cream is not the same standard as the chocolates this will hurt the brand image. Also the exclusivity of the ice cream must be similar to that of the chocolates. Perceived quality by the customer is determined by the exclusive image and premium price, all of these factors must be harmonised if the brand image is to remain unharmed.

Abel has been neglecting the following:

- Traditional family "way of doing things", Abel is going against all his peers.
- Long term cost of expansion in terms of profitability because of interest repayments.
- Repercussions of brand repositioning; it is easier to move from an exclusive market to a more common one rather than the other way around.
- Shareholders are being neglected as profitability is falling. Some effort must be made to console them.
- Perceived quality may fall, strict controls over levels of quality must be maintained.
- Control over the increasing shops will be hard to maintain.
- Loss of family identity. Moving towards a more corporate image.

Neglecting some of these issues such as the shareholders may lead to problems in the long term. Other factors such as the family identity will be quickly forgotten, yet all of these merit consideration, they deserve more respect than to be simply disregarded.

4. Track the changes in C3 (capital cost covered) and EVA (economic value added) for Pieta over the last ten years.

YEAR	Net Profit	Cost of Equity	Cost of Debt	Cost of Capital	C^3
1980	282	809*0.13 = 105.17	409*0.11 = 44.99	150.16	1.878
1981	308	885*0.12 = 106.20	420*0.09 = 37.80	144	2.139
1982	387	1043*0.17 = 177.31	460*0.11 = 50.60	227.91	1.698
1983	636	1241*0.18 = 223.38	655*0.14 = 91.70	315.08	2.019
1984	723	1488*0.23 = 342.24	885*0.16 = 141.60	483.84	1.494
1985	779	1735*0.28 = 485.80	1196*0.17 = 203.32	689.12	1.130
1986	951	2002*0.21 = 420.42	1423*0.17 = 241.91	662.33	1.436
1987	793	2217*0.20 = 443.40	2011*0.12 = 241.32	684.72	1.158
1988	975	2661*0.26 = 691.86	2088*0.13 = 271.44	963.30	1.012
1989	1123	2594*0.23 = 596.62	3607*0.16 = 577.12	1173.74	0.957
1990	1372	3113*0.25 = 778.25	4402*0.16 = 704.32	1482.57	0.925

Table 1: Capital Cost Covered (C^3) Per Year

$$\textbf{CAPITAL COST COVERED} = \frac{Net\ Profit}{Sales} \times \frac{Sales}{Assets} \times \frac{Assets}{CostofCapital} = \frac{\text{Net Profit}}{\text{Cost of Capital}}$$

Year	Net Profit	Cost of Capital	EVA
1980	282	150.16	131.84
1981	308	144	164
1982	387	227.91	159.09
1983	636	315.08	320.92
1984	723	483.84	239.16
1985	779	689.12	89.88
1986	951	662.33	288.67
1987	793	684.72	108.28
1988	975	963.30	11.70
1989	1123	1173.74	-50.74
1990	1372	1482.57	-110.57

Table 2: Table to show the changes in Economic Value Added (£000's)

ECONOMIC VALUE ADDED = Net Profit - Cost Of Capital

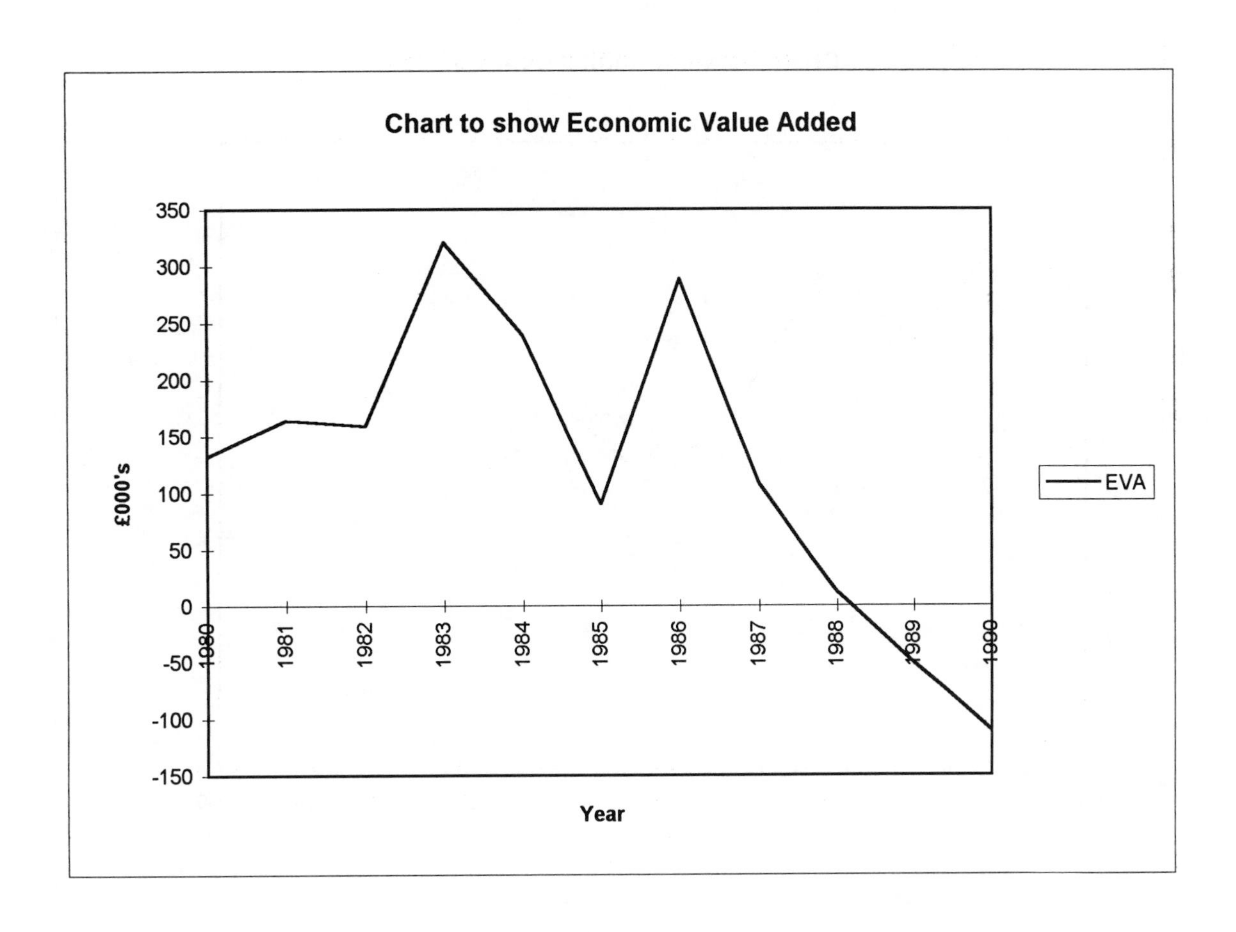
Chart to show Economic Value Added
350
300
250
200
150
100
50
0
-50
-100
-150
£000's
1980
1981
1982
1983
1984
1985
1986
1987
1988
1989
1990
Year
EVA

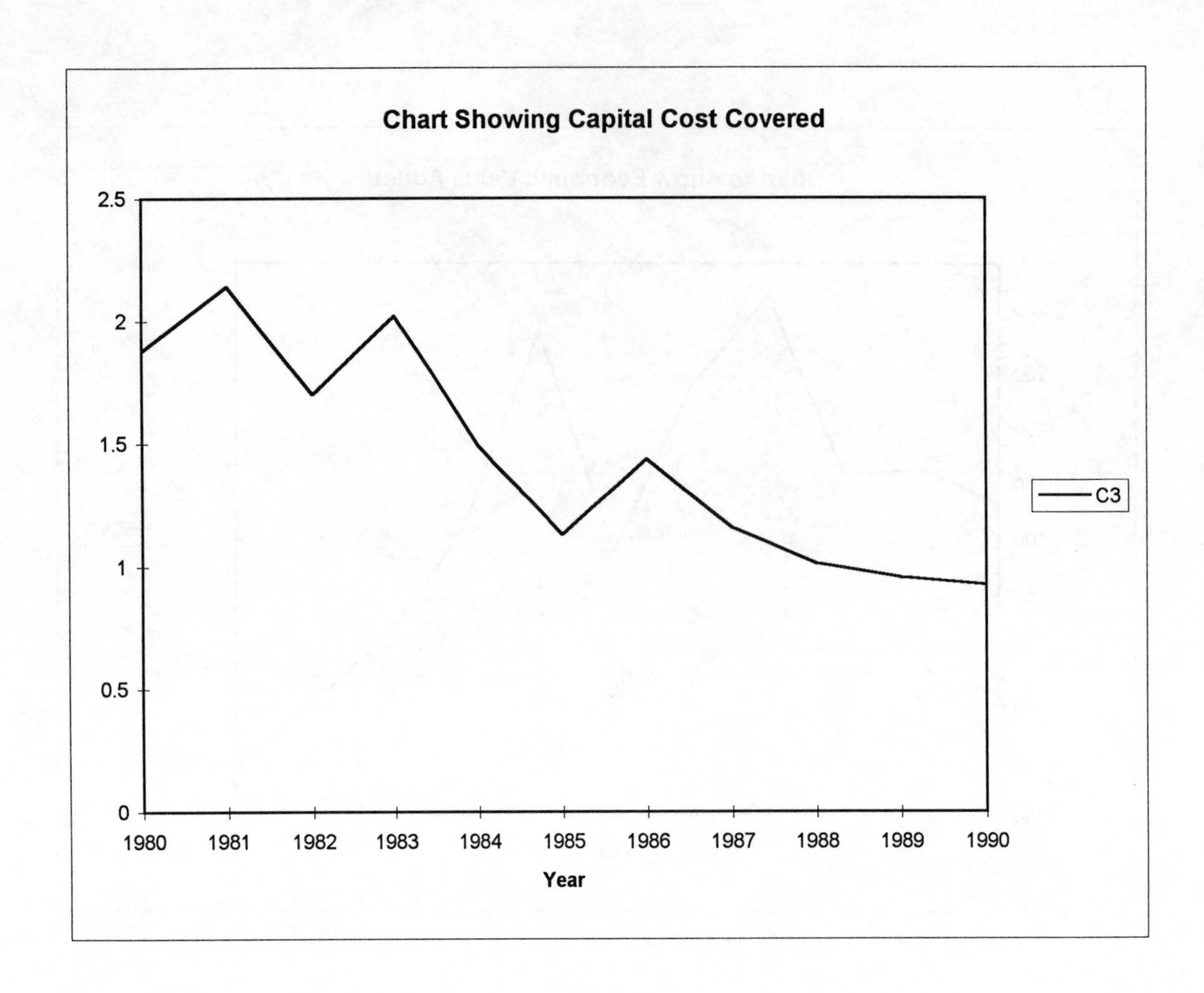
Chart Showing Capital Cost Covered
2.5
2
1.5
1
0.5
0
1980
1981
1982
1983
1984
1985
1986
1987
1988
1989
1990
Year
C3

5. Comment on the C^3 EVA trends and compare them with the impression given by the growth in profits and sales. What strategies of Abel's explains the performance that the C^3 and EVA reveal? Should the trend be changed , and, if so, how could it be changed?

At a glance Pieta's sales, gross profits and net profits have risen drastically between 1980 and 1990, such that over that decade net profit has risen from 282 in 1980 to 1,372 in 1990, nearly a five fold increase. However, whilst this initial analysis looks very impressive, it does not portray the whole picture. In order to fully analyse the performance of Pieta the Capital Cost Covered (C^3) and the Economic Value Added (EVA) needs to be considered. C^3 looks at the organisations ability to pay back interest charged against debt accrued to purchase assets which generate profits and the EVA calculation directly compares the cost of capital against profit, such that they validate each other. These calculations were performed and supplied in the previous part of the case study. You will notice that between 1980 and 1988 the C^3 and EVA calculations were within reasonable boundaries, i.e. the C^3 positive and above 1 and the EVA positive. It can also be noted that during this period these figures rose and fell, which is largely due to the increase and variability of profitability and capital in terms of equity and debt. Had the levels of capital stopped rising whilst profits continued to rise then the C^3, EVA and overall performance of Pieta would be particularly impressive, but in real terms up to 1988 performance has stagnated, although the organisation has expanded. After 1988, however, the C^3 calculation fell below 1 and the EVA calculations went into the negative, the implications of which are that profits do not cover the cost of capital and no economic value is being added to the business through its operations. This indicates a need for change such that the figures fall within the accepted boundaries.

The fall in performance in the C^3 and EVA figures can be accounted for by Abel's strategy of expansion through franchising, increasing the number of his own shops, refurbishing existing shops, selling to M & S, direct mailing and exporting. However, this expansion has not been done through organic growth (i.e. through re-investment of profits), but instead it has been financed through the increase of equity and debt capital to Pieta. Moreover, after 1988 expansion through the increase of equity and debt capital was no longer economic because insufficient profits were being generated as a result of the investment/expansion strategy. A contributory factor to the fall in these figures is the reduction of CTN franchise sales from 1,303 tonnes in 1989 to 1,259 tonnes in 1990 which generate net profits of 14% and the increase in own shop sales from 11,845 tonnes in 1989 to 14,753 tonnes in 1990 which only generate net profits of 6%, less than half that in franchise shops. To a large extent the results could be blamed on insufficient market research before expanding Pieta's operations.

In order to improve the trend the company must increase profits whilst decreasing debt and equity capital. This could be done through dropping the export activities and direct mail activities and allocating its resources to a more profitable activity such as own shops or CTN franchises. Moreover, the shops in poorer locations could be sold off as confectionery, tobacco and news shops with a Pieta franchise within them. This would have the effect of paying back capital through the sale of the poorer located shops which would then produce a higher rate of net profit (14% instead of 6%) through the sale of Pieta products.

APPENDIX 1

			1990	1989	1988	1987	1986	1985	1984	1983	1982	1981	1980
LIQUIDITY RATIO		Total Long Term Debt	4,402	3,607	2088	2011	1423	1196	885	655	460	420	409
	B	Total Equity	3,113	2,594	2661	2217	2002	1735	1488	1241	1043	885	809
	A/B	Debt/Equity ratio	**1.41**	**1.39**	**0.78**	**0.91**	**0.71**	**0.69**	**0.59**	**0.53**	**0.44**	**0.47**	**0.51**
GEARING RATIO:	A	Total Long Term Debt	4,402	3,607	2088	2011	1423	1196	885	655	460	420	409
	B	Total Assets	7,515	6,201	4749	4228	3425	2931	2373	1896	1503	1305	1218
	A/B	Gearing Ratio	**0.59**	**0.58**	**0.44**	**0.48**	**0.42**	**0.41**	**0.37**	**0.35**	**0.31**	**0.32**	**0.34**
GROSS PROFIT MARGIN		GROSS PROFIT	9064	6891	5803	4696	4066	3005	2405	1961	1568	1215	1285
		SALES	**15551**	12826	10887	8821	7091	5653	4270	3461	2783	2222	2262
		GROSS PROFIT MARGIN	**58.29**	**53.73**	**53.30**	**53.24**	**57.34**	**53.16**	**56.32**	**56.66**	**56.34**	**54.68**	**56.81**
NET PROFIT MARGIN		NET PROFIT	**1372**	1123	975	793	951	779	723	636	387	308	282
		SALES	**15551**	12826	10887	8821	7091	5653	4270	3461	2783	2222	2262
		NET PROFIT MARGIN	**8.82**	**8.76**	**8.96**	**8.99**	**13.41**	**13.78**	**16.93**	**18.38**	**13.91**	**13.86**	**12.47**
Net profit as % of Net assets		NET PROFIT	**1372**	1123	975	793	951	779	723	636	387	308	282
		NET ASSETS	**7515.00**	6201	4749	4228	3425	2931	2373	1896	1503	1305	1218
		%	**0.18**	**0.18**	**0.21**	**0.19**	**0.28**	**0.27**	**0.30**	**0.34**	**0.26**	**0.24**	**0.23**

Overview Case VIII
GTE: Competition Comes Calling

Synopsis

The case begins as Kevin Murphy, a salaried General Telephone and Electronics (GTE) sales consultant, stops at a Smile Gas Station in Durham, North Carolina. The manager of the gas station wants to have a pay phone installed. He had previously had a GTE pay phone but had it removed in anticipation of buying a pay phone from a private firm. However, the firm had gone out of business, and the manager was left without a pay phone. This had resulted in his losing business to a competitor's station across the street.

This scenario sets the stage for a look at the public communications market which has seen dramatic changes since the deregulation of the telephone industry in 1984. What had once been a sleepy, neglected business has suddenly drawn the interest of literally hundreds of small companies who, as a result of FCC and judicial rulings, have had this once monopolistic market opened to them.

In 1989, the pay-phone market in the United States will generate approximately $6.3 billion in revenues. Despite the size of this market, however, the telephone companies such as GTE had generally neglected this business prior to deregulation. Pay-phone operations were generally lumped into general telephone operations and were not accounted for separately. Further, the business was demand-driven in that there were many more requests for pay-phone installations than the telephone companies granted. GTE approved only about two of every ten requests made for pay phones.

However, deregulation and FCC rulings changed all this. The FCC ruled that any person who purchased a coin-operated telephone had the right to connect it to the local telephone network. This ruling created a new product and a new market: the customer-owned coin-operated telephone (COCOT). As a result, many entrepreneurs set up private pay-phone companies to sell pay phones to individual businesses. These firms included everything from one-person businesses to large publicly traded telephone companies. Further, the implementation of the "equal access" provisions of deregulation meant that AT&T no longer had a monopoly on long-distance service. This allowed the entry of other long-distance carriers and set the stage for competition between those carriers for long-distance customers. As a result, COCOTs could offer commissions to businesses for using their pay telephones and also the businesses could earn commissions from the long-distance carriers for selecting their service.

Armed with these commissions, the COCOTs entered the industry with a vengeance. The COCOTs targeted established pay-phone locations and offered owners commissions significantly above those offered by GTE. The case relates a series of steps taken by competitors and counter measures taken by GTE to respond to the competition. At the conclusion of the case, Kevin Murphy has left the Smile Gas Station and is preparing to attend GTE's first sales meeting for its sales consultants who work in the south-eastern area. GTE realises that it must improve its marketing strategy to respond to the new competition in the public communications market.

Teaching Objectives

1. Acquaint students with the public communications market.

2. Provide students with an opportunity to apply concepts presented in Part VIII.

3. Allow students to recommend changes in GTE's marketing strategy.

Study Questions

1. What kind of service does GTE sell?

Using the text's discussion, students will identify GTE's services as both people-based and equipment-based. GTE's telephone equipment provides the communication service at the core of the product offering. Much of its work is automated. Its people are also involved however in providing operator services and repair and maintenance services. These jobs are both skilled and unskilled. The telephones also serve both personal needs and business needs. As with Smile Gas, businesses want the phones to provide additional services to their customers and to draw traffic into their businesses. The phones satisfy both personal and business needs for the users. Students will also note that GTE's service provider's objectives have changed because of competition. Whereas the company previously did not really focus on pay-phone profitability, it now must do so.

2. How do the characteristics of GTE's services affect its marketing efforts?

The services GTE provides are certainly intangible. An electronic telephone call is not tangible. Neither are the operator and maintenance services. Because consumers have come to believe that telephone calls are a commodity, a telephone call is a telephone call no matter who sells it, the industry has moved to price competition. This means that the operator and maintenance services, which are not commodities, have taken on more meaning in the marketing equation.

GTE's services are inseparable from the equipment and people who deliver them. Both the businesses or the users care who provides the personal services. They want well-trained, courteous operators and skilled maintenance workers. This means that GTE must emphasise employee training. Note that Kevin is going to the first-ever sales meeting. GTE must also train its salespeople. Their professionalism will reflect on the quality of service the customer can expect from GTE. The way the salespeople conduct themselves can also differentiate GTE from competition, which may be using part-time salespeople.

Both the people and the equipment will be variable in their performance. Although telephones have become very reliable, GTE will want to work to make its phones as reliable as possible. It will also want to stress the availability of its repair service. Public phones do take much abuse. It will want to train its employees to provide a uniformly high level of service and to standardise that service.

Because its services are perishable, GTE will want to monitor demand and staff its operator and repair services to meet peak demands. If GTE advertises 24-hour repair service, it must have the staff to back up that claim.

3. How should the concepts of internal and interactive marketing shape GTE's marketing strategy?

As noted, GTE must train all of its workers, not just the salespeople, in marketing. This internal marketing is important in any service business, and especially where competition is fierce. All of GTE's customer-contact employees must understand their contribution to the quality of the customer's service experience. This ties to interactive marketing. All of the customer-contact employees must be trained to manage buyer-seller interactions. Customers will look at both the technical quality of the telephone call but also the functional quality of the personal interactions.

4. What changes should GTE make in its marketing strategy? Be sure to address each aspect of the marketing mix and the issues of managing differentiation, service quality, and productivity.

The case focuses on GTE's competitors as seen from an industry point of view, that is a group of firms who offer products that are close substitutes. Students should realise however, that there is a market point of view in which cellular telephones, mobile phones, and pagers also compete to serve the customer's need for "mobile communications."

Given the information in the case, it can be argued that the new competitors who have entered the pay-phone market are probably short-term profit maximisers who wish to take advantage of the suddenly available market opportunity. The case indicates that many of these competitors are small operations, even operating out of pick-up trucks, which will take almost any step to make a sale. Although there are certainly larger and more reputable companies operating in the market, the opening of the telecommunications market has attracted many opportunists. As to competitors' strategies, students should realise that the pay-phone market is a mature market and the product is seen by customers as a commodity. This situation requires, therefore, that entering firms attempt to take established business away from the telephone companies. As the case indicates, the new competitors are targeting established locations. GTE and the other telephone companies have already installed phones where they think they will be most profitable. Thus, they have identified the best customers for the new entrants. Therefore, the new firms are simply "cherry picking" by trying to take established locations from the telephone companies.

Students should see that these new firms have both strengths and weaknesses as they enter the competitive arena. A significant strength is their lack of overhead. GTE and the other established telephone companies have large sales and service networks. They have large office staffs and other support facilities. The new firms do not have this kind of overhead burden. Further, in many areas, telephone companies, like other utilities, are often seen in a somewhat negative light by many customers due to their previous monopoly position and the perceived lack of customer service. Therefore, the new entrants have a psychological advantage. Also, because the new entrants are not regulated, they have more freedom to act and react than does a publicly regulated telephone company.

However, some of these strengths are also weaknesses. The overhead that GTE carries brings with it the ability to provide prompt, high-quality customer service. Obviously, a start-up firm operating out of a pick-up truck does not have this kind of established service capability. The problem, however, as we will see in later questions, is that customers do not really see the service aspect of the business. Like residential customers, they are simply used to having the phones work and assume that all work equally well. Because the service has been a commodity, customers are not educated to ask the right questions or to be concerned about the right issues with regard to the product.

5. The telecommunications industry's deregulation has caused the marketing situation GTE faces. Does deregulation promote economic efficiency?

On one hand, the answer is obviously yes. The new competitors, although some may be unprofessional, have sent GTE a wake-up call. The firm is going to have to do a better job in all areas because of the competition.

On the other hand, the text indicates that a key ingredient in the success of deregulation is the presence of well-informed buyers. For years buyers did not have to worry about telecommunication services. Now they must, and many are uninformed. This makes them susceptible to disreputable firms, or it may lead to their making decisions that are not in their own best interest. Long-distance service has become so complicated that few customers really know what they are paying or if they are really saving any money.

This discussion points out again the importance of the promotion part of GTE's strategy. It must educate businesses and consumers in its market areas about public communication services so that they can make informed choices.

Teaching Suggestions

Because students may not be familiar with the pay-phone market and may not have thought much about pay phones, an interesting assignment with this case is to have them survey their daily environment for pay phones. How many pay phones are there on the college or university campus and who provides those phones? Has the number of phones been increasing or decreasing in recent years? Can they find pay phones around the college or university which are provided by different firms? They might be interested in contacting some of the alternative providers to see what they can learn about their businesses and how their businesses are going. They may also be interested in talking with representatives of the regulated telephone company to find out how the pay-phone business is going in your area.

There is also a substantial amount of innovation in the pay-phone market which may be of interest to students. Public fax machines are being installed in many shopping centres, airports, and other high-traffic locations which allow customers to send fax documents much as they would make a pay-telephone call. Some companies are also experimenting with pay phones which allow a person making a local call which is not answered to insert an additional quarter. The additional quarter allows them to record a message. The computers at the telephone company record this message and re-dial the number the person called every fifteen minutes for up to four hours. If the party being called answers, the computer will play the recorded message for them. These kinds of product innovations in addition to the increasing competition are making the pay-phone market a very interesting place to operate.

Additional Information

In June 1993, a GTE official reported that the Public Communications group was maintaining a stable market share and doing very well. GTE has adopted a strategy of focusing its sales efforts on the high-volume, profitable accounts. It no longer targets small, one-phone installations with its salesforce. It services these accounts with its service technicians.

GTE reduced its salesforce by one-third and segmented the market as follows:

Government. This segment includes military installations, public hospitals, government office buildings, and prisons. Prisons have become especially profitable accounts. Laws require that prisoners be allowed to make telephone calls, and they make a lot of them.

Retail. This segment includes large retail stores, hotels, and motels.

Convenience. This segment includes convenience stores, petrol stations, and restaurants.

GTE focuses only on profitable accounts in these three segments. It has also cut costs, removed low-paying phones, and cut needless commissions. It now pays commissions only on local coins-in-the-box, that is coins in the box generated by local versus long-distance calls.

GTE also pays more attention to the customer. It has learned that service is the key to differentiating itself from competition. Customers learn to appreciate the value of good repair/maintenance service.

To educate customers, GTE has developed a pamphlet that it calls the "GTE Pay Phone Guide." The pamphlet presents a series of questions about pay phones and gives information on GTE's answers to each question. There is a place after each question where the customer can record if competition has an answer for that question, such as "Are repairs performed free of charge?" In this way, GTE tries to educate the customer and help that customer compare GTE's and others' services.

Many smaller competitors have gone out of business or have been purchased by larger companies. Peoples is still the largest competitor. It has branched out into cellular phones, installing the phones in rental cars. A person renting a car from a rental car firm may request a cellular phone. The person then pays on a per-minute basis for use of the phone.

Many firms are also offering a debit card. The phone user makes payments to create a debit balance on his/her debit card. Then the person can use the card to charge calls even on phones that aren't set up to accept credit cards. In the US, AT&T is still the only company that allows a person to pay for a call in coins because only its operators have equipment that lets them "hear" the coins and determine how much has been deposited.

Jokes and Quotes

Retail is detail.

If money doesn't grow on trees, how come the banks have so many branches?
ANON

In an age robbed of religious symbols, going to the shops replaces going to the church... We have a free choice, but at a price. We can win experience, but never achieve innocence. Marx knew that the epic activities of the modern world involve not lance and sword but dry goods.
STEPHEN BAYLEY

To open a shop is easy, to keep it open is an art.
CONFUCIUS

There were three stores next to each other all competing for business. One day, the owner of the middle store saw an enormous poster hanging outside the store. On one side that read 'Gigantic Sale Now On! and outside the other an equally large poster reading 'Biggest Sale Ever'. The shopkeeper dashed into his store, came out and put up a small sign that read, 'Entrance to Sale!'
JOKE

An elderly shopkeeper was dying, with his family around his bedside. The old man asked 'Is Joseph here?'
'Yes, father, I'm here,' said Joseph.
'Is Amy here?' the dying grocer demanded.
'Yes dear' said his wife. 'I'm right here'.
'Is Barbara here?' the old man persisted.
'Yes, grandfather,' the young girl said. 'We're here. We're all here'.
The grocer sat bolt upright in bed and shouted 'Who the hell is looking after the shop?.
JOKE

Shopping malls are liquid TVs for the end of the twentieth century. A whole micro-circuitry of desire, ideology and expenditure for processed bodies drifting through the cyber space of ultracapitalism.
ARTHUR KROKER

They also serve who only stand and wait.
JOHN MILTON

Consumption is the sudden or gradual destruction of a valuable article obtained from a retail trader or other final producer.
A. F. MUMMERY

You cannot bore people into buying your product. You must interest them into buying it. You cannot save souls in an empty church.
DAVID OGILVY

A man without a smiling face must not open a shop.
CHINESE PROVERB

The Customer Is Always Right
Shopping Days to Christmas
This Famous Store Needs No Name On The Door
Complete Satisfaction Or Money Cheerfully Refunded
H. GORDON SELFRIDGE

A hapless bridegroom explained to a court why he broke into a contraceptive machine 'It was our wedding night and my wife wouldn't let me get into bed until I had a contraceptive. Unfortunately, neither of us had any change.
TRUE STORY